The World That Fear Made

EARLY AMERICAN STUDIES

Series Editors:
Daniel K. Richter, Kathleen M. Brown,
Max Cavitch, and David Waldstreicher

Exploring neglected aspects of our colonial,
revolutionary, and early national history and culture,
Early American Studies reinterprets familiar themes
and events in fresh ways. Interdisciplinary in character,
and with a special emphasis on the period from about
1600 to 1850, the series is published in partnership with
the McNeil Center for Early American Studies.

A complete list of books in the series
is available from the publisher.

THE WORLD
THAT FEAR MADE

Slave Revolts and Conspiracy Scares
in Early America

JASON T. SHARPLES

PENN

UNIVERSITY OF PENNSYLVANIA PRESS

PHILADELPHIA

Publication of this volume was aided by the C. Dallett Hemphill
Publication Fund.

Published by
University of Pennsylvania Press
Philadelphia, Pennsylvania 19104-4112
www.upenn.edu/pennpress

Printed in the United States of America
on acid-free paper
1 3 5 7 9 10 8 6 4 2

Library of Congress Cataloging-in-Publishing Data

Names: Sharples, Jason T., author.
Title: The world that fear made: slave revolts and conspiracy scares in early
America / Jason T. Sharples.
Other titles: Early American studies.
Description: 1st edition. | Philadelphia: University of Pennsylvania Press, [2020] |
Series: Early American studies | Includes bibliographical references and index.
Identifiers: LCCN 2019045143 | ISBN 9780812252194 (hardcover)
Subjects: LCSH: Slave insurrections—United States—History—17th century. |
Slave insurrections—United States—History—18th century. | Slave
insurrections—Caribbean Area—History—17th century. | Slave
insurrections—Caribbean Area—History—18th century. | United States—
Race relations—History—17th century. | United States—Race relations—
History—18th century. | Caribbean Area—Race relations—History—17th
century. | Caribbean Area—Race relations—History—18th century.
Classification: LCC E441 .S527 2020 | DDC 306.3/62097309032—dc23
LC record available at https://lccn.loc.gov/2019045143

For Tim and Dee

CONTENTS

INTRODUCTION

The Cup of Wrath Is Almost Full

There is a puzzle in the history of early American slave rebellions that offers a view of the hidden workings of slave societies and how fear coiled the springs of exploitation, resistance, and power. The mystery is the dissimilarity between two events—one a spontaneous uprising, another a planned insurrection—in the heart of coastal South Carolina rice country, roughly ten years apart, each involving more than one hundred enslaved people. In the first, in the predawn hours of a Sunday in September 1739, a core group of about twenty desperate people near the Stono River broke into a store, seized weapons, and killed two white storekeepers. They chose not to march ten miles north to strike at the heart of the regime in Charleston, where the slumbering townspeople would have made easy targets (fig. 1). Instead they tried to flee almost three hundred miles south to St. Augustine in Spanish Florida to secure their legal freedom through a policy that welcomed them as refugees.[1]

As the group advanced along the road and raised a banner, about eighty more people joined from among the several hundred who were enslaved in plantation labor camps in the immediate area. The insurrectionary force plundered some of the houses they passed and burned them as they left, killing about two dozen enslavers and sparing the lives of others. They made it to the next river but succumbed to the colony's militia in the open field. As a Royal Navy captain reported shortly after these events, this rebellion "was not general"; it was limited to "only . . . part of the Country." He also observed that this revolt was homegrown, contrary to British colonists' usual suspicions. He did not yet see reason to think that it was "stirred up by the Spaniards" or any other agitator, despite later speculation to the contrary. In South Carolina's largest rebellion before the chaos of the

Figure 1. In 1739, rebels near the Stono River took up arms within striking distance of Charleston, but they preferred to march away from South Carolina's seat of power toward the autonomy promised in Spanish Florida instead. Detail from *A Compleat Description of the Province of Carolina in 3 parts* [. . .] (London: Edward Crisp, [1711?]). Courtesy of the John Carter Brown Library at Brown University.

American Revolution, these insurgents rejected slavery through personal escape rather than general massacre and political takeover.[2]

In the second event, ten years later and ten miles away, a different group of enslaved people appeared in the highest court of the colony, the council chamber in Charleston, to confess their plans for insurrection in January 1749. As they described their intentions, however, they painted a picture of planned violence that looked rather different from the Stono Rebellion. An enslaved boatman named Agrippa stood before the governor of South Carolina and six of the most powerful men in the colony to reveal that hundreds of enslaved people would rise at the end of the week. The governor ordered costly countermeasures. He forced common white men to put down their work so they could mobilize as a militia to patrol by foot, horse, and boat. He also stopped all traffic at Charleston's harbor and stationed two Royal Navy vessels nearby. Normal business ground to a halt for two weeks.[3]

The uprising did not occur. Agrippa and six other enslaved informants described the plan, termed a "conspiracy" or "plot," and implicated 104 enslaved people and thirteen white laborers in joining it. Two white men, transients believed to be connected to the Spanish, seemed to have proposed the plot and organized it for enslaved people, whom white society deemed at the time to be natural followers incapable of the necessary strategic vision. They appeared to initiate conspirators by swearing them to secrecy with formal oaths, creating a network of confirmed conspirators that stretched to the enslaved "Headmen" on many rural plantations who recruited the "Cleverest Slaves" in their employ. The informants insisted that racial massacre was the goal—to "kill the White People"—and that Charleston was the target, where they could take advantage of the concentrated white population. The masterstroke of the plot was to "set the Town & [powder] Magazine afire and in the Confusion kill the white People," using fire to draw victims into the streets to be ambushed before heading to the frontier for freedom.[4] Why was the Stono Rebellion of 1739 so different from the plan for rebellion that informants warned about in 1749?

The rest of the puzzle comes into view when we expand our compass to include the rest of the anglophone American colonies. Dozens of times, enslaved informants confessed to "conspiracies" or "plots" that included plans for insurrection and visions of violence that were strikingly similar to Agrippa's revelations. In many, they said that they would set diversionary fires and ambush the white people who rushed to extinguish them. In Barbados in 1692, investigators believed that conspirators would have "sett the towne on fire in severall Places . . . to amuse [distract] the inhabitants" and lure them into a slaughter.[5] In New York (1741), a series thirteen fires prompted investigators to announce that plotters set them with the intent of ambushing "the white people [who] came to extinguish them, [to] kill and destroy them."[6] In Jamaica (1744), it appeared that conspirators planned to light fires in a town "first at one End of it, and then at the other," so that when "People ran in Confusion to the same, they were to be stab'd and destroy'd."[7] In New York, in the tense winter of 1775, an investigation in the Hudson Valley found that plotters planned to "fire the houses, cry fire, and kill the people as they came out."[8] In South Carolina in 1822, investigators claimed that conspirators wanted to "set the town on fire in different places & as the whites come out . . . slay them," in Charleston's iconic Denmark Vesey affair.[9] The centerpiece of the South Carolina plot of 1749—to blow up the powder magazine and use the distraction to massacre the townspeople—had more in common with these revelations of *intended* violence than with the progression of *actual* violence in the Stono

Rebellion, when insurgents followed the road away from Charleston and burned rural plantations only after the fact.

The idea of an ambush at a diversionary fire was just one of several recurring features in conspiracy confessions that had more in common with Agrippa's confessions than with the Stono rebels' actions. During several conspiracy scares in slave societies of North America and the Caribbean, informants said that conspirators took direction from outside agitators such as Catholic spies (another element of Agrippa's confession), swore oaths to one another to maintain secrecy (witnessed by Agrippa's enslaver), and circulated lists of conspirators. In terms of tactics, some said that they timed the averted rebellion for a holiday such as Easter, St. Patrick's Day, or Christmas, and that they would coordinate the uprising with French, Spanish, or Native American invaders. Often the initial informer claimed to alert the community within days of the planned insurrection, as Agrippa did, in a dramatic turn worthy of the early modern stage. They described common goals of massacring white men and raping white women. Above all, they said, conspirators appeared to aim for a social inversion by which they would take the names of leading planters and replace them at the heads of families, estates, and government. While Agrippa's confessions certainly had some connections to the Stono Rebellion, they also must be understood as part of this related but distinct phenomenon—the slave conspiracy scare—which grew from different historical forces and generated a different set of effects on the world. These were events of information and misinformation at least as much as they were insurrectionary events.

The distinctiveness of conspiracy allegations is evident when we expand our comparison to what actually happened in most revolts in seventeenth- and eighteenth-century America. When groups of rebels took up arms against their oppressors, their insurrections usually began at one or two plantation labor camps and typically remained limited in scope. Out of fear of reprisals, many hundreds of people enslaved in the immediate vicinity did not join. When larger numbers of enslaved people accepted the risk of joining insurrections, which happened only a handful of times in the Americas, they usually did so in viral fashion, from plantation to plantation, rather than in a premeditated, simultaneous rising as part of a clandestine network.

Rebels also pursued tactics and goals different from those professed by informants for alleged conspiracies. They usually killed very few white people and rarely committed sexual violence, contrary to enslavers' expectations of massacre and rape. Generally, they prioritized plundering for provisions and escaping from the zone of colonization rather than going out of their way to murder white people or to conquer colonial centers. They did not jeopardize their opportunity for individual success with complicated plans for overturning the social order. They set fire to buildings to deny their adversaries shelter and to intimidate pursuers with billowing spectacles; there is little evidence that they initiated rebellions by setting diversionary fires to draw inhabitants out of buildings into an ambush.[10] These limited conflicts, a sensible strategy in situations of extreme domination, allowed rebels to seek autonomy in regions inaccessible to their former oppressors—mountains, swamps, forests, and even Spanish settlements. The Stono Rebellion corresponded to most other rebellions with its limited initial participation, its viral spread, and the primary goal of escape more than massacre, even if it did not square with the confessions of Agrippa in 1749.

The initial answer to our puzzle—why did the violence of South Carolina's 1739 rebellion differ so markedly from the predicted violence of 1749?—is that these were two distinct types of events, which have been conflated from the beginning. During investigations into possible plans for rebellion, enslavers forced enslaved informants to speculate about violence that *might* occur or *could have* occurred instead of describing something that actually *did* occur. For white people in early America, the only significant difference between a conspiracy and a rebellion was the stage to which the insurgent activity developed. In their minds, when enslaved people did take up arms in rebellion, magistrates retroactively explained it as having originated as a "conspiracy" that they had failed to detect. (When the rebellion did not engulf the whole colony, as with the Stono Rebellion, they expressed relief that the original conspiracy somehow misfired.) An "insurrection" or "rebellion" is properly defined as collective violence that actually occurred, whereas a "plot" or "conspiracy" is a representation of violence that was supposedly planned but appeared not to come to fruition because enslavers anticipated it and arrested the alleged "conspirators."[11] This distinction is the beginning of the answer. The rest requires recognizing that slavery was, at its core, a system of fear.

Violence and Fear in Slavery

Enslavers systematically used terror against the Africans and African Americans whom they enslaved as a strategy for trying to command obedience.

"Fear," theorized the slavery apologist Bryan Edwards, was the only "impulse to action" to which an enslaved person could respond. Individual enslavers wielded the lash, the most obvious instrument of attempted terror, not to mechanically prod enslaved people so much as to inflict freshly stinging examples of what could befall them if they displeased an enslaver. The historian Edward Baptist has aptly characterized this as a system of torture for compelling labor and outward obedience from enslaved people, and a seventeenth-century traveler also described this as a system of "torment[s]" and "excessive tortur[e]s." Enslavers throughout the colonies terrorized enslaved women and men with rape and its lingering trauma, and they threatened them with the possibility of physical pain, humiliation, confinement, or reassignment to difficult labor. They also used the chattel principle to threaten to separate families through sale, and they could send an individual to a new enslaver who was more sadistic or whose position in the economy involved a more grueling labor regime. In wielding these instruments of fear, enslavers deliberately exploited people's human instinct to avoid doing whatever might lead to pain or loss.[12] Coercion in slavery depended on fear of violence: it occurred when enslavers convinced the people whom they enslaved that they could be assured of specific negative outcomes, particularly in the realm of basic needs, if they did anything other than what was bid them. But in doing so, white people generated the unintended consequence of their own fear of black people.[13]

Enslaved people experienced another form of terror from colonial governments. They faced the possibility of painful death and mutilation at the hands of the state, which had less interest in preserving their value as property, whenever it claimed to act for the public safety of white people. Enslaved people experienced this as a compound fear because the public display of dismembered corpses had religious implications, as Vincent Brown has shown.[14] They also continued to experience the terror long after the grisly spectacles had vanished from sight because, as Marisa Fuentes has observed, their daily travels carried them through a landscape of crossroads and market squares that retained their traumatic association with punishment.[15] Colonial governments meant these punishments to influence the living, to terrorize onlookers into changing their calculus for actions in the future. With executions after one uprising, an enslaver shared this hope that the grisly spectacle would "leave a Terrour on the Minds of all the other Negros for the future" to prevent them from rising again, and Enlightenment thinkers agreed that terror could maintain the standing

Figure 2. Enslavers wielded terror in an attempt to control the people whom they enslaved, publicly displaying the tortured bodies of rebels. Joshua Bryant, *Five of the Culprits in Chains, as They Appeared on the 20th of September, 1823*, 1824. Engraving in Bryant, *Account of an Insurrection of the Negro Slaves in the Colony of Demerara on the 18th of August, 1823* (Georgetown, Demerara, 1824), plate 12. Courtesy of the John Carter Brown Library at Brown University.

order. Enslaved people carried an accretion of violent experiences and traumatizing examples that enslavers and colonial governments deliberately deployed to try to control them.[16]

Historians have been coming to grips with the centrality of deprivation, pain, and trauma to enslaved people's lives.[17] The scholarship of Saidiya Hartman, Nell Irvin Painter, Wendy Warren, Edward Baptist, and Sowande' M. Mustakeem, among others, emphasizes the all-encompassing violence of enslavement. This corrects views that ignored the considerable constraints on "the world the slaves made" and minimized violent encounters in "the world they made together." The world of white violence and black trauma that scholars have come to recognize was, in truth, a world made and sustained by fear.[18]

This emphasis on violence and trauma has led some scholars to see that the bodies of enslaved women and men were a main site of political resistance against oppression. Survival was the most fundamental struggle. The slaving regime imposed scarcities that directly threatened people on the brink and also pitted them in competition for limited resources.[19] In fear of punishment, many resorted to subtle forms of resistance that could not easily be ascribed to them but that achieved human-scale victories: they preserved something of their bodies for their own use by taking food, feigning or exaggerating illness, destroying equipment necessary for production, or working less vigorously when unobserved. These were realistic ways for vulnerable people to attempt to meet basic needs and to cope with the pervasive pain and terror of enslavement.[20]

When possible within the considerable constraints of enslavement, slaves asserted personal control of their bodies as resources, at the expense of enslavers, through their movement, adornment, enjoyment, and depletion. Many attempted to forge bonds of mutual responsibility at funerals, religious occasions, and illicit social gatherings where they could discuss their shared plight with a few trusted souls.[21] Some even temporarily fled their enslavers for days or weeks as a way to preserve their bodies from work or to visit family members held in captivity on a distant plantation.[22] These clandestine activities were moments of freedom: as political scientist and Africana studies scholar Neil Roberts has theorized, given the impossibility for any human being to experience perfect liberty or absolute domination, we should look for historical freedom in enslaved people's acts of "flight" from one pole to the other, along paths both real and metaphorical that led from oppression toward relative autonomy. This array of responses showed just how wrong enslavers were when they proclaimed that slaves lacked the mental capacity to resist.[23]

A small number of enslaved people, driven to desperation, took the dangerous path of rising in open rebellion against their oppressors even though they risked almost certain death.[24] From the ancient world to the modern, as David Brion Davis has observed, "revolts appear to have been extremely rare" because large-scale insurrections lacked a clear exit strategy and brought violent crackdowns against rebels and bystanders alike.[25] Some followed a slightly less dangerous path away from domination: they permanently fled their enslavers. Self-liberated fugitives could seek safe harbor by forming illicit settlements in swamps and mountains, known as maroon communities, hidden or inaccessible to colonizers who would re-enslave them. Others took refuge among American Indians beyond the colonial frontier or among the transient populations and people of color in urban seaports.[26] In times of war and other interimperial tension, a significant number fled across battle lines or imperial boundaries, took refuge, and later participated in battles against their former oppressors.[27] Within the severe constraints of enslavement, terrorized enslaved people selected from this array of resistance strategies to respond to the violence and trauma of their exploitation. The most violent and visible of these approaches, however infrequent, in turn struck fear into their tormenters.

For their part, enslavers feared that the violence and terror with which they attempted to control enslaved people also sowed the seeds of their own destruction. They wielded enormous power, but they were also aware of their regime's vulnerabilities.[28] Enslavers understood that they surrounded themselves with people whom they exploited, and they recognized that they furnished implements, such as machetes for cutting sugar cane, that could be used as weapons. They knew that as a practicality they sometimes had to turn their backs, as shown in the rare visual admission by an illustrator in figure 3. In time, they worried, enslaved people in desperation would answer their tormentors' persistent violence by erupting into armed rebellion. An artist who depicted Tacky's Rebellion in Jamaica (1760), without having witnessed it, represented this reversal as an insurgent bursting into a domestic space (fig. 4). The insurgent brandishes a machete that the artist has morphed into an Ottoman scimitar, with implications of tyranny, barbarity, and a threat to English liberty.[29] Such transformations of New World phenomena through references to threats white people perceived from the Old World, as in this fantasy illustration, contributed to enslavers' heightened fears. Absent from either of these deeply flawed depictions, each predicated on a harmful stereotype, is the violence and fear experienced by enslaved people in reality.

When revolts occurred, enslavers located their origins in slaves' desire for vengeance. When South Carolina's colonists tried to make sense of the Stono Rebellion of 1739, some presumed it was "revenge for particular severity's [that slaves] conceived they had received from their Masters and overseers."[30] They pointed to insurgents' decision to spare the life of one of the enslavers whom they encountered because supposedly "he was a good Man and kind to his Slaves."[31] After another rebellion, in Antigua, the colony's governor thought that the enslaver whom the rebels beheaded was probably "guilty of some unwise act of severity or . . . indignity." After

Figure 3. Enslavers knew that they exploited people in ways that left themselves vulnerable to insurrectionary violence, as when this overseer turned his back to an enslaved cane-cutter's machete. *Cutting Down the Sugar-Cane*. In Amelia Opie, *The Black Man's Lament: or How to Make Sugar* (London, 1826), 16. Courtesy of Cotsen Children's Library, Department of Rare Books and Special Collections, Princeton University Library.

all, he mused, the people who revolted were from the Gold Coast region of Lower Guinea and therefore, he unsoundly generalized, "Obedient to a kind Master, but implacably revengefull when ill treated."[32] When Bryan Edwards remembered Tacky's Rebellion, he thought that insurgents' "emotions of fear and revenge" clouded their ability to discern which enslavers were "innocent," deserving quarter, and which were "guilty."[33] Enslavers predicted general massacre because they knew they were guilty of brutalities. Recognizing a "just Law of Retaliation," they acknowledged that they deserved the worst fates that enslaved people could give them.[34]

Figure 4. In this image, inspired by Tacky's Rebellion (1760), an enslaved man uses a tool of his oppressor to surprise him in a domestic space. The artist has emphasized the curve of the blade, suggesting an Ottoman scimitar and alluding to associations with tyranny and barbarity. François Anne David, *Souleve-ment des Negres a' la Jamaïque en 1759*. Engraving, after the drawing by le Jeune, in David, *Histoire d'Angleterre* (Paris, 1800), 3:plate 5. Courtesy of the John Carter Brown Library at Brown University.

The radical thinker Thomas Tryon played on enslavers' fear of vengeance to advocate for better treatment for enslaved people. He wrote an imagined dialogue between a man and his enslaver. Adopting the voice of a slave, he noted that enslavers mistreated enslaved people with "great Tyranny, Injustice, and cruel Usages," including by "gratif[ying] their raging Lusts . . . [with the rape of] our Women." He cautioned the enslaver that this violence "stir[red] up . . . wrathful Qualities in us" and noted that enslaved people had already formed "several horrid Plots and Conspiracies" to "kill and destroy you." The corresponding solution, he wrote, was to treat enslaved people more humanely—although notably not to free them—to "disarm the Rage of the fierce Wrath."[35]

Enslavers heeded Tryon's warning that "the Cup of Wrath is almost full," and they watched for warning signs that enslaved people were about rise. They established legal and policing apparatuses organized around the possibility of insurrection. Their own fear was the wellspring of slave law.[36] Their hypervigilance prompted them to interpret as sinister whatever they glimpsed of slave life and overheard of their conversations. At times, enslavers' fear boiled into an intensity that gave conspiracy scares a head of steam, and the findings of those investigations appeared to affirm what enslavers had always suspected: it seemed that their slaves had been wanting to kill them all along.[37]

The Conspiracy Scare Phenomenon

The conspiracy scare phenomenon emerged from this combination of enslaved people's traumatic experience of terror and enslavers' awareness of their culpability and exposure to the people whom they exploited. On at least ninety-six documented occasions before 1790 (see Appendix, table 1), colonial officials in eastern North America and the British Caribbean believed that they discovered evidence of a "slave conspiracy"—a detailed plan for insurrection coordinated by a network of enslaved men—just in time to avert the uprising.[38] Often they ended up convincing themselves that they regularly dodged ambushes at decoy fires and averted a world turned upside down. Two questions about conspiracy scares motivate *The World That Fear Made*. How and why did white colonists, with the coerced involvement of enslaved people, create these particular fears and come to believe in them? And how did people remake their societies in relation to fear and navigate the world that it conjured?

The creation and logic of conspiracy scares has eluded explanation partly because historians have been using conspiracies to debate the degree of slaves' resistance or acquiescence to enslavement. In the mid-twentieth century, recovering examples of collective political consciousness was historiographically urgent as the United States struggled openly with racial injustice on many fronts. Troubled by misguidedly sanguine portrayals of enslaver-enslaved relations, Herbert Aptheker and others argued for enslaved people's perpetual resistance by cataloging rebellions and rebellion plots in North America and the Caribbean that appeared ready to explode into revolution.[39] This scholarship sometimes confused the matter by conflating the distinct but related phenomena of insurrections and conspiracy scares.

Conspiracy scares were recognized as a distinct phenomenon when Bertram Wyatt-Brown and others offered early voices of skepticism about rebellious intentions by emphasizing that these events were important as white community rituals. More stridently, Michael P. Johnson has argued that the iconic Denmark Vesey plot in South Carolina (1822) was not an imminent rebellion so much as a fabrication by politically motivated judges.[40] Johnson's skepticism has ignited new debate about other high-profile conspiracy scares—in each case, did slaves intend to revolt, or did enslavers falsely accuse them?[41]

The World That Fear Made views this question as an artifact of archival power, forged in fear. We must remain constantly aware of chattel slavery's extreme relations of power, which were even more warped in the courtroom during a crisis. Officials applied tortures that were meant to terrorize enslaved informants and extract information from their trauma. They converted this physical violence into what Marisa Fuentes has called "epistemic violence" by wielding pens that reduced asymmetrical exchanges to summary caricatures of purported plans for rebellion. In the end, officials inscribed the enslaved in ways that obscured their full humanity in the conventional record.[42] Fear in many forms was a crucial ingredient in the manufacture of these distortions: white people's fear of slaves' violent resistance, colonial officials' fear of failing to protect the white population, and enslaved people's fear of punishment, loss, death, and religious violation at the hands of the enslaving regime.[43] We must pay attention to how these threats and forms of power interacted at crucial sites of knowledge creation, such as in street conversations, jailhouse collusions, tortured confessions, courtroom confrontations, and print shops.

In these interactions animated by fear, enslaved people and their enslavers navigated their immediate predicaments by thinking across broad landscapes of ideas and experiences. They used conceptual guides from Africa, Europe, and other colonies in America. They evaluated these ideas within broadly regional developments such as demographic changes and interimperial wars, and they applied them to explain and influence local dynamics among enslaved people and colonists. Each of these layers had implications for the others in generating conspiracy scares and constructing their findings. Using these shifting scales of Atlantic history, it is possible to map the dynamics of fear between colonial enslavers and the vulnerable people on whom they preyed. This book's archaeology of the discourses that informed conspiracy scares may assist the efforts of other scholars who wish to read between the lines of these trial records to recover more details of life in enslavement.[44]

This angle on conspiracy trials has much in common with studies of early-modern witch-hunting. Trauma, racial anxiety, and wartime fear are at the center of Mary Beth Norton's interpretation of the Salem witch trials. Other scholars of European inquisitions and witch-hunting have noted how extreme power relations between magistrates and suspects, often society's most vulnerable members, generated false confessions and expansive networks of accusation. Investigators both of witchcraft and of slave conspiracy fixated on a shadowy countersociety that threatened to replace elements of the status quo with abominable opposites, and confessing suspects in each scenario used vocabularies that simultaneously reflected their own understanding of the world while also speaking to magistrates' expectations of conventional scripts and stock characters. Very often, in both situations, a governing class shored up its power by preying on weak links of acquaintanceship between informers and victims.[45]

Applying this approach to understanding slave conspiracy scares in the anglophone colonies is more effective if we examine them in a geographic frame that includes both the Caribbean and North America. In a zone we might call the Greater Caribbean, tied together by the connected labors of exploited people of African descent, we must include the wharves and workshops of New York, Charleston, and Bermuda; the rivers and fields of the Chesapeake Bay and the Carolinas; and the sugarcane fields and cattle pens smothering Barbados, the Leeward Islands, and Jamaica.[46] While it would be tempting to look at figure 5 as depicting a comparison between North America and the Caribbean, perhaps showing greater fear in one area, on closer inspection it represents the two regions' interconnection. The territories' formal political separation in 1776, at the start of the American Revolution, has obscured their earlier circuits of migration, trade, and information. That shared anglophone culture was one ingredient that made conspiracy confessions sound strikingly similar across these regions, and enslavers in each place learned from the others' experiences with conspiracy scares. These two regions of the British American empire, furthermore, experienced parallel and shared developments, such as war, that impinged on enslaved people's constraints and opportunities as well as enslavers' everchanging awareness of their own vulnerability.

Conspiracy scares varied in size and intensity. In minor scares, judicial authorities at the county and parish level interrogated informants, sometimes torturing them. In these cases, white colonists' fears remained in check and coerced informants did not implicate more than a handful of suspects convincingly enough for the court. Although comparatively small in scope, these ordeals still terrorized local enslaved populations with public whippings or the exemplary execution of one or two alleged ringleaders. In major conspiracy scares, in contrast, judges at a colony's highest level investigated for weeks, if not months, and forced informants to help them arrest dozens or hundreds of suspects. These tribunals usually sentenced some convicted conspirators to banishment, requiring their enslavers to sell them out of the colony, and sentenced others to grisly spectacles of execution, dismemberment, and display, terrorizing thousands of black people in an effort to defuse white fears. Some went into hiding or fled to another colony.

These different kinds of scares produced an archive that ranges widely in terms of format and level of detail. Investigators collected hundreds of pages of enslaved people's testimonies in some cases, but in others they only summarized that evidence as a synthesis of what they deemed to be true. These two sets of documentation lend themselves to in-depth explorations of the contributions of enslaved people and their enslavers to conspiracy scares. When we lack such detailed information about an investigation's findings, we can use other governmental records to examine patterns in colonial officials' actions in response to a perceived threat and to characterize their fear. Sometimes we can complement our knowledge of governmental actions with laypeople's narrative descriptions of the plot in

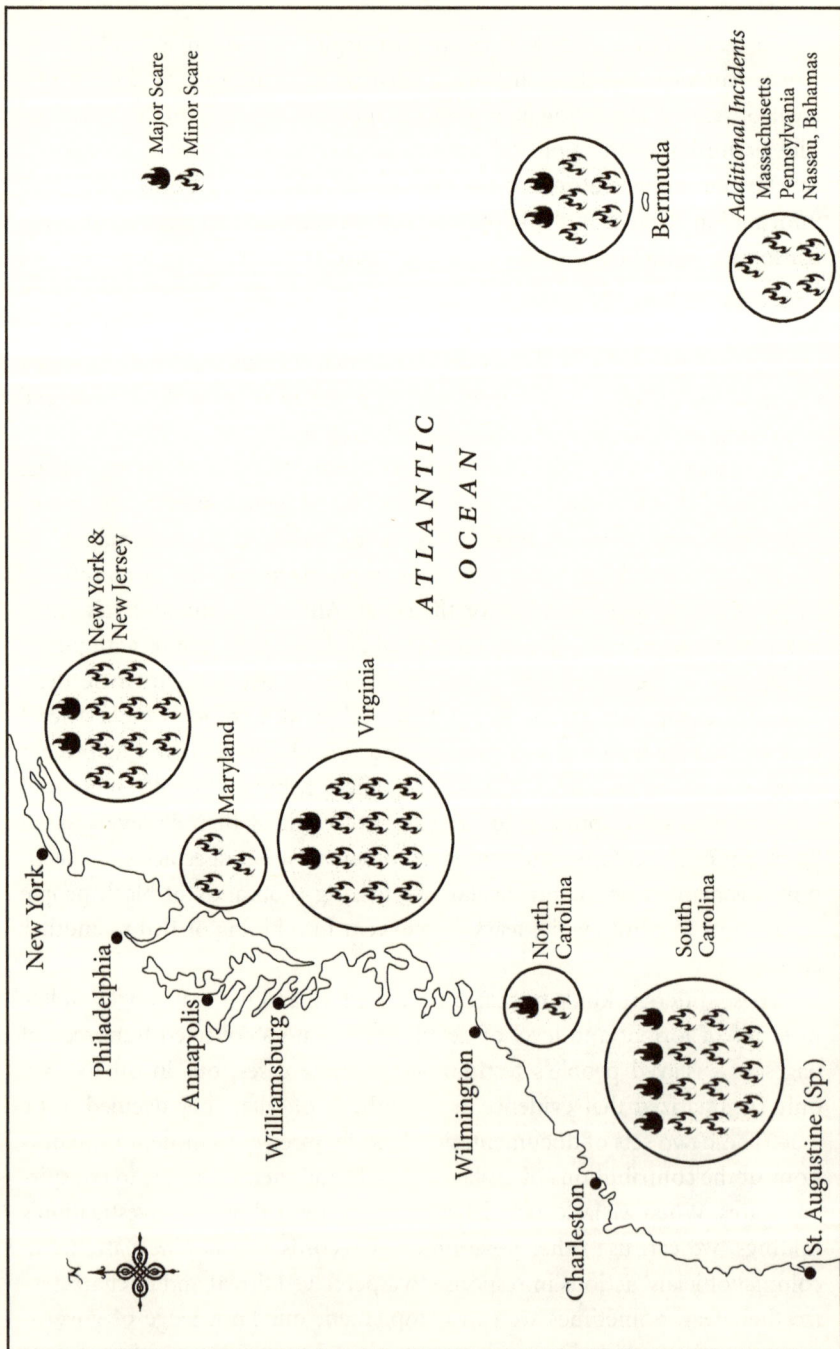

Major Scare

Minor Scare

Additional Incidents
Massachusetts
Pennsylvania
Nassau, Bahamas

Bermuda

ATLANTIC
OCEAN

New York &
New Jersey

Maryland

Virginia

New York

Philadelphia

Annapolis

Williamsburg

North
Carolina

South
Carolina

Wilmington

Charleston

St. Augustine (Sp.)

N

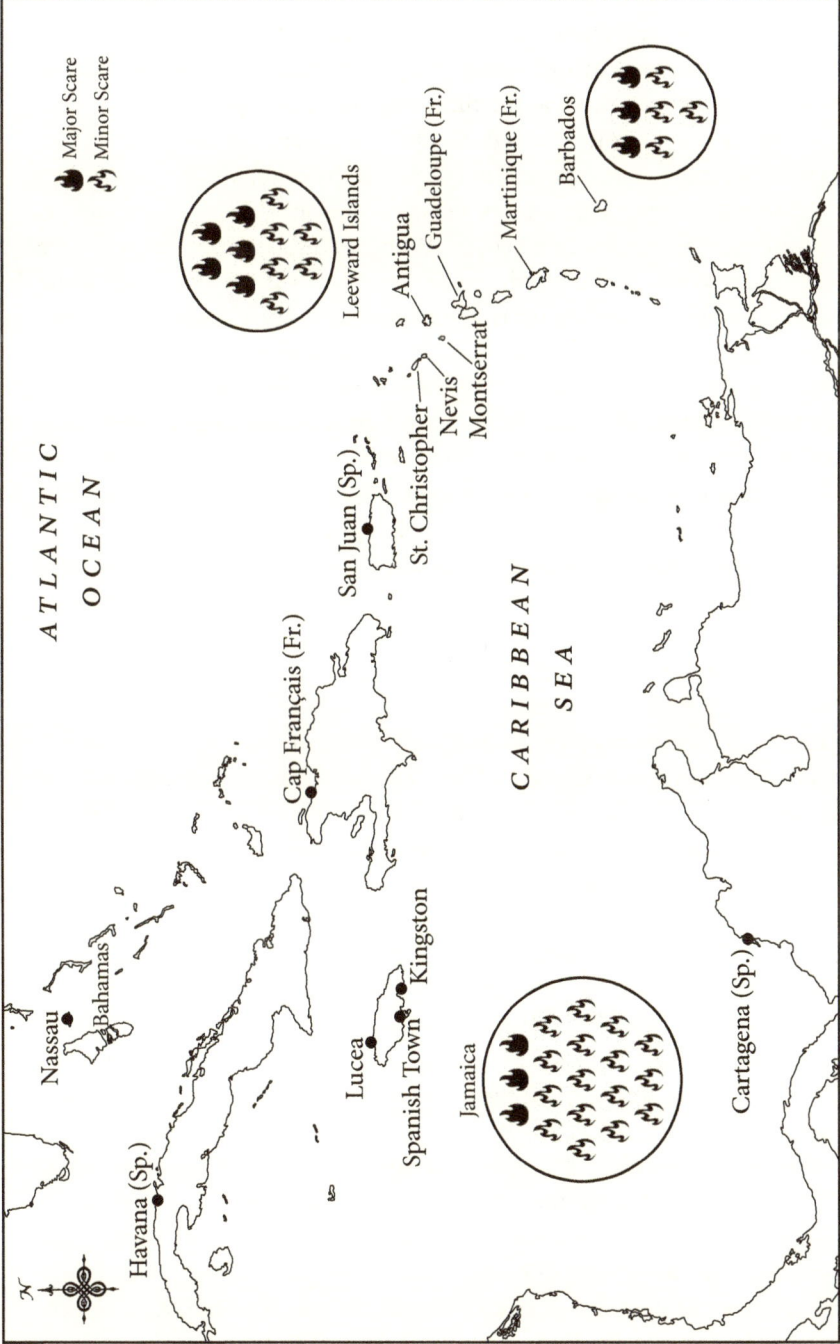

Figure 5. Map of known slave conspiracy scares in Anglo-America, 1655–1786. Source: Appendix, table 1.

newspapers and correspondence. Finally, because governmental archives are incomplete, we learn of some conspiracy scares only through newspapers or histories written at the time. I exclude any reported rumors that did not worry authorities enough for them to accept the costly disruption to white people's economic and public life in the colony.

Colonial governments did not make the decision to investigate lightly, because false alarms could be costly. White colonists wanted to avoid the lost chattel value of convicted people, the neglected livelihoods of white men who mustered in the militia, the economic loss of a closed harbor, and the sapped public finances of a colony in emergency. In government, assembly chambers typically voiced these financial concerns because their elected members controlled the purse strings in colonies under royal control, such as those at the heart of this book. On the other hand, smaller chambers known as councils were appointed by the king and tended to emphasize potential risks to white people's physical security because they assisted governors in protecting his subjects. Assemblies, councils, and governors attempted to balance these concerns as they directed governmental responses to rumored uprisings and supported investigations.

Judicial authorities sought the facts of the matter even if the conclusions they drew were often incorrect. Each colony used a slightly different investigative body, sometimes inconsistently, deploying county courts, high criminal courts, courts-martial, and ad hoc tribunals. Always, however, judicial authorities tried to "get the Truth out," as South Carolina's council put it in 1749, because of the high costs of false alarms. To do this, they attempted to fairly evaluate informants' evidence, accurately identify possible conspirators, and uncover information that would quash any imminent rebellion. In nearly all cases, investigating judges simultaneously generated this information and decided the innocence or guilt of individual suspects. They did not think as much about the suffering that they caused the enslaved people whom they ensnared in investigations or the trauma of thousands more living in its shadow. The highest cost of conspiracy scares was in black lives.[47]

Investigators used coercion and torture to compel suspects to confess. Those who turned informant recognized that their route to power lay in offering investigators the right information to curry favor with them. They provided evidence against jailed slaves and named new suspects in exchange for promises of pardons, monetary reward, or even freedom. As a suspect named Cudjoe explained to a jailer, "Fellows to Save their own lives would

Say any thing against him."[48] Some turned informant out of fear for their own lives and in order to protect their loved ones by redirecting the inquiry away from their home quarter, in a local kaleidoscope of social tensions that went far beyond the fundamental conflict of exploitation. They did this at a steep human cost: those who did turn informant gave evidence that enabled colonial authorities to terrorize still more enslaved people. Informants scoured the jail for information that could help them, and they presented it in the courtroom in crafted performances. The most powerful informants drew on their torturers' assumptions about the nature of slave insurrection. They deployed potent idioms against other suspects, incorporating stereotypes that touched sensitive nerves. They found that their own route to power depended on getting investigators to believe them. Playing directly to their fears was one way to accomplish that.

Conspiracy investigations were not clear windows through which enslavers could look out onto enslaved people's politics. They were more like the warped and bubbled glass of an eighteenth-century pane, distorting white people's views of enslaved life and partially obscuring it with their own fearful reflections. If we bring those distortions of the record directly into focus, we can see that they have disguised significant dynamics of fear for enslaved people. We can also see that they have naturalized, through enslavers' fear and archival power, many embellishments and racialized visions of the threat of insurgent violence from the perspectives of white colonists. Our clearer vision shows us that enslavers had less confidence in their "mastery" than they claimed, articulating their perceived vulnerabilities, and it also gives us a better understanding of enslaved people's human experiences of terror and trauma and their array of responses to it. Violence's less-visible counterpart, fear, influenced a person's perception of the realm of possibility. This could shape decisions, inspire actions, and govern social relations. At the same time, a person with some awareness of others' fear could use it to exercise power to attempt to oppress them, to subvert them, or to survive.

CHAPTER 1

Making Sense of Strangers

The Invention of Anglo-American Slave Conspiracy

An enslaved man named Ben faced a harrowing decision in Bridgetown, Barbados, in October 1692, at the beginning of the largest and most devastating conspiracy scare of the seventeenth century. He had no good options left when four militia officers found him guilty, hung him up in chains, and starved him almost to death to get him to speak about the alleged plot. Ben saved himself and his loved ones by turning king's evidence and by dubiously confirming for the court that it had discovered a secret plan for coordinated insurrection exactly one day before it would have engulfed the island. The officers expanded the investigation with Ben's testimony against acquaintances, describing him as "altogether the meanes of the farther discovery" of many new suspects. As a result, two hundred to three hundred enslaved people experienced the trauma of arrest and interrogation by the militia officers, and they faced the real prospect of joining the scores whom the court banished, castrated, hanged, burned alive, or starved to death. At least 114 enslaved people died painfully at the hands of the judges, and others were left terrified and in mourning.

As the militia officers took down Ben's coerced confession, they transposed that information into a distinctly European projection in a table appended to a report of four manuscript pages (fig. 6). Demonstrating English fears more than African goals, they recorded conspirators as members of militia units in a rebel army in a format that exactly mirrored the colony's regiments of horse and foot. The table also represented the projected postinsurrectionary world, with the anticipated "disposeall of the Government" positions among rebels and, simultaneously, conspirators' claims on gentlemen's very identities. A horizontal line connected each

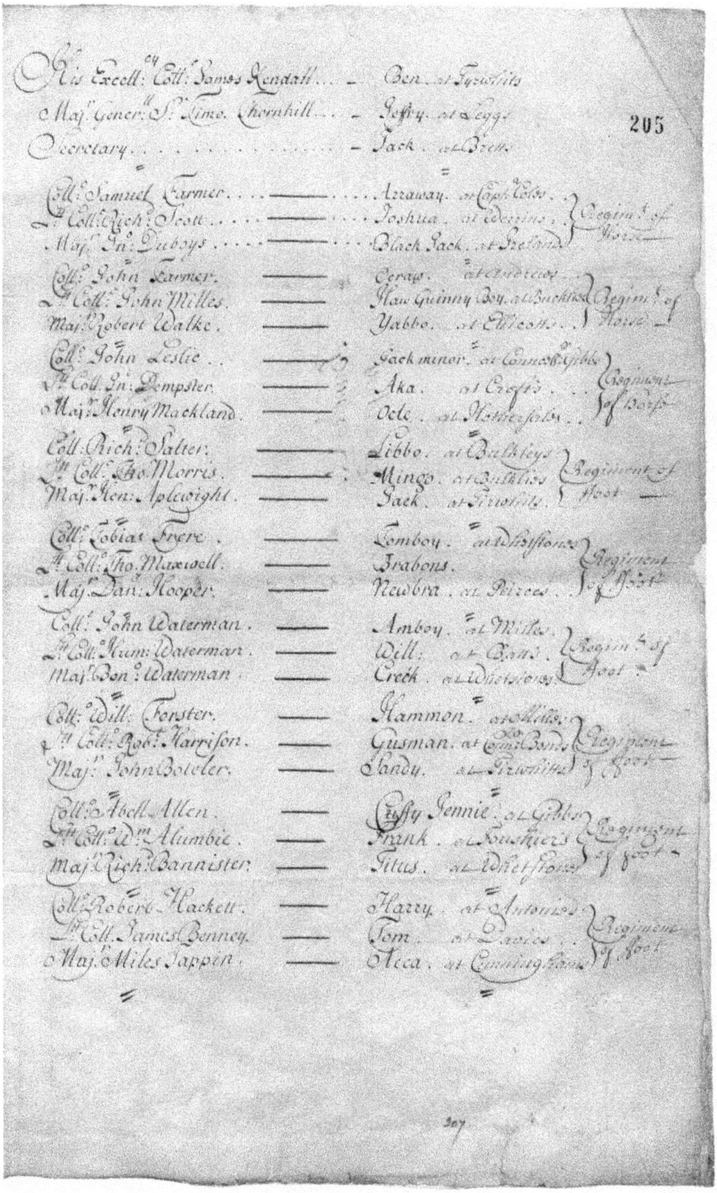

Figure 6. Investigators in Barbados in 1692 recorded the names of principal alleged conspirators in a format that mirrored the colony's structure of militia officers. List of Alleged Conspirators, in Tobias Frere et al., Report on the Conspiracy, encl. in James Kendall to the Lords of Trade, November 3, 1692, Colonial Office series 28/1, 205, National Archives of the United Kingdom, Kew, London. Courtesy of the National Archives of the United Kingdom.

enslaved man's name to that of the gentleman he intended to supplant. Ben apparently placed himself in the position of "governor" to increase his value to information-hungry investigators and to enhance his power to bargain for his life and redirect arrests away from his loved ones.

The essence of the "discovery" of a slave conspiracy—that is, the fabrication of official knowledge about an alleged plan for insurrection—is best captured in this cross-cultural reframing and intimate but imbalanced negotiation between fearful investigators and a desperate informant. Magistrates were helpless to know anything about the potential rebellion unless they extracted information from an enslaved person whose assistance they compelled through calculated terror. But when they turned English ears to African voices, they heard them imperfectly. They evaluated informants' ideas and recorded aspects of them that aligned with their own notions of possible forms of insurrection. Questioning led informants down paths laid by European expectations. Accordingly, the court determined on slim evidence that Ben and his accomplices planned to seize masters' arms in the dead of night, meet at the principal settlement of Bridgetown, set fires around town to lure sleepy men outside into a slaughter, and then supplant them as heads of existing households and government. Even though this scene would look familiar in the eighteenth century, in this seventeenth-century moment it was a new, conjunctural pastiche of English and African ideas.[1]

The problem of incomplete understanding across cultural chasms was particularly pronounced in the seventeenth century. English planters were just beginning to enslave Africans in large numbers and exploiting them so violently that they drove some in desperation to take up arms, turning colonists' minds toward anticipating some greater form of vengeance. English colonial officials were still novices to the practice of racial slavery and had no immediate framework for understanding this new possibility of large-scale African insurrection. Colonists had slender experience with slave rebellions and were still inventing the category of "slave conspiracy." Moreover, in this earliest period of English slavery, they freely admitted that they could not comprehend the languages that captive strangers spoke within their homes, and they only barely recognized diasporic African social and political activities in the slave quarter. At this point, enslaved Africans were still domestic "strangers" to the English through cultural and linguistic distance, as well as across the gulf of incomprehension that divided people of extreme power differentials. When colonial officials attempted to make sense of this new possibility of slave insurrection, they instinctively borrowed from realms of ideas beyond the practice of slavery.

Barbados's slave conspiracy scare of 1692 is an ideal focal point for understanding how enslaved Africans and English investigators developed the fears of insurrection in the seventeenth century that would haunt colonists in the eighteenth. After all, it was the largest and best-documented scare of the seventeenth century after several similar events with more fragmented records in Bermuda (1656, 1661, 1673, and 1682); Barbados (1659, 1675, 1683, and 1686); Jamaica (1683, 1685, and 1687); Antigua (1687); and Virginia (1687). This chapter uses the ample record of Barbados in 1692 and other shards of evidence from the seventeenth century to expose how English colonizers came to believe they understood the intentions of enslaved Africans, and how traumatized Africans contributed their own perspectives in ways that enflamed the fears of their tormenters.

Enslaved informants, under coercion, provided some information about life in the slave quarter and offered visions of what an insurrection might look like. To do this they drew on African conceptual lexicons, or banks of concepts, that shaped their contributions similarly to but more fluidly and creatively than what we sometimes call cultural "frameworks." Colonial magistrates, for their part, listened to Africans' ideas with reference to their own conceptual vocabularies from distinctly English and American experiences. They borrowed from theories of domination and resistance in their reading knowledge of ancient Roman slavery and their experience with American indentured servant rebellions. They used ideas of treason and insurrection from the dominant political ideology of antipopery, which guarded the Protestant realms from Catholic plotting, and they considered its colonial manifestations in violent encounters with Native Americans and the Irish. These spectral fears from other realms enabled them to decide to bring terrible violence against hundreds of alleged plotters and to terrorize the island's enslaved population.

Why did enslavers and enslaved people combine this particular mix of conceptual vocabularies to think through the social consequences of the violence of colonial slavery? And how did colonial enslavers borrow guiding concepts from them? The case study of Barbados's conspiracy scare of 1692 illustrates that guiding concepts entered the production of knowledge at many points in the unequal exchange between magistrates and suspects. Although investigators wielded power through coercion and inscription, thus favoring English concepts, they had to select ideas from among those deemed relevant by informants who generated them through their own diasporic African conceptual guides. Thus the final conspiracy findings did not originate with just one group but were a product of unequal coauthorship between Africans and Europeans. This began with how investigators restrained suspects and posed questions, and it continued with how informants in turn understood those queries and decided how to answer: they looked for any possible correspondences between enslavers' apparent interests, their experiences of colonial social structures, and relevant ideas from their own available diasporic African frameworks.

When investigators in turn evaluated coerced informants' cautious responses, they processed them by thinking with analogies at several levels. First, English magistrates favored and adapted confessed information that resembled their own experiences of colonialism. They anchored ideas from these remote lexicons in the social reality of the exploitation they perpetrated in colonial slavery. More importantly, however, they also favored aspects of African confessions that corresponded to one or more familiar guiding concepts from the seemingly relevant English lexicons of ideas that they had at the ready. Thus, the investigators and informants developed their findings by drawing analogies to each other's ideas at the intersection of diasporic African and colonial English ideas about, and experiences of, political organization, class conflict, ethnocentrism, and expectations of vengeance.

The Machete and the Whip

The human anguish of Africans' enslavement, which English colonists inflicted to generate profit, established the fundamental conditions for conspiracy scares. Violence was at the root of fear. English violence in the forcible relocation and enslavement of Africans transformed the economies of Bermuda, the Chesapeake Bay, and the Caribbean. English whips threatened enslaved Africans within households and drove them to perform backbreaking work in fields of tobacco and sugar. Enslaved Africans, desperate to survive, sometimes violently resisted their oppressors in uprisings. Those who were using machetes to cut sugar cane could turn and wield them as cutlasses. Others lifted hoes and axes or seized the guns of overseers. However infrequent, these small uprisings caught the attention of English colonists and unnerved them, as they recognized a new vulnerability for themselves: potential large-scale insurrection.

Large insurrectionary conspiracies by Africans became a realistic possibility in the eyes of English colonists only after a period of sweeping economic and social transformation that increased the populations of exploited people. Tobacco drove the economic development that changed the social profiles of Bermuda and Virginia, and sugar had even greater effects on Barbados, Antigua, and Jamaica. Bermuda was the first colony in English America to enslave Africans and the first to codify slavery, in 1623, in support of an economy of tobacco export and mixed agriculture. By the 1670s, fifteen hundred of the eight thousand people who lived there were enslaved. Barbados underwent its own labor revolution from 1640 to 1660, when English planters discarded an experiment in poor-quality tobacco cultivation for more profitable—and labor intensive—sugar monoculture. Sugar cultivation rewarded enormous capital investments in labor, land, and processing machinery. During this economic realignment, planters relied increasingly on purchasing enslaved Africans as changes in Atlantic labor markets made it more difficult and less profitable to use indentured servants from the British Isles. High death rates in the tropical climate only amplified the demographic effects of these economic changes. From the 1640s to the 1670s, and accelerating in the 1680s, the European population dwindled from 35,000 to 19,600, while the African population soared from 20,000 to 46,600 and beyond, almost entirely through the torment of the transatlantic slave trade. Virginia, the Leeward Islands, and Jamaica embarked on similar economic and social transformations later in the seventeenth century.[2]

Enslaved Africans took the lead in demonstrating that rebellion was possible. They rose up most frequently on slaving ships during the Atlantic crossing in response to the disorientation and despair of enduring dehumanizing treatment that included family separation, confinement, and rape. In 1654, for example, a resident of Barbados relayed news of the arrival of a ship on which sixty souls perished in an unsuccessful revolt, retaining only twenty members of its human cargo. As more slaving ships arrived from Africa, Barbados's enslavers probably heard about the other nineteen known shipboard revolts from 1640 to 1690.[3] Upon arrival in the Americas, enslaved people likewise resisted their condition in ways big and small. Only the greatest uprisings survived in the record and, although they were concerning to colonists, they resulted largely in fugitives living in self-organized societies outside the zone of colonial control, a phenomenon known as marronage, rather than racial massacre or political takeover. In

Barbados, Irish servants and enslaved Africans escaped to "the Thicketts & thereabouts" in the 1650s, finding freedom on the run. As they provisioned themselves through raids that left behind a trail of "Murthers, Roberies & divers other mischiefs," they caused such consternation among white colonists that the settlers fortified their houses, and the colony declared a day for "a General Hunting" of them in 1657. Facing similar resistance in the early 1670s, the Virginia Assembly worried that the strength of their own maroon groups beyond the frontier would inspire others held in bondage to "fly forth and joyne with them."[4]

People who rebelled on plantations sought to escape from slavery and to live autonomously in frontier regions, not to slaughter their enslavers, as exemplified in Jamaica. To destroy the English and seize the colony was not guaranteed success. The attempt would surely provoke the colonial state's violent retribution and white people's outraged vigilantism. Therefore, as Jamaica transformed into a slave colony, on the occasions that Africans at frontier labor camps rose up, they attempted to join existing communities of Maroons, as these people identify ethnically today, in the mountains in the 1670s and 1680s. In 1673, for example, enslaved people killed twelve English people in remote St. Ann Parish, robbed the few neighboring settlements for provisions, and created an opportunity for two hundred people to flee to the mountains. For years, the colony of Jamaica sent expeditions against the growing communities of Maroons, whose entrepreneurial plundering posed the greatest threat to settlers' security in the remote northern parishes.[5] In 1678, rebels at one plantation "Set Upon the Family" only four miles outside of the government seat of Spanish Town, a tempting target, but they did not go for what colonizers considered the main prize. Again, in 1685, at an estate just fifteen miles outside of Spanish Town, a group of insurgents broke into the main house to seize weapons and provisions. They murdered one white man and injured another, while a woman escaped out the window. As the violence unfolded, the insurgents' numbers grew to 130 assailants from the home quarter and 20 more from satellite farms. Despite their proximity to Spanish Town, the rebels did not attempt political takeover or massacre of white people but instead prioritized survival and autonomous living in the island's inaccessible interior. They set fire to the "Canes Houses & Works" to cover their escape and "Fleed into the Woods" toward the mountains, "Destroying little Families the[y] Met in their Way."[6] Jamaica's numerous small insurrections informed the horizon of possibility throughout colonial America: in Bermuda, for example, a recently arrived enslaved person bragged that "when he was in Jamaica, he killed . . . many people" and would do so in a fresh plot on this new island.[7] Despite rebels' personal goals, colonists took these risings as evidence that a larger-scale reckoning was forthcoming unless they remained vigilant for plans as they formed.

As some Africans took up arms against their enslavers, colonists noticed that elite planters had created dangerous conditions for their neighbors by concentrating and traumatizing large groups of exploited people who might answer violence with violence. In Barbados, for example, the leading cadre of 175 planters (7 percent of the property-holding population) held 61 percent of the island's enslaved people and concentrated them in plantation workforces of about one hundred to three hundred people. In contrast, thousands of middling and small planters held, on average, fourteen enslaved people per estate. The elite planters, therefore, held most responsibility for creating the utterly novel labor regimes that made slave insurrection likely; their pursuit of private gain by exploiting enslaved Africans inadvertently created a public problem for white neighbors.[8] Shards of evidence indicate that ordinary colonists pressured governing officials to act decisively against the possible uprising by enslaved Africans by punishing alleged conspirators. For example, in Bermuda in 1673, when a court-martial whipped and branded the confessed conspirators and then released them back into daily life, "some disorderly persons" threatened vigilantism that would "maim or kill" them to enact their own vision of justice.[9] Wealthy slaveholders, having monopolized political offices, faced popular pressure to defuse a public problem for which they held responsibility. They looked for conspiracies before they materialized and scapegoated enslaved people who were legally powerless.

African Speech and English Ears

Enslaved people from different African origins attempted to communicate with each other to grapple with the anguish of enslavement, even as early as their confinement on slaving ships.[10] English planters worried that any easy communication among Africans would allow them to coordinate their responses to enslavement. Insurrection appeared most threatening, settlers agreed, when enslaved people from different parts of a colony coordinated in advance in a conspiracy. Where such communication seemed unlikely, especially in the first decades, colonists considered themselves secure. But as Africans beat paths toward one another, English colonists revealed their unease by discussing their own security, circumscribing enslaved people's activities, and commenting on alleged conspiracies and actual uprisings alike.

At first, some English colonists professed that enslaved people could not organize collective violence because they could not understand one another's languages and, in a naive oversimplification, because they harbored ethnic animosities toward one another. In truth, they did experience profound dislocation in separation from familiar people and societies, which their African enslavers began with slaving wars, captivity, and forced marches to the coast, and which Europeans cruelly amplified during the Atlantic voyage.[11] As a resident in Barbados in the late 1640s explained it, the enslaved Africans "speak several languages, and by that means one of them understands not another." Indeed, Barbados's first comprehensive statute to police enslaved people (1661), even following the island's first recorded slave conspiracy scare (1659), did not reflect white people's concern about Africans' communication and planning for rebellion so much as about small-scale crimes like robbery, murder, and especially flight.[12] The governor of the island agreed with this sentiment but added a note of caution that, although enslaved Africans' "different tongues and animosities have kept them from insurrection," any new creole (American-born) generation would more easily conspire to rise up. A visitor to Jamaica made the same prediction that "in the next age" creoles would share a "generall understanding" of English that would enable conspiring in "private consulltation together."[13] These commentators might have added that a sufficient number of people from a single language group, such as prisoners of war captured all at once in Africa, presented similar conditions for plotting. Communication among people from different backgrounds was difficult but not impossible, and forced migrants were desperate to seek solace somewhere. Their attempts to do so frightened enslavers and caused them to "discover" conspiracies, whether real or imagined.

Africans' attempts to overcome social isolation through interplantation communication were central to how enslavers understood the plots' viability and the colonists' vulnerability. In Bermuda, a court-martial in 1656 identified ten African conspirators (including one free man) as ringleaders of a plot that involved "the negroes in this Island" for a coordinated colony-wide massacre, "cutting off and distroieing the English in the night." The governor rued that colonists endangered themselves in carelessly tolerating enslaved people's "night walking and meeting together." He attempted to master white fear by regulating black movements with a pass law, which required enslaved travelers to carry an enslaver's written permission, and by striking terror into undocumented travelers by permitting their execution "then & thiere without mercye." Even the mere threat of this sudden violence dampened the effectiveness of enslaved people's search for solace in this isolating and dehumanizing system.[14]

In Barbados, in 1659, colonists "discovered" a similar conspiracy seemingly aimed, as a newsletter put it, at "massacring . . . all the English whom they could find upon that Island." Whether this threat was authentic or not, colonists identified Africans' interplantation communication as the dangerous mechanism for plotters, "some going from Plantation to Plantation" in "a correspondency." Incidentally, the news writer salaciously added that it appeared to locals that "the Spaniard had a finger in this Plot" because of a taunt during a chance commercial encounter in Cape Verde that Barbados would feel "the sting of Spain" when its enslaved people "cut off the English" and became "masters of that place." The Spanish weaponized this fear of rebellion and invasion against the English of Barbados, using enslaved people's torments and resistance to needle the English, at the cost of causing anguish for the enslaved people who bore the human toll of counterinsurgent judicial violence. This incident crystallized for Barbadians the possibility of island-wide African insurrection and inspired the governor to create militia parades intended to be "seen amongst the Negroes once a year" to try to terrorize them into obedience and to remind white people that their unified violence was the mechanism by which they maintained mastery. This martial display was largely a symbolic statement of values, however. The real battle recurred nightly with enslaved people's clandestine visiting, which white people could make more difficult but that they found impossible to fully police.[15]

In the 1670s colonists in Bermuda and Barbados, as well as in Virginia and Jamaica, continued to identify enslaved Africans' interplantation communication as a potential basis for colony-wide conflagration. At precisely the moment when Virginia planters invested heavily in African slavery, radically increasing an exploited and suffering population, the governor warned against those agonizingly separated individuals' "unlawful . . . combinations" on Saturdays and Sundays when they gathered to find some freedom within slavery. Records of these gatherings rarely exist, but it is evident from white people's concerns that they happened all the time. In Bermuda, when another conspiracy scare occurred, the governor outlawed enslaved people's gatherings and tightened restrictions on unsupervised traveling off plantations.[16] In Jamaica, after two rebellions in 1673 and 1675, the island's governing council chose to emphasize the importance of restricting "by all wayes imaginable" the "Correspondence" and "Communication of the Negroes one with another," even though these particular revolts involved only one or two estates. White people's alarm upon "discovering" plots and experiencing revolts focused their minds on attempting to control enslaved people's movements.[17]

In Barbados, a major conspiracy scare in 1675 also seemed possible only because of Africans' interplantation communication. According to published news pamphlets, the scare began at the Gyles plantation on the windy bluff overlooking the port of Speightstown when an enslaved woman named Anna (later known as Fortuna) told the white woman who legally owned her that in the garden she overheard an eighteen-year-old enslaved man say some suspicious things. Perhaps Anna was either afraid of how a civil war would dislodge her slender hold on some security in life, or hopeful for a reward of freedom to improve her lot within this slave society. The man whom she accused faced questioning and, frightened for his own life, confessed to a planned revolt. He claimed it was intended to occur "in the dead time of the Night," using planters' alarm to increase the urgency of his additional information and the value of his assistance. Out of desperation, he implicated several acquaintances from neighboring estates whom he knew because they came from the same linguistic group in Africa, and who also matched planters' expected profile of conspirators as ethnic brothers. To coordinate the time of the rising, one of the suspects confessed that they would signal each other from the hills with trumpets "made of Elephants Teeth and Gourdes," in another African mode of communication that the English grimly realized they could not decipher. White people worried about the apparent menace of Africans' cross-island communication that desperately compliant informants confirmed was at the center of this conspiracy, and so the Barbados Assembly immediately attempted to prohibit any further gatherings of enslaved people, making it riskier for them to create those valuable pockets of freedom and self-organization within slavery.[18]

Unlike with prior conspiracy scares, the published accounts of this 1675 Barbados case provide an early glimpse into white colonists' beliefs about *how* exactly insurgents would enact their massacre: we get an indication, made fuller in the confessions of 1692, of early tropes. Whites were afraid that conspirators supposedly wanted to create a simultaneous distraction by setting "fire [to] the Sugar Canes." Burning the cane, we know from other sources, was always disconcertingly loud, "as if two Armies, with a thousand shot of either side, were continually giving fire, every knot of every Cane, giving as great a report as a Pistoll."[19] The enslaved informant who included this detail described a way to terrify white people moments before killing them, much as enslaved people experienced in torturous executions. In this vision of planned rebellion, having woken up their enslavers in confusion, the conspirators would then "run in and Cut their . . . Throats in their respective Plantations." Some said their goal was racial massacre —to "Murther all the White People"—while others planned to challenge white men's mastery over women, both African and English, by "spar[ing] the lives of the Fairest and Handsomest Women," who were wives and daughters of the planters, "to be Converted to their own Use" (raped). After the carnage, rebels would install a man named Kofi as king. The governor and twelve militia officers arrested at least 107 enslaved people, terrorizing them and their loved ones. They executed at least 42 of them through tortures intended to frighten other enslaved people into obedience, and they sentenced many others to be sold out of the colony into a new system of slavery away from anyone familiar.[20]

Beyond the trauma of physical violence and psychological terror, white people focused on the role of black communication and created lasting impacts for enslaved people in two more areas: enslaved men's opportunity to engage with the Christian religion and to develop trade skills such as carpentry and blacksmithing. Colonial agents of Barbados appeared in person to the Lords of Trade, the body in England that regulated the colonies, to explain that Christian missionization efforts would exacerbate white people's vulnerability to black rebellion by making it "necessary to teach them all English." It seemed well established, they explained, that "the diversity of the negroes' languages" was their "greate[st] security" from insurrection plots. The Lords of Trade agreed to allow Barbadians to find a different way to Christianize the enslaved, even as an early antislavery advocate insisted that ancient Rome's example proved that even non-Christians would still revolt and, furthermore, that the colonial agents had it backward: "the late Plot" in Barbados (1675) would not have occurred were a greater "number of the Negro's [*sic*] here . . . Christians."[21]

Horrified by what appeared to be the narrowly averted overturning of power, the governor of Barbados pointed to the unchecked circulation of enslaved craftsmen as one of the factors that facilitated the alleged 1675 conspiracy. A few years before the trials, enslavers had begun training Africans in the skilled trades and entrusting them with leadership positions.[22] From the perspective of an enslaver, it made economic sense to train a person who would be enslaved for the remainder of his life, always generating additional revenue. Some enslaved people who got this opportunity could use it to make a more autonomous life for themselves. Nevertheless, the Barbados Assembly worried that this trend gave too many enslaved Africans unsupervised mobility, and they revised the slave code in 1676 to prohibit "any Negro Man or boy to worke at any of the Arts and Trades." It is evident that this provision reflected white peoples' concerns about black peoples' physical movement, rather than the economics of protecting white craftworkers, because the rest of the clause restricted further forms of mobility and communication. It prohibited gatherings of enslaved people from different estates, limited communication with horns or drums, ended the hiring out of enslaved people to other sites, and reemphasized the requirement that enslaved people have passes to travel.[23]

In the 1680s, Barbadians continued to identify enslaved people's clandestine communication and gatherings as the mechanisms that would lead to island-wide insurrection rather than the more manageable, if frequent, isolated risings and flights. In 1683, a white hoaxer played on the islanders' unease with communication among enslaved people. Early one morning a rumor flew around Bridgetown that enslaved people of the populous leeward coast had a "design to rise upon and destroy the Christians." White militias mustered, compelled to acknowledge enslaved people's potential power of insurgency, but the light of day revealed this to be a false alarm for white residents. Nevertheless, for the enslaved population, even just the rumor was a dangerous event. Colonial officials whipped four or five men "for Example sake," deliberately terrorizing onlookers, and burned one of them at the stake who had wielded his captors' fear against them with the moralistic warning that "the Negroes ere long would serve [kill] the Christians." The prankster meanwhile played on white islanders' anxiety about communication in this moment of fright by forging notes in the voices of enslaved conspirators and tossing them "in fields, High-Waies, hedges and in houses." (Scattered notes such as these were a common feature of alleged Catholic plots in England.)[24] In the only surviving example of this hoax,

the anonymous author demonstrated an awareness of the value of communication for enslaved Africans: "Brothers, Our design is discovered but not
be dishartned, lett us begin the next Sunday about Midnight, do not lett us
mind the Packett or Companies for I understand some Brothers are in hold
[jail] and if wee do not begin wee shall all be brought in trouble [named as
accomplices and arrested], and withal lose Our lives, if not then sometime
next week, for wee will have it, for wee have done for our Brothers here,
methinks long the time, for wee have most of all Countries of Our Side,
therefore bee not afraid."[25] The author's admonition, in the voice of an
African, that conspirators should "bee not afraid" acknowledged everyone's
awareness that the colonial state tried to use terror to control enslaved black
people and make would-be rebels apprehensive of taking further action.
The content of this forged note also confirmed that settlers were thinking
of slave rebellion in terms of a confraternal conspiracy that bridged "all
Countries"—and all languages—of enslaved Africans, despite planters'
attempts to re-create the fracture of Babel. Furthermore, the scattering of
notes in different places spoke to fears of widespread interplantation communication, particularly when enabled by literacy. The militia officer who
collected this sample reassured his correspondent (and himself) that it was
a joke by noting, dismissively, "the incapacity of the Negroes to read or
write such thing." His inability to imagine literate Africans gave him an
opportunity to turn this moment of fear ultimately into one for expressing
confidence. Nevertheless, the joke was cutting because it played on colonists' increasingly deadly and costly suspicions that enslaved people actually
were capable of coordinating in other ways.[26]

At the same time, Antigua, Virginia, and Jamaica were completing their
transformations into slavery-based colonies that forcibly assembled large
populations of exploited, suffering, desperate people. Slave conspiracy
scares became more common in the 1680s as colonists noticed a political
crisis developing in England around the increasing likelihood of a line of
Catholic successors to the throne of a mostly Protestant realm. Such a situation invited political instability and division among white people, in a self-
inflicted reversal of their own strategy to divide and control enslaved Africans. In Antigua, in 1687, it appeared to white officers that some enslaved
people coordinated with a maroon community to "cut of[f] and Destroy
the Christian Inhabitants" and "make them selves masters of the Contry."
The insurrection would begin, informants said, "by firing the plantacons to
Amuse [distract] them" so that the rebels could "in the Hurry to fall on

them."[27] In Virginia, also in 1687, settlers in the Northern Neck discovered "a Negro Plott . . . for the Distroying and killing his Majesties Subjects" with the goal of "Carrying it through the whole Collony." Predictably, Virginia's governing council issued and enforced rules against enslaved people "Walking and Ramling on broad" on Saturdays and Sundays to "meete in great Numbers." It also prohibited self-organized "ffuneralls for Dead Negroes" because enslavers worried that these ceremonies were occasions for enslaved people to gather from several plantations to plan resistance. This prohibition made it more difficult for the living to commune with ancestors, to seek access to their spiritual power, and to recreate the generational continuity that transatlantic enslavers had shattered.[28]

From the earliest conspiracy scares starting in the 1650s to the more numerous investigations in the late 1680s, colonial officials identified communication as the key to enslaved individuals' ability to unify and coordinate a colony-wide insurrection. White people worried aloud about it and established regulations against it, while black people continued to try to communicate. White people blamed it when they believed they discovered an imminent large-scale revolt. As time went on, judging from the increasing numbers of convicted conspirators, they appear to have sought it out so forcefully as to get desperate informants to describe communication and identify people as participants.

The Cage and the Quill

Once English colonists decided that enslaved Africans were "plotting," what did they think they were up to? As the best-documented seventeenth-century conspiracy scare, Barbados's investigation of an alleged 1692 plot lends itself to examining how African informants and English investigators collaborated unequally to create knowledge about the alleged conspiracy. A manuscript summary of the findings provides details of the features of African insurrection that white officials found plausible—exactly the mechanisms by which they believed their power could be overturned—some of which had already appeared in earlier investigations of the preceding four decades. Barbados's report of 1692 was the clearest crystallization of seventeenth-century white fears and African warnings about insurrection. This report is detailed enough to serve as a focal point for discerning the overlapping influences—some of them rather surprising—that led African informants and English investigators to arrive at this particular projection.[29]

In the courtroom, the true center of activity in the production of knowledge, the supremely unequal encounter between desperate suspects and information-starved investigators constrained the findings. From there it is possible to proceed outward into several informational realms of influence brought to bear by African informants and European judges—from the slave quarter and African memories of the old world, to planters' libraries and ideas about indentured servants, to the religious politics of England and its amplification in colonial experiences with Irish servants and Native Americans in captivity and at the frontier. But it is necessary to begin in the place where ideas from each of these realms ultimately became braided together.

The courtroom was the point of intersection for many ideas that produced conspiracy findings, through face-to-face, adversarial collaboration between a handful of enslaved informants and white militia officers who turned to each other out of necessity for self-preservation. In Barbados in 1692, this began with the routine trial of an enslaved man. Hammon was caught sneaking up to the jail in Bridgetown to tell two prisoners, Sambo and Ben, that they "should not discover [reveal] any thing" about some concealed crime. Major John Duboys drove the process of discovery by promising Hammon reprieve if he divulged everything he knew; already, a colonial official's desperation limited Hammon's possible responses. It must have been an agonizing decision, and Hammon could not have fully foreseen the destructive effects it would have on hundreds of people and their families. In exchange for saving his own life, he identified himself as the mastermind of an intended rebellion and implicated three people: Ben, Sambo, and another man from jail, Sampson.

Governor James Kendall, otherwise helpless to avoid the threat described by Hammon, made the expensive and therefore weighty decision to launch an investigation by appointing a court-martial of four militia officers: Colonel Tobias Frere, Lieutenant Colonel Richard Scott, Lieutenant Colonel Thomas Morris, and Major John Duboys. Frere, the senior officer, was a member of the governing council and held a "plentiful estate" because of his family's early arrival on the island and exploitation of coerced labor. Scott settled permanently in Barbados in the 1680s to inherit his father's estate, and he joined Frere on the governing council in 1695. Morris, aged fifty-one years, called himself a merchant and served in the colonial assembly to represent the parish encompassing Bridgetown. Duboys, the junior officer who started it all, remains a mystery. These four investigating judges met in Mary Stowe's tavern from October 10 to November 21, 1692, to conduct examinations and trials and to synthesize their findings with the assistance of a clerk of the court.[30] Noting the vulnerability of planters to large-scale insurrection, out of self-preservation they found it imperative to arrive at accurate details about the means, locations, and participants of the imminent rebellion. Their lack of understanding governed their decisions. Unable to directly observe evidence of enslaved people planning an insurrection, they depended heavily on local informants. Indeed, in many slave colonies, magistrates changed juridical practice to allow testimony from persons without legal standing because they were generally in positions to witness or hear about transgressions.[31]

The investigating judges, desperate for information, used torture to attempt to terrorize suspects into becoming informants, forcing them to make an impossible decision. They sentenced the first convicted conspirators to be "gibbeted alive," or hung up in chains, to die slowly of thirst, starvation, and exposure (fig. 7). Ben and Sambo endured four days of this agony before relenting, demanding that they be "promised Life" in exchange for the "Clear confession of the whole matter" that enslavers craved. Ben opened the investigation widely. The judges also gibbeted at least seven more suspects in a search for informants. Blinkered by belief in the efficacy of torture, investigators claimed that these torments and the "publique examples" of decapitating, dismembering, and burning corpses of convicted conspirators—with severe implications in some African religions for access to the afterlife—induced "Severall confessions" that filled in the membership and picture of the plot.[32] Suspects faced an excruciating choice when pressured to confess and give up names. The records of other conspiracy scares indicate that many suspects went to their deaths while maintaining their innocence or attenuating their confessions, with the effect of limiting the investigation's damage. In Barbados, the small number of informants who impeached dozens of new names, as Ben did, acted understandably out of self-preservation. Ultimately, they brought the arrests of hundreds.

Although coercions and rewards compelled some enslaved suspects to become informants in this impossible situation, these African participants had more influence than investigators realized. This torture could not control their confessions or guarantee their accuracy. Severe physical and mental stress encouraged a victim to provide some kind of information, accurate

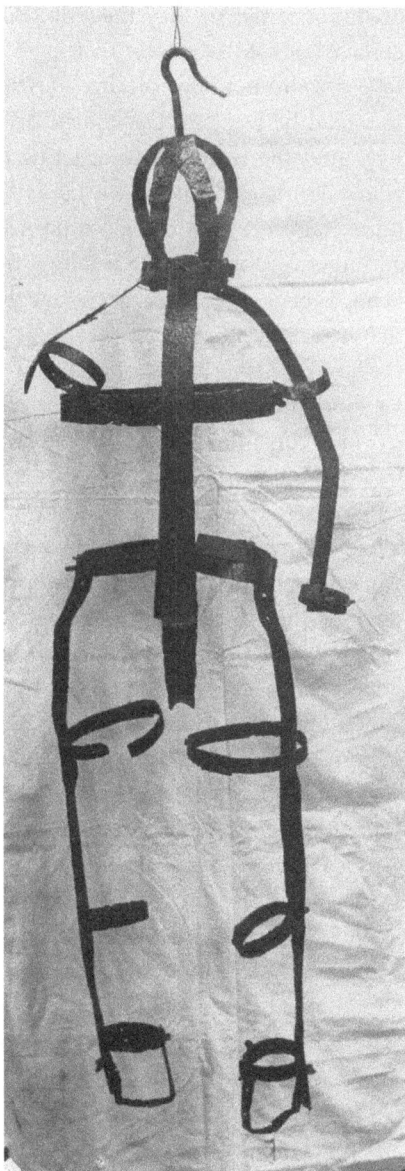

Figure 7. Enslaving regimes sometimes used torture to induce enslaved people's confessions, while terrorizing onlookers, by hanging them in iron cages (gibbets) to die of thirst, starvation, and exposure. Gibbet used in St. Vadier near Quebec in 1763 [. . .]. Courtesy of the Photography Collection, New York Public Library.

or not, in order to allay the pain. But despite the coercion, the words that enslaved people used were their own, drawn from their own mental worlds. Judges could not have dictated their confessions even if they thought doing so would be prudent. Dependent on African input to avert the threat, they measured the words of informants to make sure the confession was "the whole Truth, and not . . . a Lie." Without extant examination notes, it is difficult to ascertain the give-and-take that transpired between informants and interrogators, but the resulting official report is a record of what Frere, Scott, Morris, and Duboys evaluated to be true after measuring the words that Africans spoke. Given the dire stakes of a possible threat, combined with the heavy costs in the event of a false alarm, we can take the official report as an approximation of what the four judges deemed to be true.[33]

The conspiracy they arrived at through coerced coauthorship was baroque but formidable. Whites were forced to envision their own security weaknesses. It seemed to be three years in the making, to the horror of white men responsible for policing enslaved people for the security of the white population, but it was "discovered" just in time to prevent the insurrection "the Night before," as a sensationalist broadside would boast. Such "Miraculous" timing was common in initial confessions of similarly well-documented slave conspiracies of the eighteenth century because, functionally, it inflated the value of information offered by a man bargaining for his life. From the judges' perspective, conspirators managed to maintain three years of secrecy by swearing oaths to one another that, "God dam your Body Bloud and Soul," if a man revealed the plot he would immediately be stabbed and his "Soul [would] burn in hell."[34] The membership of conspirators who allegedly swore this oath appeared from forced confessions to be mainly creole craftsmen and gang drivers who directed the labor of others. In reality the complex social and political life of the slave quarter undergirded this list of "plotters," with informants protecting loved ones and casting blame on enemies and distant acquaintances. But the court viewed the final artifact through European eyes, as evidence that the enslaved people they "most trusted" had betrayed them. This shook their confidence in having complete mastery and reminded them how little they really knew about even the American-born people they exploited.

Most of the conspiracy report focused on the projected scene of averted violence rather than the mechanisms of planning. It appeared that conspirators would take up weapons "from their masters" to murder them "secretly in the dead of the night" and then prepare for the main assault. Those in the rebel cavalry would seize horses "out of their Masters Stables." Insurgents would strike the decisive blow at Bridgetown, converting whites' usual advantage of dense settlement to a handicap. They would "sett the towne on fire in severall Places . . . to amuse [distract] the inhabitants" who tried to save buildings, thereby drawing them into an ambush. Fittingly for a confession led by militia officers, they warned of a reversal of the colony's apparatuses of attempted control. An enslaved man employed at the public armory confessed in anguish, while hanging in chains, that he would have furnished arms, ammunition, powder, and cutlasses on the night of the projected revolt. It also appeared that rebels would take control of Needham's Fort. Conspirators enlisted "four or five Irish men," whose liminal status as Catholics made them another object of domestic disquiet for the English. They would ply guards with drink and let in the African rebels, who would use the cannon to take control of the harbor. Upon victory, white colonists were horrified to learn, the conspirators who participated in the rebellion would take on "the Sirnames and Offices" of leading gentlemen, as well as their estates and workforces, claim "many of the best houses" in town and—"what was most desireable"—the white women. When these findings reached the public, "the People" of the colony went "into so strange a consternation" that Governor Kendall worried he could not quell their "fears and Jealousyes [suspicions]" that an insurrection was imminent. Popular fear among white colonists forced him to investigate more thoroughly and to extend what he regarded as an expensive ordeal. The enslaved people would bear the brunt of it with their lives, loved ones, and lingering trauma.[35]

The Daily Battles and Africa's Wars

Tortured enslaved suspects who regained some control over their personal fates by "confessing" described possible insurrection in terms of their own perspectives on colonial American realities of domination, exploitation, resistance, and diasporic African community-building. As investigators evaluated this information, Africans' reference to those immediate and observable realities in Barbados tethered the more fantastical findings of conspiracy from Europeans' imaginations to anchors of seeming plausibility. In this way, some ideas from distant conceptual vocabularies—ancient slave revolts, colonial servant unrest, Catholic insurrectionary conspiracies,

Irish rebellions, or Indian warfare—appeared to people at the time to be locally relevant because they resembled something about life in Barbados. Informants' terror prompted them to give information that judges shifted and evaluated in European schemas to arrive at pictures that, once revealed, amplified their own fear and increased terror for the broader enslaved population.

Desperate informants, thinking about how colonial officials regularly terrorized them, described a threatened reversal of two of the colonial government's technologies of control—organization as a militia and desecration of bodies—that the members of the court intuitively understood. When investigators decided that conspirators would organize themselves into "regiments of foot and . . . regiments of horse," the idea gained credence by corresponding to the colony's primary institution for policing enslaved people and suppressing insurrections. Similarly, when the exchange between informants and investigators settled on a scenario in which plotters would have "scattered" the governor's "flesh . . . on the Earth," they must have thought about the very spectacles of execution and dismemberment that officers of the government frequently used to terrify enslaved people, including eleven whose decapitated bodies were "dragged through the streets" for allegedly conspiring in 1675. The feared seizure of the fortress, cannon, and naval vessels, as revealed in 1692, likewise would have reversed the colony's best imperial weapons for defense from invasion and insurrection.[36]

Enslaved informants mined their own experiences of terror to author confessions that struck fear into white people. Their daily experience of enslavers' attempted domination and their resistance to it inspired them to threaten reversals of those strategies, or prepared investigators to think that they heard them. Africans' use of these ideas also contributed to the shared creation of the report because they described American social realities that ultimately anchored the more fantastical elaborations of similar ideas from English colonists' lexicons. For example, the allegation that conspirators would appropriate enslavers' horses in fact reversed how enslavers used their horses to dominate laborers and to pursue fugitives from slavery. The official finding that conspirators would seize lineal names, take over families, and rape their wives and daughters received support from how enslavers terrorized enslaved women and men with rape, renamed forced migrants, and refused to recognize enslaved people's independent families. Informants struck fear back into white people by painting picture of a reversal of fortune that violated white patriarchal authority and scrambled white lineages. At stake in rape, according to early modern English law, were patriarchal concerns about maintaining claims to chains of dependence and about propagating one's lineage. The idea of Irish-African collaboration in deception was anchored by local awareness of times that Irish servants and enslaved Africans escaped together and lived "in rebellion" in inaccessible regions of the island such as deep caves and wooded gullies. The idea of a decoy fire was supported by the practice of exploited workers sometimes using arson, an anonymous "weapon of the weak," to preserve their labor, destroy agricultural buildings, or even harm enslavers. Informants' threats and investigators' fears gained power from the combination of these associations with local patterns of exploitation and resistance.[37]

The mental worlds of West Africa also contributed ideas to informants' confessions. Although some were born on Barbados, the informants lived in societies densely composed of Africans who had been wrested from the slaving frontiers of kingdoms in the Gold Coast and the Gap of Benin. The interconnected regions, forming Lower Guinea, furnished about half of Barbados's enslaved arrivals in the 1670s and 1680s.[38] The anguish of African dislocation caused them to *attempt* to rebuild community, however fractured it necessarily remained under the crush of enslavement. These forced migrants could not recreate Africa in America, but they did draw on a combination of local and transatlantic resources and memories in building Afro-Caribbean communities. Consequently, informants used ideas from a realm of Afro-Caribbean political cultures and practices that fell outside the view of enslavers when asked to confess or to corroborate the plot. For example, enslaved people chose their own surreptitious leaders on such a regular basis that informants could agree quite easily that, in this case too, conspirators would choose a governor or a king for the conquered colony. When a puzzled overseer glimpsed this usually out-of-sight practice in Antigua in 1687, he needed an enslaved guide to explain that a man being carried on the shoulders of others had just become "a grandy man" or "Governor" for the slave quarter. The overseer's vision was doubly obscured, first by the social distance his violence and power created between him and his victims, and then by his cultural unfamiliarity with African ways, which was more pronounced in the seventeenth than in the eighteenth century.[39]

Warfare in seventeenth-century West Africa only vaguely resembled the violence predicted in Barbados. If informants described methods of war based on their own military backgrounds, the English judges accepted and recorded only the most familiar aspects in their evaluations. In the dense forest of the Gold Coast, as in the maze of waterways of coastal Lower Guinea, armies moved like chess pieces along a network of narrow paths. Victories in these small-scale conflicts came when they ambushed enemies at choke points. More familiar to Europeans would have been the clashes of armies on the open savannah of Lower Guinea and the swift might of the Oyo Empire's cavalry. People from these areas knew that kingdoms sometimes organized fighting forces into town-based units, each directed by a captain, somewhat like the militia familiar to people in America. Forces that reached villages struck swiftly and killed women and children to reduce the demographic viability of political rivals, sometimes burning the village as they left. In Barbados, enslaved informants may have referred to these oath-based political formations, ambuscades, cavalries, and demographic-sapping strategies when colonial English investigators asked them about plans for massacre. If this is the case, however, when investigators listened, they heard contorted versions that conformed more to their own expecta-tions of massacre and rape, decoy fires, nighttime ambushes, and sworn oaths of conspiracy. These few points of congruence between African mili-tary history and ideas from English conceptual lexicons gave informers and investigators ways to believe they understood each other.[40]

The Learned and the Vulgar

Practices of slavery and the dynamics of West Indian economy and society informed some Africans' confessions, and also anchored enslavers' inter-pretations. Two class-oriented conceptual vocabularies of the English fixed the court's attention on vengeance, diversionary fires, and social inversion: histories of classical slavery and experience with colonial servant uprisings. Knowledge of Roman history entered investigators' lives through Greek and Roman classical histories in translation, "Englished" by the turn of the seventeenth century, which would have been common knowledge for young men such as Frere, Scott, and Morris, whose families groomed them to join polite society. Such preparation was all but requisite for well-to-do Englishmen, not least because the classics were seen as a useful "parallel or mirror," as historian Daniel Woolf has put it, for understanding the early modern world. In America, knowledge of Rome was a marker of status.

Planters spent a great deal on books, particularly in the Caribbean, where they spent per capita twice as much as mainland colonists did. Throughout the colonies, the most widely held titles included Livy's *History of Rome*, Florus's *Roman History*, Plutarch's *Lives*, and Diodorus Siculus's *Historical Library*, among summary histories of the ancient world. When English planters read these works and believed they gained an understanding of the arts of domination and resistance, they actually developed a false sense of mastery. They encountered abundant examples of the detection of slave conspiracies and the results of insurrection.[41]

One category of ancient touchstones consisted of alleged slave conspiracies that the Roman state believed that it quashed before they could come to fruition as rebellions. Even though enslaved people in the Roman Empire were not racialized, nor even necessarily of African descent, this class-oriented conceptual lexicon supplied English judges with several guiding concepts for making sense of enslaved Africans' descriptions of Barbados. Readers of Livy learned that in 420 BCE enslaved informants confessed that a group "had conspired to fire the cittie" in several places "farre asunder." While inhabitants were "busily occupied, here and there, to save their houses," readers learned, the rebels would "surprise the Castle and Capitoll." In another example, readers of Livy found that rebels planned to use a day of "solemne games and plaies," while inhabitants "were busie in beholding the spectacle," to "massacre" them in a sudden "hurly-burly" in 198 BCE. The magistrate reportedly executed five hundred alleged conspirators. In each of these cases, informants earned monetary reward and freedom.

English political thinkers also knew of Catiline's attempt to seize power by force in a conspiracy against Cicero and the Roman Republic (63 BCE). Many supporters mobilized as a rebel army and, reportedly, enslaved people too promised to assist him in setting fire to Rome in several quarters. They would use the "uprore and tusselyng . . . to more easely murder the citizens" who "endeavored . . . to quenche the fire." As playwright Ben Jonson imagined in the tragedy *Catiline His Conspiracy*, conspirators agreed that arson was ideal to "fright" and "terrifie" the victims, with "that confusion" bringing "the chiefe slaughter." These guiding concepts helped investigators make sense of informants' descriptions of potential insurrection, as they assembled a report that charged Barbados's conspirators with the cunning use of a distraction and of fear tactics to facilitate massacre. English colonists knew that Africans' demographic superiority in several parts of

America gave enslaved people an advantage when enslavers were preoccupied.[42]

Another category of ancient touchstones included slave rebellions that involved large numbers of people who took up arms. Investigators used these events, too, to develop questions for enslaved informants and to interpret their compulsory responses. Their familiarity with these ancient rebellions guided them to believe that enslaved Africans had vengeful motives, widespread participation, desire for complete takeover, and planned usurpation of symbols of authority.[43] In William Fulbecke's digest of the great historians, readers found that Spartacus "assumed to himselfe a regall pompe and title" and wanted to "possesse himself of the Capitole [at Rome], and to erect a monarchie." In this way, as Fulbecke's interpretation reflected wider anxieties about status in late sixteenth-century England, readers lingered on how these insurgents intended not just personal autonomy and vengeance but also a complete reversal of social order. As readers who found useful historical examples in classical Rome, Barbados's investigators could apply these conceptual guides to locally rooted information to produce a report stating that enslaved people intended total insurrection and complete control of the island.[44]

Outside of the library, planters first applied and developed these theories of class conflict in practical experience with indentured servants. Exploited servant populations made implicit threats that preceded those of enslaved Africans and helped colonists conceptualize the motive, means, and aims of domestic plotting in America. Planters assumed that laborers, when mistreated more than usual, clandestinely consulted each other about retaliating against their social superiors. The Barbados government investigated significant servant plots allegedly aimed at massacre in 1634 and 1647, and Virginia magistrates did so in 1661, 1663, and 1687. Each of these alleged servant plots predated the earliest large-scale slave conspiracy scares in Bermuda (1656), Barbados (1659), and Virginia (1687). Magistrates drew connections from the earlier examples and the more familiar populations of poor Europeans to understand this new challenge posed by unfamiliar Africans.

Fundamentally and most significantly, planters believed that subordinated servants had the desire to collectively resist their exploitation and had at least some ability to do so. Vengeance against poor treatment appeared to planters to explain why English servants occasionally rebelled, as when Richard Ligon accounted for a servant plot in Barbados (1647) as originating with servants' "extreme ill usage" by their captors and their "daily complainings . . . of the intolerable burdens they labour'd under." These servants, able to communicate among themselves more easily than Africans, appeared to "conspir[e] with some others of their acquaintance, whose sufferings were equal." Even so, investigators seized on one uncorroborated confession that the colony's bursar, Guy Molesworth, instigated and orchestrated the servant plot. As a royalist, he was a politically convenient scapegoat.[45] In Virginia, too, English servants whom planters asked to explain their insurgency appeared to foreground their miserable poor conditions and their desperation to raise grievances in a system that lacked recourse. In York County, in 1661, some gathered to "talk of their hard usage" and complain about meager rations, which apparently led to talk of protesting in a small revolt. In neighboring Gloucester County in 1663, planters learned that servants gathered at a "Little house in the woods" to consider how to use an armed revolt to win a reduction of their service time by one year. From these experiences, propertied elites learned to expect coerced laborers to resent their abuse and to present the greatest threat by gathering from different estates.

Planters tried to assure themselves that laborers, who appeared to be "natural" followers, could not organize themselves without an outside agitator of higher stature. Propertied English colonists sniffed that only "persons of quality" and "Gentlemen of good Condition" could catalyze laboring classes of allegedly so little native ability. In Bacon's Rebellion (1676–77), gentleman-instigator Nathaniel Bacon appeared to critics to organize just such an underclass because his banner attracted a few hundred servants and enslaved people. His "rebellion" was really a civil war against the sitting governor, fought primarily over the colony's pace of expansion into Native American territory. Nevertheless, published accounts emphasized Bacon's charismatic leadership and blamed him for "encourag[ing] the Tumult" and "seduc[ing] the vulgar and most ignorant People," who supposedly would have stayed quiet without a well-heeled leader.[46]

When planters experienced fear because they were helpless to assess enslaved people's organized resistance, they grasped for models and had ready examples in translated and abridged classical histories. Their expectations for slave conspiracies and slave rebellions attributed motives of retribution to the insurgents and a desire to adopt their oppressors' symbols of power. The histories portrayed enslaved plotters using decoy fires to facilitate large-scale insurrection in the confusion. Perhaps these ubiquitous models were enough to guide American enslavers in viewing their enslaved populations as vengeful underclasses who coveted their enslavers' stations and had cunning tactics. But planters also developed a theory of exploited laborers' motives and weapons through their experience with indentured servants. Servants came together and talked about their plight, a step made easier by their shared language, and demonstrated to planters that they had an inclination to rebel. Planters applied their assumptions about the inability of such "brutish" people to organize themselves effectively, and their susceptibility to taking someone else's direction, and theorized that they would be most successful with capable outside leadership. As it turned out, Catholic priests seemed to the Protestant English to be experts in leading impressionable flocks. And the Church of Rome appeared to relish using violence against Protestants.

The Jesuits and the Neighbors

White people's experience with religious violence infused the coerced confessions of enslaved informants. Barbados's mainly Protestant officials, as with counterparts in Bermuda, Virginia, and Jamaica, lived alongside neighbors and servants who they knew or suspected to be Catholic, while a cresting wave of publications, correspondence, and migrants' firsthand experiences brought England's violent confessional politics to the colonies in exactly these years. The kingdom's predominantly Protestant subjects worried feverishly about attempts by English Catholics to massacre neighbors and complete a revolution during the monarchies of the Francophile Charles II (r. 1660–85) and his brother James II (r. 1685–88), a professed Catholic. Some Protestants believed that, as one militant anti-Catholic put it to a dinner companion, "we are likely to be over run with Popery." The Protestant ascension of William III and Mary II in the Glorious Revolution (1688–89) only heightened the perceived dangers of Catholic plotting and introduced outright hostilities with the French and Spanish. Given widespread fears of Catholic subversion in the decades surrounding the Glorious Revolution, officials in the American colonies took keen interest in news of Catholic intrigues in the primarily Protestant realm.[47] They also drew on stereotypes of Catholic rebellion plots in England to flesh out their images of what a slave uprising planned with the same dexterity might look like. This existing conceptual vocabulary of politico-religious violence that was available to colonists provided conceptual guides in visions of conspiratorial planning, diversionary fires, indiscriminate massacre, and social reversal.

White colonists' beliefs about Catholic insurrection in England were perhaps best encapsulated in revelations about the so-called Popish Plot of 1678. This conspiracy scare in London began when Titus Oates, a peripatetic troublemaker, came forward with an elaborate false confession that convinced Charles II. He claimed special knowledge of an imminent Catholic rebellion based on his conversations with Jesuits and other plotters, but in fact it was a fabrication designed to play on the king's and the populace's long-standing fears. No one unraveled the deceit for several years. At first Oates was a hero. Publishers capitalized not only with pamphlets but with collectible playing cards available as packs or "in sheets to adorn studios and houses." As a myth that was widely believed, the Popish Plot is an excellent window onto assumptions about Catholic insurgency because Oates perfectly distilled and fully articulated fears that had long been circulating.[48]

As in many other Catholic conspiracies that also made up this frame of reference, the abortive uprising described by Oates would commence when plotters set fire to London in several places at once in predetermined combinations of important streets. The diversion would enable the Catholic English to surprise their Protestant neighbors and slaughter them. Oates's confessions played on popular assumptions that Catholics were behind unexplained fires: Jesuits, whom an anti-Catholic polemicist termed "those grand *Incendiaries* in all senses," supposedly received training in the production of smoldering fire-starting devices called fireballs. He also pointedly confirmed popular suspicions of French or Catholic design behind the Great Fire of London (1666) by relating a Jesuit's boast that his coconspirators had used "700 Fire-Balls" with the help of "fifty or sixty Irish" and "several Frenchmen." This appeared to confirm the popular suspicions of Londoners that, as one declared, "This doth smell of a popish design." A justice of the peace at the time of the Great Fire claimed to see a man carrying fire-starting materials in his pockets; a doctor claimed to see a mysterious man toss a fireball into a shop that then burst into flames; and another eyewitness to an alleged arsonist said "methought he looked something Jesuit-like." Parliament's investigation into the cause of the fire turned up many accusations, but authorities did not give credence to these stories, and they issued an official report that the fire had started by accident. No massacre followed the Great Fire, according to Oates, because they preferred to use it as a distraction "to plunder what they could," bagging a small fortune of £14,000.[49]

In the Popish Plot, Oates played on Protestant Londoners' wariness of neighbors whom they knew or suspected to be Catholic. Oates reported "a List of 20000 Catholicks in London" who would rise at a moment's notice to "cut the Throats of a hundred thousand Protestants." As another polemicist reminded readers, Catholics were natural followers and in thrall to the pontiff, "obliged to rebel at any time upon the Popes pleasure." Many English were captivated by the idea of Catholics slipping into neighbors' houses and slitting "their throats . . . in their beds." These potential turncoats, literary historian Elizabeth Dolan has observed, were much like fire itself in the minds of English Protestants: both "familiar" and "unpredictable and dangerous." This domestic Catholic enemy blended in with loyal subjects, making it easier to lurk in the shadows and breach Protestant households. In America, these conceptual guides assisted investigators in making sense of informants' references to fire and war in a colony that viewed itself as besieged by an internal enemy whom it violently exploited.[50]

Control of the realm at the highest levels and in households seemed to be at stake for Protestant English in a potential Catholic insurrection. Oates claimed that conspirators would take the titles and offices of leading Protestants, as he revealed in a list purportedly drawn up by the pope. A similar list proved appealing as a way for investigators to represent many goals of the Barbados plotters. Rape was commonly predicted as part of any Catholic insurrection. The prospect focused men's minds on the vulnerability of households, which were fundamental to social order and assurances of lineal purity. One author warned men to expect "troops of Papists ravishing your wives and daughters" in his illustrated broadside of a stereotypical Catholic insurrection, which included "a City . . . set on fire in divers parts," massacre, conversion, political takeover, and French invasion (fig. 8). Such widespread predictions of insurrectionary rape in London provided models for men in Barbados to meditate on their own vulnerability to this blight of early modern warfare. The prevalent Catholic example helped enslavers think through how their rape of enslaved people could very well be turned back against them by their victims.[51]

Magistrates in early Barbados who held suspicions about their Catholic neighbors had remarkably similar concerns about the growing population of Quakers. Members of the Society of Friends had begun arriving in Barbados in the 1650s, some for worldly profit but many for the opportunity to

Figure 8. London would have fallen in a Catholic rebellion conspiracy that included the familiar steps of decoy fires, popular insurrection, invasion, rape, and massacre, according to seventeenth-century Protestant English stereotypes, as illustrated in this broadside. *A Scheme of Popish Cruelties; or, A Prospect of What Wee Must Expect Under a Popish Successor* (London, 1681). RB 183932, Huntington Library, San Marino, California.

spread their teachings in England's most important overseas possession. In general, many Anglican English took unease at Quaker egalitarian tendencies and rejection of traditional Christian rituals. Pamphleteers frequently linked Quakers to England's politico-religious arch nemesis, the Roman Catholic Church. English polemicists identified Quakers as potential insurgents, alongside Catholics, in the event of French or Spanish invasion. In *The Quakers Catechism* (1655), Richard Baxter suggested that "these Papists have begotten this present Sect of Quakers" and that "here and there a Papist [is] lurking to be the chief Speaker among them."

During periods of acute unrest in England, such as on the eve of the Restoration in 1660, pamphleteers accused Quakers of planning insurrections in England. It did not help that George Fox, the sect's founder, once said that "the outward sword might have its place in fulfilling God's purposes on earth." The pamphlet *One of Antichrist's Voluntiers Defeated* (1660) blamed Quakers for the fire that consumed houses in Oxford in 1659. Rumors also alleged that they wanted to execute a similar arson plot in Middlesex. In a Devonshire town, inhabitants woke up one night to cries that the Quakers, together with other radical groups, were about to "not only . . . cut the Throats of the Godly in that Town, but the throats of all the Godly in the Nation that Night." Newsbooks relayed rumors of other nonconformist risings throughout 1659 and into the 1660s. As the Governor of Barbados commented to the Lords of Trade, "It is most certain that they are all Jacobites and many of them papists in masquerade." Indeed, Virginians suspected their Quakers of collaborating with the French and Indians on their frontiers during the next war.[52]

After Barbados's conspiracy investigation of 1675, the Assembly announced that it had found a link between the alleged conspirators and the island's Quaker population. The Quakers appeared, like Catholics, to be external agitators organizing enslaved conspirators. The assemblymen placed new restrictions on the religious sect at the same time that it revamped the slave code in 1676, citing Quakers' "designes with the slaves." The *Act Preventing Quakers from Admitting Negroes to Meetings* (1676) threatened steep penalties for Quakers who allowed enslaved Africans to continue worshiping with them. When imperial administrators objected to the "severe" restrictions on Quakers, the assembly explained that this "mo[st] deceitful people" had already assisted enslaved people in "combin[ing] against Us" by offering a venue for plotting "under pretence of converting of them." Investigators who in 1675 believed that they tracked the slave plot, "about three years" in the planning, back to the year 1672 must have noticed that the date coincided with George Fox's visit and successful advocacy for setting up slave meetings for worship. Even during his visit, colonists charged that the Quakers "ha[d] a Design to teach the Blacks to rebel." The anti-Quaker laws of 1676, 1678, and 1681 attempted to defuse these perceived threats. At the same time, though, they renewed the conceptual associations that Anglican settlers made between rebellious slaves and troublesome "popish" Quakers. Enslavers' expectations from past "plots" by religious minorities provided a rich vocabulary for describing how exploiting Africans could come back to haunt them.[53]

Native Americans and the Terror of Domestic Invasion

English colonists assumed that popish agents were sent by foreign Catholic powers to form alliances against them with non-English, non-Christian— soon to be called nonwhite—attackers.[54] Their experience of violence with some American Indians, and their reading about colonists' other conflicts with Indians, furnished ready ideas for them about how an ethnically non-English population under the right leadership could massacre colonists. Although English fears of Indian powers focused on an enemy who came from without, settlers often called the wars "rebellions" and described the raids in terroristic terms. The sudden, unexpected violation of domestic spaces, especially houses, by Indian raiders clearly resembled the "intestine" threat later posed by enslaved Africans. In some cases, English colonists considered Indians to be subjects, like the Irish, whose rebellion would be tantamount to treason. They also believed that in their "utter brutishness" they were susceptible to following evil leaders.[55]

English colonists regularly charged the French with inciting Indians to attack them in both North America and the Caribbean. Dismissing Indian powers' geopolitical strategy and complex deliberative internal politics, many English assumed that in matters of war Indians easily took direction from people of higher status. The French appeared willing to use the special suasion that Catholics, particularly priests, had with so-called brutish populations. The French seemed to parlay this into devastating Indian attacks against the English colonists. The English vastly overestimated the level of coordination among their enemies, and they often attributed Indians' independent raids to French provocation.[56]

With the Carib Indians flexing their strength in the Eastern Caribbean, the English feared that even islands were not safe from the violence wrought by their Catholic enemies' unholy alliances with Indians. The Carib insinuated themselves into Leeward Island colonists' imaginations almost as a domestic threat. They enjoyed such ready access to the English islands in their canoes that they tormented colonists, in the words of the governor of the Leeward Islands, to the point of living "in perpetual fear of a skulking enemy which comes in the night . . . like a thief." It seemed to these Antigua settlers that Catholic powers relished the chance to turn non-English, non-Christian fighters against them. The violence horrified them, reminded them of their vulnerability to invasion, and gave them a model for what could happen with a Catholic European power's leadership of desperate enslaved people. With this vision of potential gory vengeance, enslavers looked warily toward the enslaved population and reasserted attempts to control it through violence and terror.[57]

Meanwhile, Barbados and other Caribbean colonies were aware that New England struggled to suppress its own anti-colonial Indian rebellion in Metacom's War (1675–76), also known as King Philip's War, taking its names from two appellations for the leader of the Wampanoag Indians at the time. Barbados received shipping and news from New England almost as frequently as it received arrivals from home in the British Isles. During the war it was "nothing but ill news." Governor Jonathan Atkins of Barbados relayed in one missive his intelligence that New Englanders were "much infested by the Indians . . . [who] made great Destruction." A month later the news arriving in Barbados did not improve: he expressed astonishment that "ships from New England still bring advice of burning, killing, and destroying daily done by the Indians." With the onset of the frontier violence in Bacon's Rebellion (1676–77), he framed these distinct Native American conflicts as part of a common "infection [that] extends as far as Maryland and Virginia, where they"—an ethnically essentialized mass of Indians in the Eastern Woodlands—"have likewise done some mischief." Twenty-one printed accounts of Metacom's War propagated scenes of Wampanoag success in using terroristic violence against settlers. It was a model that portrayed an alienated people's resistance to English colonization. Reports emphasized how Indians attacked English settlers by setting fire to their houses and forcing them out into the open where they could be slaughtered or, "if they were Women," they could be raped to "satisfie [the assailants'] filthy lusts." Indians intended this fiery violation of domestic spaces to terrorize the English population, and indeed they drove refugees from inland settlements to coastal towns.[58]

Commentators at the time believed that New England settlers' obvious powerlessness in the early stages of Metacom's War, and their resulting horror and trauma, could shed light on Barbadian colonists' own experience of alarm in the conspiracy scare of 1675. Physically stitched together within the same pamphlet, one of these accounts of the New England war contextualized how readers encountered news of Barbados's plot. *A Continuation of the State of New-England, Being a Farther Account of the Indian Warr*, [. . .] *Together with an Account of the Intended Rebellion of the Negroes in the Barbadoes* (1676) mostly conveyed news about the atrocities of Indians in New England, but the printer used the leaves that remained after folding to include a letter that described Barbados's own travails. The Barbadian correspondent framed his own experience in reference to New England's when he observed that both groups of colonists "tasted of the same Cup" in facing planned rebellions. The account from New England referred to Metacom's War as "a Conspiracy to cut off the English" in violation of their acknowledged subjection to the English sovereign. Barbadians viewed enslaved Africans as more comprehensible through this lens of New England's war, believing that they gained the power of understanding non-English, non-Christian subject peoples by witnessing the sufferings of their New England brethren.[59]

Planters in the West Indies received at least one thousand captive Narragansett, Wampanoag, and Nipmuc from Metacom's War. These rebels, now enslaved, carried trauma that Caribbean enslavers expected to burst into vengeance, feeding into their existing expectations that exploited Africans would push back. The Indian captives arrived offshore at Barbados and Jamaica with documents of enslavement that certified that they had "conspire[ed] . . . in [the] Rebellion" with the intent to "totally destroy Exterpate & Expell . . . [English colonists from] within the Collony & upon the Continet."[60] Ultimately, colonial officials found their insurrectionary potential too alarming. The Barbados Assembly determined that they were "a People of too subtill Bloody & Dangerous nature" to suffer safely. It passed an act to ban them and did so, as the Barbados governor recalled, "with reference to [the averted conspiracy]." Any planters who did not send their enslaved New England Indians out of the island faced fines equivalent to twice the value of an enslaved African. Jamaica's council matched Barbados's policy. A New Englander reported that wherever a ship of enslaved

New England Indians went, colonists "would not buy them." English settlers in slavery-based colonies learned about Powhatan, Carib, Wampanoag,
and Narragansett tactical use of fire, apparent interest in massacre, capture
of women and children, and seeming incitement by Catholic European provocateurs. With a vision of Indians' effectiveness in terroristic destruction,
particularly in domestic spaces, white settlers in slavery-based societies
imagined the capabilities and inclinations of their own enemies within:
enslaved Africans and indentured Irish.[61]

The Rebel Irish and the Catholic Powers

For the English, the Irish represented another ethnic version of the broader
conceptual vocabulary of Catholic violence from which colonists borrowed
guiding concepts to make sense of enslaved Africans. English horror at what
they heard about the Irish Rebellion of 1641 became a touchstone for them
to understand the seeming Irish capacity for violence. In this case, real
violence occurred. The undeniable reality of some aspects of the resulting
depiction gave undeserved credence to other, more dubious allegations of
Irish motives and exaggerations of their violence, all of which appeared to
confirm some deep-seated ideas about potential Catholic insurrection. Sir
John Temple supplied the delivery mechanism for this frame of reference
by establishing a formidable Protestant interpretation of the conflict in his
book *The Irish Rebellion* (1646). His work went through at least ten editions,
appeared as cheaper abstractions in 1660, 1679, and 1689, and influenced
popular martyrologies: it saturated English understandings of Ireland.[62]
Temple estimated with great hyperbole that rebels massacred three hundred
thousand Protestants in simultaneous risings throughout Ireland. In the
book's gruesome scenes, Irish insurgents took delight in setting fire to Protestant victims and their homes. They did so under the tutelage of foreign
priests, friars, and Jesuits who infiltrated the realm, "charmed the Irish,"
who supposedly could not organize themselves, and served as expert plotters of insurrections. Temple asserted that the plot was "sealed up no doubt
with many execrable Oaths, the great engines of these times." He also hinted at a perverse social inversion that motivated conspirators: the leading
Catholic Irish supposedly divided up the titles of the English Protestant
elite and nominated a king, Phelim O'Neill, who would "settle the whole
power of the State in the hands of the Natives." After the burning and

massacre, Temple concluded, the conspirators would replace the kingdom's English place names with their Gaelic originals.[63]

English colonists in Barbados received this frame of reference by way of the printed word and as tens of thousands of Irish servants arrived, many through forced migration. Traffickers procured many through warfare, in a mechanism resembling the enslavement of Africans, especially during England's frantic attempt to reclaim control of Ireland after rebellions of the 1640s. The English loathed the Irish nearly as much as they did Africans. For the rest of the seventeenth century, colonial planters reluctantly purchased the forced labor of Irish servants and tended to treat them worse than servants from other regions of the British Isles. In conjunction with English colonists' indirect memories of the Irish Rebellion and other violence, these Irish servants embodied English fear of Catholic rebellion with their physical presence and gave that fear a protoclass dimension. In the 1650s, Irish servants with no other recourse against suffering conducted themselves "Rebelliously & Mutinously" and led the governing council of Barbados to note that some enslavers were "in fear of their Lives by their Servants." What's more, Irish servants' evident companionship with Africans and their shared resistance activities encouraged planters to link fears of the Irish rooted in the British Isles to the local Irish-African situation in Barbados. In the 1650s, "several Irish servants and negroes" left their estates to establish a rebellious maroon community together in an uncultivated corner of the island.[64]

Irish servants took self-liberating actions that made English planters distrust them in times of war. For example, Irish servants in the English Leeward Islands repeatedly tried to leverage their Catholic faith into political alliance with a foreign power by rebelling against the English colonists only when Catholic France attempted its own invasions. Irish servants were wisely apprehensive of rising up without involvement by a third, Catholic combatant. Consequently, English colonists' concerns about invasion combined powerfully with anxieties about an Irish enemy within. In Barbados, militia officers noted in 1657 that this "Juncture of time, of Warr" with Catholic Spain, prompted them to forbid even free Irish inhabitants from having arms or ammunition in their homes because they were "of the Romish Religion." With the prospect of a French invasion in 1660, the governing council maintained "an exact list of the Irish" and flagged "the names of turbulent and dangerous spirits," whom they disarmed.[65]

English colonists of the Caribbean were right to worry. When the French entered the Second Anglo-Dutch War (1665–67), the Irish of the island of St. Christopher (better known today as St. Kitts) rebelled and "robbed, plundered, and almost utterly consumed" the estates of the Protestants. This insurrection left the colony ripe for a successful French invasion. When the English attempted to recapture the colony, they reluctantly armed some remaining servants and included them at the rear of the force. Some of the Irish seized the opportunity and "fired volleys into the front," killing more "of our own [English] forces" than the French did. After more incidents like this, Governor William Willoughby grumbled that although Irish colonists now swore allegiance to the English sovereign he only "believe[d] them till an enemy appear."[66]

Irish leadership of a colony-wide rebellion appeared to come to Barbados in 1686 when island officials entertained African accusations that Irish servants were planning to revolt. The ordeal further linked the two subjugated peoples in the minds of officials, and more importantly it incorporated the existing conceptual lexicon of Irish rebelliousness directly into local interpretations of Barbadian social unrest. The threat of an Irish rising in Barbados seemed realistic to planters in early 1686, with Catholic power ascendant in England in the wake of James II's defeat of a Protestant pretender, the Duke of Monmouth. Meanwhile in Barbados, an enslaved informer revealed that several conspirators intended to meet to plan a massacre that would "destroy all Masters and Mistrisses of Familyes." The attorney general took depositions and arrested twenty-two enslaved Africans. Some enslaved informers deflected investigators' attention away from African quarters by implicating "some White servants," leading to the arrest of eighteen Irishmen for a "combinacon [of] the Irish servants and Negroes." In time, however, investigators decided that the evidence they collected showed nothing more than exhausted complaints or drunken boasting. They acquitted the Irish suspects, who appeared not "soe far guilty as was first suspected." However, they sentenced many Africans to death as examples to terrify the enslaved population into submission, and with that same state-sanctioned violence they managed the free white population's fear of retribution for its collective exploitation of enslaved people. In looking for a conspiracy combining Catholics and slaves, Barbadian officials nearly found one, and convinced themselves to instrumentally traumatize the most vulnerable people of their society, revealing their utter contempt for African lives.[67]

Soon again, colonial officials showed willingness to conflate fears of religious violence, Irish insurgency, and African rebellion when Edwyn

Stede, governor of Barbados, "discovered" a Catholic insurrectionary plot on the island in February 1689. In order to solidify his own power, Stede played on English colonists' well-developed fear of a combined invasion and insurrection. To claim to discover a Catholic conspiracy was a politically astute move fifteen days after he received a report that William III's Protestant coup was likely to succeed in ousting James II. Stede jailed two prominent Catholics—Sir Thomas Montgomery, a merchant and attorney general, and Willoughby Chamberlain, a wealthy planter—and collected depositions that mixed accurate information, garbled hearsay, and realistic exaggerations.[68] He marshaled the most damning pieces of information to charge that they planned an insurrection among the "poor Irish servants and freemen," whom they organized by "a list taken of some that were at mass." On the appointed day, "the Magazine was . . . to be blowne up" and a French invasion would land, having been coordinated through clandestine communication by traveling priests and a French admiral. The goal appeared to be to install a new "popish governor" and to convert the colony's Protestant inhabitants by wielding "fire and faggot," threatening Protestant colonists that they "must turn, run or burn." What's more, Tobias Frere, already a member of the governing council and soon to become an investigator in the 1692 slave conspiracy, saw suspicion fall on Edward Burke, a Catholic Irishman and formerly a "bought servant" of Frere's late uncle and benefactor, for helping the two ringleaders "in fetching and entertaining the Jesuit." Frere and the council of Barbados also arrested "three Portuges Negroes" who did "openly profess themselves Roman Catholick" and were "often seen at Mass." The council members predicted that these three men might "seduc[e] and dra[w] of[f] the Negroes and other slaves of this Island to that Religion" and engineer "wicked attempts and designes" of insurrection. The Catholic menace and African threat were not only analogous; they merged into one for Tobias Frere.[69]

Stitching It All Together

English colonists generated their own fears about slave insurrection, with African input, when they chose in the seventeenth century to embrace the violence of racial slavery. Through the forced migration of Africans to America, the English created utterly novel labor regimes in Bermuda, Barbados, the Leeward Islands, and Virginia. With these radically new social formations in the early period of colonial English slavery, they concentrated people from unfamiliar places. When English colonists exploited these enslaved Africans to an unusual degree, they believed that their victims would turn vengeful and dangerous. They grew particularly alarmed when enslaved Africans visited each other and communicated in attempts to overcome the alienation of their forced migration and to form new communities of their own.

English colonial officials, charged with the security of white people, conceived of the potential dangers posed by abused Africans by referring to other familiar threats. When they investigated rumors, they selectively listened to coerced informants describe a mix of diasporic African political culture and the practices of power in racial slavery. They made sense of the things revealed to them in light of scenarios more familiar to them—rebellions of the ancient world, protest by indentured servants, contests between Catholics and Protestants, war with Native American powers, and ambivalent dealings with the Irish—drawing out common threads of instigation, arson, massacre, surrogation, and sexual violence. They stitched these together into an emerging conspiracy theory portraying an essentialized underclass that lacked ability but held sinister social and political aims. They projected motivations of enslaved people rooted in vengeance against maltreatment; they ascribed to them goals of massacre and envious replacement of social superiors; and they assumed enslaved people's incapacity to accomplish these things without guidance from inflammatory leadership and, at times, coordination with foreign Catholic powers.

Colonial investigators and enslaved African informants arrived at these projections somewhat unwittingly but not at all accidentally. Rather than adopt European frames of reference wholesale, colonial investigators chose *not* to borrow some of the most prominent elements of Roman histories and Catholic fears. They rejected ideas that failed to resemble their experiences of local colonial sociohistorical developments or to resonate with their existing frameworks, and which contradicted enslavers' interest in domination. Investigators did not ascribe motives of religious conversion to African conspirators despite predicting they would borrow tactics from Catholic insurrection. They recognized, either from direct observation or through informants, that the enslaved population was largely non-Christian and non-Muslim and held religious beliefs that did not demand expansion into unconverted populations. Nor did the idiom of militant conversion accord with Europeans' own histories of Roman conspiracies and the Irish

Rebellion, which emphasized massacre and social inversion. In addition to these incongruities, it was overwhelmingly expedient for investigators to deny enslaved Africans strong politico-religious affiliation in insurgency when they justified their domination by identifying them as a "heathenish . . . sort of people."[70]

Similar disjuncture explains why colonists did not take up the language of "war" so prevalent in Roman and Greek histories. Readers of Florus and Plutarch encountered the "bondmens warre" in Sicily and the "Spartacus War," conducted by an "Army of slaves." Enslavers did not use this legitimating language when describing averted rebellions, even when depicting enslaved conspirators in militia regiments, because it served their dominant position to deny the possibility that enslaved people could be independent. Even in Jamaica's later protracted military struggles with Maroons, the colonial assembly referred to these self-ruling polities as "in rebellion" and sent expeditions for "reducing the rebellious negroes." The limits that colonists placed on how they projected "slave conspiracy" demonstrates that although existing lexicons of ideas provided many core concepts, political expediency constrained their power.[71]

The new conspiracy theory was a global hybrid with African, English, and American antecedents. Their sources of borrowing were no coincidence. The geopolitical context of the time—politico-religious conflict, and the resulting colonial wars—prompted colonists to turn to those particular discourses to explain the new problem of slave insurrection. The underlying situations in early modern England, Ireland, North America, and the Caribbean shared deeply fundamental similarities that facilitated the borrowing of ideas related to domestic threats. Religious crisis, frontier exposure, and underclass alienation—just like the new expansion of African slavery— contributed to shaky colonial social structures made up of people from distant places of unclear loyalties, leaving populations vulnerable to violence from within and weakened in defending against incursions from without. Although no one at the time reached this explanation, they inadvertently articulated it by robustly imagining slave conspiracy to be interlinked with these threats outside of the nascent institution of English racial slavery. Anglo-American ideas about racial violence, often taken as innate to slavery, grew from historically specific preoccupations with political precariousness, frontier vulnerability, and religious violence in the late seventeenth century.

Slaveholders who cultivated the poisonous fruit of this new hybrid conspiracy theory of the seventeenth century cast its seeds into other colonies in the eighteenth century. Like an invasive weed that took to local soils, this dangerous new organism inspired dread in English colonists and terror in vulnerable Africans. This happened when colonial officials relayed their experiences in published histories and news sheets, giving coherence to the new conceptual vocabulary of American racial slave conspiracies, and rendering older, more remote lexicons unnecessary. Eighteenth-century English Americans applied these ideas even as they closed the ethnic and linguistic distance with enslaved populations, which turned from African to African American, because they still failed to comprehend the people across the chasm of violent racial victimization. English colonists used the new, deadly hybrid lexicon of ideas when its logic flagged particular historical conditions for danger.

CHAPTER 2

Studying the Horizon

The Stories and Circumstances That Conjured Demons

After Barbados's major conspiracy scare of 1692, the colony's assembly hoped to avoid the financial burden and human toll of executing every single convicted enslaved person. It sought to recoup convicted conspirators' monetary value to enslavers by selling them to other colonies and forbidding them to return. Some enslavers congratulated themselves for their humanity in these arrangements, while others took cruel delight in separating families because they knew that "an Exile from their wifes and children is almost as terrible to them as death itself," recognizing the value that forced migrants from Africa placed on reconstituting social connections.[1] The ship *Carolina* headed for Jamaica, where enslavers were advancing the colony's internal frontier and had strong demand for more captive laborers.

But Jamaica's governing council had already learned of Barbados's travails. When the *Carolina* arrived, the Jamaican authorities received the enslaved convicts straight into the town jail and directed their consignors to send them away. Two decades earlier, with the scare of 1675, Jamaica's council responded in a similar way when Barbados's assembly tried to do the same thing. Noting the "great hazard," it threatened a fine steeper than the purchasing price of an enslaved person for each convicted Barbadian whom a white Jamaican purchased. In time, colonial legislatures learned to send convicted conspirators to the ports of rival empires because British enslavers preferred purchasing captives directly from Africa, out of suspicion that any whom colonists passed along from other places had committed overt resistance.[2]

If Jamaicans believed that they quarantined themselves from a spreading insurrection, they did not appreciate that the *Carolina* exposed them to something else: information. Below decks, captives brought the experience of surviving a harrowing investigation. Above decks, their captors brought their own perspectives on how a plot had formed, what it would have entailed, and how it was discovered. Both sides had stories to tell. Even if ports turned those ships away, as they did in Jamaica in 1676 and 1692, another ship always arrived with people who shared eyewitness or secondhand stories of conspiracy. Colonial officials gained knowledge of other colonies' conspiracy scares because of expanding informational networks in the first half of the eighteenth century. Export-oriented, slavery-based colonies formed the heart of an economic system in which ships circulated along commercial arteries. This infrastructure enabled enslavers to purchase histories of conspiracy scares, exchange news in correspondence and other colonies' newspapers, and listen to the rumors that sailors swapped in port.

In Jamaica, news of the shocking extent of Barbados's apparent plot reminded English colonists of their own vulnerability to enslaved Africans. Jamaica's governing council braced the island for its own possible uprising. The prospect of insurrection in Jamaica seemed likely in the context of war with France, ongoing Maroon rebellions, the temporary quartering of prisoners of war, and a cataclysmic earthquake that erased the principal port town from the map. These risk factors in 1692 made sense to white Jamaicans because of their familiarity with conspiracy scares and rebellions of the preceding forty years. As the Christmas holiday approached, during which enslaved people enjoyed more autonomy, the council ordered additional patrols and extra night watches. These policing institutions enabled white Jamaicans to manage their own fear by threatening violence against black Jamaicans, terrorizing them.[3]

In the eighteenth century, histories of conspiracy scares conveyed the seventeenth-century paradigm forward into new investigations, even though the classical, religious, and ethnocentric origins of that paradigm largely became obscured. As the frequency of conspiracy scares outpaced actual rebellions in the eighteenth century, most news accounts propagated the fantastic doomsday scenarios generated through unequal coauthorship with terrorized informants and reified by official investigations. These accounts constrained their vision and provided colonial officials with tool kits of guiding concepts for understanding possible rebellions in their own local circumstances.[4]

As in Jamaica, this bundle of assumptions influenced when and where conspiracy scares occurred in the eighteenth century. Both consciously and not, colonists evaluated their own security according to principles from this paradigm. Thinking of accounts of earlier rebellions, they ascribed violent tendencies to African-born enslaved people who could communicate and plot when clustered by ascribed ethnicity. Consequently, they discovered more conspiracies during rapid demographic shifts. Likewise, having theorized that enslaved people required outside instigators to organize themselves, and that they tended to coordinate with simultaneous invasions, English colonists tended to worry about possible conspiracies more often when at war with another European empire. Measurable changes in demographic balance and military affairs corresponded to the timing and frequency of conspiracy scares in noticeable clusters.

As white people repeatedly exorcised their demons by terrorizing enslaved people, they recorded and reported their experiences for people in other colonies and a later generation. They worked from established theories of enslaved people's insurrectionary politics and then published their own experiences in what appeared to be confirmation of this growing body of "common sense" by the middle of the eighteenth century.

Found in Story

When Valentine Morris investigated a conspiracy in Antigua in 1736, he compared his own colony's predicament to similar examples "that can be found in Story" or taken from "Memory or Reading." Starting with personal experience, his mind turned to 1729, when he assisted in an investigation of another plot to massacre the island's white population. At that time, in fact, he and other members of the governing council reminded each other about a small rebellion in 1701 that "many of us . . . must remember" and that brought "terrible Consternation" to white colonists. As with his seventeenth-century predecessors, Morris had a lexicon for thinking about slave conspiracy drawn from "all Rebellions that I have heard or Read of." He composed a memorandum to justify the continued judicial killing of enslaved people in the fourth month of trials because some enslavers started to object to the destruction of their "property." Morris drew comparisons between Antigua's situation and historical examples. He referred to two old chestnuts from anti-Catholic ideology, the Irish Rebellion (1641) and the

St. Bartholomew's Day massacre in France (1572), and to the more recent
assassination plot against William III of England aimed at reinstalling James
II (1696). He also mentioned early modern political conspiracies in Venice
and Portugal that inspired brutal crackdowns. Morris's touchstone comparison, though, was Barbados's major conspiracy scare of 1692. Unlike predecessors in the seventeenth century who were limited to making oblique
comparisons to analogous situations, Morris and other investigators in the
eighteenth century could look back to prior slave conspiracy scares for clues
about what to expect.

Morris drew the most direct comparison to Barbados's alleged conspiracy
of 1692 because it was the most frightening comparison he could conjure. He
proclaimed that the alleged Antigua conspiracy presented an even greater
danger to white people, using fear to prevail on other members of the governing council to agree to continue the executions as an instrument of social
control that worked by terrorizing enslaved people. Much of his comparison
was a distinction without a difference. In Antigua the conspirators appeared
already to have crowned a new king; in Barbados they planned to install a
new governor. In each island they appointed officers with militia titles, but
only in Antigua did they specify where those units would muster. Morris
simply had more information about the Antigua conspiracy because he performed the interrogations there. In the biggest difference, the Antigua rebellion would begin with a gunpowder explosion beneath a ballroom floor,
whereas in Barbados the opening gambit involved several decoy fires around
town, but both visions were adapted from the annals of Catholic plotting
against Protestant England. Other aspects of the two conspiracies did not
differ at all, including plotters' alleged desire to assume the names of former
enslavers and to lay claim to their estates. Morris's comparison shows that he
knew about other colonies' conspiracy scares.[5]

Slanted memories of seventeenth-century conspiracies and rebellions
circulated well into the eighteenth century. Publishers profited on the
anguish of others by granting readers a glimpse of enslavers' fears and enslaved people's trauma. The fixity of print and the original investigations'
imprimatur of judicial authority combined to mask the shortcomings and
uncertainties of the findings. The more salacious the details, in any case,
the more profitable the story. When readers peered at refracted versions of
Barbados's conspiracy scares of 1675, 1686, and 1692, generic conventions
made them appear similar, linked, and easily explainable as a natural struggle of "slaves" against "masters."

Nathaniel Crouch's *The English Empire in America* (1685) reached a mass audience as a small, cheaply printed book that went into many editions and served as a source text for later histories. Crouch maintained the old position that enslaved people allegedly could not conspire because they "do not understand one anothers Language," but he admitted that he had seen enslaved Africans overcome those linguistic and ethnic divisions when tormented by enslavers. Identifying the anguish of enslavement as the fundamental origin of resistance, he explained that Barbados's enslaved people were "used with such severity" that they formed "a great conspiracy against their Masters" in 1675, or at least vocalized complaints to startle their enslavers and to negotiate for lessened burdens. He projected a deep fraternal bond onto them and marveled that the investigators managed to unlock it "the day before it was to be acted." Crouch horrified readers and then assured them that even though the large population "might prove dangerous," the colonial counterinsurgency kept them in "strict aw" by putting alleged conspirators to death "as a Terror to the rest." Just as officials terrorized enslaved people to manage white fear, Crouch managed readers' horror by describing the colony's violence against its most vulnerable people all over again.[6]

In the early eighteenth century, John Oldmixon's similarly popular *British Empire in America* (1708) went through several editions and established a transhistorical typology of racial insurrection in his accounting of Barbados's travails. He announced that "the Negroes . . . began early to enter into Conspiracies against their Masters," preparing readers with a sense of dread of attempts to come. Accuracy eluded him most of the time. His version of a plot from "about 1649" sounded real enough: to cut enslavers' throats and claim the island because of a "universal" desire of revenge for daily violence. But he conflated two events from Richard Ligon's *History of the Island of Barbados* (1657): a major servant conspiracy of 1647 and an enslaved group's discussion about burning down an enslaver's house in 1650.[7]

Oldmixon also mischaracterized Barbados's conspiracy scare of 1686, leaving out Irish involvement, and described the major conspiracy scare of 1675. He asserted facts that were far murkier than he knew, but that horrified readers with a great reversal, when he parroted existing pamphlets' assertion that "the Planters were to be kill'd, their Wives to be kept for the Chief of the Conspirators, their Children, and white Servants to be their Slaves." His mix-up speaks to the power of generic conventions, especially

horrifying ones, as much as to his ethnocentric attitude.[8] Subsequent historians who relied on Oldmixon endorsed his conflation of these events by
publishing the same mistakes into the 1760s.[9]

As for Barbados's conspiracy of 1692—the touchstone for Valentine
Morris forty-five years later—Oldmixon based his extensive treatment in
British Empire in America on a combination of oral interviews, governmental records, and a contemporary broadside. He used enslavers' fear, and
enslaved people's suffering and terror, to profit from white readers' fascina-
tion with potential reversal. Readers learned of its long planning, organized
under self-selected officers "to form themselves into several Regiments of
Horse and Foot," and the plan for the most trusted slaves to simultaneously
massacre their masters and to "kill the Governour." All of this reflected
Edmund Bohun's original broadside account, *A Brief but Most True Relation of the Late Barbarous and Bloody Plot* (1693).[10]

Printed accounts encouraged readers to lump past slave conspiracies
together and stereotyped enslaved Africans' protest as vengeful and violent.
This logic was clear when Oldmixon wrote about the Barbadian slave plot
of Christmas 1701. He linked it into a longer tradition and, implicitly,
invited his readers to join him in conflating several events and constructing
an essentialized category. "The Blacks then form'd," as he put it, "another
Design to burn the Bridge Town, and seize the Forts." He added almost no
detail, suggesting that readers had learned all they could about this event
from his previous descriptions of earlier ones. He completed the logic by
summarizing what he believed he knew about "the Negroes," in the
abstract. They seemed to him "generally false and treacherous" toward
the people who enslaved them rather than duly subjecting themselves to
the authority of social betters, just the kind of "sullen and cruel" people
who would rebel. Concluding his discussion of Barbadian slavery, he generalized that "what has been said of Barbadoes, with Relation to Servants and
Slaves, may serve for Jamaica." Place did not matter for him as much as
race and condition did. This reading provided plenty of evidence, however
faulty, for the supposedly vengeful nature and violent impulses of enslaved
Africans. He cautioned, "Their numbers render them very dangerous."[11]

An alternative view recognized enslaved people's rebellion as a desperate
assertion of rights. Thomas Tryon, the radical thinker, drew a causal link
from enslavers' exploitation and violence to enslaved people's attempted
rebellion, and he pleaded for a less severe slavery. The Reverend Robert
Robertson, based in Nevis, voiced the idea that, having "heard strange

Stories of their Rebellions in Barbadoes," perhaps the philosophical assertion of a "natural Right and Liberty [was] not altogether unjustifiable."
Another chronicler reported that enslaved people "frequently plotted the
destruction of their masters . . . but their plots were constantly discovered,"
and then he offered a warning to enslavers. With the benefit of a long view,
the chronicler observed that when enslavers attempted to terrorize enslaved
people into submission by inflicting "terrible punishments . . . on the ringleaders," they inadvertently "increase[d] the disaffection of the rest, and
laid the foundation of fresh conspiracies."[12] These authors tried to use fear
of rebellion to get enslavers to ameliorate conditions for vulnerable people
with little recourse of their own. They did this from a social position that
allowed them to voice warnings of comeuppance without suffering the
violence and terror of a conspiracy investigation. Unfortunately, however,
raising the prospect of rebellion actually reminded enslavers of their vulnerability, reinforcing the cycle of fear and violence that produced conspiracy
scares. These histories gave eighteenth-century investigators access to
coherent theories of insurgency, developed in the seventeenth century, for
them to consider and to apply when making sense of new contests between
enslavers and the enslaved.

Smoke and Fire

In the first half of the eighteenth century, enslaved people's resistance and
rebellions reinforced some assumptions and challenged others in what
white people read about the skewed findings of seventeenth-century investigations. Along the way, white colonists initiated many conspiracy scares
that produced findings influenced both by white people's memories and
enslaved people's actions.

In Anglo-America from 1700 to 1750, enslaved people's most common
collective rebellion manifested as living as "maroons." Enslaved people liberated themselves by force or by stealth and fled to inaccessible regions
beyond the reach of colonial authorities, usually swamps, mountains, and
thick forests. Groups of maroons sometimes raided outlying colonial settlements for supplies and when defending their freedom against colonial expeditions to re-enslave them. Colonial officials called these frontier conflicts
"rebellions," conducted by the "Revolted Negroes," but they bore a closer
resemblance to colonies' frontier struggles with Native American tribes

Figure 9. Maroons, self-liberated people who lived in regions inaccessible to enslavers, defended their autonomy through masterful ambushes in difficult terrain. J. Merigot, *Maroons in Ambush on the Dromilly Estate in the Parish of Trelawney, Jamaica*, 1801. Aquatint print, after a painting by Francois-Jules Bourgoin. © The British Library Board. Shelfmark Maps.K.Top.123.59.

than to domestic insurrections. Maroon bands tormented frontier colonists with raids in South Carolina in 1711 and 1733, and in Virginia in 1713 and 1729.

In Jamaica these self-liberated people, who embraced the name Maroons, installed themselves in the island's mountains in the seventeenth century. In the decades leading to 1739, they grew more powerful, raided enslavers' settlements, and sent refugees fleeing in terror. Until that time, one resident reflected, "I never knew what fear was." Their boldness dampened enslavers' ardor for expanding the frontier on the island's interior. Jamaica's Maroons repelled every colonial expedition sent against them (see fig. 9). Sometimes they had only to let the colonists bushwhack endlessly before the intruders accidentally discharged their weapons into their own party. Finally the island's two Maroon polities forced the colonial government into treaty settlements in 1739. Jamaica's assembly later recalled "the expense of blood and treasure, [and] the alarms and dangers to which we were continually exposed during that horrid rebellion," using the contemporary term for this frontier warfare in Jamaica's interior. The groups' ongoing independence and military success confronted colonists with their own impotence against Africans in arms, showing them that they should be wary of those whom they had enslaved.[13]

As important as these examples of freedom were, most enslaved people did not liberate themselves and join maroon groups. They found autonomy in other ways. After all, survival itself was a challenge in societies of scarce resources and the unrelenting crush of enslavement. As displaced persons, enslaved Africans were understandably reluctant to abandon loved ones and social networks, however fragile, that they had just rebuilt. Rather than flee to swamps and mountains, most sought autonomy by moving in the other direction—into the slave quarter—away from direct supervision and toward self-authored cultural and political practices. To create more time and energy for this zone of semiautonomy, they used "weapons of the weak" to influence the terms of their burden of labor, by breaking tools, feigning illness, or pretending incompetence. Some took temporary refuge by absenting themselves from a slave labor camp for a few days to visit family and friends, but never so long as to become fugitives in the eyes of enslavers. These human-scale victories meant a great deal to people teetering on the brink of survival.[14]

To rise up in domestic insurrection was, therefore, a tremendous risk for enslaved people. Nevertheless, a small number viewed it as a recourse. Insurrections—in which groups of people took up arms against their enslavers in the confines of the site of their enslavement—appear in the record inconsistently. Perhaps a dozen occurred in the first half of the eighteenth century, based on traces in the archive, but a reliable count is not possible. Large conflicts in mainland North America did draw the notice of colonial officials, for they were both rare and concerning to enslavers, but many smaller uprisings may have gone unrecorded. In the Caribbean, and particularly Jamaica, the archival record is more frustrating in its hints of frontier uprisings in the context of the emerging Maroon war, but often without much detail. For example we know of an uprising in Westmoreland Parish in 1711 but can only guess as to whether participants numbered, perhaps, two hundred to four hundred rebels from one or two plantations as in the rebellions of three decades earlier. The absence of comment suggests it was not larger.[15]

Many rebellions occurred at fraught moments in interimperial Anglo-Spanish relations. Several occurred during the War of Spanish Succession (1702–13). In Antigua in 1701, and in Queens County, New York, in 1708, small groups of enslaved people on single farms rose up and murdered their enslavers and enslavers' families. In Antigua, the rebels fled into marronage, but in New York they were captured and executed by enslavers in an attempt to use terror to claim mastery over the rest of the traumatized enslaved population.[16] In 1712, rebels set fire to an outbuilding and skirmished with a militia. Authorities identified forty-three participants. The "Spanish Indians" were suspected as the ringleaders because of "having the most understanding to carry on a plot." Subsequent memory considered this "a Plot to set Fire to the Town" that began when insurgents "burnt down a House in the Night and killed several People who came to extinguish the Fire," even though little in the contemporary record suggests that this was an ambush.[17] In 1713, shortly after the war's conclusion, a group in Middlesex County, Virginia, plundered a storehouse and used firearms to resist arrest and to flee successfully to the swamp.[18]

The largest insurrection of the first half of the eighteenth century that loomed in Anglo-American enslavers' minds occurred in the Danish West Indies on the island of St. John in 1733–34. One thousand enslaved people liberated themselves, took control of the island for most of a year, and repelled Danish soldiers. They faltered only when French and Swiss soldiers arrived from Martinique to reestablish chattel slavery. This most successful example of an insurrection that converted domestic spaces of enslavement into bloody sites of self-emancipation provided chilling proof to colonists that their apprehensions were well founded. The rebellion elicited comment throughout the Caribbean and from Georgia to New Jersey.[19]

Colonists noted these instances, however small in scope, and recognized that they should be uneasy about their place atop the realms that they believed they controlled. For enslaved people, these episodes could give hope, but more often they ended in sorrow. The colonial state punished them with deliberate savagery to establish control through terror, often killing even noncombatants.

In striking contrast to these few moments of insurgency, at least thirty-three conspiracy scares occurred in Anglo-America from 1700 to 1750 (see Appendix, table 1). As judicial affairs of public import, these conspiracy scares left paper trails in government records or at least newspapers. This state-sanctioned violence, by which white people managed their fear through scapegoating and inflicting terror, far outstripped insurgent violence by enslaved Africans whether we measure it by the frequency of events or the numbers of people killed, maimed, or banished. As Figure 10a shows, conspiracy scares occurred more frequently in some decades than others. Inspecting these peaks and troughs can suggest the need to examine decades of war, for example, such as the Seven Years' War or the American Revolution. But the more incisive questions come from the regional patterns shown in Figure 10b. Why did South Carolina and New York (with New Jersey) experience a disproportionate number of scares in the 1730s and 1740s? Why did Jamaica also experience a disproportionate number of scares in the 1760s, but the Carolinas did not? Why did white people become more alarmed in the mainland colonies than in the island colonies in the 1770s? The full explanation stretches across several chapters of this book, but the foundation is laid by examining patterns in the late seventeenth and early eighteenth centuries. These subtler patterns show that the theories of slave insurgency that European colonists developed in the seventeenth century—their fear beliefs—influenced those patterns of outbreaks.

Local white populations succumbed to conspiracy scares when the dangers of slavery itself appeared to combine with threats to English colonists from outside the institution of slavery. Although enslavers correctly identified the possibility that enslaved people could revolt, and news of rebellion amplified their fears, colonists actually treated slave conspiracy as one element in a larger matrix of their security concerns. The bigger picture for white people included the threat of hostile invasion by European armies, privateers, Indians, or maroons, and underpopulation in understaffed outposts. Colonial officials in a locale assessed broader shifts in a colony's or region's security situation, always cognizant of how those changes might lead to insurrection. Enslavers tended to investigate possible conspiracies when they noticed swift rises in African populations or plummeting numbers of whites. They also worried about insurrection when they perceived threats of invasion by European powers, and they tended to investigate rumors at times they believed the colonial government failed to police slaves adequately; they tended to feel safer when they had confidence in slave patrols, colonial militia, or professional garrisons that could strike terror into an enslaved population.

Above all, colonists succumbed to scares most often when they perceived *change* in these climatic conditions. Moments of accelerated change

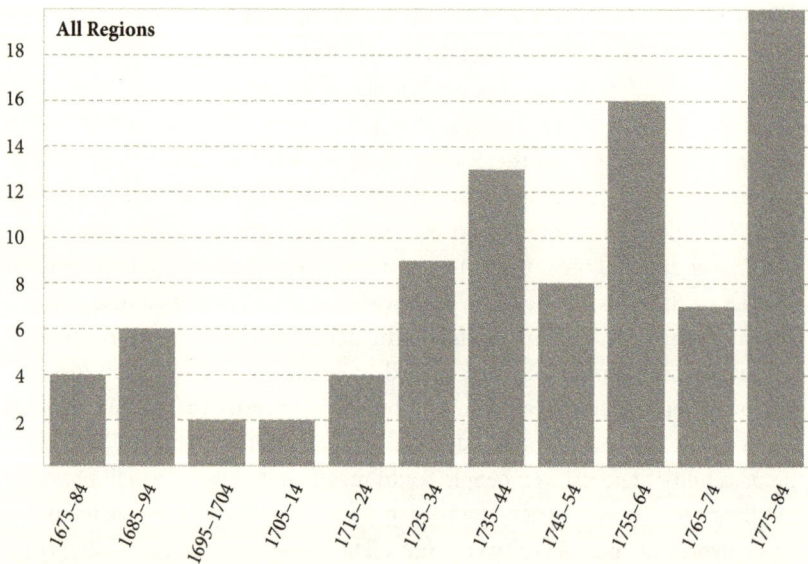

Figure 10a. Frequency of slave conspiracy scares in Anglo-America, by decade, 1675–1784. Conspiracy scares occurred more frequently in times of political turmoil and when war threatened colonial societies that were composed of large numbers of enslaved people. Source: Appendix, table 1.

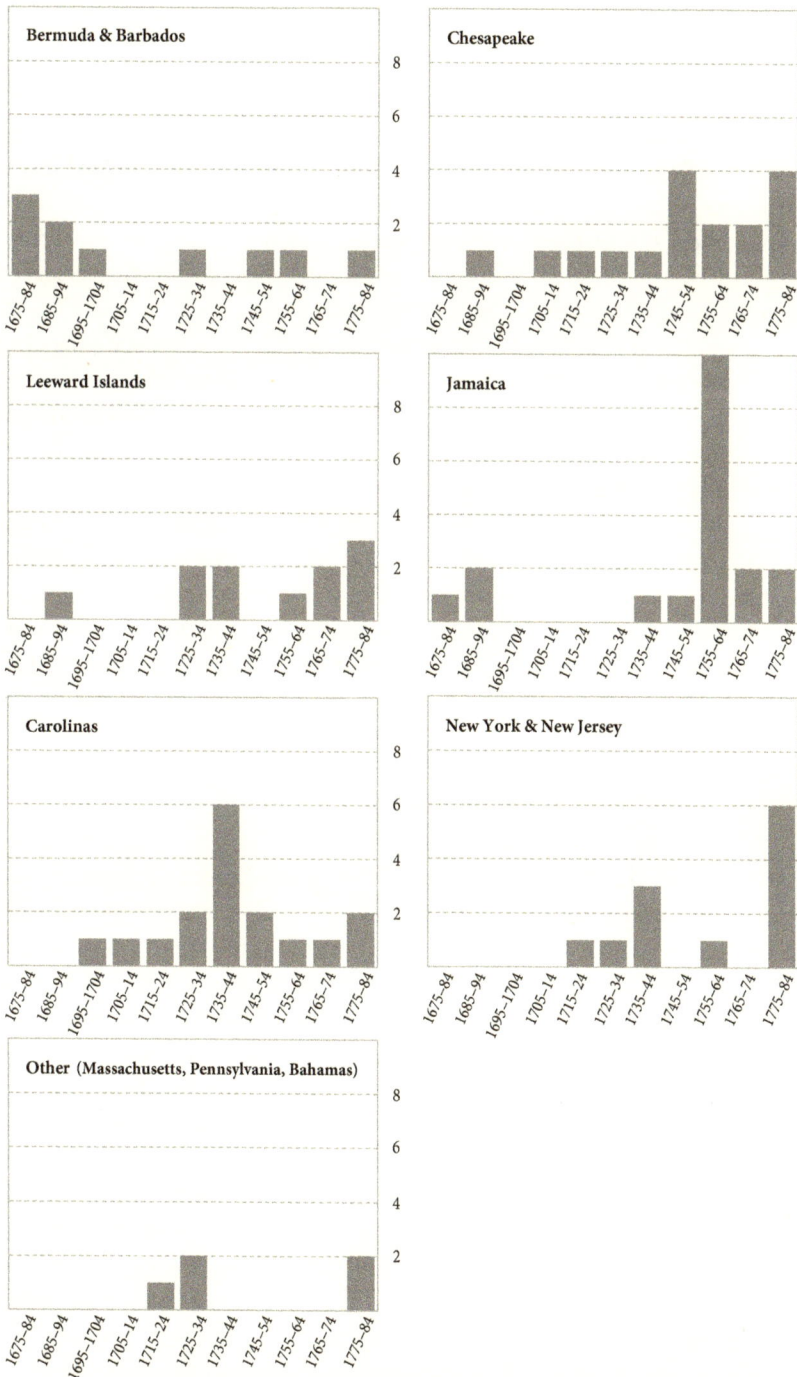

Figure 10b. Regional variations in frequency of slave conspiracy scares in Anglo-America, by decade, 1675–1784. Some regions experienced more conspiracy scares at certain times because facilitating factors, such as war, affected them disproportionately. Source: Appendix, table 1.

carried the most psychological meaning because they attracted notice. Enslavers became acutely aware of their vulnerability when altered circumstances called their attention to the realities, otherwise safely lodged in the ordinary background of the day-to-day, of how their contempt-fueled exploitation traumatized enslaved people. Colonists' exaggerated perceptions of change ushered in conditions that led them to pressure enslaved communities into contributing to conspiracy scares.

Geopolitical conditions affected the likelihood of conspiracy scares but never perfectly determined them. While there are identifiable patterns in enslavers' alarms, there are no easy, algebraic explanations for events driven by interactions among large numbers of individuals, enslaver and enslaved, whose fears interacted with one another's. Indeed, scares could occur at times and places deemed unlikely according to the climatic factors identified here. Personalities, sheer accident, and other entirely contingent factors sometimes happened to initiate conspiracy scares within these amplifying conditions. Changes in the conditions of demography, policing, and warfare did not *cause* locales to become enflamed with fear, but they did furnish an environment in which sparks of suspicion easily caught fire.

Unsettling Populations

Demographic changes help to explain why certain times and places experienced more conspiracy scares. Enslavers frequently expressed the accurate belief that by exploiting a significant proportion of the population they put themselves in danger, especially in colonies such as Jamaica where enslaved people comprised between 70 and 90 percent of the total population in the eighteenth century. White enslavers found black minorities almost as threatening as they did black majorities, particularly when North Americans used examples from the Caribbean to think through the implications of their violence. William Byrd wrote that slaves who arrived in great numbers in Virginia could "do as much mischeif [sic] as in Jamaica." He warned that Virginia's thousands of Africans waited only for a "Cataline [sic]" to "kindle a Servile War," as in antiquity, for them to slay their enslavers and "tinge our Rivers as wide as they are with blood." He proposed a ban on further importations from Africa. Even though enslavers in Virginia and New York never tipped the demographic balance to favor an enslaved majority, they nevertheless believed that they discovered conspiracies of a scale similar to those of the island colonies. But the simple fact of slave majorities does little to explain why conspiracy scares occurred at some moments and not others.[20]

Enslavers believed that captive Africans turned to violence more readily than creole (American-born) cohorts. "Africanity," historian Jennifer Morgan has observed, "rather than enslavement" seemed to planters to cause rebellions in the early period.[21] Enslavers noticed a valid pattern even if their explanation revealed loathing for Africans and denied responsibility for this violent system. Most revolts occurred among populations dominated by African-born slaves, as was the case in Jamaica and on slaving vessels still within sight of the African coast, but not, as white colonists would have it, because of any inherent violent tendencies. Rather, captive Africans often knew freedom in former lives, in some cases they possessed military training, and they had fewer family ties and investments in local society in the quarter at risk in rising up. Enslavers' distrust of African-born slaves led a polemicist in Jamaica to argue for radically constricting the forced migration of captive Africans to the island. He aimed not to end slavery but only to reduce the number of new Africans in Jamaica: "Let us be Wicked still," he assured his profit-minded readers, "but let us not be Fools." Without parental intervention by Parliament, the island's greedy enslavers would endanger themselves like "children . . . who are playing with Edge-Tools, which they cannot manage, and should be prevented from cutting themselves." He pointed to a slave conspiracy quashed "the other Day" as evidence of the danger. British slave traders, he winked, could bring their dangerous cargoes instead to New Spain to make profits while weakening the enemy.[22]

Consequently, large influxes of newly enslaved Africans frightened colonists more than did a natural increase in population among African Americans born into slavery. Enslavers understood that the Atlantic crossing was filled with agony and sorrow, and they worried that it was a precursor to desperate violence.[23] They tended to initiate conspiracy scares when they perceived floods of traumatized Africans. The first step to demonstrate the correlation is to use the estimates made in the Trans-Atlantic Slave Trade Database, itself based on a combination of documentary records and mathematical estimations.[24] The second step must approximate colonists' imperfect human perceptions of this data: the lived experience of seeing an unusual number of slaving ships in port or captive bodies in coffles. We can estimate what residents would have viewed as "normal" at any given moment through rolling averages for the previous five years' and ten years' number of annual arrivals of captive Africans. Any surges in numbers as compared to these two norms should reveal what contemporaries may have found especially noticeable. Enslavers who perceived a rapid influx of suffering Africans did not automatically act on their disquiet by discovering conspiracies, but they had a much greater likelihood of doing so.

Rapid demographic changes made conditions ripe for scares. Barbados experienced five conspiracy scares in the seventeenth century. Enslavers initiated two major investigations, in 1675 and 1692, and two minor inquiries, in 1683 and 1701, at moments when they imported numbers of captives from Africa that usually reached 120–224 percent of at least one of the norms (see Appendix, table 2). In 1675, for example, slaving vessels brought an estimated 3,600 Africans to Barbados, a number larger than those in recent memory. The ten-year norm for arrivals (based on 1665–74 data) was 3,015, and the five-year norm was 2,300 (1670–74); the arrivals for 1675 were 120 percent of the usual annual figure for the previous ten years, and 158 percent of the average for the five previous years. Likewise, the 1683 conspiracy scare came at a moment when the forced arrival of Africans comprised 224 percent of the ten-year norm and 190 percent of the five-year norm, based on colonists' experiences during 1673–82. In 1692, forced African immigration reached 117 percent of the five-year norm when a major scare occurred. In 1701, arrivals were 190 percent of ten-year norms and 148 percent of five-year norms. Only one of the scares, in 1686, occurred at a time when Africans did not seem to be arriving in numbers that would drastically change the colony.

In Virginia, enslavers demanded investigation into their first major slave conspiracy scares, as distinct from servant plots, soon after purchasing enough captive Africans to triple the enslaved population from an estimated 3,000 people to 9,345 people (1680–90).[25] Early in the eighteenth century, Virginians experienced their largest conspiracy scares. In 1710, enslavers launched a major investigation just after a period when new arrivals exceeded norms for five years in a row (see Appendix, table 3). Virginia's governor declared that "by Their Dayly Encrease [they] Seem to be The Most Dangerous." At precisely this moment, an illness also swept through the colony and reduced the number of white men available for defense. The combination of developments, as well as alarm about a possible French invasion, worried white people and led to a conspiracy scare in which justices of the peace across four counties in Virginia arrested at least twenty-nine enslaved people, in a network of almost as many enslavers' households. The scare's wide geographic footprint led Governor Alexander Spotswood to warn white Virginians that they could no longer count on Africans' "Babel of Languages," as the recent investigation showed that "freedom Wears a Cap which Can Without a Tongue Call togethar all Those who Long to Shake of[f] The fetters of Slavery."[26] White Virginians took devastating action again in 1722. Directly after purchasing traumatized new captives in the years 1718–21 in numbers 226–493 percent of norms, they investigated a rumor of conspiracy to "kill murder & destroy very many."[27]

South Carolina's first conspiracy scares occurred in the two decades when its African population quadrupled from 2,600 to 11,900 (1700–20). Colonial officials noticed that "the number of negroes do extremely increase in this Province, and . . . the white persons do not proportionally multiply," and they believed that they discovered a slave conspiracy in 1713. Between 1715 and 1718, the Charleston residents' dread mounted as they witnessed enslavers purchasing unusually large numbers of captive Africans, successively 157 percent, 354 percent, and 250 percent of recent years' arrivals. With additional stressors of political strife and an invasion scare, white colonists took alarm at local signs of enslaved people's daily struggle for autonomy and launched a conspiracy investigation in 1720.[28]

White colonists in Antigua began discovering conspiracy scares when they quintupled the enslaved population from 2,100 to 12,900 (1678–1707), almost entirely through forced African immigration rather than Afro-Caribbean births.[29] Elsewhere in the Leeward Islands, enslavers also purchased large numbers of traumatized Africans in the 1720s and 30s (see Appendix, table 4). They launched a major investigation in Nevis in 1725, just as captive Africans arrived in numbers around 200 percent of the ten-year and five-year norms; white people launched another one in Antigua in 1729, when arrivals measured 203 percent and 149 percent of recent numbers, and again in 1736, when arrivals were 144 percent and 223 percent of recent experience. Another scare in St. Christopher, in 1738, also coincided with enslavers' increased exploitation of newly captive Africans in the Leeward Islands.[30]

Catastrophic population decline among whites also stoked their unease and facilitated scares. In Bermuda in February 1730, white inhabitants believed that enslaved people were coordinating a widespread poisoning campaign. Enslaved people sometimes used poison, whether derived from pharmacology or religious objects, against one another and as a weapon of the weak against oppressors. However, it is difficult to ascertain the actual extent of poisoning because an epidemic swept through Bermuda in the same years, 1729–31, and reduced the population by 7.8 percent among whites and 6.4 percent among blacks. Compounding the Bermudian slaving regime's concerns, a garrison departed the island at the same time. To stop the alleged poisoning conspiracy, colonial officials questioned many suspects, burned a woman, hanged a man, and sold several people into exile in Spanish America.[31]

Another swift scything of the white population encouraged the exposed-feeling survivors to wield state violence against the even more vulnerable people whom they enslaved. In 1733–34, in New Providence, the Bahamas, an epidemic ripped through the population and brought an annual decline of 4.8 percent among whites. The colony's council worried that the collapsing population rendered the islands indefensible, particularly with the recent departure of their garrison. At the same time, the black population grew by 7.5 percent annually. In this worrying demographic scenario for white people, the governor of the Bahamas easily believed the revelations of an enslaved man, Quamino, who found himself in jail for having killed a soldier. Quamino's remaining recourse was to declare that he knew about an imminent insurrection. His revelation played on white people's dread and gave him the power to summon the governor to his jail cell in the middle of the night to personally evaluate his revelation that "a great number of our Negro's . . . appointed Sunday . . . to rise & destroy all the white Inhabitants." Quamino, having witnessed countless spectacles of terror by enslavers, told the governor that the plotters planned to kill him first "in order to strike the greater terror in the people." The governor arrested and tried several people. He made that decision precisely as the white population collapsed in an epidemic, the black population grew, and the garrison departed.[32]

*   *   *

In this period when American enslavers wrested Africans from across the ocean, they tended to trust creole slaves more than they did Africans. Formerly, some enslavers had worried that if enslaved people learned English the common tongue would remove a supposed barrier to conspiring. As enslaved people inevitably developed "very good English," to some white people this actually seemed to render people of African descent less strange and more comprehensible. Indeed, enslaved people could be adept at manipulating enslavers by donning the personas that they wanted to see. Enslavers now hoped that among these creoles they could discern the "trusty" from the "subtle" ones. James Knight, who wrote about his experience in Jamaica, reported "many Instances of great Fidelity" in creoles that included occasional revelations of the "Rebellious designs of other Negroes." Some portrayed themselves in this way, even as "loyal" to their enslavers, as a means of self-preservation. Thirty years later, Edward Long estimated in the abstract that perhaps ten thousand of Jamaica's enslaved people, or 5 percent, were "sensible . . . and trusty." In normal times, enslavers exploited the men whom they believed showed outward "loyalty" as craftsmen and drivers. Long warned that many others "artfully" used presentations of loyalty to "play upon" their enslaver's ego for favor within this system of deprivation.[33]

In these understaffed imperial outposts, enslavers sometimes relied on this logic to defend their colonies by arming the very people they had been exploiting. Colonizers experimented with arming "confidential Slaves" in almost every conflict of the eighteenth century.[34] From his vantage point in Jamaica, Knight estimated that creoles and so-called "privileged" slaves or skilled workers (overseers, drivers, and tradesmen, who had "a kind of Property to defend") would be the safer choice for serving in the militia, not least because they were socially invested in the status quo through the "Friendship and Alliances they have Contracted." Later, in moments of crisis such as during Tacky's Rebellion in Jamaica (1760), individual enslavers tested these theories by handing weapons to some of the people whom they personally enslaved in last-ditch attempts to defend their small fiefdoms. Thomas Thistlewood made this gamble without losing his life, but Edward Long reported that when another enslaver handed weapons to twenty people, they immediately deserted him to join the rebels. They took advantage of his dependence on them for manpower, made more acute by the ongoing rebellion, and they elected a path of resistance blazed by the first rebels. Experiences such as this gave the lie to the myth of slave loyalty.[35]

At times, white people doubted their ability to understand and control enslaved people, which always had been wishful thinking. Enslaved people's sudden acts of resistance, such as flight, theft, and poisoning, periodically shook their faith even in "the fidelity of our most trusty slaves." As Oldmixon asserted in *The English Empire in America*, even though African-born "Foreigners" still seemed to be the most dangerous group of slaves for enslavers, the "Numbers and [enslaved] Condition" of American-born creoles made them "still dangerous" to the people who enslaved them. They sometimes chided themselves and each other for "Putting too much trust in Negroes," as a resident in Charleston did after the Stono Rebellion (1739).[36] When conspiracy scares generated accusations against both African field hands and creole drivers, enslavers expressed dismay at this further evidence of flaws in their judgments and especially those of their neighbors. A year after a major conspiracy scare in Antigua (1736), a plantation manager vowed "not [to] trust them so much as we have done," and after another scare in Jamaica in 1776, a resident was aghast that "even the Creole Negroes" joined and that "the most dangerous enemies were in [enslavers'] houses with them."[37] Their astonishment demonstrates that they generally expected creoles not to rebel even if they were aware of the possibility.

Where creoles dominated enslaved populations, their enslavers tended not to launch as many conspiracy investigations, at least in the first half of the eighteenth century. Historians have used the creolization of the enslaved population of Barbados to explain why it did not take up collective arms in rebellion against enslavers at any point in the eighteenth century.[38] In addition to the significant obstacle of the military power of their oppressors, Jennifer Morgan proposes that "the growth of family ties. . . . magnified the potential dangers [to enslaved people] of violent resistance to slavery."[39] Other historians who conflate conspiracy scares with rebellion have also pointed to the notable absence of investigations in the eighteenth century, except for two—one in 1701 and one in 1778. If we shift this to a study of fear, it is indeed still curious that Barbadian enslavers felt themselves so secure, given that they treated the island's enslaved majority with just as much contempt as in other colonies and caused immeasurable suffering. The geopolitical answer is that the island's far southeastern position in the Caribbean removed it from direct involvement in eighteenth-century wars. The demographic answer is that from 1700 to 1770 the enslaved population increased more through births than through the Atlantic slave trade, except for a brief reliance on imports in the 1750s.[40]

Likewise, white Virginians initiated fewer conspiracy scares after 1730 in part because the enslaved population increasingly consisted of people born in the colony rather than forced to emigrate from Africa. Looking back, the largest scares—those of 1710 and 1722—occurred when less than 50 percent of the enslaved population had roots in Virginia. The colony experienced no major conspiracy scares in the decades after 1730, when creoles comprised 65 percent (in 1740) to 80 percent (in 1750) of the enslaved population. During these decades, relatively few enslaved people arrived directly from Africa. The change came not in the rate of population increase but in sources of growth, from forced migration to natural increase, creating different perceptions for white people of the likelihood of insurrection.[41]

In time, as enslavers saw that informers implicated American-born suspects more and more often, they questioned their confidence in creoles who seemed at once vaguely familiar and threateningly alien. They convinced themselves that even the most submissive-seeming creoles were hiding private thoughts behind masks. In the nineteenth century, demographic developments no longer ushered in dark clouds of fear as much as did other climatic factors such as the Haitian Revolution (1791–1804) and abolitionism, distracted policing institutions, and the possibility of invasion during wartime.

Policing Terror

Enslavers' policing practices, which changed as much as demographics, also help to explain why conspiracy scares occurred in certain times and places. Slavery was a form of incarceration without bars. Enslavers tried to enforce their claims to controlling enslaved people's bodies in the carceral landscape through armed guards and surveillance along racial lines.[42] The more that enslavers in a colony had confidence in their militia's ability to terrorize enslaved people with effective policing, and to defend against invasion, the fewer conspiracy scares they initiated. The most apprehensive white populations were those with such demographic deficits that they could support only ragtag military forces.

Calculating that a larger free white population would add up to a stronger militia, colonial officials in the Greater Caribbean attempted to attract white settlers through special programs. Colonial assemblies taxed enslavers, recognizing on some level that they created the possibility of insurrection, and used the money to attract new white immigrants. They hoped ideally to draw families in a belief that they would be "the most likely to Continue in a Place." A representative scheme in Jamaica targeted British boys and girls aged eleven to fifteen who had such "weak impressions of their own Country, they will soon wear off." These plans generally

Figure 11. White residents of the British West Indies did not have confidence in the islands' militias. Lampooned here are islanders who endanger each other by improperly holding firearms. Details from Abraham James, *Martial Law in Jamaica*. Etching and aquatint with hand coloring. Published by William Holland, [1801 or 1803]; reprinted ca. 1824. Courtesy of the Lewis Walpole Library, Yale University.

failed, as with German-speaking Palatines in 1709 and Scots in 1740. Those immigrants who did arrive often settled in towns rather the frontier. According to a contemporary tabulation of the cost of attracting new white settlers, in the course of twenty-five years enslavers in Jamaica paid £16,308 to bring only 250 heads of household. These plans did not succeed and enslavers in most of the island colonies continued to worry that insufficient staffing for militias opened their vulnerability to insurrection by the enslaved people whom they abused.[43]

Enslavers in Jamaica, South Carolina, and the Leeward Islands also chronically lacked confidence in their militias because they failed to organize the institution effectively (fig. 11). Pessimists generally did not appreciate the fear with which enslaved people regarded them because, as James Knight noted, "when they See the White People Muster or Exercise, . . . it strikes an Awe and terrour into them."[44] Laws did more to indulge enslavers in shirking duty than to discipline them as a militia: laws exempted office-holders from service, established uselessly small units of four to six men to bestow vanity officer titles, and permitted militiamen to neglect regular musters because fines were negligible. Edward Long recollected in his *History of Jamaica* (1774) that the militia's performance was "in so much confusion" during the insurrections that cascaded across Jamaica in 1760. Their poor discipline was little bulwark against their fear of the self-liberated African rebels on the battlefield. In a panic, "they began to discharge their pieces at random, and in such disorder," that their commander shouted out, "For God's sake, gentlemen, do not shoot one another!" Archibald Campbell, governor of Jamaica, remained pessimistic in 1782 when he wrote that "no lasting support can reasonably be expected from the Militia of a sugar colony." Instead, he believed, for "sure defence," the white inhabitants of sugar colonies must rely on "Regulars alone."[45]

Professional soldiers, colonists believed, were the better instrument for terrorizing enslaved people into seeming submission. Militias may have struck more fear into enslaved people because they had fewer checks and more incentive for capricious violence, and did more day-to-day policing, but white colonists took greater confidence when redcoated professionals were around. White inhabitants were themselves impressed with parades of professional soldiers. The assembly of Jamaica noticed that where soldiers were barracked their presence seemed to "over-aw[e] the negroes." Knight, describing Jamaica during the War of Jenkins's Ear (1739–1748), recognized that terror was his weapon when he believed he saw a "Visible Alteration" in enslaved people near "the Regular forces"; the mere "Appearance of them . . . Struck a Terror into Them." Accordingly, "they will shun a Person cloathed in Red either on foot or on Horseback; for which Reason Some Gentlemen," out of their own fear of enslaved people, "put on a Coat of that Colour, when they Travell."[46]

In the 1730s, as Maroons continued to repel colonial invasions, Jamaicans credited the presence of professional troops with having "prevented many Insurrections" by slaves who would have revolted and fled to the mountains were it not for "the name and sight of them [soldiers]." Consequently, when conspiracy scares occurred, colonists turned to professional soldiers and the Royal Navy when possible. The deployment of professional soldiers in Antigua in 1736 was "heartening to us," one inhabitant wrote, "and intimidating to the slaves." After a 1765 scare in Jamaica, Thomas Thistlewood cheered the presence of professional soldiers when "about 40 troopers past thro' the Estate" with "Trumpetts playing." Therefore, garrisons figured into Caribbean colonists' plans to prevent conspiracy scares. As Long later wrote, these garrisons protected colonies "not so much from French or Spaniards, as against the machinations of the many thousand slaves." The island colonies frequently petitioned the king for additional garrisons even in peacetime. During conspiracy scares, governors also hailed naval vessels for assistance. The arrival of the navy, Knight noted, was the best way to convey to rebellious slaves "an Idea of the Strength, and Power, of the English Nation, and [to] Strik[e] an Awe and Terrour into them." Caribbean enslavers recognized that their power depended on fear, and one instrument of fear was the imperial state.[47]

However, in a telling exception to the rule of chronically weak West Indian militias, enslavers in Barbados maintained a strong corps and, unsurprisingly, experienced only two conspiracy scares in the eighteenth century. The turning point came in the mid-1690s with a regularization of the colony's institutions for attempting to subordinate its enslaved population. Most crucially, two thousand disbanded professional soldiers arrived to live at the island's slave labor camps on agricultural plantations at a cost to the colony of £36,000. These militia tenants comprised a policing force that did not depend on unreliable and conflicted individual enslavers to enforce slave governance. As much as enslavers were apprehensive about neighbors' enslaved people, out of necessity they negotiated with enslaved workers in an informal economy of labor relations, however lopsided and violent the terms. Perhaps in an effort to divide and conquer, the Militia Act of 1697 also tapped certain enslaved men for military service if enslavers found them "worthy of great trust and confidence," as judged by each regiment's colonel. As part of enslavers' broader strategy of fostering enslaved people's surveillance of one another on behalf of the regime, this introduced another incentive of status and autonomy for individuals to stand out as "trusty." Such militarization and fostering of divisions among the enslaved made a successful rebellion seem less and less possible, inspiring confidence among whites that they could rally to suppress rebellion. They did not look so hard for conspiracies to detect.[48]

In the mainland colonies of the Carolinas, Virginia, and New York, a large population of arms-bearing white men opened the possibility of forming effective militias for enslavers to police and terrorize enslaved people. At first, early in the eighteenth century, militias failed to inspire confidence among white people. Immediately after Virginia's conspiracy scare of 1710, the governor pronounced the militia to be "so Imaginary A Defence." His successor characterized it as "perfectly useless" and cried out that "the People are so stupidly averse to the only means they have left to protect themselves" from threats that included European invasions, Indian raids, and African insurrections. He missed the golden opportunity for reform that arrived immediately after he left office. A major scare in 1722 provided a crisis that his successor, Hugh Drysdale, exploited in his first address to the Virginia assembly. He focused on strengthening the militia and preventing enslaved people's social gatherings as "the surest method to prevent any fatal consequences that may arise from their evil Designs." He explained that militia musters would put on a terrorizing "shew" for enslaved people to prove that they would be "terrible to . . . slaves, formidable to the Indians, and in a Condition to oppose all Enemies." The performance was at least as much for white people's sake, in kinesthetically confirming their sense of mastery to themselves.[49]

In Virginia in the 1730s and 1740s, Governor William Gooch did the most to strengthen the militia's ability to terrorize enslaved people. He took inspiration when fifteen enslaved people fled to the Blue Ridge Mountains in 1729 to find freedom as maroons. "I am training and exercising the Militia in the several Counties," he wrote, "as the best means to deter our Slaves." Within a year, colonists' lack of confidence in the militia together with intimations of war with Spain catalyzed simmering dread into a conspiracy scare. They noticed "Meetings & Consultations of the Negros in several Parts of the Country" and arrested people to examine them. At first it seemed that enslaved people were discussing a rumor that King George had emancipated them, as sometimes circulated in slave societies, but upon forceful examination they generated evidence of a "Conspiracy . . . to Rise in Arms against their Masters." It appeared that four ringleaders led two hundred people in selecting "Officers" to lead the insurrection. Gooch vowed to strengthen the militia. During the 1740s he vigilantly exercised it and kept his thumb on the county-level officers to strike fear into enslaved people. He also oversaw Virginia's other major policing institution, a new system that paid white men to patrol and thereby retained veterans in the positions year over year. Patrollers had power, independent of the enslavers who claimed to own someone, to initiate searches of slave quarters and to arrest undocumented enslaved persons discovered away from their residence. They were empowered to terrorize enslaved people by their independence from the more subtle negotiations between enslavers and the enslaved on whose labor they depended.[50]

South Carolina's enslavers signaled a lack of confidence in the colony's policing institutions in the first half of the eighteenth century. The assembly established a system in 1704 and made sporadic revisions in 1720, 1734, 1737, and 1740, often in response to conspiracy scares. The acts between 1704 and 1740 did not follow a linear progression so much as they zigzagged through attempts to find new solutions to the problem of neglected patrols. Loopholes enabled absenteeism and grand juries repeatedly complained of neglected patrol duty. Many enslavers trusted themselves to keep tabs on the people whom they directly enslaved, but they dreaded the people whom their neighbors enslaved. Nevertheless, they left it to each other to police them. The assembly's revision of 1740 was the one that stuck. It came in the wake of the Stono Rebellion, which enslavers considered to be frighteningly destructive and nearly successful, and a related conspiracy scare. The 1740 law revealed new heights of concern about the shortcomings of the existing patrol system. The assembly required every militiaman to participate in patrolling, reduced each circuit to fifteen miles, posted maps of patrol districts at churches, and mandated better patrol records. These measures signaled great unease in 1740, but this was the last major revision of the eighteenth century. Sometime after the mid-1740s, assemblymen in South Carolina gained enough confidence in the patrolling system's terror-izing surveillance to stop trying new things. At the same time, conspiracy scares became relatively infrequent.[51]

When enslavers had confidence in their ability to surveil and terrorize enslaved people, they assuaged the fear that inspired aggressive crackdowns. But changes in geopolitical winds could bring other conditions, such as war, that challenged white people's confidence in the illusion that they could maintain complete domestic control.

War on the Horizon

Enslavers' attitudes toward wartime were another powerful factor in facili-tating conspiracy scares. White colonists worried that they could lose domestic control if they faced external pressure from invasion forces. They believed that a foreign enemy could either inadvertently distract masters from keeping their slaves in subjection, making the time ripe for insurgents, or choose deliberately to coordinate with them to open a second, internal front. In reality, most enslaved people probably viewed wartime with trepi-dation because foreign powers who raided English slave colonies usually took more interest in abducting enslaved people as spoils of war than in liberating them. Nevertheless, English colonists believed they saw a link between "Foreign Attempts" and "intestine disorders" because those insur-gents who did take up arms usually made their attempt during times of war.[52] This kernel of truth encouraged enslavers to calculate in geopolitical terms the external pressure that their rotted-through societies could withstand. Conspiracy scares, far more frequent than revolts, also appeared to white people to confirm their suspicions because they compelled informants to confess about the link.

Since the seventeenth century, white enslavers held the fundamental but flawed assumption that enslaved Africans were congenitally unable to organize themselves. Many enslavers looked upon enslaved Africans with disgust as natural born followers, "brutish," much like servants or peasants in Europe, who waited for someone of the so-called better sort to give them direction and harness their labor. Bryan Edwards, the Jamaican enslaver and historian, thought about this while he read his copy of Long's *History of Jamaica*. He endorsed Long's theories of the "brutal . . . manners" of Africans by filling the page's margins with his belief that enslaved people in ancient Rome "lost not only the habit, *but even the capacity* of deciding for themselves, or of acting from the impulse of their own minds."[53] Self-emancipated individuals who led rebellions and enslaved informants who confessed to planning a conspiracy regularly challenged this theory of African inability. Perhaps enslavers dismissed the insurrections that did break out as somehow unsuccessful because they resulted not in revolutionary reversals but in flight to the frontiers, a sensible goal for such vulnerable freedom seekers.

In conspiracy scares, colonists overlooked many indications of enslaved people's intellects by assuming that an outside agitator of greater leadership ability deserved credit for the organizational aspects of the plot. Magistrates did not fully appreciate that they produced their findings primarily through fearful and unequal exchanges with slaves. Many slaves confessed (or many masters surmised) that insurgents planned to revolt in concert with a Spanish, French, Indian, or Maroon invasion, and that a provocateur infiltrated an otherwise content slave quarter to coordinate the uprising. Some commentators scoffed that even if a conspiracy successfully came to fruition, the insurgents would not have the talent to consolidate their gains in the aftermath. One white author, in the voice of a free black person, claimed that "it wou'd be an unsurmountable Difficulty . . . to maintain our Possession." Another dismissively found it "rediculous to suppose that they could keep Possession of the Town [New York] if they had destroyed the white People." Others theorized that ethnic animosities would drive a self-liberated society into civil war. Before the Haitian Revolution proved enslavers wrong, they took comfort in the myth of enslaved people's natural inability. The myth of enslaved Africans' inability underwrote the link that enslavers perceived between foreign enemies and domestic insurrection.[54]

Colonial officials usually referred only in passing to logic they found so obvious, but some explained in detail the relationship between foreign and domestic enemies. In seventeenth-century Virginia, Governor William Berkeley sketched a schematic of the colony's weakness "at our backs" during the Third Anglo-Dutch War (1672–74). He warned that the militiamen who ought to "defend the Shoars and all our Fronteirs" would possibly shirk their duty because of "fearfull apprehntions of the dainger they Leave their Estates and Families in, Whilest they drawne from their houses to defend the Borders," opening themselves up to "Many Servants besides Negroes."[55] In the eighteenth century, when some colonists of then-slavery-free Georgia learned that neighbors were petitioning for the introduction of slavery, they immediately pointed to "how miserable would it be to us, and our Wives and Families, to have one Enemy without," meaning Spanish Florida, "and a more dangerous one in our Bosoms!" Another remarked that Georgians were "so frightened by three kinds of enemies, namely Spaniards, Frenchmen, and Indians and still," illogically, "would bring in a fourth, that is, Negroes or black slaves."[56]

Enslaved people's latent threat of rebellion during an invasion worried imperial planners to the point of reconfiguring the empire's geographical footprint. Later in the eighteenth century, after experience with several conspiracy scares and the terrifying series of revolts in 1760, Edward Long pondered where exactly to situate two new military posts in Jamaica. In a private memo, he noted that two considerations competed for attention: "Security against Insurrections" and "Security against foreign Invasions." The location and style of defense against these two threats required diametrically different military configurations, just as when attempting to fight a war on two fronts. To defend against invasion required a handful of strong coastal garrisons, while to suppress a rebellion called for "a chain" of strong houses "along the interior range of the Country." Later generations of white Americans and British West Indians into the nineteenth century continued to view potentially powerful domestic insurgency and the possibility of invasion as linked threats, particularly as they learned about alleged slave conspiracies that would have exploited this particular vulnerability of enslavers' claims of control.[57]

Nonwhite invaders could also loom in the fears of white English settlers. American Indians and self-liberated maroons did use military means to press their claims to autonomy. Enslavers worried that they could attack a colony in coordination with a slave insurrection, particularly if secretly backed by a European power. In Maryland in 1687, white colonists entertained a rumor that Indians would pummel their frontiers while enslaved people rose from within, all under the supervision of the French and their inside man, Lord Baltimore, a Catholic. New York's slave insurrection of 1712 occurred at the same time that white colonists expected the French-backed Haudenosaunee to attack the Hudson Valley and a European invasion force to arrive "by Sea." Petitioners in South Carolina, situated among several Indian powers in the Southeast, referred in general terms to the province's precarious security situation "surrounded by numerous Tribes of Indians from without, & exposed & lyable to the Insurrections of their own Slaves from within."[58]

Maroons appeared threatening to colonists not only because they gave general "Encourage[ment]" to enslaved people but also because they challenged colonial taxonomies of race and power. Maroons challenged colonialism and slavery by their self-claimed autonomous existence, and implicitly, as enslavers noted, by inspiring enslaved people to continue the struggle. But enslavers worried more about the combined threat of maroon military strikes from the interior frontiers with coordinated insurrectionary conspiracies within domestic spaces. In the eighteenth century, white Jamaicans shared rumors that Maroons were communicating with the Spanish of Cuba or the French of Saint-Domingue, who "granted them many Supplys." When the Maroons forced the colony to sue for peace, James Knight observed that the treaty was reached just in time before the War of Jenkins's Ear: "I shall leave every one to conjecture what the condition of Jamaica would have been when threatened with a Foreign invasion [by the Spanish Empire] . . . [and with] such Enemies within their bowels [Maroons] to have excited and supported their slaves in a Rebellion."[59]

At least one man did conjecture what would happen if invaders, Maroons, and enslaved people joined forces. A pamphleteer who urged more humane treatment of enslaved people in Jamaica warned that the island would soon erupt. White fear and black threats appeared capable of building pressure for amelioration, but in fact most enslavers took an approach of instilling more terror. He characterized the recent insurrections and conspiracy scares in St. John (1733–34), South Carolina (1739), and New York (1741) not as enslavers' triumphs but as uncomfortably near misses. The rebels had potentially strong "Numbers," he pointed out, but they could not organize themselves: "Their only Want was good Leaders," he condescended, and "good Commanders." One day those leaders would show up, whether from the Jamaica Maroons who knew "the Art of War," the French, the Spanish, or even—he suggested with an arched eyebrow— the Moroccans, whose "Prince looks upon all the Black People in our Plantations as his Natural Subjects."[60] The combination of insurrection and invasion seemed formidable to enslavers, whether insurgents' support came by sea, from the frontier, or even from the mountains. White people's fear of external enemies compounded their feelings of vulnerability to the enemy within, sometimes erupting in conspiracy scares in which they used terror to regain a feeling of mastery.

Dangerous Neighbors and Internal Enemies

White people acted on suspicions far more often in wartime because of the perceived link between military invasion, outside instigation, and insurrectionary conspiracies. Sixty-eight of the ninety-six known conspiracy scares from 1650 to 1790, including sixteen of the twenty-three major scares, occurred during wartime or during the interimperial hostilities that preceded war. Most occurred during three wars: twelve at the height of the War of Jenkins's Ear (1739–48; especially 1739–42), fifteen in the Seven Years' War (1754–63), and nineteen in the American War of Independence (1775–83). In turn, enslaved people's implied threats and their enslavers' fear hamstrung the ability of English colonies to wage war.

Wartime did not automatically trigger conspiracy scares. Three main variables influenced whether enslavers investigated rumors of revolt in any given place affected by war. First, a locale's proximity to a theater of conflict or to an enemy's staging ground facilitated white people's fear of insurrection. Just as often, mercantile ties to rival European powers also increased many colonists' sense of vulnerability to invasion. Commercial routes between Charleston and St. Augustine, New York and Havana, Bermuda and St. Eustatius, or Kingston and the Spanish Main provided communication corridors that temporarily became constricted during wartime and fostered rumors.[61] In fact, to spread fear was one technique of warfare. Colonists watched for signs as best they could because they expected not to have clear warning in advance of an enemy fleet's arrival. For example, during the War of the Quadruple Alliance (1718–20), colonists in Charleston, South Carolina, expected "an invasion design'd by the Spaniards" to arrive from Havana "every hour" because several contacts there reported the departure of a large naval deployment. These insidious rumors combined with internal division within the regime during a political rebellion against the proprietary government, accentuating enslavers' sense of vulnerability to an insurrection by rebels who took advantage of their distractedness. An investigation determined that conspirators planned to kill "all the white people," and that the "whole Province" narrowly escaped "utter extirpation" in a plot to capture the town in "a new revolution." Invasion scares often correlated to insurrectionary scares.[62]

Second, enslavers were more easily alarmed when they perceived a degradation in the quality of the military presence. In places where enslavers distrusted their militias, however traumatic such policing actually was for enslaved people, colonists valued access to the British army and navy, even though they could not control the size and duration of deployments. During wartime, military presence increased when naval vessels defended Caribbean ports and when regiments amassed in preparation for an amphibious offensive, but it also could suddenly depart on an expedition or dissolve with the end of the war. Conspiracy scares sometimes coincided with the departure of soldiers and naval squadrons, and enslaved suspects sometimes confessed (or their interrogators surmised) that plotters aimed to take advantage of the temporarily reduced defenses. For example, an informant in Barbados's major conspiracy scare of 1692 claimed that the rebels timed their imminent rising with the departure of English soldiers to invade French Guadeloupe and Martinique. When a large ship appeared off the coast during the investigation it triggered an invasion scare in this distracted and valuable island.[63] On the eve of the War of the Spanish Succession (1702–13), another purported conspiracy in Barbados coincided with the abrupt departure for Jamaica of ten warships that had just arrived from England, which left Barbados without its best defense against insurrection and invasion at precisely the time twenty-two hundred French soldiers arrived in the region at Martinique with a fleet rumored to number fifty warships.[64]

A final key variable to facilitate conspiracy scares was whether the British military won victories or suffered defeats in nearby theaters. Resident slaveholders commented in letters on their awareness of military developments and their concern about the impact on their own lives. The large number of insurrectionary scares that occurred during the War of Jenkins's Ear resulted largely from fighting a losing war against a foe with an overwhelming military presence around the Caribbean. The Seven Years' War, by contrast, was not just a winning war for the British but one they fought with a greater military mobilization. The French, moreover, did not pose the same regional threat as the Spanish did in the slave-dependent West Indies. British enslavers in the Caribbean nervously took notice when Spain entered the war.

The example of the 1730s and 1740s serves to demonstrate how these factors combined to encourage conspiracy scares. A military engineer in Jamaica at this time noted that the island colonies were "Situated amid dangerous and Potent neighbors": Jamaica was just south and west of Spanish Cuba and French Saint-Domingue, and the English Leeward Islands sat down-current from the French islands of Guadeloupe and Montserrat in the eastern Caribbean. Meanwhile, South Carolina contended with the French and Indians by land and the Spanish of St. Augustine and Cuba by sea. In the decade before the War of Jenkins's Ear colonists intermittently took alarm at rumored invasions. James Glen, governor of South Carolina, remembered from a safe vantage point many years later that his colony faced potential invasion on several fronts in the 1730s: "The People of this Province were Annually alarmed with accounts of intended Invasions, & even in time of profound Peace they were made [to] believe that the Spaniards had prepared Embarkations for that purpose at St Augustine & the Havanna, or that the French were marching by Land from Louisiana with more Men than ever were in that Country to drive us into the Sea. Sometimes the Negroes were to rise & cut their Masters Throats at other times the Indians were confederating to destroy us." During this period of heightened attention to vulnerability to Spanish attacks, and increased attention to souring Indian relations, enslavers turned inward toward a population they believed they could control, and they discovered several purported conspiracies.[65]

Two flashpoints in Anglo-Spanish tensions correlated with clusters of conspiracy scares. During the Anglo-Spanish conflict of 1727–29, not everyone was sure whether they were actually at war. Governor Gooch of Virginia asked his brother repeatedly in private letters to confirm whether "we should have Peace, or War should be proclaimed." Spanish guardacostas seized British shipping to inhibit smuggling. Scares occurred in 1729 and 1730 in Antigua, Bermuda, Virginia, and South Carolina as interimperial tension ratcheted up in the Caribbean and the borderlands of southeastern North America.[66] In the second flashpoint, in 1734, more rumors brought concern that "the Flame of a War" might flare up in Europe and quickly spread to America.[67] Four conspiracy scares occurred in South Carolina, New Jersey, Pennsylvania, and the Bahamas. A fifth almost erupted in St. Christopher when an enslaved man was accused of setting six houses on fire in the town of Basseterre. In the largest example, from Somerset County, New Jersey, a drunk enslaved man issued a veiled threat to an English colonist and, upon interrogation, confessed that hundreds of enslaved people would rape and massacre the white population and then escape to "the Indians in the *French* Interest." Meanwhile, Governor Gooch continued to beseech his correspondents to give him any hints about European wars that would spill into America.[68]

At the outbreak of the war, in a rare instance of collective uprising, self-liberated rebels reminded colonists of South Carolina about the link between war and insurrection. The Stono Rebellion, with which this book began, occurred on the same weekend that news reached Charleston about the long-anticipated war with Spain. This inauguration of open hostilities set the tone for fears of insurrection during the war. Three months later, magistrates investigated accusations of slave conspiracy. Charleston resident Robert Pringle experienced this and decided that "we shall Live very Uneasie with our Negroes while the Spaniards continue to keep possession of St. Augustine." Rumors circulated without foundation that a Spanish spy had instigated the rebels.[69]

But the prosecution of the war could not have inspired confidence among British enslavers in the region. The only real British triumph came quickly, with the capture of the Spanish trading entrepôt of Portobelo on the Isthmus of Panama in December 1739, but this victory was soon overshadowed by an embarrassing parade of military failures in the Greater Caribbean. James Oglethorpe's siege of St. Augustine failed in the summer of 1740. The attempts against Cartagena (spring 1741), Guantanamo (summer 1741), and the Portobelo hinterland (spring 1742) all failed to make headway. In July 1742, the Spanish attempted invasion of Georgia exacted some damage and greatly alarmed Carolinians.

During the military fiasco of 1740–42, South Carolina's proximity to Spanish territory and vulnerability to invasion stoked the anxieties of enslavers, bringing three conspiracy scares. In June 1740, simultaneous to the "Inglorious Expedition" and "Miscarriage" at St. Augustine, in the words of Robert Pringle, an enslaved informer warned of an insurrectionary conspiracy "the night before it was to be put into execution." The threat seemed authentic when 150 unarmed slaves gathered the following day, even though slaves often assembled in large numbers for other reasons. The militia arrested fifty of them and hanged them ten at a time during the next five days in an effort to use terror to assert control. Five months later, a catastrophic fire consumed three hundred houses in Charleston and burned for six hours, sparking murmurs of imminent insurrection. Pringle asked his correspondent to "please excuse this Incorrect Confus'd Scrawl" of indecipherable prose because he was "very much fatigued both in body & mind having slept but very Little." Guards locked down what remained of the smoldering town by keeping their posts "Constantly night & Day." Enslaved people, mindful of the recent spectacles of terror, must have steeled themselves for a conspiracy scare. Contrary to expectations, though, no one discovered incendiaries. The fire reminded a "very apprehensive" Pringle of the "great Risque we Run from an Insurrection of our Negroes."[70]

New York City, entangled with the Greater Caribbean through trade, experienced similar conspiracy scares in the winters of 1741 and 1742 precisely as the British invasion of Spanish America faltered. In 1741, during a series of thirteen mysterious fires, a simple inquiry into a burglary erupted into a conspiracy scare, tied to rumors of a Spanish invasion, that brought convictions against 114 enslaved people. A year later, in another New York scare, an enslaved man named Tom admitted to setting fire to a house. To extricate himself from his hopeless legal predicament, he collapsed into confession about a much larger conspiracy. He used one of the few weapons left—threatening words, calibrated to stoke enslavers' fear—to regain some control over his fate. He claimed that "several others . . . advised him . . . in order to set the whole Town in Flames" so that the region's enslaved people could simultaneously "murder the White People." Tom succumbed to pressure and tried to save himself during repeated coercive examinations by implicating "four or five" others "by name positively." However, whether moved by conscience or confused about the English legal system's incentives, he then recanted and admitted that "he did it out of his own Head." When he found that this undid his leverage, and he was slated for execution, he tried to implicate more accomplices. Under continued examination it appeared to these unusually insightful investigators that "every other Story differ'd and varied from the last." Nevertheless, many white colonists remained convinced that "no doubt many other Negroes were concerned with him" because the contours of the plot he described made too much sense. A strengthened policing force patrolled the streets.[71]

At the same time, as the war entered its third disastrous year in 1741–42, enslavers in South Carolina discovered domestic bogeymen. First, magistrates uncovered their own alleged arson plot in August 1741 during a military conflict that had turned decidedly sour. Then, in March 1742, the colony's assembly indicted the white prophet Hugh Bryan for preaching to enslaved Africans, prophesying the "Destruction of Charles Town and Deliverance of the Negroes from their Servitude." Upon news of the Spanish invasion forces landing in Georgia, Elizabeth Lucas noted, "We were greatly alarmed in Carolina," where she managed slave labor camps for a family rooted in the Caribbean. The colony's governing council believed it was infiltrated by a Spanish spy who was helping to plan an imminent invasion of South Carolina. By the Christmas holidays, the colony had suffered another year plagued by anxieties about Spanish invasion and enemies within. On the evening of December 23, colonists attributed a fire at the magazine to possible slave conspirators and went looking for them. If an enslaved person did set the fire, that rebel inadvertently created an atmosphere of dread for other enslaved people who had survived several scares in a few years and witnessed horrifying results. White people had more resources to try to manage their own fear: when a British warship arrived, a merchant in Charleston expressed relief that it would "keep our Domesticks in awe."[72]

Jamaica's colonists were living in a similarly gloomy theater of war. Their fear ebbed and flowed with the movements of soldiers through its ports. A correspondent there lamented that his was "a Country *Surrounded* with *Enemys*, Especially at this juncture." The island hosted the launches of ill-fated attempts against Cuba and Panama in 1741–42. The arrival of a two-thousand-soldier expeditionary force in 1742 gave enslavers temporary confidence that enslaved people would not revolt. After repeated disappointments in the region, however, the naval fleet and twelve regiments of soldiers quitted Jamaica for England. The colony's defensive capability deflated to a nervous reliance on its militia and garrison of a single regiment. In October 1744, four months after France entered the war, Jamaican magistrates launched a major investigation when an enslaved man known as Hector and his wife revealed a plot to lure enslavers to decoy fires for slaughter. Then, in 1745, they believed that they discovered an even larger conspiracy.[73]

White colonists looked hopefully to promises of increased military presence. After Jamaica's two conspiracy scares in two years, and with the wartime threat redoubled by France's entry, the island's governor assured the assembly that they could expect to receive another regiment. A white resident predicted that without these reinforcements his fellow enslavers would continue to feel "insecure, and [be] under perpetuall alarms." He prescribed "10 or 12 sail of the line at least . . . be constantly kept there during the War." He ventured that if the army and navy did not adequately protect Jamaica, "I shall not be Surprised if the Negroes . . . dispossess us of it," provided that the Spanish did not do it first. Jamaican colonists' sense of vulnerability finally subsided when military deployments returned. Through the last years of the War of Jenkins's Ear, Jamaica's garrison doubled from six companies to twelve. With this reassuring buildup, the colony experienced only one insurrection scare, in 1755, before Tacky's Rebellion (1760) enflamed fears on the island and the end of the Seven Years' War (1755–63) required another postwar removal of regiments.[74]

Enslavers in the Greater Caribbean recognized that their reliance on large populations of exploited people compounded their own vulnerability in times of war. Local and colonial officials who took responsibility for subjects' security believed they discovered slave conspiracies when they noticed developments around them, particularly demographic changes and the souring fortunes of war, that seemed to increase their vulnerability. They handled their episodic alarm by exacting a human toll: to manage their own fear they wielded terror against enslaved people in extreme violence. The official findings of their investigations damaged enslaved communities far afield because, as with histories of seventeenth-century events, news of eighteenth-century scares informed and even inspired new investigations in other colonies.

The Plot Printed

As more conspiracy scares occurred in the eighteenth century, more examples informed enslavers' assumptions about the nature of slave insurgency. Especially after 1730, printed news accounts of contemporary conspiracy scares supplemented their historical memory. One colony's experience quickly became another's lesson. Valentine Morris, who previously had drawn ideas from "memory, or Reading" when overseeing Antigua's major investigation of 1736, participated in the panel of judges who published an account of their findings. The pamphlet, *A Genuine Narrative of the Intended Conspiracy*, described a threat that appeared more solid on paper to white readers than the mixture of coerced confessions, desperate recriminations, and hearsay that enslaved people knew lay beneath it. The report indicated that 132 convicted conspirators would have exploded "a Quantity of Gun-Powder" at an upcoming ball in order to wipe out the leading planters, echoing the Gunpowder Plot (1605), and then descended on the town from three or four directions. The plotters agreed to the plan, the authors explained, by swearing oaths to each other at suppers, dances, and funerals—just as masters had long feared—and divvied up their enslavers' estates, officer titles, and very identities. For readers who did not buy the pamphlet, publishers reprinted it serially in newspapers.[75]

Other newspapers screeched that some plotters "administered the Sacrament . . . according to the Rites of the Bishop's Church" and compared the plan to "the *Gunpowder plot*," echoing the anti-popery literature that Morris admitted consulting, or compared this plot as he did to Catiline's conspiracy in ancient Rome, weaving these frail threads into a misleading theory about the nature of insurgency that proved dangerous for enslaved people because it animated new investigations.[76]

In flesh, not paper, Josiah Martin, who presided over the executions of forty-one conspirators, shuttled between Antigua and New York as he continued to fulfill his duties on the island while beginning to establish a residence in Rockaway in 1738. He willingly shared his own details of "the grand Affairs which I suppose you have heard of" when writing to correspondents and presumably when speaking with neighbors in New York.[77] His cousin, Edward Byam Jr., served in Antigua's assembly during the conspiracy scare and lost at least two enslaved people. By 1739, Byam secured a government position in New York. Others of lesser means, including sailors, contributed to the intercolonial conveyance of Antigua's faulty findings, even if their words are lost to the record.[78]

White people's intercolonial communication about conspiracy scares reached a turning point in the early 1730s with the advent of many colonial newspapers. Whereas some colonists received scribbled news of discovered conspiracies from family, friends, and business contacts, many more received published versions of letters acquired by printers. Publishers in Boston, New York, Philadelphia, and Williamsburg regularly reprinted items from both the mainland and the West Indies, including newspapers

such as the *Weekly Jamaica Courant* and *Barbados Gazette* that survive only
as a fragmentary archive. British papers, in turn, used American reports to
convey mostly the larger-scale conspiracy scares. Magazines consolidated
these news items and, if we gauge by output of the *Gentlemen's Magazine*,
printed more than one article per year summarizing insurrectionary events
and fears. One reader in Philadelphia in the late eighteenth century kept an
impressively thorough catalog of conspiracies and rebellions in the Caribbean and North America, with citations to the newspapers, magazines, and
works of history where he found the details.[79] White people in proximity to
these newspapers and magazines received regular reminders of the fact of
their own vulnerability, participating in a common white culture of fear.
Black people were an unintended audience for these publications. Their
low rates of literacy did not keep them from hearing and mourning the
news and dreading the day such uncontrollable witch hunts troubled their
own neighborhoods.

A survey of extant newspapers from 1730 to 1750 reveals that conspiracies dominated the pages more than revolts, influencing the lessons that
white and black audiences took.[80] Beginning in 1736 the number of
conspiracy-related news items far surpassed coverage of revolts. To draw a
comparison, major conspiracy investigations in Antigua (1736), New York
(1741), and Jamaica (1744) generated much more coverage than did actual
rebellions in South Carolina (1739) and Jamaica (1745). The investigation in
Antigua generated at least twenty-three news items in American papers, and
the New York conspiracy scare of 1741 produced at least fifty contemporary
accounts in American papers and, subsequently, as many as fifteen retro-
spective references. By contrast, the 1739 Stono Rebellion in South Carolina
generated four reports in extant American newspapers. Almost all other
news items between 1736 and 1749 referred to minor slave plots—in Maryland (1740), South Carolina (1740, 1741, 1749), New York (1742), and Jamaica
(1744). Perhaps conspiracy scares lent themselves to more extensive coverage because they generated unfalsifiable stories, conditioned with the
would-haves and could-haves of the subjunctive mood. Coerced informants, as a matter of survival and exercise of power, encouraged their tormentors to imagine doomsday scenarios.

Printers profited by commodifying black trauma. While some readers
took interest in news of actual and averted rebellions because it helped
them predict market and shipping conditions in those colonies and networks, many surely took the reprinted correspondence as entertainment.

Printers published longer and more detailed letters to give white readers what they believed they wanted to read. They revealed this in their decisions to pick up salacious details, such as secret priests and attempted role reversals, more often than tamer accounts available about the same alleged conspiracy. These stories, extracted through torture, owed their existence to human suffering. Upon export, they thrilled white readers with the prospect of a world turned upside down, while assuring them that it had always been right-side up.

One could hardly find a more complicated group authorship than that of a published conspiracy narrative. Printed accounts relied on magistrates' questions and informants' explanations in the courtroom and varying levels of mediation such as investigative reports, proclamations, and word of mouth. With each shift between mediums, conspiracy tales took more and more guidance from generic conventions. When a printer set his type into the frame of the press, his was only the latest in a series of artificial framings and narrations, albeit the most concrete, far reaching, and long lasting of them. Printers sold white readers a narrative arc that they craved, and it also taught them to continue to expect it. These satisfyingly black-and-white accounts by enslavers and colonial officials papered over the cacophonous cross talk of conspiracy scares in the courtroom.

Printed matter amplified the voices of enslavers who communicated their version of events to readers in other places and later times. As a durable medium, printed texts also preserved one strain of the cultural scripts with which the powerful spoke about events. As scholar Adam Fox concluded in his study of early modern England, "No one . . . could help but repeat material and articulate forms which derived from these [printed] sources."[81] Cultural scripts such as this pervaded the early modern world, in dying speeches, execution sermons, and evangelical conversion experiences. During conspiracy scares, too, published and whispered narratives infused conspiracy investigations by similarly furnishing "a stock of images and themes" for understanding one's own experience.[82] Even though the powerful endorsed these cultural scripts, the powerless could learn from them how to manipulate their oppressors.

Readers of published conspiracy narratives encountered four recurring lessons about how insurgency and counterinsurgency appeared to work, often in agreement with notions from the seventeenth century. First, it seemed from many accounts that conspirators usually intended massacre and sexual violence against leading enslavers and then the takeover of the colony as their own. Second, it appeared to white audiences that plotters received instruction from outside agitators, would use decoy fires to ambush victims, and organized themselves into a militia structure that they sometimes recorded on paper. Third, readers encountered newspaper accounts that often hewed to a narrative structure of a lucky discovery or revelation by a faithful slave at the last possible moment. For example, readers took comfort that an informant in St. Christopher in 1734 "had a peculiar Regard for his Master, disclosing the Plot," and were thus reassured at the appearance that "trusty" enslaved individuals, if not the whole population, could be counted on after all. The neighbors' slaves seemed to be the problem.[83] Fourth, readers learned that colonial leaders almost always discovered and suppressed imminent revolts, a fact represented graphically in published lists of executions and banishments at the ends of accounts.

New York's major conspiracy scare of 1741, which occurred during the souring War of Jenkins's Ear, also owed a great deal to this circulation of printed information. John Peter Zenger's newspaper had recently published findings of Antigua's 1736 conspiracy, which similarly featured oath-taking, companies of officers, arson, and racial massacre.[84] In turn, as New York's investigation proceeded, Zenger regularly summarized its progress for the use of printers in other colonial port towns, particularly Boston and Philadelphia. The printed story line adhered to white people's expectations that a white instigator "contrive[d] and encourag[ed]" the plot, in coordination with the Spanish, to "kill and Murder all the Male Inhabitants thereof (the Females they intending to reserve for their own use)."[85] Enslaved people in other port towns received this news with dread as it arrived, and it sometimes contributed immediately to new conspiracy scares, as in New Jersey and South Carolina.

Daniel Horsmanden, New York's lead investigator, decided to sell his own story and that of the trauma of enslaved New Yorkers. Horsmanden fronted several hundred pounds and partnered with the newly arrived printer James Parker to reframe the ambiguous evidence on a printing press furnished by his patron Benjamin Franklin. Horsmanden wanted *A Journal of the Proceedings in the Detection of the Conspiracy* (1744) to repair his reputation, which was under assault by some enslavers who were upset that the court had destroyed so much of their property by sentencing enslaved people to death. Horsmanden and Parker sold the documentary history of the trials, a large-format showpiece, as "a useful lesson" and "a necessary Memento" for New Yorkers' "Memories." Too expensive, even Franklin could not sell it. Parker slashed prices to recoup some of his lost investment as soon as a cheaper London reprint undercut it in 1747.[86]

Several publishers competed to deliver this sordid tale at a fraction of the cost, trafficking in a story produced by torturing enslaved people, and profiting from a whole community's trauma. *The Annals of Europe for the Year 1741* covered the conspiracy. It played up the charge of outside instigation and exaggerated the incidence of arson that had led to the investigation, claiming that fires broke out day by day, "in different Parts of the Town, and so on to four or five, and sometimes six in a Day," much worse than New York's revolt of 1712 "about forty Years ago."[87] In a popular trickster tale and travel narrative, when Bampfylde Moore Carew arrived in New York he was greeted with "a great Number of Gibbets, with Blacks hanging upon them." His disorientation faded when, "on enquiring, he found the Negroes had . . . entered into a Conspiracy of burning the whole City." He concluded the scene with an assurance, satis-fying and encouraging to white people, that the plot was "timely discov-ered," "great Numbers were executed," and examples were "hung up to terrify the others."[88] In the following decade, William Smith's *The History of the Province of New-York* reminded readers of the city's 1712 rebellion and 1741 conspiracy scare. In 1712, nineteen slaves had "burnt down a House in the Night, and killed several People who came to extinguish the Fire." Viewing this through the lens of 1741's findings, Smith cast it as a botched "Plot to set Fire to the Town" and create "an Insurrection of the Negroes."[89] In a broad political history of the British colonies, William Douglass informed readers that "at sundry times in the city of New-York there have been negro conspiracies, more than in the other colonies," in which conspirators "se[t] the town on fire."[90] Each of these publications profited anew on stereotyping enslaved people as failed rapacious rebels who seethed with vengefulness.

In Jamaica, Governor Edward Trelawny scanned his copy of Horsman-den's original publication, *A Journal of the Proceedings*, and found it exceed-ingly useful. When he investigated the possible slave conspiracy in December 1744, he checked the list of alleged conspirators at the back of the book. He found that a man in Jamaica, named Hanover, was noted as someone "indicted and not to be found." As newspapers in Philadelphia and Boston reported with satisfaction, the governor ordered Hanover's arrest and sent him back to New York. By July 1745, according to city records, "Hannover a Negro Man" was in the jail beneath city hall.[91]

According to a correspondent, conspirators supposedly planned to massacre "all the white People" in St. John Parish by setting the town on fire, "first at one End of it, and then at the other," so that when "People ran in Confusion to the same, they were to be stab'd and destroy'd." Colonial authorities apparently learned of the plot from an enslaved informer named Hector, who received freedom and a £30 annuity as a reward, under circumstances lost to the historical record. Surely, however, he did not do this out of a loyal "Regard for his Mistress," as colonizers' accounts insisted, balking at the prospect of "her being [one] to be murder'd."[92] Rather, coercions and incentives usually left little other recourse to enslaved individuals in legal jeopardy. On the basis of Hector's confession, the militia assembled and found a social gathering of "a great many Negroes" and arrested "12 or 14 of them" to be hanged, burned alive, or banished. One correspondent warned that, as drivers who managed gangs of enslaved labor, these men "had such an Influence over the others" that they would have brought the parish to its knees.[93]

Hector had his own story to tell as an alternative to colonial and British periodicals' conventional narrative. As soon as he received his freedom and annuity, according to his petition to the King of the England, he found himself "in daily danger" from slaves who "often assaulted him." He moved to England without his wife, whose freedom he could not afford to purchase. Even though he changed his name to Thomas Edwards, his bloody reputation preceded him. He could not "get into business" because of animosity from black Jamaicans in London who understood better than most the devastation he had caused. Back in Jamaica, his wife still received harassments of her own. Feeling helpless, he petitioned the king to redeem her and send her to London, and to increase his annuity to match London's cost of living. Edwards's experience of the conspiracy scare did not center on his supposed "Regard for his Mistress." From his perspective, his harrowing decision to assist white Jamaican authorities resulted in a real change in legal and material circumstances, but it also failed to insulate him from slavery's propensity to rip apart families. His decision blocked him from one of the sources of strength for displaced people: his membership in an ethnic community. Slavery and its conspiracy scares ensnared him even at a distance and in freedom.[94]

The Last Word

The colonial officials who took responsibility for discovering and investigating slave conspiracies noticed when circumstances around them changed in ways that they believed increased their vulnerability to insurrection. Having facilitated the exploitation of enslaved people, they prepared themselves for retribution. Governors and council members already tended to view slavery in a framework of imperial conflict, but they also harbored specific beliefs about conspiracies that directed their eyes toward ships on the horizon and strangers in port. They investigated hunches more often when ships brought unusually large parcels of newly enslaved Africans who were so traumatized as potentially to take desperate, violent measures. They scanned newspapers and asked correspondents for hints about war and peace in Europe and they extrapolated the consequences for their colonial outpost. In colonies with stable white populations, they took comfort in the visible patrols and militia musters whose capriciousness in wielding power was so chilling to enslaved people. In sugar colonies with severe death rates, enslavers took heart in seeing soldiers clothed in red who struck fear into enslaved people. When colonial wars did break out, they recalculated the evolving likelihood of raids or invasions because enslaved people did sometimes press for autonomy by playing European powers against one another in times of interimperial conflict. Enslavers recognized that their reliance on large populations of abused and anguished laborers compounded their own vulnerability. Noticing outside threats that reminded them of their vulnerability, magistrates and enslavers applied these ideas to take stock of their societies and sometimes to initiate investigations.

Colonial officials developed this understanding of slave insurrection by reading and hearing about the outcomes of other conspiracy investigations and sometimes by bringing their own experiences. Histories of seventeenth-century uprisings and conspiracy scares reminded mid-eighteenth-century readers about the very real possibility of insurrection but shaped their expectations with exaggerated findings that papered over the violent, coercive creation of information. News in the 1730s and 40s enabled readers to compare situations in other slave societies to their own experiences and perceptions. Doing so in real time encouraged them to view other colonies' strife as part of a larger conflict that pitted "masters" against "slaves" throughout colonial America. With every tale of a conspiracy scare, publishers commodified black people's trauma and sold white readers a small, inoculating dose of other colonists' fear and a prescription for using violence and terror to overcome it. These testimonials helped to reinforce a paradigm for colonists' thoughts on the most threatening forms of slave insurrection. In some cases, printed accounts of other times and places clearly inspired colonists to take devastating action against enslaved people.

Readers and writers of slave conspiracies, and interrogators and confessors, all participated in a genre. Enslavers looked for stock characters such as foreign agents, Catholic spies, loyal slave informants, and unrepentant conspirators who died stoically without confessing. They welcomed familiar story arcs in which conspirators planned months or years in advance, loyal informants warned magistrates in the nick of time, and then officials restored a colony to tranquility by executing or banishing scores of enslaved people, "which hath set a Period to that trouble," as one governor tellingly concluded.[95] Having recognized that slaves might seek revenge for exploitation, colonists recentered themselves in the story by emphasizing the victimhood of white people in the predicted massacres. Very few white colonists actually suffered violence at the hands of enslaved people, but a great many projected themselves into that position by playing out counterfactual scenarios.

In the hands of enslaved individuals, as we will see, these generic conventions empowered some to navigate moments of extreme precariousness in the jailhouse and the courtroom. Some gave confessions that referred to conventional elements such as mysterious fires, vengeful massacres, officer titles, and inverted social orders. Desperate individuals used these cultural scripts to manipulate enslavers' fears, empowering themselves to escape worse fates, but levying chilling costs on others.

CHAPTER 3

Seeking Truth Through Terror

Coercion and Survival Inside the Courtroom and the Jail

Billy arrived in New York with a reputation for being "very expert at Plots."[1] He had just escaped with his life from Antigua's conspiracy scare of 1736 by making the harrowing decision to turn informant. In New York, white people identified him not with that personal trauma but with the danger he seemed to present: in 1741, in a new conspiracy scare, they imprisoned him in the overcrowded basement of the city hall. Although these two colonial outposts differed in their economic configurations—one a sugar island, the other a maritime town and imperial center—they shared a fundamental reliance on the violence of chattel slavery and the system of fear that it generated for black people and white people. Billy's improbable path out of one investigation and into another, and how he learned along the way to use his constraints for self-preservation, all illustrate how suspects, informants, and investigators with human impulses, fears, and failings propelled major conspiracy scares. As this chapter shows, Billy was not alone.

In Antigua's scare of 1736, Billy first came under suspicion early in the investigation when an informant mentioned social gatherings of his acquaintances at the house of his enslaver. In these early days, the judges were desperate for the names of unidentified conspirators and a picture of the plot. They ramped up their coercive techniques on the jailed enslaved people over whom they held total physical power. They sentenced a group of convicted men, including Billy, to be gibbeted alive—to die of thirst, starvation, and exposure in hanging cages. Billy gained some degree of control over his situation by agreeing to turn king's evidence immediately after his sentencing, having seen others do the same when fitted into iron cages. He gave the names of at least fifty acquaintances as new suspects because his possibility of reprieve depended, precariously, on how the investigating judges regarded his usefulness. He also served as a trial witness against at least fourteen people, including a longtime rival for whom he had a "great hatred." Three of his victims the judges burned at the stake, and eleven they banished to Spanish America, selling them away from loved ones.[2]

Robert Arbuthnot, the justice of the peace who led this investigation, and other fearful magistrates were desperate to understand the potential danger. Together with terrified informants who were struggling to survive, they assembled a collage of evidence that suggested a scene horrifying to white people. They decided that conspirators planned to strike the colony's center at St. John's Town. The conspirators would have exploded gunpowder hidden beneath the ballroom floor as the wealthiest enslavers celebrated the anniversary of the king's coronation, catching them "at the heights of their mirth," as one resident put it to his brother. Companies of hundreds of insurgents would have descended on the town from several directions to kill the remaining white people in the streets, take over their households and identities, erect a new government, and install an African king. Colonial authorities arrested and questioned several hundred suspects from October 1736 to March 1737. They pressured 32 to become informants in exchange for reduced punishment or material reward, and used them to bring convictions against 132 people, 88 of whom were executed and 44 banished through sale. They terrorized thousands more around the island.[3]

Improbably, Billy found himself threatened by a second conspiracy scare in New York. He arrived there because his enslaver sold him northward in 1738, which was meant as a milder punishment than death or sale to Spanish America. Parallel to Billy's forced migration, news of Antigua's conspiracy arrived through published reports and word of mouth. Josiah Martin, for example, presided as a judge over forty-one executions in Antigua in 1736 and then established a residence in Rockaway, New York, in 1738. He willingly shared his own details of "the grand Affairs which I suppose you have heard of" when writing to correspondents and presumably when speaking with neighbors in New York.[4]

New York's conspiracy scare began late in the winter of 1741. A two-week series of unexplained fires frightened town-dwellers, and a vocal segment of the white population demanded the preemptive, blind arrest of enslaved people. Daniel Horsmanden, a justice on the Supreme Court of Judicature, with other investigators and coerced informants generated an eerily familiar story that the blazes were meant as decoy fires to facilitate

an uprising. Suspects alarmed their interrogators with the plausible com-
monplaces that they would have massacred the white men, kept "all the . . .
wives for themselves," and "take[n] the country" with the assistance of a
Spanish invasion. They allegedly planned this over sumptuous feasts, issued
oaths to new recruits and recorded them in "a List of Names of those
who were to rise," and appointed some to be "captains" over "several
Companies"—features all present in Antigua's plot. Their principal orga-
nizers, they said, were two white tavern keepers and two Catholic priests.[5]

During this crisis, Bill, as most of his new black acquaintances now
called him, came under suspicion because of his confessed experience in
Antigua's conspiracy and his rumored participation in a rebellion on the
Danish island of St. John in 1733. Bill was arrested when another desperate
person seized on the governor's promise to pardon anyone who confessed
and impeached new suspects. Bill arrived in jail to find that, as in Antigua,
the thronged and sweltering cells were an incubator for informants' trial
testimony and suspects' collusion on defense. Bill confided to a fellow prisoner, Pedro, that he "understood these Affairs very well" and coached him
that "unless he . . . did confess and bring in two or three, he would either
be hanged or burnt." As in other scares, the only way to escape was to
contribute to a cascade of accusations. He even prompted Pedro with some
names "as proper ones to be accused" and suggested that it was best to
mention fire because it "would make the Judges believe him."[6]

When Pedro appeared before the judges he confessed that he drank
once at the plotters' tavern, learned there about the conspiracy to "burn
the town and kill the white people," and joined that night by taking an
oath; he adhered to the broad outline established by earlier suspects. He
answered the judges' demand for names by implicating a personal rival,
using the jail for information, and accusing three men he saw there. For his
part, Bill pleaded guilty and indicated that he would say more if pardoned.
He did not receive the opportunity. The court was alarmed by his apparent
recidivism after the Antigua plot and sent him to the stake. Nevertheless,
Bill continued to try to save himself with a stunning confession. While the
flames rose around him, he accused two white soldiers, "reputed Papists,"
of instructing a slave to set fires and to "do it with some wet Cotten" as
with a Jesuit's slow-burning fireball because "that will make no Smoke."
Bill also impeached nine more men, five of whom were newly implicated,
and dangled the possibility that he "heard that other soldiers were concerned." In amplifying colonists' fear, he hoped to increase the value of his

claimed knowledge and leverage it into reprieve. Such tactics sometimes worked.[7]

Bill protected only his ally from jail. He said that "Pedro . . . is innocent for what he knows," not realizing his confidant had already betrayed him. A few days earlier, Pedro had revealed to the justices that his own confession "was not true" and that he had developed it based on advice from Bill. Bill's impulse to navigate the investigation by colluding in a false confession actually provided Pedro with precisely the *other* type of information that the judges coveted: a report on one's cellmate. In the jailhouse one could not so easily distinguish friends from foes, particularly when white fear tightened the screws of black terror.

Bill died violently while "lifting up his Hands and Eyes" in one last attempt to earn reprieve. He "cried aloud, and several Times repeated the Names" of those he had accused. That night the constables arrested two of the five new enslaved suspects, the others having eluded capture. They also arrested a white soldier who, in turn, confessed and served as a valuable new trial witness. Pedro won release two weeks later for his assistance. In the end, New York's investigators questioned 172 people, 20 of whom were white. The Supreme Court of Judicature found 114 guilty, including 81 who confessed for the reduced sentence of banishment. They sold as many as 90 people to Spanish and Portuguese territories and ordered the judicial murder of 30 enslaved people and 4 white people.[8]

This chapter uses the cases of Antigua and New York to explain how desperate people, such as Bill and Pedro, and their counterparts Robert Arbuthnot and Daniel Horsmanden, created conspiracy scares through their interactions in the investigative process. By the 1730s and 1740s the unequal coauthors drew on generations of memory of insurrectionary scares and sometimes even personal experience to inform their encounter with the investigation. Although colonies differed in their specific mechanisms for investigating slave conspiracies, they did share similar juridical cultures and beliefs about the nature of slave insurgency. As the cases of Antigua and New York demonstrate, colonial authorities placed suspects and informants in such peril that some took extreme measures with the few tools at their disposal. They spoke directly to enslavers' fears, they used information from jail, and they mustered as many signals of credibility as they knew. Desperate suspects and informants pursued a spectrum of strategies, but each person struggled to escape with his life, even if one man's success worked at cross-purposes to another's.

Hunches and Discoveries

In both Antigua in 1736 and New York in 1741, suspects for small crimes seized on the system's incentives to make accusations of more serious crimes, playing on enslavers' fears to save themselves. On the morning of Monday, October 11, 1736, justice of the peace Robert Arbuthnot of Antigua oversaw what seemed to be a routine slave trial for gambling. The magistrates met in a house in St. John's Town, home to fifteen hundred white residents and the center of business on an island in which five thousand white people enslaved nearly all of the twenty-three thousand black people. In Antigua, as in New York, most ordinary slave trials occurred in front of a panel of three justices of the peace, with no jury. In themselves, such trials threatened serious physical harm to suspects.[9] During this summary trial, a white resident recalled overhearing one of the suspects mention a "List of Officers and Soldiers." This piqued Arbuthnot's suspicions. He tried to leverage the gamblers' fear of punishment for the smaller charge into revelations about a potential insurrectionary conspiracy, but each man on trial denied knowing anything helpful.[10]

When Arbuthnot continued asking around, he became suspicious of a playful exchange between Jack, a cooper, and Dorothy Douglas, his enslaver's sister. He mentioned that another man, Court, had been crowned king at a recent ceremonial gathering. She bantered: "What, Court is King, and you are to be one of his Officers?" Jack replied: "Yes, Court is King and I am to be one of his Generals." He insisted he was only joking, but enslavers who were aware of previous plots took alarm at hearing of a crowned slave king who might lead European-style companies of insurgents. The next morning, Arbuthnot searched the room where Court's enslaver housed him. He discovered only money and a drum, not weapons or powder. By chance that night, a plantation manager noticed "five or Six" black men in earnest conversation at the house's back gate. He thought he heard one of the figures mention something about "Powder & Shot," and heard another—Court—respond "I have none." If only the eavesdropper had known about Arbuthnot's inquiry and that morning's search of Court's room, he would have realized that these men were discussing those events, probably with an eye toward self-preservation. Instead, he reported the exchange a few days later when he learned that Arbuthnot was looking for evidence of a rebellion conspiracy.

Arbuthnot continued his informal inquiry by choosing people to interview based on their reputations. Lacking an informant, he called on

Emanuel, whom he regarded as a "sensible" Christian and "honest Slave." He asked him leading questions, such as "whether he thought the Negros were not arrived to a much Greater height of Insolence than he had Ever Observed," and listed the men whom he had arrested. Emanuel did not need immediate physical coercion to understand Arbuthnot's expectation of cooperation. He protected himself by trading on his reputation as a Christian, turning informant, and later serving as a witness at the first trials in the persona of a trustworthy person. On the other hand, Arbuthnot used other enslaved people's negative reputations against them. He arrested Tom Limerick and Fortune on a hunch that "if any thing Criminal was going forwards . . . , they were Probably Concern'd in it." Two weeks later he sent Fortune to the stake.

Arbuthnot wove together these loose threads of vague hunches and suspicious moments into a report that he presented to the island's assembly and governing council on Friday, October 15, four days after the original inauspicious gambling trial. The governor ordered the soldiers and militiamen to keep guard and maintain nightly patrols around the island, especially in St. John's Town.[11] Based on Arbuthnot's preliminary findings, on October 19 the assembly appointed a four-man tribunal, composed of two members of the assembly, one member of the governor's council, and Arbuthnot himself, the justice of the peace who had started it all and now found his stature elevated.[12]

*　　*　　*

Four years later and eighteen hundred miles away, in New York in 1741, a parallel sequence of suspicion, discovery, and coerced confession led to tragically similar results. The City of New York was better described as a town, where 9,000 white people enslaved 2,000 black people, surrounded by farmland in modern-day outer boroughs where another 21,800 enslavers exploited 3,300 more slaves.[13]

New York's conspiracy investigation began as an attempt to explain an unusual cluster of ten fires in three weeks. The first fire consumed the governor's residence at Fort George on March 18. Initially, the governor reported, it seemed to be "accidentally done by a plumber." By April 6, however, white people in the streets developed their own theories as they fought three fires in one day. One elite New Yorker wrote to his stepson in Jamaica, who was soldiering in the War of Jenkins's Ear, "Five of these fires happening [on] one day, with many other Strong causes of Suspicion[,] render it Likely that all or most of them have been on purpose." Speaking to widespread assumptions linking arson, outside agitators, and insurrection, some cried out that "the Negroes were rising" because they saw a black man running away from the fire.[14]

Popular outcry led to the indiscriminate jailing of enslaved men, particularly a handful recently arrived from the Spanish Caribbean. White New Yorkers issued a call to "take up the Spanish negroes," who had been recently captured and auctioned off by a privateer in the War of Jenkins's Ear, and who now lived in the vicinity of two of that day's fires. "The people," the governor later recalled, were in "the utmost Consternation and Confusion [emotional disorder]." They took matters into their own hands, as Justice Horsmanden explained in his documentary history of the trials. "Many people" acted on their "terrible apprehensions" by taking custody of almost any black man they "met in the streets" and bringing him to jail. As white people took action, the governor attempted to "appease their fears" with a nightly twenty-five-man militia patrol, which he noted to be prudent "Especially in Time of Warr." He explained to imperial officials, that he regarded New York to be "a frontier province," long considered a plum prize for the Spanish, and in particular danger if the War of Jenkins's Ear expanded into "a French warr," as it did in 1744. Looking for a Trojan horse, the sheriff led a canvas of town for "any strange Lodger or suspicious Persons."[15]

Direct evidence of an insurrection finally emerged from the usual type of figure—an unfree person who, charged with a lesser crime, found a way out of jeopardy by revealing the greater danger of a planned insurrection. Mary Burton, a sixteen-year-old indentured servant, was unusual in confessing because she was female and white, but like others before her she was disempowered as a servant and was first involved in a smaller burglary investigation. Authorities already suspected that John and Sarah Hughson, the tavern keepers who held Burton in servitude, were responsible for fencing stolen goods for enslaved people. When Burton had a chance encounter with Anne Kannady, whose husband was a constable, Kannady dangled the prospect that if Burton revealed the hidden goods she "would free her" and give her harbor. Burton testified the next day to expose a burglary ring centered at her master's tavern, but she did not say anything about a slave insurrection. Indeed, she did not yet have occasion to do so because the fires had not occurred and primed people's imaginations.[16]

In April, after the fires, Burton accepted the city's promise of a pardon, stipend, and freedom, all of which she received, for identifying the arsonists behind this new and more serious crime.[17] She explained the blazes by building on white residents' outcry against enslaved people. Burton added her own specific and legally actionable information to sharpen the references to shared assumptions about slave conspiracy. In front of a grand jury, which had been convened to investigate the fires, she claimed that the plan the conspirators hatched at Hughson's tavern was to "set fire to the town . . . in the night" so that "as the white People came to extinguish it, they would kill and destroy them." The insurrectionists, she said, would make Caesar, an enslaved man, into the governor, and Hughson the king. This testimony, which launched the rebellion conspiracy trials, relied on a precise rendering of three of the main tropes about slave conspiracies: organization by a free white instigator, the use of decoy fires, and the elevation of a new governor or king for the conquered province. The Supreme Court of Judicature took over the investigation—instead of the usual bench of three justices of the peace and five freeholders for serious slave crimes— when it appeared that free white defendants would stand trial as the alleged instigators of the usual enslaved suspects. White people's public pressure and Burton's initial hints combined to launch a coercive investigation that in turn forged a sinister interpretation of what the slaves intended that winter.[18]

Cascading Accusations

In Antigua, elevating the investigation from one man's hunch to an institution's duty added irreversible coercive pressure. Judges applied judicial, psychological, and physical coercions to extract information. As a matter of survival, some of Arbuthnot's initial suspects now made the heart-wrenching decision to turn informant by accusing others of conspiring. If they identified enough previously unknown conspirators, described their methods, and served as trial witnesses to convict them, then colonial authorities promised them lighter punishment (banishment instead of execution), pardon, or even stipendiary rewards. If they did not, they faced agonizing deaths.

The gallows cast a long shadow that influenced each moment of the proceedings. The execution spectacles of plots past, such as Antigua's in 1729, formed an emotional backdrop of terror. Throughout the British colonies, magistrates who discovered plots insisted on using the spectacle of execution to "deter others from the like bloody and wicked attempts for the future" and "leave a Terrour on the Minds of all the other Negroes for the future." As men of the Enlightenment, they considered terror to be a salutary emotion by which rulers maintained the standing social order.[19] In keeping with this, the judges in 1736 ordered the first deaths to be horrifying spectacles of mangled bones and charred flesh. The first three victims were broken on the wheel. Torturers pinned them to a rack on the ground (fig. 12) and crushed their limbs with blows from an iron bar. They writhed for hours. The judges sent ten other men to be consumed in flames at the stake, a grisly punishment that they considered fitting for treason.[20]

Terroristic examples such as these weighed on men in custody. The prospect of the gallows served as a startlingly effective psychological prompt when legally powerless enslaved people faced enraged white examiners. Questioning under such conditions built up massive cognitive pressure until it forced some suspects to break their silence. In these coerced confessions, suspects did not necessarily convey accurate information. Instead, they gave a confession, better characterized as instrumental than informational, in order to alleviate physical and mental stress. The speaker no longer valued accuracy so much as *any* action that promised to allay the pain.[21]

Judicial torture was not part of the common law tradition in the British Atlantic world. Nevertheless, during conspiracy scares such as this one, investigators occasionally forgot themselves. The Antigua justices congratulated themselves on their restraint in torturing suspects only three times after receiving formal authorization from the assembly. They "Declined further to use it," they explained, because the results were "Fruitles[s]" when they broke a man on the wheel and received only an admission of guilt. Despite their avowed humanity, out of dissatisfaction with the paucity of information from men who burned at the stake in the first week of the investigation, the judges demanded that the next group undergo a more prolonged and agonizing death "in Order to produce Discovery's." They gibbeted these convicts, killing them over days, not hours, by thirst, starvation, and exposure in iron cages that towered over the public market in St. John's Town. The cages faced each other "in a Quadrangle, so that [the victims] cou'd see and speak to one another," forcing them to visualize their own suffering.[22]

Although the judges only ever sentenced ten men to hang in the cage, they nevertheless received a staggering windfall of information. They took

The Execution of Breaking on the Rack.

Figure 12. Enslaving regimes tortured convicted conspirators by breaking their limbs, sometimes using a wheel instead of the rack shown here, to induce confessions and to set a horrifying example. *The Execution of Breaking on the Rack*. Engraving in John Gabriel Stedman, *Narrative, of a five years' expedition, against the revolted Negroes of Surinam*, vol. 2 (London, 1796), plate 71. Courtesy of the John Carter Brown Library at Brown University.

down at least fifty new names in the final confessions of two men as they withered away. They compelled three others to turn king's evidence and to serve as star witnesses for the next several months. These informants alone furnished sixty pieces of trial evidence in the fraction of records that survive. As more suspects turned king's evidence, they accused a wider network of people and set in motion a cascade of arrests. Initially, just three witnesses convicted ten men in the first week of trials. In the next two months, several new witnesses convicted ninety men. At the end of five months, thirty-two informants brought 132 convictions.[23]

*   *   *

In New York, as soon as Mary Burton described a rebellion conspiracy led by white agitators in April 1741, the Supreme Court of Judicature took charge of the investigation in conjunction with the grand jury. Justice Horsmanden and his fellow justice Frederick Philipse interrogated enslaved people immediately upon their arrest in the belief that "the Truth would bolt out," especially if "under great Terror." In the early days each suspect denied knowing anything. The justices tried to assuage colonists' fear in the streets by turning to torture to force convicted men to contribute information about enslaved people's possible vengeance. They strung up two enslaved men who were found guilty of a burglary, Caesar and Prince, in chains, and gibbeted them to induce a conspiracy confession, but the two men "very stubbornly" refused to do so.[24]

The prospect of punishment encouraged another suspect to break her silence: Margaret (Peg) Kerry, an Irish sex worker and the mother of Caesar's child. In a roughly parallel trial, she and the Hughsons, the aforementioned keepers of Hughson's tavern, which Kerry and Caesar frequented, faced charges of receiving the stolen goods from Caesar and Prince. She almost saved herself on May 7 when she devised a confession that squared the mysterious fires with her burglary-related conviction by using an anti-Catholic trope. In the distraction of fire, she said, New York's plotters would not only "kill them all" and appoint a white instigator as "Governor," but also "steal, rob and carry away all the Money and Goods they could procure." This echoed Titus Oates's fabricated but widely believed confession that Catholics orchestrated fires such as the Great Fire of London (1666) to loot Protestants' homes. At this pivotal moment, Kerry's

greatest impact on the investigation was to name ten people as alleged conspirators. She implicated one enslaved man who had died before the investigation, two who were about to be gibbeted alive for burglary (Caesar and
Prince), a free white instigator who had already fled town (John Romme, a
neighbor of the Hughsons), and—crucially for investigators—six previously unsuspected enslaved men, who were taken up that night. One
month later, despite her information, the court executed Kerry and the
Hughsons on the charge of rebellion conspiracy that she helped them
develop.[25]

The black men in custody experienced a deeper terror, created by even
greater power imbalance, and understandably tried to save their own lives
by accusing acquaintances. Sandy, one such jailed suspect, faced this grim
choice at age sixteen. After a week in jail, on May 22 Sandy became the first
enslaved person to confess and to turn king's evidence for the rebellion
trials. The justices promised him that "the Negroes which confessed the
Truth and made a Discovery, [would] certainly [be] pardoned, and shipped
off," urging him not to be guided by stories that enslaved people who "told
all they knew" were still hanged after the 1712 rebellion. He immediately
accused Fortune, who in turn confessed on the spot and joined him as
king's evidence. Sandy relied on well-worn ideas about slave conspiracy in
revealing the oath and describing companies of insurgents who gave themselves officer titles such as "captain." When the grand jury asked Sandy
"what the negroes proposed by rising and doing all this mischief," he raised
the familiar specter that the goal was to "kill all the gentlemen, and take
their wives." With these confessions and tropes, Sandy and Fortune provided clinching evidence for the prosecution of a man named Cuffee, who
had been arrested in the initial sweeps, and his acquaintance Quack.[26]

Quack and Cuffee, the first two people found guilty of the insurrectionary plot, refused to confess until overcome by the terror of being strapped
to the stake to burn. Horsmanden described the scene as one of "great
Noise and Confusion" by an "impatient" crowd. He believed he saw "great
Terror" on the condemned men's faces and directed his secretary to record
useful information from their confessions, which he found especially credible because extracted through fear, "confirmed in the Midst of Flames,
which is the highest Attestation." The "Mob press[ed] forwards to hear and
interrup[t]" with follow-up questions. (At this point, the governor's scribe
accidentally wrote "fear" instead of "hear" as he prepared a copy for the
supervisory Board of Trade in London.)[27]

Quack and Cuffee strategically gave information that they hoped would horrify investigators with the enormity of the conspiracy and ideally tantalize them into sparing them to serve as informants. They confirmed that Quack set the fire at the fort, that the conspirators were bound by an oath, and that John Hughson, the tavern keeper who had received stolen goods, was "the first Contriver of all." They described the incriminating activities of twenty-eight people by name in a two-part strategy. First, they bolstered their credibility by agreeing with the investigators' hunches: they confirmed the involvement of twelve men who were already in jail, two who served as king's evidence (Fortune and Sandy), and two whom the court had already killed (Caesar and Prince). Then they proved their value as informants by freshly impeaching ten new people. They tried to ensure their continued survival by hinting that the dimensions of the conspiracy were larger than anyone realized. Quack said that Hughson planned to "bring down Country People in his Boat," and both men claimed to know the names of "40 or 50" more conspirators, if only they were removed from the stake and given the chance to elaborate. The two men almost saved their own lives with this information. The governor sent word to temporarily stay the execution, on their likelihood of "producing great discoveries," but the sheriff believed that the crowd grew so insistent that he could not retreat to the jail with the condemned men. He proceeded to burn Quack and Cuffee. The fear and anger of white people in the crowd encouraged him to perform public violence that restored their sense of mastery by terrorizing enslaved onlookers. Perhaps the black audience found their own alternative lessons, though, such as the barbarity with which they would be treated if they did not turn informant sooner.[28]

The investigators vastly expanded their net on the basis of Quack's and Cuffee's dying confessions of May 30. That afternoon they arrested seven of the ten newly accused people, the others having heard and fled. On June 8 and 12, a second wave of accusations quickened the pace of arrests, primarily based on the confessions of two people. One, named Jack, was already in jail because of Sandy, but Quack's and Cuffee's deaths must have shaken him. He impeached at least nine new suspects and served consistently as a trial witness, garnering a pardon and transportation out of the colony. The other, an enslaved man known as Tickle (alias Will) who was arrested because Quack and Cuffee accused him at the stake, confessed on June 12 and implicated at least ten new suspects.[29] Each successive wave was larger and more powerful. By late June, almost all of the nineteen men whom Jack and Tickle accused in turn confessed or pled guilty, as did eight more implicated by other informants. Under formidable pressure, they found a way to mitigate their torment in Governor George Clarke's June 19 proclamation that he would pardon and banish anyone who confessed within two weeks and revealed new names of still more conspirators. He immediately noted that "every day produces new Discoveries." Jailed suspects seized the governor's offer, and a torrent of accusations brought the arrest of fifty-eight new people and created a shortage of space in the jail. The justices enlisted private lawyers to help them keep up with recording confessions, which they now accepted in abbreviated form to save time. They ultimately questioned 172 people and elicited eighty-one confessions.[30]

Trials

The investigating judges who extracted names and information from informants concurrently governed the trials of suspects and orchestrated witness testimony against them. In Antigua, they used a trial procedure that balanced their strategy of issuing terrorizing punishments with their respect for legal process, however skewed, and awareness that enslavers considered enslaved people to be valuable property. Initially the judges allowed onlookers at the trials, but they noticed that "Masters were prone to . . . Excuse their Slaves" and to assist in their defense by "asking questions" when their own slaves were under scrutiny. Several wished to preserve the value of their human chattel through acquittal. Perhaps they also had a personal incentive to perform as their slaves' benevolent patron at court and wrest back dominion over persons and properties about whom the government was suddenly making decisions. The judges grumbled that this "much retarded" the proceedings, but perhaps their greater concern was that enslaved suspects were "imboldened by their Masters['] presence, and Witnesses [were] intimidated." They soon closed the trials to everyone but jailers, constables, and witnesses, hoping to reassert control of the power dynamics between the court and the accused slaves.[31]

Judges convicted suspects on the basis of stunningly slight evidence. By this time several colonies had relaxed their prohibition on using evidence from enslaved people. Starting with cases of insurrectionary conspiracy, they overcame their reluctance to use information from people who could not swear an oath in the court of law, and whose words might destroy another white colonist's human property.[32] During Antigua's conspiracy trials, the suspect and the witnesses attended all together in the courtroom without legal representation. The witnesses were usually "Produced Joyntly," which happened to help them give consistent and effective testimony that would prove their worth to the judges. Others were "Call'd in" as needed if their names unexpectedly came up. This allowed the judges to check, in the event of a dispute, that "all the Witnesses do agree," even if the situation forced them to manufacture their agreement on the spot. A witness always gave evidence in the presence of the suspect on trial, and frequently the accused disputed their testimony. Often, suspects and witnesses interjected comments to impugn one another's credibility, for example by tarring the adversary as "a great Stealer of Goats" or having "a Mind to [the suspect's] Wife."[33] Several defended themselves at trial by making "Obstinate Denyals of Every thing." Others refuted key details in the testimony against them: at least eight denied attending one particular weekend social gathering at Francis Carlile's plantation that was thought to be a major conspiracy meeting. Some of them said they had not visited the estate in question "since Mr. Carlile's Death [in 1734]"; others said "these 4 or 5 Years," and in a few cases, "in his [the defendant's] life time."[34]

In order to send an enslaved man to the flames in Antigua, the court required only two witnesses to provide "positive evidence," meaning eyewitness accounts of a conspiratorial oath or material support for the plot. Circumstantial evidence could strengthen the case, but the court insisted on procuring two pieces of positive evidence before sending any man to his death. On weaker evidence, the court sentenced a man to banishment to Spanish America. Their sale out of the colony was not only a cost-effective punishment but also an intentionally cruel one; as a colonial official wrote under similar circumstances in another colony, "an Exile from their wifes and children is almost as terrible to them as death itself." These requirements in testimony held for other colonies as well.[35]

Witnesses knew that judges evaluated their performances throughout their months of testifying. They were rewarded on a sliding scale from lighter punishment (banishment instead of execution) to pardon, a monetary prize, or even freedom. The Antigua justices waited until the conclusion of the trials, when they evaluated witnesses' performances to revise earlier promises upward or downward. Ultimately, they pardoned ten witnesses and allowed them to continue living in Antigua, of whom three received cash and two garnered freedom on top of it. Other informants did not fare so well: four were executed as convicted conspirators, one was sold to slave traders in a Spanish colony with other convicted plotters, and nine were sold to enslavers in British North America—including Billy, who became known as Bill (or Will) in New York.[36]

*   *   *

In New York, the investigation and trial proceedings likewise dwelled at the intersection of respect for the rule of law, the property rights of enslavers, and the court's self-assigned prerogative to terrorize the enslaved population. After the windfall of new suspects from the dying confessions of Quack and Cuffee, the court tried the alleged conspirators in groups of four to eight on most days for two months. As an unusual consequence of the Supreme Court of Judicature's involvement, the accused were tried before a twelve-man jury of white freeholders. The city's leading lawyers prosecuted the suspects based on evidence wrenched from the terrified informants by Horsmanden and Philipse. They obliged white informants to give sworn testimony, forced black informants to give unsworn evidence, and compelled the words of the deceased into service by reading back the last recorded words of executed convicts. The prosecutors made their cases against the handful of free white suspects, such as Hughson, on the basis of white testimony and whatever information from enslaved people could be sworn into the record by constables, jailers, and participants in the linked grand jury proceeding. The prosecutors and justices did not need to scrub hearsay and speculation from the testimony because the jury was charged with deciding for itself which of the presented evidence to take into consideration and which to discard. Jurors relied on "common sense" about the nature of planned insurrection, which they developed from the information about conspiracy scares that circulated widely by the early 1740s.[37]

The accused defended themselves without counsel against a battery of the town's best lawyers. Enslaved people could not afford the legal representation that a jury trial usually allowed. Some defendants benefited from Spanish interpreters and from people who claimed to understand the pidgin English of native Africans.[38] Enslaved defendants were hampered by an incomplete understanding of how to win a jury trial and were surely intimidated by the stakes. They knew at least to "stiffly" deny the evidence against them, but they supposedly said "nothing material in their Defence" in Horsmanden's estimation. Unfortunately, the surviving fragments of the manuscript trial record cannot corroborate his dubious recollection that the New York suspects "asked the Witnesses no material questions" except for "now & then a few trifling Questions." Antigua's counterexample gives us reason to doubt his opinion.[39]

When the court invited them to produce witnesses who could speak "to your Characters," some of the accused got their enslavers and other white patrons to vouch for their "very good Character" and history of having "behaved very well." Horsmanden noticed in New York's trials that enslavers had an interest in protecting the value of their investment in an enslaved person, especially, he noted, skilled tradesmen. At a minimum, enslavers preferred that convicted conspirators whom they claimed as property be sold out of the colony to recoup more of the loss. They had more success petitioning the court for this when the convicted conspirator enjoyed a reputation of good character, as sworn to in the foregoing trial.[40]

A few defendants got their enslavers to testify as to an alibi for the time of the fire, such as when Quack said that he was "employed most Part of that Morning . . . [and] that he was hardly ever out of their Sight all that Morning."[41] The so-called Spanish Negroes offered the most robust defense with broad alibis. Antonio de la Cruz, for example, got his enslavers to explain that because of his severe frostbite they "believed it was not possible" for him to go "down stairs" all winter, let alone outdoors. These men probably developed this line of defense together in jail, as suspects often did, considering that they got their own enslavers to give similar testimony as to being "sick in his house till some time in March," "sick all the winter," and hobbled by frostbite at a "farm in the country."[42]

Horsmanden noticed that in some cases enslavers guided suspects with "Advice and Instruction with Respect to their [courtroom] Conduct." Perhaps Gerardus Comfort's sons-in-law had coaching in mind when they volunteered to translate pidgin English on behalf of Jack, mentioned earlier, whom their family enslaved. They claimed that having worked so many years with him in the cooper's shop they "could make a shift to understand his Language," which the court found "perfectly Negro and unintelligible." In speaking with him, they used their "Influence over him" to convince him "to make an ingenuous Confession." He brought the arrest of seven new suspects and then served as a trial witness.[43]

Horsmanden recognized the legal alliance that formed between suspects and their enslavers under these circumstances. He noted that according to

"§ 20" of the published report from Antigua's investigation, the investigating judges learned to keep suspects' owners out of the courtroom because their mere presence could shift the trial in favor of the defendant. The "very Sight" of one's enslaver in the courtroom reportedly "buoy'd" suspects and gave them greater resolve to defend themselves. After the trials, when Horsmanden reflected on enslavers' conflicted motives, he admitted that allowing defendants to call them as witnesses—a regular feature of a jury trial, but not normally in a slave trial—was "perhaps . . . too great an Indulgence" in "Matters of so much Consequence to the Publick."[44]

The Treacherous Jail

Jailhouse conversation was the source of the stunningly consistent testimony that impressed investigators in Antigua, New York, and elsewhere. Conspiracy scares often owed their findings to the physical restraining of so many suspects in an overcrowded makeshift jail. Suspects waited there for the court to determine their guilt or innocence, while convicted conspirators languished there until execution or banishment. Stripped of familiar support networks, the incarcerated tried to regain some power by reaching out to a range of other participants: some tried to help one another through collusion, others combined against each other, and a devastating few formed their alliance with the investigators. Informants used these jails to note the identities of prisoners who were already under suspicion so as to include them in their testimony, in order to enhance their own credibility and indispensability in the eyes of the judges who would determine whether they earned a reprieve from bodily punishment. Little did investigators know that the internal consistency in their findings owed a lot to what happened in these jail cells.

To consider Antigua first, the physical circumstances of the holding pen provided witnesses and suspects many opportunities to draw inferences that structured their stories in the courtroom. Prisoners easily exchanged information because the building that served as the jail in 1736—the "tenements adjoining the Guard-house"—was better suited for short-term imprisonment of debtors and fugitives from slavery than for a conspiracy investigation that required the isolation of suspects and witnesses.[45] Jailers kept the prisoners in five rooms, split between the upper and lower levels of the building, with a total capacity of about fifty people. One prisoner in "an upper Room in [Gaol]" communicated to another in "the Room under him," through "a large hole in the Floor, which he Could run his hand through." Clearly, those who built these jail spaces did not intend them for a conspiracy investigation. Insurrectionary scares occurred only intermittently, and no other use of the jail in colonial America required the same expansive capacity and relative isolation. In the three rooms that held trial witnesses, according to an officer's report, "Sentrys" kept guard "night and Day" and "Several Soldiers" stayed "between every two Evidences." The witnesses remained there for weeks and months at a time while waiting to serve at the trials of newly jailed suspects. The deficiencies of the jails allowed prisoners to communicate unbeknownst to their jailers.[46]

In addition to the physical environment, the system of overlapping prisoner populations allowed inevitable leakages in sharing information among prisoners. Suspects and witnesses rubbed shoulders in this overcrowded and underguarded space. This gave them opportunity to collect and create information. Newly arrested suspects stayed in confinement for as long as it took to discover and marshal evidence against them. Convicted men returned to jail to await the execution of their sentence, usually for one to four weeks. Other convicts, awaiting their banishment, remained in confinement for several months so that the entire group could be transferred at one time to a single merchant. All the while, new suspects continued to arrive as informants made fresh impeachments.[47]

Prisoners who shared information with each other often did so to their own detriment. Their jailhouse confidants, once in the courtroom, gained an advantage by repeating to judges what they had heard in confinement. For example, at one trial, an informant claimed overhearing a prisoner say that he would have fled from justice if given the chance. Another informant claimed that a jailed suspect confided in him that he was in fact guilty. Others went beyond onetime informing and chose to serve as spies in jail. They posed as men awaiting banishment and drew their cellmates into compromising conversations. As convicted conspirators, these spies had strong incentives to ferret out new information: most produced satisfactory results and were spared their lives, but one of them, Frank, failed to generate new findings and was burned at the stake. Under this pressure, a spy turned even a tasteless joke into evidence against a flippant prisoner who darkly quipped one day, while several men were burned at the stake, "that they had done all the Roast Meat." He was sentenced to banishment.[48]

The jail swirled with information and misinformation about the apparent conspiracy—all of it useful for spies and informants, yet dangerous for suspects who chatted in unguarded moments. Some jailed men, wary of eavesdroppers, took precautions in their conversation. One was overheard to reprimand two others that "they were turn'd Fools or Children to Confess their Guilt in a place where they Did not know their friends from their foes." Others knowingly played to eavesdropping spies and jailors. Three men loudly complained to one another that certain other people from their plantation "ought to have been brought to Town, instead of them, for that they [the persons still at large] were more guilty than they [the jailed suspects] were." Their ruminations caught the ears of a spy and the attention of the judges, who then took up the new suspects and eventually found them guilty (one banished, one burned).[49]

Despite these dangers of being overheard, prisoners attempted to help each other by sharing information about what they gleaned of the judicial process. They consulted about "what Signifies Confessing to the Justices" and reassured each other, incorrectly, that "Two Witnesses are not Sufficient to take away a Negro's Life, nor three, Nor hardly four" (a misunderstanding that originated with a spy).[50] Some prisoners consulted one another about the temperament of the judges. One newly arrested man, "as Soone as [he] came into [Gaol]," asked cellmates "if they had been tried" and what exactly had happened in the courtroom. A prisoner who had just been convicted related "what the Justices said to him" and reported that "the other Justices were easyer with him than Colonel [Valentine] Morris." Were it not for Morris's zeal, he objected, "the rest of the Negro's would all get Clear."[51] But prisoners seemed to believe that jail keepers could provide help, and guards sometimes entertained their requests. Soon after arriving in jail, Cudjoe, a carpenter, asked a guard "to Stoop Down, that he might Speak with him . . . not to be overheard." He confided that he "was afraid" that other prisoners would concoct lies about him to win reprieve, but the guard misguidedly advised him "by no means, to Say any thing that was false to Save his life." Two weeks later, Cudjoe was burned at the stake.[52]

In these whispered conversations, general advice slipped into outright collusion. Some of the suspects attempted to coordinate their stories to protect one another. "When you go before the Justices, keep one Tongue, and don't Confess any thing against the Johnson's, but Die like Men," one suspect reportedly said to two of his cellmates. Another man, newly arrested, apparently tried to get his story straight with others upon his arrival by speaking with someone in the room upstairs through the hole in the ceiling. From above, he received instructions to deny several specific allegations. His efforts backfired; soon he was executed.[53]

When testifying against any suspect, witnesses bolstered their credibility in the eyes of judges by populating their stories with people who it was obvious had already drawn suspicion. They did this because the judges would kill them or sell them away if they were proved false. We can measure this in the patterns in how witnesses mentioned third parties in the extant record. They did this 269 times (excluding references to other witnesses and the alleged ringleaders Court, Tomboy, and Secundi). Most of the time, trial witnesses referred to people they saw in jail, whether or not they knew them prior to arrest.

The most effective version of this testimony incorporated the names of prisoners who had already been found guilty, whether executed or still languishing in jail. Witnesses invoked the names of the deceased seventy-eight times. This gave their stories credibility because it built on what investigators already believed to be true, and it also allowed witnesses to make claims that the dead could not contradict. At least thirty-one times, witnesses named living conspirators, already convicted, who still sat in jail awaiting their fate of banishment or execution. This was a riskier move, but a determined witness could usually overpower the protests of a convicted conspirator whose credibility already suffered in the eyes of the judges. In addition to fingering convicted men, whether dead or alive, witnesses also found power in mentioning the names of prisoners who still awaited trial. They used the names of jailed suspects at least 103 times. They incorporated newly jailed men into their testimony perhaps to avoid stale scenarios with familiar dead conspirators. Although witnesses correctly noted the cloud of suspicion hovering over these new inmates, they may have regretted their decisions later when only some of the men were deemed guilty at trial. Many were released or acquitted.[54]

Although it may appear to us that witnesses tried to limit new arrests by overwhelmingly naming suspects who were already in jail, in fact their decisions were far from heroic and did not come from the solidarity that powerful white people projected onto the enslaved population. They came from terror and they preyed on others trapped in this vise. Witnesses named dead, convicted, and jailed men in order to help prosecuting judges achieve convictions at trial. By doing that they would survive the investigation. If these witnesses named dead people because they wanted to *limit* the investigation, they missed their chance during the pretrial examinations at which interrogators demanded fresh impeachments. At the trial stage, witnesses' indispensability to judges rested on their avoidance of patent falsehoods and their achievement of convictions. They knew that the judges valued witnesses who gave plenty of detail yet seemed never to perjure themselves. The tactic of naming dead, convicted, and jailed "conspirators" in trial testimony helped witnesses reach that standard, rendering them worthy of reprieve and reward in the eyes of the people who held their lives in the balance.

*   *   *

As in Antigua, the jail in New York that held accused and convicted conspirators served as both a coercive instrument and an incubator for inaccurate information about the plot. The jail was a large common "dungeon" in the basement of City Hall meant really to hold debtors temporarily (fig. 13). It was poorly equipped to investigate a group of people suspected of conspiracy because it allowed prisoners to communicate. Consequently, the city council temporarily installed walls to create smaller compartments, or "Pidgeon holes," to separate witnesses from suspects and from each other as much as the "scanty Room in the Jail" would allow. As in Antigua, however, New York's cascade of arrests "throng'd" the jail with prisoners beyond capacity. As many as seventy people were confined by the middle of June 1741, and more than one hundred at the end of the month, with the population "daily multiplying."[55]

The justices recognized that confinement itself could coerce suspects into giving information. As the Virginia council put it during its own conspiracy investigation a decade earlier, jailing suspects for a length of time "under a Strict confinement and the Terror of a prosecution" increased the pressure on them to confess.[56] In fact, in New York the first revelation of an insurrectionary conspiracy came when Mary Burton, after "Standing mute & Obstinately refusing" to speak about the fires, was threatened with imprisonment.[57] Similarly, an enslaved man named Adam who turned himself in preemptively for the governor's proclamation of mercy, but who said "as little as possible" to earn it, would "beg" to continue each examination, evidently to delay descending back into the jail.[58] Horsmanden counted on revelations "bolting" out at the shock of confinement, and prisoners took

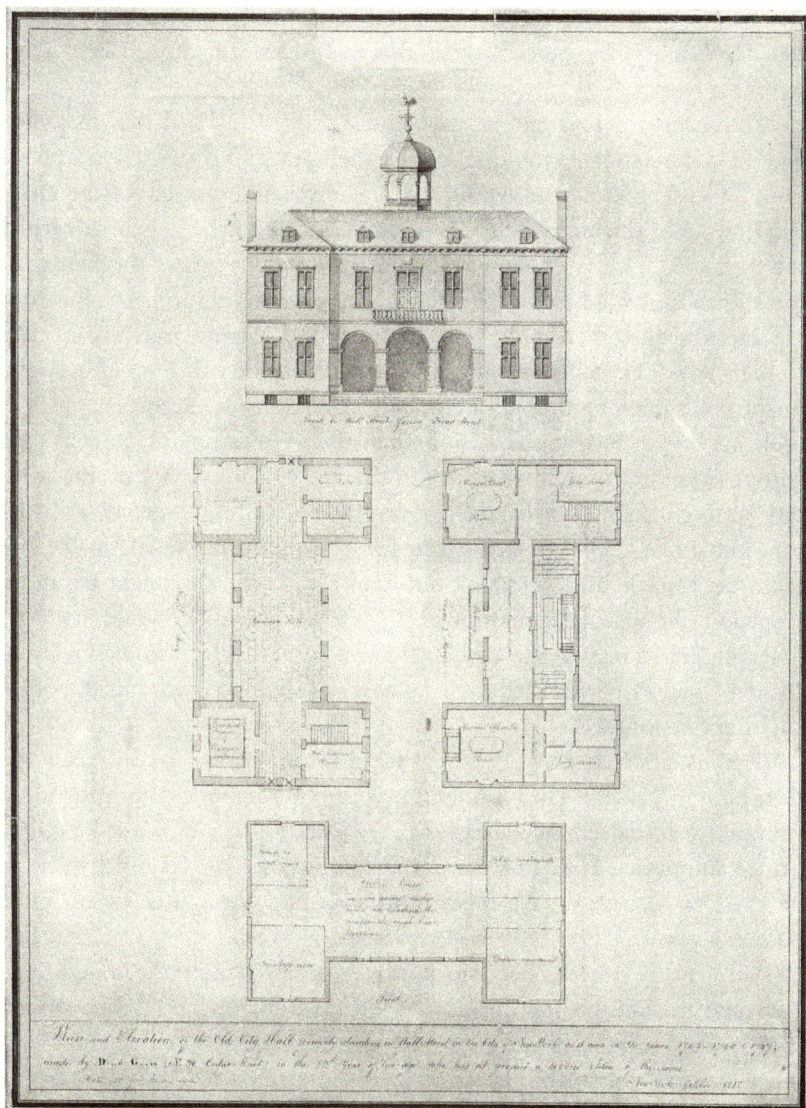

Figure 13. In New York's conspiracy scare of 1741, the Supreme Court of Judicature met on the upper floor of City Hall and jailed accused and convicted conspirators in retrofitted compartments in the debtors' prison in the basement. David Grim, *Plan and Elevation of the Old City Hall Formerly Standing in Wall Street in the City of New York as It Was in the Years 1745 & 1746 & 1747* [. . .], 1818. Drawing. Negative 27567, New-York Historical Society.

advantage of those expectations. When their captors implored them for so-
called voluntary confessions, they falsely admitted guilt to qualify themselves for mercy.[59]

The justices used a spy in jail because they recognized that prisoners
had an understandable impulse to seek each other's help. The spy in New
York was a servant named Arthur Price who was imprisoned for the unrelated crime of stealing goods. He began service early on when he earned
the trust of Peg Kerry enough for "frank Talk and Openness" in their conversation through a hole in the door that separated her compartment from
his. He told the jailer about their conversation, which largely revealed a
woman who knew little about any plot but dreaded that other suspects
might say something to make her seem "as black as the Rest." The justices
took her vague statements of apprehension as meaningful morsels that
"dropt from her in accidental Talk in the Jail."[60] Four days later the jailer
put Sarah Hughson, the daughter of tavern keepers John and Sarah Hughson, into Price's cell. She insisted to Price that "she did not know of any
Plot." As Price helped her think out loud about why she might be under
suspicion, she speculated about which enslaved men in her world might be
dragging her into this. She mentioned two in particular whom she "mis-
trusted," and Price reported their names. One was arrested, but the other
could not be found.[61]

The justices recognized Price's value in "pumping out the Secrets of the
Conspirators" and began putting him with other prisoners and providing
rum punch to loosen their tongues. They placed him into the same cell as
Cuffee and passed in a "Tankard of Punch now and then, in order to chear
up their Spirits, and make them more sociable." At Cuffee's trial, Price
related a conversation that involved nothing about an insurrection but
instead a rivalry between two associations of enslaved men (the Long Bridge
Boys and the Smith's Fly Boys, based on town landmarks). Horsmanden
later stitched together this glimpse of enslaved men's self-organization with
other suspects' confessions about "several companies" led by "officers" and
"captains" to arrive at the conclusion that this geographical division represented the insurrectionists' two self-organized military districts. Price kept
up his espionage for only two weeks before the prisoners clammed up,
having noticed his frequent departures for court.[62]

In more ad hoc fashion than this spy's, suspects in confinement also
reported on each other's conversations to gain favor with the court. Often
the incriminating evidence pointed more to their desperate attempts to

navigate the investigation than to any actual planned rebellion. Some whispered to one other that, unsurprisingly in this draconian slave regime, they were not completely innocent of any violations. One prisoner threatened another that he would "kill him" if he said "any Thing" at court, an understandable threat from a vulnerable man, even an innocent one. As in Antigua, some prisoners conferred about how to handle their predicament. A suspect named Cambridge strategized with his cellmates that "if they did not confess, they should be hanged." He falsely confessed "through Fear" and wrongfully accused new suspects, devising his believable confession from "a common Talk . . . that Hughson was concerned in a Plot with the Negroes." Others surely did the same but never recanted.[63]

Informants who were desperate to save themselves used the jail to identify people whom they could credibly accuse, as others did in Antigua. Peg Kerry tried to reserve this tactic for a later time by claiming in her initial confession that she did "not now remember" the names of everyone she could implicate but she would "remember their Faces again if she should see them."[64] She was executed before she could, but other people who were jailed at a later date did just that: they gave confessions and testimony by noting who already sat in prison. In essence they reprised other informants' earlier impeachments. This mutual corroboration had the effect of increasing late-coming informants' credibility in the eyes of the justices and jury. Consider the example of a man named York, who gave a confession one day after the governor's promise of pardon. He named twenty people, most of them already deemed guilty: two trial witnesses, four men who had already been executed, three who had pleaded guilty and sat in jail waiting to be sold out of the colony, seven who had just been found guilty and awaited sentencing, one who had died years before the scare, and finally— providing the only utility the court had for York's confession—three in jail who awaited trial. For neglecting to freshly identify new suspects, York was hanged. To take another example, Caesar gave a confession two days after the governor's proclamation. Of the twenty-three whom he impeached, nine had already been executed and eight were already in jail. He introduced only six new names to the investigation, but that was enough to recommend him for banishment rather than execution.[65]

Incarceration, and close confinement in particular, created an environment that perpetuated major conspiracy scares and crystallized faulty knowledge about them. Incarceration, as an instrument of coercion, encouraged confessions and recriminations. It brought together suspects into a physical prison where they exchanged information about the "find-ings" of the investigation, formed shaky alliances with one another, and sometimes secretly joined forces with the investigators as spies and informants—all ways that desperate men tried to empower themselves. In this setting, informants produced evidence they would not have otherwise known, including the identities of the likeliest suspects and the evolving story line of conspiracy that they collectively coauthored.

Presenting Evidence and Taking Its Measure

The grisly outcome of these investigations and trials may seem to us to have been a foregone conclusion, but at the time colonial authorities wanted to accurately understand the alleged threat. They wanted both to avert the danger to white society and to avoid the financial and human cost of too many miscarriages of justice. To their dismay, they almost never found physical evidence of a planned uprising. In Antigua, searches did not yield any weapons caches and only ever turned up stolen goods (the same was true for New York). After one such raid, Robert Arbuthnot surmised that the resident must have "Received Notice [and] . . . had just [enough] time to Strip his House and Put Everything Out of the way." Nevertheless, the investigating judges persistently asked about the location of the gunpowder that was meant to be the centerpiece of the conspiracy. One informant tried to placate the court by saying he saw a covered package "which by the Shape he took to be a bottle & imagined but Do's not know it was Powder." Months later, when they believed they had finally tracked down the fabled ten-gallon keg, they went to seize it "but the Powder was Gone." They were chasing shadows cast by coerced confessions.[66]

Without physical evidence, investigators had to turn to enslaved infor-mants to understand these hidden crimes of speech and planning. To distin-guish truth from lies, colonial judges (and, in New York, the jury) applied some familiar tests from English jurists' tool kits and adapted them to the new situation of racial slavery. Handbooks instructed justices of the peace that in situations lacking "open and evident" proof they should evaluate "half proofs" as possible "good causes of suspicion." Under normal circum-stances, a judge or jury considered category-based markers such as suspect's or an informant's gender, age, religion, free or unfree status, and race to estimate a person's natural propensity to lie. Even though investigators believed that enslaved people's race, unfree status, and criminality diminished their credibility, they were forced to rely on them for information. They attempted to discern who among this suspect group demonstrated "a greater Stock of Sincerity than most of his Colour," as Arbuthnot said of one informant, by learning about people's reputations and sizing up their personal demeanors. They also evaluated informers' stories against their own version of common sense, the "Probability of the Matter," rooted in memory and news of insurrections and conspiracy scares.[67] Ironically, by following a seemingly rational path for evaluating information, investigators arrived at exaggerated irrational conclusions about the nature of the threats they faced. At every turn, they tried to decide whether a suspect who confessed was truthful or deceptive.

Having already assigned a doubtful moral character to enslaved people by brutalizing, racializing, and criminalizing them, investigators believed that they had to evaluate a suspect and potential informant on the basis of personal reputation. White patrons, particularly a person's enslaver, could intervene successfully for a suspect or informant by vouching "as to his character." In the eyes of the court, enslaved people's legal identities were already subsumed to those of their enslavers. A reputable sponsor could lend his own credibility if he commanded social authority within white society and perhaps even intimidated the court. Enslaved persons who served convincingly as trial witnesses tended to be backed by enslavers who already held a great deal of social power. Quamina, for example, a man enslaved by Josiah Martin, benefitted from his enslaver's stature as one of half a dozen members of the colony's royally appointed governing council. Martin, "being wrote to" on two occasions, vouched for Quamina's trustworthiness. He "Gave a very good Character of his Slave Quamina and Spoke very Indifferently of John Sabby [the suspect on trial]." During another trial, Martin again vouched for Quamina and proclaimed him a "Dispassionate Fellow" who he believed would "not . . . impeach any[one] wrongfully." Quamina's hand grew only stronger when Martin joined the tribunal halfway through the ordeal. Other trial witnesses also benefitted from the intervention of their enslavers. In fact, three of the four most devastating informants were backed by enslavers in powerful offices: two by investigating judges, three by members of Antigua's council.[68]

As a check on enslavers who tended to insist on their own slaves' innocence and credibility, investigators used additional methods to evaluate suspects and potential informants. English legal procedure recommended looking into a person's known associates, lifestyle, criminal history, and "common fame." For example, before the formal investigation, on the second day of his one-man inquiry, Arbuthnot identified Court as a new suspect but was "quite a Stranger to him and his Character." His enslaver, Thomas Kerby, speaker of the assembly, gave a good account of the waiting man's "Fidelity and honesty" over thirty years of servitude. But within a few days, Arbuthnot collected common reports from other white men that Court was actually "a Dark Designing, Ambitious Insolent Fellow." He decided that Kerby "was in great Measure blind to his Faults." Less than a week later, in the first act of the formal investigation, the judges sent Court to his death as the plot's ringleader.[69]

Evaluating a suspect's or informant's personal demeanor was perhaps the most common way that investigators, judges, and juries attempted to sort truth from falsehood. A common legal guidebook of the time advised that "the very Speech, Gesture and Countenance" of suspects and informants could reveal more than neighbors' (or enslavers') testimonials to their character. Those in command in the courtroom believed that they were skilled in detecting truthfulness or guilt by observing a person's facial expressions, even though they had to peer across a power divide that included racial ideas about the body. For example, during Arbuthnot's informal inquiry he thought he noticed "much Sifting" in the body language of Jack, who probably could not disguise that he understood the danger of this interview. When the trials commenced, Arbuthnot orchestrated Jack's conviction based on his own assessment even though his enslaver "gave a very good Character" of him. He sent him to burn at the stake.[70]

Body language was a factor over which some people had more control. Some enslaved people had life experiences that enabled them to present a personal appearance that boosted their perceived credibility in the gaze of judges. Witnesses who could use their bodies to signal credibility were rewarded by judges. Consider the courtroom performance of Attaw, a thirty-three-year-old man. His work as a gang driver at the sprawling Parham plantation gave him experience managing competing demands and presenting well to powerful white men. In the courtroom, Attaw testified against Cudjoe. When the suspect denied some of the accusations, Attaw "laid his hand upon his heart[,] looking Cudjoe in the face, and wish'd that God might Eternally Damn him, if what he said of Cudjoe was not true." As he locked eyes with Cudjoe, the other four informants in the room must have studied the court's response. The second witness, Dick, took his cue from Attaw and after giving his evidence also "laid his hand upon his heart[,] looking upon Cudjoe, and wish'd that he might never Enter into the Kingdom of Heaven, if all that he had said of Cudjoe was not true." While this asserted link between lying and damnation reflected judicial oath-taking among Akan-speaking Africans, these invocations of "God" and the "Kingdom of Heaven" were also crafted for the judges' Christian ears. The judges marveled at the demonstration of sincerity and scribbled the drama into their trial minutes. Cudjoe was burned at the stake. Attaw was pardoned but remained enslaved.[71]

*   *   *

In New York, as in Antigua, the investigating justices and the jury would have preferred not to rely on enslaved people for information because, in their estimation, their social and racial status suggested a predisposition toward dishonesty. They understood white informants, on the other hand, to be inherently more trustworthy even when other social markers such as class and gender worked against them. All of this mattered because courts, whatever their considerable blind spots, usually worried about whether they were getting things right. A key legal advantage that justices of the peace and colonial officials saw in relying on white people was that, as Christians, they could almost always give sworn testimony.

In New York, Mary Burton's whiteness had a value for the investigating justices that exceeded her perceived inadequacies as a young woman and an indentured servant, opening a path for her to become a star witness in New York. White witnesses who testified at such length were highly unusual in slave conspiracy trials in the eighteenth century, but Burton claimed to have spent enough time with enslaved black men that she saw them conspire. White people in marginal positions, such as overseers and their wives, indentured servants, sex workers, and jailers, occasionally had relevant information precisely because they interacted with black people more frequently. These white informants typically provided early tips—or, more accurately, suspicions—rather than claimed intimate knowledge of the inner workings of a conspiracy. In Burton's case, her ability to give sworn testimony enabled justices to convict the suspected white instigators, who were immune to the unsworn testimony of enslaved persons. Nevertheless, for slaveholders who lost property when her testimony led to the deaths of enslaved men, her status as a servant and a sixteen-year-old woman at times fostered their concern that she might be lying. The investigating justices chose to privilege her usefulness as a sworn witness and convinced themselves of her truthfulness by scrutinizing her gestures for seemingly commonsense markers of transparency and by measuring her story against what they already believed they knew about how New York slavery operated.[72]

In the main, however, Daniel Horsmanden and the other justices had to rely on "some of the Confederates them selves" to illuminate "Such works of Darkness." He was frustrated by what he perceived to be "the Difficulty of bringing and holding them to the Truth." While Horsmanden did solicit white people's assessments of enslaved persons' characters, he also trusted himself to accurately evaluate a person's demeanor.[73] It was a gut feeling—"it is hard . . . how to describe it"—but he believed that he could read black faces. He thought he noticed that black people who were feeling guilty exhibited "an odd knack or . . . way of turning their eyes inwards, as it were." Their faces may have been flashing with fear, anger, contempt, despair, or guilt over something else, but only they could say. In his supreme confidence, Horsmanden announced that in one case "Patrick's Visage betrayed his Guilt," while in another case, he said the man's face displayed "Truth and Innocence." In the latter case, Horsmanden elaborated that the man, named Cork, normally had the "Disadvantage" of a "naturally suspicious Look" but that during his interrogation he flashed "a chearful, open, honest Smile." He announced that Cork's momentary "Beauty" and "handsom[eness]" came from his honesty, shining through his natural "Deformity." Horsmanden evaluated speech in similarly racialized and subjective terms. He complained that many non-native English speakers erected a communication barrier of "unintelligible Jargon" as a "Craft[y]" tactic "to conceal their Meaning." In reality, feigning inability or noncomprehension could help someone avoid becoming more entangled in the scare.[74]

These perceived signs of credibility—social status, individual reputation, personal demeanor—meant nothing if a person's story did not add up. It mattered what informants said. Magistrates measured informants' words by asking two questions: (1) Were they consistent with other information? and (2) Did they basically make sense? The first of these "tests" compared informants' stories to each other. If several informants' "respective Testimonys Tally & agree," Horsmanden mused, "what better Evidence can be desired or expected?" He admitted that some of the claims of the informant Mary Burton initially "Stagger[ed] ones belief," but he ultimately found satisfaction that "every thing that has come from her, has in the Event been confirmed." He took particular satisfaction that her "Testimony has been confirmed by Several Negroes in Flames . . . [at] the Stake," which he considered to be strong proof.[75]

The other gauge of an informant's story was to measure it against commonsense assumptions. Magistrates considered the likelihood that the crime being described could actually be committed. In the case of slave conspiracy, they took account of how the information fit with their knowledge of past rebellions as well as the peculiarities of the local security situation. For example, colonists already believed that outside instigators helped enslaved people to organize effective conspiracies and to coordinate with invasion forces. In the first two months of New York's investigation of 1741, John Hughson seemed to be the agitator, and the Spanish-speaking men of color whom New Yorkers captured at sea and enslaved appeared to be intermediaries for facilitating a Spanish invasion as part of the War of Jenkins's Ear. However, Hughson only partially fit the profile of the white leader: in other slave conspiracies, secret Catholic emissaries were more convincing as instigators. "The Old proverb," Horsmanden wrote to a colleague, held that "There is Scarce a plot but a priest is at the Bottom of it." Indeed, in mid-June Governor Clarke received a letter from James Oglethorpe, engaged against the Spanish in Georgia, that confirmed as much. Oglethorpe related a Spanish prisoner's confession (or terroristic boast) that his empire had sent "many Priests" disguised as doctors and teachers "to burn all the Magazines & considerable Towns in . . . English North America." White New Yorkers searched the town for "Popish priests lurking about."[76]

Enslaved men in jail picked up on this expectation and used it in their confessions to devastating effect. Within days of the letter's arrival, one such prisoner, named Tom, confessed to learning that the "very great Sin" of insurrection would not damn him because "there was An Old Man in Town . . . that could forgive [sins]." Immediately, the governor reported to his superiors in London that "two of the Negroes have confest" to hearing about "the hand of Popery" in the plot, generating speculation that the Hughsons were Catholic and harbored "a Man who is said to be a Romish Priest." At the end of June, the constables arrested John Ury, a white teacher who knew Latin and allegedly used his school as a cover for "a private Conventicle." Mary Burton immediately added to her deposition that this man, "shewn to her in Prison," was someone whom she often saw at Hughson's tavern and who frequently remarked that "he could forgive . . . a great deal [of] Sins." When Adam, mentioned earlier, was arrested at about this time, he was shown the same man (Ury) and wisely gave a confession that echoed the charge that Ury "was one of the Two Priests who could forgive Sins."[77]

Thus, within two weeks, white people's expectation of a priest's leadership was matched by the testimony of informants who identified the culprit. One informant said that he "swore the Negroes of the Plot." Another described the plotters' incendiary devices—"balls, which we were to set fire to and throw . . . , which sticking fast would set fire"—as fireballs for which Jesuit plotters were dreaded. Ury was found guilty and hanged. In the ensuing month, the constable arrested several white men, "most of them (it is thought) Irish Papists," the governor reported. By stoking English Protestants' fear of Catholics, enslaved informants shifted some of the burden of the terrorizing experience of this investigation to white people who lived at the margins of New York society. When an informant's story conformed to conventional understandings of slave insurrections, it spoke to jurists' imperative to evaluate it in terms of commonsense probability.[78]

Learning Curves

Suspects faced an agonizing choice when considering whether to become informants. They could save their own lives and redirect the investigation away from loved ones, but they did so at the staggering cost of creating misery many times over. We gain a rare view of a range of informants' evolving approaches in Antigua's scare of 1736 because investigating judges recorded the trials as a series of dated entries. The trial transcripts contained each witness's evidence as they appeared in turn against the convicted conspirator. Some cynically manipulated the proceedings, while others attempted in good faith to recall events that seemed in retrospect potentially conspiratorial. Many coped in inconsistent ways, some days sealing the fate of another suspect, but other days restraining their testimony, whether out of fear of being falsified or out of moral disgust. At some point, almost every informant invented evidence or recast events that they had not found relevant at first. The descent into dissimulation was a path by which a powerless victim discovered some degree of control over his or her situation.

Jemmy, enslaved by Thomas Hanson, was the sincerest and least vindictive of the witnesses. He entered the investigation's orbit when his sister Philida was arrested for making "virulent Expressions" about their brother Tomboy, who had been broken on the wheel as a ringleader. Philida unwittingly expanded the investigation when she mentioned that Tomboy had gone to social gatherings at the cabin of a man named Treblin on a plantation outside of town. The judges took these visits to be conspiracy meetings. When Jemmy confirmed his sister's information about their infamous brother's social activities, he entered service as an informant for the judges. But Jemmy did not invent evidence, as best we can tell, and he did not even become convinced that he had seen any behavior that could appear conspiratorial in the new light of this line of questioning. Instead, he testified in a patent attempt to maintain his own innocence while shedding light on what transpired. Perhaps he set this bearing so as not to follow the fate of his brother, who confessed—only to be tortured to death on the rack.

The result is a collection of evidence regarding social relationships that is probably the most accurate portrayal of what was actually going on, but which the judges could use only as circumstantial evidence. Jemmy divulged all he knew about the suspects: that one was "very great with" Tomboy and "used to keep Cocks for him"; that another was at a specific gathering "Dancing a Dance called the Cutts"; that a third was at another gathering "Standing & leaning Over the Table"; and that someone else often had drinks at Tomboy's house. Nearly everyone he informed on had been a friend of his brother, circumstantial evidence that mattered only because Tomboy was branded a ringleader. When the judges pressed Jemmy to recall something about plotting and oath-taking, he unhelpfully explained that he "went Out to Dance" and "heard Nothing of the Plot while [he] was there." Jemmy's refusal to describe plotting displeased the judges, who stopped asking him for testimony. Other witnesses were not as scrupulous when poised precariously on the sliding scale of punishment and reward.[79]

At the other end of the spectrum, Quamina prosecuted a rivalry by capitalizing on the trust the court placed in him and his enslaver, the powerful council member Josiah Martin. He ingeniously generated his evidence from a single tale that was difficult to falsify. He maintained that John Sabby, a mulatto carpenter at the plantation of John Pare, had hosted private conspiracy meetings "three Sunday's Run[n]ing" in the weeks before the scare ignited. No other witnesses mentioned these meetings at Sabby's. As later came to light, the people enslaved at Martin's and Pare's labor camps had been feuding for months before the scare. The "great Quarrel" began when a person enslaved at Pare's plantation was "Ill treated" by someone from Martin's. The two groups refused to interact with each other for the next five months. Surely Quamina knew that he was indicting a man from a plantation with which his home quarter was at odds.

Quamina continued to use the story of private meetings at Sabby's to bring the conviction of five more men from the Pare plantation and several others from neighboring estates. He produced daily convictions with his story that Sabby invited conspirators to his house each Sunday to renew their oath and commitment to the conspiracy. On December 8, he provided the only eyewitness evidence against four creole men from plantations near Pare's: a gang driver and his brother (banished), a neighboring carpenter (burned), and a cooper (banished). On December 9, Quamina gave the only evidence against an old man on Pare's plantation who he claimed pledged "with all his heart" and tried with Sabby to poison Pare. He was sentenced to banishment. On December 10, Quamina provided the decisive evidence to condemn three more of Pare's people: an ironworker (burned), a Coromantee field hand (banished), and John Sabby himself (banished). On December 11, he again gave the only positive evidence against the creole carpenter of a plantation neighboring Pare's. Thereafter he issued only sporadic evidence, but he used the familiar oath-at-Sabby's scenario one more time against Billy Sabby (John Sabby's brother, a pipelayer) and Cudjoe, an expert in boiling sugar, to send them into banishment.[80]

Informants could learn as they went. Another Jemmy, who like Quamina was also enslaved by Martin, overcame his initial reluctance in early trials and became an indispensable witness in the investigation. At first he approached the questioning with forthrightness and claims of innocence reminiscent of Hanson's Jemmy. Under mounting pressure and physical coercion, however, he provided testimony that led to twenty convictions. It all began when Martin's Jemmy and his brother Tony were arrested on the second day of the conspiracy scare. They adamantly maintained their innocence even as they awaited the assembly of iron cages where they were sentenced to die.[81] After Jemmy was "hung up in Gibbets for 12 hours," he made "a full discovery" and agreed to become king's evidence in exchange for a pardon. Tony did not strike such a deal, and Jemmy gave evidence against him. When the executioner broke Tony's limbs on the wheel, the tormented man finally uttered dying incriminations that were written down and later used to condemn other men at trial. Both brothers stridently tried not to aid the investigation's expansion, but each faced torments that made them say things they never thought possible.[82]

Even when his depleted body was taken down from the cage, Jemmy was not yet a star witness. He only gradually took up his next role, trial witness, which required him to personally face each suspect and speak the words that brought their condemnation. His earliest recorded performance at trial was hesitant and self-doubting. Incrementally, however, he became fully entangled in maintaining a web of stories about the alleged conspiracy.

At his first trial, Jemmy observed the example of two other witnesses (one of them, by chance, with a vendetta against the suspect) before he haltingly offered that he, too, "Seems Confident that he saw [the suspect]" at the supper in question. At another trial two days later, Jemmy again hesitated. He began by naively wracking his memory for useful evidence. Several months earlier, he recalled, the suspect excused himself from a large supper to speak with the now-dead ringleaders, which in hindsight Jemmy "Supposed to be about the Plot." Come to think of it, Jemmy continued, that day someone drank a toast to "King" Court. The judges pressed him further and "Asked if Robin [the suspect] had Ever told him any thing of the Plot." Jemmy bowed to the mounting pressure of the judges' insistence, the courtroom's warped power relations, his memory of twelve hours in gibbets, and sorrow and anger about his brother's recent death. "Yes," Jemmy replied, "[Robin] Asked me if I knew any thing of the Affair[.] I told him, Yes," and Robin said he knew about it too. The judges demanded a clear answer, and Jemmy finally "insist[ed] upon it that Robin Knew the Plot perfectly well and Robin himself told him so." Robin was found guilty and sentenced to banishment.[83]

Jemmy was now initiated into the dark art of giving false or embellished evidence. He provided positive evidence against eight more suspects in the next two weeks.[84] But his learning curve was steepened by the resistance of the people he testified against. They adamantly denied his charges. This presented a serious danger to Jemmy as a convicted person whose fate the judges would determine based on his ability to garner convictions in which they could have confidence. Jemmy must have recognized the threat to his life because he changed his tactics. By his sixth trial (at the end of his first week) Jemmy was constructing his evidence more carefully. First, he shifted the site of oath-taking to a different, smaller plantation gathering to avoid further challenges to the details of individuals' attendance. Second, to enhance the setting's credibility, he populated the scene with five recently executed principal conspirators who would be unable to contradict his version of events. Despite his precautions, however, Jemmy was challenged again, this time by a judge who observed, for reasons unrecorded, that "if Morgan's Ned [who had expired in the gibbets the day before] was here he would tell Jemmy he told a great Lye."[85]

Jemmy dispatched with the judge's objection in a flash of brilliance. "Morgan's Ned one Day in [Gaol]," he retorted, "preached to his Fellow Prisoners & Endeavour'd to Influence them by, Fasting, reading, Preaching, praying, giving the Sacrament & Absolution to them, not to Disclose the Plot." Whether or not it really happened, Jemmy reached for the unfailing stereotype that placed a Catholic priest at the heart of every plot. In formulating this charge, he began with a story that several parties agreed was basically true according to the jailer—that Ned, after his conviction, "Spirited up the other Criminals . . . not to Confess"—but Jemmy innovated the Catholic gloss on his own.[86] When Jemmy accused Ned of being a Catholic priest, he wielded the ultimate signifier of clandestine deviousness in British America. Others sought advantage at their trials by accusing each other of minor offences such as stealing; Jemmy was a star witness in part because he understood the power of calling someone a Catholic.

Jemmy became masterful at inventing unfalsifiable social settings in which suspects took oaths and made promises of arms or recruits. Now he regularly placed suspects at meetings whose other participants had been convicted and killed by the judges already. At one particular gathering, he supposedly witnessed a cabal going into a private room: four of those six plotters were now deceased, one was a witness whose testimony was already under scrutiny ("an unwilling evidence against him"), and the last was the suspect himself. In a different trial on the same day, Jemmy asserted that another suspect hosted a gathering at his own house for a startling concentration of conspirators—Court, Tomboy, Hercules, Quashee, Ned, Jack—but each of these men had been executed weeks before the trial. They could not contradict the story. Dead conspirators and small private cabals helped Jemmy give unchallenged evidence that was useful for the judges.[87]

Jemmy's performances became most creatively unhinged in the trial against a man named Ned Chester. After evading some initial queries about specific gatherings, Jemmy's testimony that day drew on some of the well-established stereotypes of slave conspiracy. He confirmed the judges' view that "Men & boys" were the conspirators, instead of women; he verified that "Attacking the Town" was the plan's central feature; and he corroborated that there was an officer list. Jemmy hit his stride and imaginatively furnished many of the plot's other distinctive elements. When he volunteered this overabundance of fantastic information, he completed his transformation from a reluctant purveyor of circumstantial evidence into a coauthor of the emerging conspiracy narrative.[88]

Judges may have compelled these men to serve as trial witnesses, but they could not control their idiosyncratic approaches to participating in this judicial violence. Some, like Quamina, embraced judicial roles wholeheartedly and performed adroitly. Others, like Jemmy (Martin), were drawn into their roles incrementally and learned from other witnesses how to enhance their performance. Many accused conspirators went unrecorded because they maintained the uncynical forthrightness of Jemmy (Hanson), who offered whatever social details about suspects he could recall but attested that he saw nothing amiss. Enslaved witnesses whom judges imperiled took action for self-preservation. Their techniques evolved along individual trajectories, but by their collective participation they braided together the legal justification for convicting many innocent men, spreading terror deeper into the slave quarter.

Outcries

In January 1737, members of the Antigua assembly became concerned that too many convicted conspirators were being executed. They asked the council for the ability to review the evidence before any further guilty conspirator was killed or any new suspect apprehended. "The Voice of the People," they said, implored them "to Cease all further Effusions of Blood." The assembly understood that convicted conspirators were "the Property's of the People"; enslavers experienced a personal financial burden when they were incompletely compensated for the loss of the people they legally owned. The assembly further recognized that their open-ended commitment to pay back enslavers threatened to create "a greater Burden of Debt than was absolutely necessary for Our Preservation" and years of taxes to pay it down. Their fear of possible insurrection, now displaced onto terrorized black people, diminished in comparison to their unease with fiscal irresponsibility. They were right to worry: one year later the governor proposed raising £20,000 through taxes, and the island remained in debt at 10 percent interest for more than a decade, all because of "the great expense [of] the negro plot."[89]

On the colony's governing council, Charles Dunbar took up the assembly's cause against his colleagues. He argued that further executions would not be "Prudent[,] Political, or Expedient" given this popular outcry. If terrorizing the subject population were the point, he observed, they had already "made Examples of" sixty-nine people by killing them "on the Wheel[,] the Jibbet[,] and at the Stake." He relayed to his colleagues the message from out-of-doors that "many People are Convinced" that many of the enslaved people who assented to the conspiracy were "Drawn in by the Art and Subtilty of the Crafty" leaders. After all, enslaved Africans seemed naturally to be followers rather than agents. He postulated that many probably took the oath "from Fears and Threats, and Others from Promises and hope of Reward," which were all tools of coercion that he and the investigators knew well, in yet another example of enslavers projection their own modes of power onto the inverted world of slave conspirators that they imagined. Only the several dozen core conspirators, he concluded, deserved death or even sale out of the colony.[90]

Valentine Morris, one of the trial judges and a senior member of the council, dismissed this "Murmering of Some without Doors, or within," as an illegitimate representation of "the Voice of the People." In any case, he countered, white people's very lives would soon again be threatened if alleged conspirators returned to the general enslaved population. Perhaps he was thinking that the small number of executions in Antigua's prior conspiracy scare of 1729, which he had overseen as a council member, failed to prevent the larger one he now faced. At that time, the council put a small number of men to death as a "proof of vigilance" to white settlers and an "intimidat[ion] . . . for the future" to enslaved black inhabitants, but declined to expand the investigation "upon account of the great Expence it would bring on the Country." Now, in 1736, he implored his colleagues to think of "Our Wives and our Infants" whose lives they now risked, he claimed, "for fear of Injuring our Fortunes." John Vernon, another council member and investigating judge, also doubted the wisdom of taking direction from "those without Doors" on the question of whether "there is . . . Safety for us at a Cheaper Rate." The governor agreed that the danger continued to outweigh the price. They denied the assembly's request to end executions.[91]

The assembly began to cast doubt on the validity of the guilty verdicts because of "the Suspicion we have of the Evidences Combining together" to achieve convictions. The council's members found this accusation to be disingenuous, "Artfully Raised" and "Industriously Spread," and they took umbrage that "Some Ill Designing Men" would throw this "Dust in Peoples Eyes" and make so many people "Uneasy." The panel of judges defended their proceedings with a statement arguing incorrectly that the informants had no reason to lie once they were promised the possibility of reprieve. The council ultimately decided to proceed with executions and, perhaps because they knew better, refused to show the underlying trial evidence to the assembly. They assented only to limiting the number of new arrests.[92]

Convictions slowed in February 1737 as the council came to recognize the diminishing returns of their increasingly costly investigation, as the assembly had urged earlier. They recognized the extraordinary terror spreading among enslaved people and suggested pausing the proceedings to "quiet their minds." In response, investigators grumbled that they had just garnered 150 fresh names.[93] The council began stepping down the extra guards and patrols that drained the assembly's coffers. The last of the executions occurred in March, bringing the conspiracy's human toll to eighty-eight souls. In April, the assembly addressed the continuing expense of holding the forty-four convicted conspirators who were sentenced to banishment. The assembly pushed for a speedy contract with merchant Arthur Wilkinson to transport the convicts to the Spanish Main, Hispaniola, Saint-Domingue, or Lisbon. He took half the proceeds and the colony's treasurer received the other half. A year later, in March 1738, the nine enslaved witnesses who received pardons but not freedom were finally released to their owners to be sold, as a "favour," to the British mainland colonies—leading to Billy's arrival in New York and his fateful jailhouse encounter with Pedro.[94]

*   *   *

The end of New York's conspiracy scare came, as it often did elsewhere in colonial America, when the town's white population grew concerned about their personal property losses. Josiah Cotton, a judge in the New England town of Plymouth, recognized that judicial violence could generate false confessions when he read about the burning of Bill and how he "impeached several others [at the stake] & amongst them some whites." He followed the conspiracy scare in the Boston news sheets and by hobnobbing with Cadwallader Colden and Chief Justice Peter De Lancey at the adjudication of an intercolonial boundary dispute. He wrote anonymously to Colden to warn him that the conspiracy investigation "puts me in mind of our New England Witchcraft in the year 1692." (Cotton was twelve at the time and convinced of its reality, although in adulthood he grew to mistrust its verdicts. Later in life he returned to the subject in his reading and thinking to understand what happened.) He cautioned that "Negro & Spectre evidence will turn out alike" because many of these confessions were extracted through "foul means, by force or torment, by Surprise, by flattery, by Distraction, by Discontent with their circumstances, through envy that they may bring others into the same condemnation, or in hopes of a longer time to live, or to dy an easier death." This is what happened, he suggested, in the "tremendous & unreasonable Tragedy at Antego [Antigua]" that first occasioned Bill's traumatic education in navigating conspiracy scares and his sale to New York.[95]

A popular outcry rooted in fear had helped to spur the investigation, and now popular pressure related to business concerns pulled back the reigns when it threatened to outpace enslavers' livelihoods. Indeed, Cotton warned New Yorkers in his letter "not to . . . destroy your own Estates" through a conspiracy scare "by making Bonfires of the Negros." Daniel Horsmanden complained that the town's white residents turned against him as soon as his inquiry touched "their own houses" and threatened to "affect their own propertys in Negroes."[96] This highlighted a fundamental tension in slavery between enslavers' individual wealth resting on owning enslaved people as private property and, on the other hand, enslavers' vulnerability to possible rebellion by each other's enslaved people. White people dealt with this tension differently depending on their experience of fear. The conspiracy scare began by initially privileging the possibility of insurrection and then, through identifying alleged culprits and supposedly cowing others through exemplary punishments, it generated a reprieve from fear and a return to valuing one's considerable investment in chattel. The human toll was staggering. White authorities killed thirty-four people and sold as many as ninety away from New York. The shipping registers point to direct sales to Madeira, Lisbon, and Newfoundland, as well as to indirect sales to Dutch Surinam, French Saint-Domingue, and Spanish Hispaniola by way of the Dutch Caribbean. According to one of the slave traders, Elias Rice, some captives discussed the events that brought them to this point, especially the tavern gatherings. Others tried to unsettle Rice by mentioning that the ship's cook was using "yellow Stuff in Shells" that resembled "Poison" of the "same Sort they saw in Guiney [West Africa]." Still in captivity, they knew that fear remained one of their few instruments, but they were quickly losing leverage as they sailed to St. Eustatius.[97]

Final Condemnation

Even though mid-eighteenth-century Antigua and New York differed in their legal systems, not to mention their economies and demographic profiles, they shared fundamental approaches to investigating the possibility of planned rebellion. In part these similarities were rooted in longstanding English juridical culture as applied to colonial spaces that were racialized and socially volatile. The specific intercolonial informational networks that matured in the first half of the eighteenth century also mattered. One colony's approach directly informed the other's: trade and migration conveyed models by which enslavers recognized and assessed similar threats and by which enslaved individuals in peril, such as Bill and Pedro, attempted to save themselves.

Judicial authorities in Antigua, New York, and elsewhere tended to uncover the threats in the course of investigating lesser crimes, and they escalated the "discovery" through torture and coercion, especially in times of heightened geopolitical insecurity. Desperate people—including enslaved suspects in the jail, as well as judicial authorities who were in the dark about the matter—used any leverage that this system of power and ideas provided. Colonial governors and investigating authorities chose to induce confessions by applying their tools of military policing, especially torture and physical confinement, with the state's authority to kill unprotected people or to set them free. Enslaved individuals attempted to deflect danger from themselves and their loved ones by repurposing several instruments inadvertently provided by the regime: exclusive knowledge of enslaved communities, familiarity with white fears, inadequate jails, enslavers' desire to protect property investments, and experiences in servitude that prepared them for the performative aspect of appearing in court.

Close confinement in jail, specifically, created an environment that perpetuated conspiracy investigations and crystallized faulty knowledge. Colonial officials incompletely understood the social nature of the crime of conspiracy, and especially that aspect of the crime's investigation. In every-day life, to be sure, magistrates who anticipated attempted insurrections fretted endlessly about communication among slaves from far-flung planta-tions: they worried about unregulated visiting, group gatherings at funerals, and communication through drums and horns. And yet during conspiracy scares, ironically, the same magistrates who tried to prevent slaves from communicating also brought them together from disparate plantations and households into confinement as jailed suspects. Whether or not these sus-pects had preexisting social connections, upon imprisonment they came to know each other through their common involvement with the investiga-tion. Collective incarceration allowed suspects—encouraged them, even —to discuss what was happening to them and whatever they knew about the purported crime that had brought them together. Conversations that necessarily centered on their predicament also tended to sound to the judges like evidence of the conspiracy's authenticity.

Terrorized enslaved men accused others, causing a cascade of arrests, and hewed their stories to precisely the scenarios that authorities most dreaded. Judges and juries assessed the veracity of these informants both in categorical terms of social status (including race, gender, and religion) and in terms under greater control of individuals and their support networks: individual reputation, personal demeanor, and consistent statements. Although each enslaved man who appeared before the court was up against overwhelming power, many grasped at opportunities to channel that power into protecting themselves by summoning their enslavers and other white patrons as character references, giving performances that catered to what they believed a white audience valued, and informing in ways that both verified old findings and shed new light for investigators without exposing oneself to falsification. These individuals—enslaved and free, black and white, suspect and investigator—and their all-too-human impulses took advantage of aspects of the system of power and ideas that enveloped them and, as a result, fanned the flames of conspiracy scares. The judges believed that the resulting "discoveries" confirmed their hunches, but they failed to comprehend that by incarcerating the powerless they did not face down their fears so much as they enacted a fantasy of mastery.

The pressures and processes of investigation, incarceration, and torture would not have produced the same abundance of knowledge for crimes other than conspiracy. Conspiracy, a crime of speech and intended vio-lence, relied heavily upon social interconnection and hushed conversations;

it was a crime predicated on community. When investigators demanded that suspects implicate their acquaintances, they pulled at threads and caused a social unraveling that began in the courthouse and affected many of the town's households and most of the island's plantation communities. With cascading accusations and arrests, trusting one's neighbor in a slave quarter could be as dangerous as relying on anyone encountered in prison. Conspiracy investigations severely undermined nascent African American communities that already struggled to cohere within the confines of slavery.

CHAPTER 4

The Risk of Relations

Community-Seeking and the Politics of Association

A secret plan for organized rebellion depended on community. Conspiracy scares involved two communities of enslaved people, one real, one idealized. The imaginary slave community was one of mythical unity. It was conjured by colonial officials who racialized people of African descent and who dreaded their collective strength, especially when they considered the tableau of rebellions and conspiracy scares since the seventeenth century. Officials in the eighteenth century projected onto the diverse people of the African diaspora a solidarity that never existed, and that is tempting to believe even today, supposedly rooted in "the Affection that naturally arises from a Fellowship in Slavery." During conspiracy investigations, if they forced informants to identify fresh suspects, they believed that they convinced them to break a deep trust. They congratulated themselves for overcoming the "extraordinary . . . fidelity of Slaves to each other," including their "best Friends and Relations," but they summoned these visions of a unified community only by compelling informants, through violence and fear, to speak certain words.[1]

The real community—or variety of communities—among enslaved people was both more fragmented and more meaningful than enslavers' flattened projection of it. As many scholars have shown, enslaved people strove to form associations out of more than just human impulses: they sought ethical bonds of mutual responsibility as strategic responses to enslavers' attempts to control people by isolating them. This community-seeking began on transatlantic slaving voyages and continued in the Americas with family formation, religious practices, property claims, inheritance, and mourning the dead.[2] Individuals overcame the vulnerability of being alone by finding allies who, if selected with care, could provide each other protection, share in strengths, and help each other stretch material resources and productively combine them. When physical flight to absolute freedom was unattainable, many people sought autonomy by "fleeing" from domination through self-organization while stationary in the quarter. Some of the day-to-day activities that we have called resistance did more than simply destroy symbols and sites of enslavement: when enslaved people broke tools, burned processing equipment, or absented themselves for the night or for the week, they "stole" back their own bodies to apply some of their mental, physical, and emotional labor to their own projects and relationships.[3]

While enslaved communities were valuable to their members, particularly around core relationships, they faced external pressure that exacerbated some of their fractures. Enslavers attempted to weaken social bridges by compelling enslaved people to deplete their bodies, confining them to certain spaces, and impeding their movements with militarized surveillance. All of this interrupted the institutionalization of social infrastructures, making it difficult for enslaved communities to productively resolve disputes over food, family, or property. Enslavers applied additional pressure by forcing people into competition for resources that they deliberately made scarce. This forced some enslaved people to victimize the most vulnerable among them, and it tested the alliances that they were striving to create and maintain. Just as insidiously, enslavers used their legal and economic power to offer "Generous Rewards . . . given to those who Discover their Practices" to tempt desperate individuals to inform on the unauthorized activities of others. Even though the vast majority of enslaved people did not accept the offer, the possibility that even a single spy lurked within a community was enough to challenge bonds among slaves and, as enslavers put it, "Render them Distrustfull of Each other."[4]

Nevertheless, enslaved people sought community. In doing the seeking, they became vulnerable to impeachment during conspiracy scares. Magistrates zeroed in on communication among enslaved people, and informers revealed meetings of people from several quarters, but these were not insurrectionary planning sessions. They articulated social networks of leaders and followers, sometimes fastened with loyalty, but this was not a guerrilla army. In reality, informants were giving hybrid information: cynically or not, they asserted that they saw "conspiratorial" activity based on a largely accurate but distorted depiction of life in the slave quarter. They usually accused mere acquaintances and rivals at the edges of core communities as a strategy to protect loved ones while satisfying the judges' desire for fresh accusations. This chapter mines the voluminous trial records of the conspiracy scares in the island of Antigua (1736) and New York City (1741) to demonstrate how real social activity and political practices in slave quarters were a basis for conspiracy evidence that investigators compelled from informants, and how the terror of the investigation in turn threatened this fragile associational politics.

Hidden community-seeking, beyond the familiar categories of marriage, ethnicity, and religion, is tucked between the lines of informants' confessions in the twinned cases of Antigua and New York. Enslaved women facilitated interplantation and interhousehold gatherings that fostered their husbands' and their own associations beyond core family and confidants. With some of these connections, enslaved men assembled patron-client networks similar to those in Africa that displaced people formed for self-preservation near inland slaving frontiers. The gatherings also fostered neighborhood identities outside of colonists' notice, such as the "Popeshead People," that emerged and then disappeared, unrecorded, with a fluidity similar to how ethnogenesis worked in West Africa. However, the cases of Antigua and New York also show that these gatherings exposed the men who were most geographically mobile and socially prominent to greater danger during conspiracy scares. The very people who were social connectors across plantation and household lines were the acquaintances whom informants usually found least anguishing to accuse of conspiring. Consequently, conspiracy scares periodically shattered fragile social and political networks; enslavers' counterinsurgency was more successful than they realized for reasons that they never fully appreciated.

Community-Seeking in the Constraints of Slavery

Enslavers tried to use social isolation to control enslaved Africans by bringing them across an ocean and enforcing a bevy of legal erasures. Furthermore, enslaved populations faced overwhelming social instability through frequent arrivals of large groups of strangers and continual departures through sale or death. But enslaved people did not allow their isolation to last. They struggled against the "prospect of social death," as historian Vincent Brown has identified it, by cautiously grasping at ways to form new communities.[5] Forced migrants' new social identification included embracing some labels and commonalities foisted upon them by their enslavers: bonds between "shipmates" in the middle passage, links among people enslaved by a common owner, and growing attachment to new ethnicities that had never existed in Africa but were ascribed by transatlantic slave traders based on ports of departure.[6] Beyond these enslaver-initiated social institutions, enslaved people also attempted to forge informal networks of association that crossed plantation and household boundaries.

On Sundays and holidays, enslaved people throughout colonial America usually benefited from suspension of labor and chose to care for themselves physically and emotionally by tending gardens to ward off starvation, going to market to supplement their own production, and traveling to visit loved ones who were enslaved somewhere else. Beyond economic and family activities, however, some also attended social gatherings.[7] Associational networks brought people into acquaintanceship regardless of particular affiliations with an enslaver's holdings, an enslaved family, or an ascribed ethnicity. White colonists knew about some of this, noting that enslaved people formed relationships with those of neighboring estates, but enslavers also clung to the idea that their plantations should be separate political units over which they ruled, in addition to economic units. In these carceral landscapes, to do any of this without the permission of one's enslaver was a significant risk.[8] Enslaved people found gaps in their captors' attempts at surveillance and control, and they crossed property lines in agricultural expanses such as Antigua and illegally took to the streets of provincial seaports such as New York to form neighborhood communities.

In Antigua, in brief respites from labor, travelers took advantage of the dark of night to clandestinely visit people who lived at other plantations in that neighborhood of the island. As in other colonies, assemblymen worried about such movements and gatherings and enacted a law that required enslaved travelers to have a "ticket," or their enslavers' written permission. But in calmer periods, justices of the peace "sometimes winked at" these regulations.[9] Indeed slaveholders could hardly enforce such draconian rules. At one point a justice of the peace in Antigua tried to drive revelers away from a weekend gathering near the Parham plantation but, as an enslaved man explained in passing at trial, "great Numbers of them Stay'd Sculking about in the Negroe Houses and in the Bushes." A plantation manager in the area complained helplessly that "Negros will ramble in the Nights to different parts" to gatherings large and small. As a white resident saw in the bright moonlight at 2:00 a.m. one night, "Several Small Partyes of Negroe Men" passed by the crossroads near his house until the resulting gathering must have numbered "at least 50."[10]

Informants in conspiracy investigations described some of these gatherings in the course of accusing their acquaintances of using the occasions to plot rebellion. If these informants lied on the particulars, they did it while hewing closely to a credible scenario to avoid scrutiny. They described gatherings that were as large as "more than 200 Negroes" and drew people from "farr Off" who sometimes traversed the distance by horse.[11] At these feasts and suppers, husbands and wives attended together, but usually only husbands were accused of using the occasion for plotting.[12] Individuals congregated at "a great Entertainment" to eat and drink, dance, and throw dice (fig. 14). Some groups seem to have been remarkably diverse, such as the American-born creoles and African-born Coromantees who dined together and danced together. Others stuck to small groups that broke off from the party into friends' cabins, plantain walks, and the edges of the property. One informant described a group that consisted of Cuffey, a plantation driver, Prince, a skilled mason, and Jack, a Coromantee field hand. Plantation gatherings provided opportunities to make acquaintance, however slender, with people who did not share categorical ethnic or occupational identities. These could be social resources and they could be liabilities.[13]

Because enslavers imposed scarcities, these social networks also facilitated conflict over property and family. For example, an enslaved man named Joe earned the ire of people enslaved at a neighboring plantation for "Stealing their things out of the Tent." Similarly, a man called Primus complained that another man, Quamina, was trying to "steal" his wife, Margaret, which may have endangered her within the household as well as fostered conflict between the men. Enslavers abjured their responsibility for the violence among enslaved people. In an impromptu treatise on solidarity among slaves, investigators in Antigua admitted that enslaved people "some times kill one another it is true" but explained it incompletely as arising "When they are Drunk & at a Play [a gathering with a feast]." Even though enslaved people created bonds of community, they did not come into ideal harmony. The violence and deprivation of enslavement constantly cut against individuals' attempts to form alliances for survival.[14]

In many ways New York City's landscape differed markedly from that of an agricultural colony such as Antigua, but there, too, enslaved people made similar efforts toward associating in the face of regulations that were

Figure 14. Enslaved people gathered from several quarters on Saturday nights and Sundays for suppers that included dancing and gambling, even if the reality was not as placid as in this idealized image. Detail from Agostino Brunias, *Negroes Dance in the Island of Dominica*, 1779. Colored aquatint. Courtesy of the Lewis Walpole Library, Yale University.

aimed at keeping them divided. Although most of the town's slaveholding households (which constituted 40 percent of all households) contained only one to three slaves, those boundaries had little spatial bearing on the associational lives of the 1,546 enslaved individuals who lived and labored within the one-third-square-mile area that comprised the main city wards.[15] No one had to go far to meet each other. However, in the daylight, groups larger than three could meet only with enslavers' permission. On Sundays and after dark, when the enslaved had more practical autonomy, it was unlawful to meet in groups at all. Enslaved New Yorkers who thought gathering was worth the risk were more easily spotted in the more intensely surveilled streets of town than in the woods, swamps, and farmland of agricultural regions.

Enslaved New Yorkers attended organized gatherings at homes and taverns after dark and on weekends. Men and women from several quarters came together and drank and toasted, feasted, and boasted together in ways that ignorant, overzealous outsiders might think resembled conspiracy. The danger of being "stopped by the watch" did not deter one man, Caesar, from trying to attend an "entertainment" in the winter of 1740, for which he was caught.[16] The lure was also great for Cato, particularly on a Sunday when he was relatively unburdened by labor, when a group near a stable told him to stop by a house "after church [got] out in the evening" because there would "be company there." Women attended as well as men. When hosts lacked the tacit permission of their enslavers, revelers went to taverns that skirted the law to serve this paying clientele, providing a venue for large gatherings. On a Monday evening at sundown, for example, people went to Hughson's tavern to "merry make," according to an informant, rather than to "talk about Fires" or insurrection. They drank and danced to tunes that one of them fiddled until about seven o'clock.[17]

In both New York and Antigua, people from town and country visited one another on Saturday nights and Sundays because they had more time and were under less scrutiny by enslavers. Towns were of outsized economic and political importance even in agricultural colonies of the Caribbean. In St. John's Town, Antigua, country people visited on Sundays and passed time with town dwellers, gambling and drinking in the streets, at market, and in dram shops. Near the small city of New York, the farms of the surrounding countryside also employed enslaved people and contributed to the social world of town dwellers.[18]

With frequent separation through sale and wide circles of sociability, family connections grew across household and plantation lines. This in turn inspired even more frequent clandestine neighborhood travel. In Antigua, one man with a spouse enslaved at a different labor camp could be found visiting her "Almost Every Day."[19] Another person identified his "home" as the plantation where his wife resided, rather than that of his own enslaver, because of "having a Wife there." As with some households in West Africa, a few enslaved men had multiple wives in Antigua. A man named Mingo was enslaved at Monk's plantation, but it was said that he spent one part of his time at Booth's plantation, "where [he] ha[d] a Wife," and another part of his time at Ash's, where both he and his brother "had Wives." That he had multiple wives was a customary sign of status, and that he also "treated . . . a Great many Town People" at his second wife's house was another signal of this man's and these women's esteem and relative means.[20]

In New York, composite households for enslaved couples were even more common in a town of dispersed slave ownership and close settlement. Most had to contend with the town watch if they braved the streets to see one another, but some were permitted by their enslavers to sleep at a spouse's residence. None of this should imply a rosy tableau of matrimonial harmony, as the pressures of enslavement could make an enslaved household simultaneously a place of relative racial autonomy and also a site of exploitation and violence by enslaved men. These composite households structured some of the social activity that investigators asked informants to describe when determining how enslaved people managed to conspire under their noses.[21]

Clandestine visiting worried magistrates because they recognized that their power rested on fostering divisions among the enslaved people who outnumbered them in Antigua and in many similar agricultural landscapes. Investigators in Antigua's 1736 conspiracy scare concluded that "Entertainments of Dancing[,] Gaming[,] and feasting," as well as solemn occasions such as "Commemorating some Deceased friend, . . . or Christining a House, or the like According to Negro Customs," all facilitated the white colonists' recent brush with disaster because these occasions provided "some Innocent pretence" for slaves to gather to plan a rebellion.[22] This theory animated the analysis of James Knight, chronicler of Jamaica in the 1740s, when he reached the bizarre conclusion that Jamaica was relatively protected from insurrection, somehow forgetting the Maroon crisis of the 1710s through 1730s. He wrote that smaller, flatter sugar islands such as Antigua were susceptible to insurrection because the ease of interplantation communication facilitated "general Conspiracies" with "great probability of Success." In Jamaica, by contrast, Knight claimed that "the chief security" against general insurrection was the "great Extent of the Country" and the island's impeding topography, which isolated plantations from one another "so that the Negroes can have no communication together, or if they had it, [it] would be almost impossible [for them to] join to Execute their Designs." Other inhabitants of Jamaica were not as confident in their landscape because "Vast crouds" assembled at Sunday markets "from all parts of the Country."[23]

Conspiracy scares sometimes jolted authorities into more strongly enforcing the laws that required enslaved travelers to carry written permission in the form of a "ticket" or pass. After Antigua's conspiracy scare of

1729, and in anticipation of the departure of soldiers and the coming Christmas holidays, nearby Montserrat contemplated restricting slaves' interplantation visiting "and Caballing together" even on the usually unfettered Sundays and holidays. In Jamaica, a 1744 conspiracy scare moved the governor to proclaim renewed adherence to the ticket law and to berate the assembly for allowing enforcement to atrophy as enslaved people continued "to pass and ramble without Ticketts."[24] But enslavers had little true understanding of what was happening when people came together for their own purposes.

Women's Gatherings

At nights and on weekends, women hosted gatherings on behalf of their husbands, operating as political actors whose labor helped to facilitate associational networks. In Antigua, Quashee, a town-dweller, held a feast at his wife's cabin on a plantation in the country and invited several townspeople. On another Sunday, Tomboy, who lived in town, instructed his wife Luzetta on Bully's plantation to treat men to punch. Women also performed the work of personally delivering dinner invitations to guests: Ned Chester sent invitations to a man named Jemmy for a feast at French's plantation, one through his daughter and the other through a friend's wife. If female hosts performed a great deal of the labor behind social gatherings, they also enhanced their own status by developing their household's access to social resources.[25] This built on women's existing centrality to enslaved societies, particularly in locales heavily influenced by forced migration from the Akan- and Fon-speaking populations of Lower Guinea (associated with present-day Ghana, Togo, and Benin) whose political culture promoted women's leadership. Women derived further power from marketing in informal economies, by controlling provision grounds and access to markets, and in spiritual functions led, as in Antigua, by "the Negro women, in particular."[26]

In New York, too, informants sometimes described enslaved women's hosting and attendance at festivities. As in Antigua, women in New York hosted their husbands and the male associates. Barbara, who was enslaved at Fort George as the governor's cook, was joined "a-Nights" by her husband Quack. As men did in Antigua, Quack invited an acquaintance named Fortune to come with him to Barbara's so he could "give him some Punch."[27] When one of Quack's visits to the fort coincided with a fire that burned it down, he came under suspicion as a prime conspirator. At his execution at the stake, in order to save his own life, Quack confessed to being "voted . . . the Person who should fire the Fort" because of his familiarity with guards who regularly allowed him to slip through.[28] No one asked why his conspiracy failed to use Barbara's connection to the kitchen to poison the governor, but then again colonists had learned to expect fire rather than poison, and they assumed that men were capable of rebellion but not women.

Enslaved women tended to avoid suspicion, impeachment, and prosecution. In published narrative accounts of conspiracy scares and actual revolts, authors throughout the seventeenth and eighteenth centuries rarely described enslaved women as rebels. Conventionally, they identified suspected conspirators to be enslaved men in so-called privileged occupations: craftsmen, gang drivers, and personal attendants. When these authors included black women, they highlighted their supposed fidelity in warning enslavers about seditious conversations they overheard. Colonial officials highlighted the stories of Fortuna in Barbados in 1675, unidentified enslaved women in Jamaica in 1744 and 1760, and two women named Susana and Kate in South Carolina in 1749. When men would rebel, the stories went, women would reveal.

Women avoided suspicion partly because informants tended not to mention their names. Trial witnesses, almost always men, mentioned hundreds of people in the available sample of confessions from Antigua and New York. Less than 10 percent of the time they mentioned women. In Antigua, informants named women only twenty-four times among the 269 names mentioned in the course of recorded testimony. In New York, informants accused women with similar infrequency: one study counted only eighteen women among the 214 people mentioned by informants in the course of questioning. They mentioned these women almost always in passing when they listed the people in attendance at social gatherings, rather than accusing them of direct involvement. One informant observed, for example, that an alleged conspirator held a gathering at a place where he "had a Wife." After she "made a Treat" and "provided a Feast" to his guests, he claimed that they took the opportunity to "tal[k] of the Plot." Investigators, apparently not recognizing this as material support for the conspiracy, hardly ever followed up on such comments.[29]

Only rarely did informants accuse women of direct participation in a conspiracy. Even then, investigators declined to question enslaved women despite these clear depictions of female involvement.[30] A woman named Obbah, for example, hosted a feast in Antigua and "herself fetched Dirt from her Sisters Grave" to mix into the rum they drank when pledging membership to the conspiracy, but she did not come under scrutiny. Another, Coobah, was said to have stored a ten-gallon keg of powder at her cabin in Antigua. Investigators searched for it and failed to find it, but they did not leave any record of arresting her. In fact, in Antigua they convicted no women, and in New York they convicted only two black women. Investigators seriously underestimated women's potential political rebelliousness and self-organization, leaving almost all of them physically unscathed by conspiracy investigations.[31]

Political Associations

Enslaved people used these associative practices to try to build social structures to shelter themselves from the battering of enslavement. Africans in America found that physical and material security was unattainable in the profound deprivation of chattel slavery, but they sought temporary material and social advantage, however fleeting, in a way vaguely familiar from the old world. A small number of leaders in Antigua and New York assembled retinues of followers for the survival of the group at the expense of other enslaved people. Enslaved patrons built these political structures by leveraging their relative access to material goods and spiritual power to build cliental relationships with men enslaved in other parts of the town or island.

In West and West Central Africa at the time, where people were more scarce than land, political leaders solidified their positions through holding "wealth-in-people." Their ability to command other people and to access new recruits through those associates conferred status on them and gave them access to labor and military defense. Leaders in Africa built retinues through a combination of taking captives from outside groups, giving gifts to loyal insiders, and protecting the people in their charge. As the transatlantic slave trade incentivized warfare and destabilized African kingdoms, wealth-in-people became even more important to new leaders' claims to power and ability to provide security for their followers. From these historical circumstances, transatlantic captives brought familiarity with the usefulness of patron-client relationships in the absence of other levers of power.[32]

In the case of Antigua, three leaders recruited sizable followings. Court was forty-five years old, born in Africa, and now identifying in the diaspora as ethnically Coromantee. He was enslaved by a prominent planter and politician as a personal servant. Tomboy was born into enslavement in Antigua, trained as a carpenter, and known to have "a very Great Awe and Influence." They both lived in town. Secundi was an Antigua-born plantation driver at the other end of the island, about ten miles away. In 1736, these three leaders drew the attention of conspiracy investigators who prompted informants to identify ringleaders. They figured into several informants' stories because of their competition over "who should bring the most Men." Tomboy confronted a hoped-for associate: "I have Asked you two or three times but you wont Come into my Company." When the prospect admitted that he instead "Promised Court," Tomboy blustered that in the end he "would Get as Many hands as Court." We know about these efforts because investigators rewarded informants who, from within, surveilled attempts to overcome and restructure social isolation.[33] Investigators believed this competition was over recruitment into a conspiracy, but these three men were actually recruiting associates in pursuit of their own social status and the survival of their group, as a re-creation of African political structures in the face of social dislocation.

Within the constraints of enslavement, leaders attempted to build wealth-in-people with the help of women who hosted associates at social gatherings. Women whose husbands were considered social leaders "treated" the associates with drinks and held suppers for them to recruit clients and maintain support. In Antigua, Court and Tomboy invited associates to plantations in the country where they had close ties and to smaller venues in town. At these occasions, they compelled some clients to assist them in hosting the others. For example, Tomboy required one associate to "tend upon him" at a feast at his wife's plantation cabin, while he invited another, a new recruit, to stay late for an exclusive drink. In the course of the evening the new associate offered Tomboy access to the people of the plantation neighboring his and recruitment of "two good Brothers."[34]

Formal gift giving also fostered patron-client relationships. In Africa, the distribution of patterned cloth, war captives, cowry shell currency, and, increasingly, firearms strengthened these cliental relationships. In Antigua, one informant alleged that Court had "A Great Deal of money & if he Could not Get his Country Men [ethnic Coromantees] by any Other Means he would give them money."[35] Attractive gifts could temporarily overcome other social obstacles in recruitment, as when two men who had a "great hatred" for each other both joined the same social retinue. Billy and Robin, both enslaved by a Mrs. Langford in town, were together one day when Robin sported a new "very good Suit of Cloths." Billy asked about the status symbol and learned that Robin was now one of Court's men and that he attended him daily. Robin, whose social status and survival were now tied to Court's success, attempted to recruit Billy. "If [you] would take part with Court," Robin coaxed, "Court would make [you] a very great Man." Billy agreed to enter the relationship, sending a goat to Court for an upcoming feast as a token of his new allegiance, perhaps seeing the arrangement as an opportunity for equal access to the gifts and favors that his rival Robin was receiving. As in patronage structures in Africa and elsewhere, the social and material success of patron and client were bound together. A leader observed to one potential recruit, a cooper in town named Emanuel, that "if you was to see me do good, you would Do good."[36]

Well-connected clients used their other relationships as currency: in exchange for treats, gifts, and the intangible benefits of the retinue, they gave their patrons access to their own circles of social dependents. As in Africa, top leaders developed relationships with well-connected men who had entourages of their own in order to gain access to their people. In Antigua, gang drivers (or "head men") on plantations provided one avenue of social access to larger groups, including the field hands whose day-to-day work and punishment they influenced. One of Secundi's recruits, for example, was said to promise "all his Master's New Negroes." On the other hand, Tomboy became frustrated when he encountered a field hand on the road to the town market one Sunday morning and asked him how many people he could deliver into his company. "I am not a head Man," the associate explained, "Jean is Over us all."[37]

Leaders could use the tug of ethnic identification to foster tentative trust when recruiting clients. The enslaved used ethnic terms such as Coromantee, Igbo, and Yoruba not because of any meaningful political or ethnic affiliation in Africa but because of their experience in the diaspora. Slave traders ascribed these labels to them based on African ports of embarkation. Enslaved Africans in the diaspora came to accept these ethnic labels as one axis of identification because of broadly shared cultural reference points and linguistic families from Africa, as well as because of differential treatment by some enslavers.[38] These diasporic ethnicities had real meaning for some people: at a supper a woman "made signs of Contempt" when she saw "so many Coromantees there." Social leaders sometimes leveraged these affiliations for recruitment. Court, who embraced his identification as Coromantee, had a special claim to associational relationships with other Coromantees who originated from the broad region of the Gold Coast of Upper Guinea and who "talked Cormantee Language [Akan]." Court was said to have deliberately reached out to "his Country Men" and also to have used the popularity of one particular client, Quou, to "get him some men" who would cautiously trust him because of their shared ethnicity.[39]

Ethnic identification was more a tool than a rule when building retinues. Even though Court and Tomboy identified with different ethnicities, each man competed for the same followers. At a supper, one enslaved man asked another "whether he would Join with Court or Tomboy," even though one was Coromantee and the other creole.[40] The plantation driver Secundi was identified as creole, but he still brought several Coromantees into his orbit, who in turn promised to recruit more Coromantees on his behalf. For example, Yorke joined with Secundi on the basis of sharing a former enslaver. He then promised to try to recruit three of his Coromantee countrymen for Secundi, a creole. For his part, Caesar, a field hand, said he would "get him all the Cormantee's he Could" for his creole patron.[41]

Although Court did not use strict ethnic belonging to limit his retinue's membership, he did rely on the political culture of his home, Lower Guinea, to claim status in Antigua. He formalized his elevated social status with a ceremony that was commonly used on the Gold Coast, as a Dutch traveler reported, to confer noble status and political authority onto a wealthy individual. "King Court," as some called him, wore regal clothing at the event in front of a reported crowd of thousands, used a specially constructed canopy, and wielded a wooden shield (ikyem) as he was trained to do by an obeah practitioner in the previous month. He took a great risk by exposing his aspirations to hundreds of potential informers. One week later, colonial officials began their conspiracy investigation on the basis of a participant's joke about this event. Officials came to interpret these unfamiliar symbols and the large gathering as a declaration of war against the colony—an understanding that a leading historian of Africa has characterized as "surely mistaken."[42] In other words, the investigators missed the more prevalent and valuable associational politics by obsessing about insurrectionary politics.

In New York, too, some enslaved men experienced elevated status according to snapshots described by onlookers. A man named Jack, for

example, carried himself "like a Gentleman" and was described as "a leading Man." These claims, shakier under slavery than in other societies, were
contested, as when one night "an impudent Boy" neglected to show him
the respect he thought he deserved.[43] In another example, Ben, who was
"no doubt . . . esteemed . . . a deep Politician" prior to the conspiracy, once
said that he had to attend a feast of mutton, goose, and fowl because "all
our Company is come down." Daniel Horsmanden, the investigator,
announced that "therefore" at the time of the plot he was "fixt upon to be
an Officer, nothing less than a Captain, a Commander of an Hundred at
least."[44] Enslaved informants described at least five other men as an "officer" or "captain" in a rough translation of social status that meant "the
other Negroes durst not refuse to do what they commanded them."[45] Perhaps these men received their positions in connection with the Pinkster
(Whitsuntide) holiday in New York, similar to General Training Day and
Election Day in New England, at which large congregations of black people
chose community leaders for the coming year.[46] Although the investigating
judges fixated on evidence that matched their expectations that plotters
supposedly hoped to install a king and a governor, only one enslaved informant ever said that Caesar would be "King." Rather it was Mary Burton,
the Irish indentured servant who became the initial informant, who
claimed—and in fact insisted—that Caesar was going to be "Governor"
after the insurrection and that John Hughson, the tavern keeper who owned
her contract, would be king. Only a suspect named London, labeled a
"Spanish Indian," agreed in a confession that Hughson "was to be Governor." He added a string of other familiar tropes, including that Hughson
kept a list of sworn conspirators and that he directed them to set fires and
lay in wait "as the People run out" to stab them and "kill as many as they
could."[47] The misguided expectations of enslavers overtook the reality of
enslaved people's tentative self-organization.

Drinking, Complaining, Toasting, and Boasting

Alcohol flowed freely at social gatherings, and it facilitated both the formal
political work of patrons and clients and the enslaved acquaintances' cautious attempts to weave together broader networks of association in both
Antigua and New York. "Where are you going," one man cried out to
another in Antigua, "won[']t you Come and Drink?" Men who drank

together swapped complaints and made boasts. In Antigua, a man named Yorke observed to his drinking companions that "the White People used him Damn'd Rough." An older man, Minian, spoke out against the person who enslaved him for "us[ing] him very Ill and hat[ing] him." These complaints were dangerous not for their content so much as for the act of conversing at all with relative strangers. Riskier were direct complaints that, if kept secret, bonded people in proportion to the amount of trust they required. A labor gang driver named Caesar howled a curse—"the Devil Damn the White People, [for] they abused him very much"—and he shared his sorrow with Secundi that "his Master had sold his Father and his Mother." Still another enslaved man, Quawcoo, boasted that he had tried to poison the overseer because of his "Ill usage beating and Starving them," but said that someone else interfered with the attempt. "I am not so well Used now," he elaborated, "as I was in my Old Masters time."[48] When drink loosened the tongue, complaints about the shared plight of worsening conditions tumbled forth and bonded acquaintances in relatively unguarded moments. But every participant and eavesdropper was a potential part—voluntary or not—of enslavers' surveillance apparatus who, faced with a legal predicament, survived by converting others' trust to their personal advantage.

In New York City, as in Antigua, people were emboldened by alcohol to take the risk of reaching out to others. Town-dwellers often convened at taverns. Officially, serving liquor to slaves was outlawed, but in practice constables enforced the ban only infrequently. A neighbor noticed that large numbers of black New Yorkers regularly congregated at shoemaker John Romme's tavern, "drinking, singing and playing at dice," often "Till two or three o'clock in the morning," a charge to which Elizabeth Romme entirely admitted. Nor did anyone disagree that the lower room at Hughson's tavern was regularly packed with about two dozen men all day Sunday and on weeknights "to frolick and merry make." They got drunk together, supped together, sometimes threw dice, and often danced to the fiddle of Ben, Jamaica, or Cuffee.[49]

Enslaved people found more safety by gathering at a private building on an enslaver's property, away from public taverns, where constables did not know to look. London was "in the street" on the afternoon of the Pinkster holiday when he ran into some drinking companions who "asked him to go and drink beer at a house." Later that day he went to a tavern. On another occasion, a man walked past a building when a friend spotted him and "called him in" to drink with "about twenty negroes" and make new acquaintances. A woman at the same house described a group of twenty to thirty people sitting around and conversing while passing the time by sharpening their knives. When their friendly chatter turned to competitive boasting, some dared to say in front of the others that their knives were "sharp enough to cut a white man's head." One woman there took advantage of the acquaintances' trust by passing the conversation to authorities for her own legal survival.[50] After all, these gatherings were outlawed and disbanded not only as a show of force to exert social control but more specifically out of fear of what might be said there in planning crimes against enslavers, including insurrection.

Alcohol, more than a social lubricant, was a key ingredient in the act of taking oaths and "drinking healths," itself a political practice of autonomous self-determination. In the seventeenth and early eighteenth centuries in West Africa, a practice of drinking alcohol mixed with blood and dirt performed several political functions. People traditionally used these oaths judicially to determine whether someone was lying, but in the upheavals of escalating warfare they also used belief in alcohol's spiritual power to overcome diminished social and political cohesion. People used oaths to solemnize personal bonds, legal agreements, and political alliances. Refugees of defeated kingdoms formed polyglot communities and built a shaky trust by swearing oaths to one another. In Antigua and New York, forced migrants faced an extreme version of this political shattering and turned to the familiar resource. They drank a "wish or health" to one another, often pledging fidelity, as one way of trying to cohere diverse and fragile communities battered by enslavement. There was great versatility in drinking a "health" or an "oath" in diasporic African political culture. They identified criminals by swearing oaths with mixtures of rum, blood, and grave dirt, made more solemn with the invocation of ancestors. One missionary in Antigua noticed that enslaved people passed around drinks laced with grave dirt to resolve "every trivial loss" of property that went unexplained. As men of the Enlightenment, enslavers did not worry about the spiritual power of oaths and obeah so much as the practices' potential to bond, inspire, and give courage to rebels. Indeed, in matters of war and peace, leaders of Maroon polities in Jamaica formalized treaties (1739) and insurgents there launched Tacky's Rebellion (1760), all by drinking oaths with similar ingredients.[51]

When African informants depicted plots, they regularly accused suspects of pledging their support for the conspiracy by swearing an oath with an alcoholic drink. In Antigua they cited such commonplace instances of oath-taking that drinking to one another's health at suppers and social gatherings seems to have been a common way for acquaintances to cautiously attempt to forge bonds. The investigators noted that suspected conspirators frequently drank together and recited the oath *without* the solemnizing ingredients of blood or grave dirt. Drinking the so-called oath reportedly happened "Two, three or four times in a Day, According as they fell into Different Company's." If these toasts were truly a promise of rebellion, one would expect the conspiracy to have been discovered months, not days, in advance. Jemmy, an informant who gave markedly straightforward answers and honest recollections, described regular drinking and toasting but never a conspiratorial oath. "I saw him Drink Tackey's health to Tomboy," he recalled, "and Round to Hercules, & Griggs Dick too in Turn, . . . & heard Nothing of the Plot while I was there." Another suspect conceded that "We Drank healths . . . but without thinking any harm."[52] Investigators listened to reports that groups drank to two leaders' honor, and they reinterpreted this associational politics as an effort to recruit friends into the politics of rebellion.[53]

Informants in desperate legal straits who eyed judges' promise of reprieve had incentive to encourage this misunderstanding.[54] They included oath-taking in their confessions partly because the solemn drinking of alcohol was a broadly verifiable social activity in the African quarter that, as with clandestine social gatherings, they could plausibly construe as conspiratorial. When informants described the oath in Antigua, the most common form was a short damnation oath prevalent among people from the Gold Coast—"Here is confusion and Damnation to all those that will Confess, or be false, and that will not stand"—that they amended to include white colonists' fantasy of racial massacre with a purported promise to "help kill or Destroy the White People, Man, Woman, and Child."[55] Judges pasted all of this information into a single menacing collage for their final report:

> The Manner of Administring the Oath, was, by Drinking a health in Liquor, either Rum, or Some Other, with Grave Dirt, and Some-times Cocks Blood, infused; and Some times the Person Swearing, laid his hand on a live Cock. The Words were Various, but the General tenor was, to Stand by and to be true to Each other, and to Kill

the Whites, Man, Woman & Child to Assist in the Execution of this, when Called upon by the Chief, and to Suffer Death rather than Discover; with Damnation and Confusion to those who Should Refuse, or having Drank and Sworn should afterwards Discover. Sometimes too, the Person Swearing Chew'd Malageta Pepper.[56]

Of course, they were correct to worry about the practice in general because it helped enslaved people organize themselves under self-appointed leaders in ways that ultimately disrupted enslavers' power structures.

In New York, enslaved men who drank together sometimes toasted one another, as in Antigua, and forged tentative bonds by promising to support each other in ways that investigators took to be conspiratorial. These alleged conspiracy oaths had three features: communal drinking, the invocation of thunder, and the kissing of a book. Hughson's tavern provided the setting for communal drinking. One informant confessed that enslaved men had been swearing oaths to each other while drinking together for at least the past "three years." For example, one night the revelers took out "a Flask of Rum" and made "some Punch" with it, after which a few people "Drank Drams, and . . . agreed to what was propos'd."[57] This was a politics of association, not insurrection, as men drank to each other's health and promised mutual support. For example, one drank and "swore" with Quack "three times; [and] then they . . . drank out their punch." The substance of what they allegedly swore to one another did not necessarily point to a plan of insurrection as much as to mutual responsibility: they promised "to be true to one another," as difficult to accomplish as that ideal was under enslavement.[58] Wary of the tentative nature of their trust, they called on spiritual power to strengthen the brittle bonds of their in-group. If they betrayed each other, whether as steadfast friends or as criminal accomplices, but not necessarily as insurrectionists, they wished that "the first thunder might Strike them dead . . . [who] did not stand to theyr words."[59] Many informants included this West Africa–originated warning that a betrayer would be punished with "thunder and lightning," or more vaguely "something of thunder," while a few others claimed that anyone who broke the oath would be "damned forever."[60] Whereas the informants in these cases claimed that suspects agreed to a plan for insurrection, we know that diasporic West Africans used these procedures to solemnize an array of personal, legal, and political relationships.

English colonial officials recognized oath-taking as a political activity. They took it as strong evidence of a person's guilt in crimes of treason, including in a rebellion conspiracy. They did not accept that enslaved people had an array of other nonviolent political uses for oaths.[61] African informants played to their English audience by claiming that oath-takers kissed a book, in reference to the English legal culture that they observed in the courtroom itself. Informants claimed that people swore on "a great book" that looked "like a common prayer book" or "a Bible." Informants said that suspects "put their hands on a Book[,] Swore[,] and kissed it."[62] In another telling, alleged conspirators "Kissed the Book" and Hughson produced "a Flask of Rum" and made "some Punch" with which some participants "Drank Drams, and all . . . agreed." Informants said that these English and African styles of swearing coexisted: alleged conspirators who were at the "other end of the room did not swear on the book," one informant said, but did so "at a distance without [the] book . . . by thunder, etc."[63] These attempts at affiliation were a broader form of politics than colonial officials could see when focusing on a supposed insurrectionary plot.

The other underappreciated way that enslaved people sought community was in the creation of new neighborhood identities that had the valence of precolonial African forms of ethnicity. These efforts, too, were often misconstrued during conspiracy scares. In Antigua, an informant described a raucous gathering at which a man "Jumped Off from the Table & Cry'd among the Windward People[,] [']good Blood Windward People never fail[']"—Windward was a particular geographic region of the island—"& he . . . & all the Windward People Rejoyced." The next morning, a Sunday, people at the same gathering "Cry'd Windward and good Blood."[64] Enslaved men from different parts of the island celebrated separate neighborhood identities. At one supper a group "Drank a health to Dickensons Bay" in the northern division of the island. On another night, an alleged plotter who supposedly took the oath of conspiracy made specific reference to his home region, Popeshead Division, when he "added the Words *In Popeshead.*" Other enslaved people declared when drinking that "Parham fellows will never fail, they'll Stand till the last" and "that after they had taken the Oath they made three Huzzas, beating their hands upon the table."[65] In Antigua, Secundi, a key social leader, identified as a Windward person even after his owner transferred him to a different region of the island. An informant also explained that Secundi was known to "Value" and "lay his Life" on one particular Windward man "& others of the Windward People."[66] A consequence of their enthusiasm for these geographically defined groups was that they separated themselves from outsiders, thus pooling and protecting resources, making these bonds useful for surviving enslavement.

Antigua's neighborhood identities were different from the ethnicities that are more familiar to historians, such as Coromantee, Igbo, and Yoruba, which were created through the slave trade and based on broad regions of embarkation from Africa. Neighborhood identities, by contrast, emerged as an initiative of the enslaved rather than from labeling by enslavers, and they operated much more like precolonial African ethnicities, even though they referred to American rather than African geographies. In fact, a person could identify both with a neighborhood and with one of the ascribed ethnicities more familiar to us today: one man, for example, "Cry'd Out good blood Windward People" and then immediately identified as Igbo by adding "I am Ebo Blood & never Faile."[67] The territorial focus of neighborhood identities was in keeping with identification among Africans in the old and new worlds at this time. Scholarship on enslaved people in Jamaica has shown that they developed strong attachments to specific places because of the desire to maintain a connection with ancestors through burial sites, a practice rooted in Africa but understandably more urgent after forced migration.[68]

Blood imagery seemed to imply a sort of permanence. This particular impulse to deepen the shallow roots of a newly constructed "ethnicity" would have been familiar in West Africa at the time. Some eighteenth-century groups in West Africa were known to amend identity and membership within a generation or two through manipulation of oral tradition and then, as with the toasts' blood imagery, to make fresh claims to deep rootedness. These groups of loosely acquainted men were cautiously grasping for the social connectedness that their enslavement had stolen from them. Their bravado reflected a wish that the small communities they were forming would never fail, but these slender associations succumbed to the investigation's demand for informers to impeach acquaintances.[69]

In New York, too, some enslaved men identified with neighborhood groups. At the time of the conspiracy scare, the Long Bridge Boys and the Smith's Fly Boys came to light as two associations that took their names from landmarks in town.[70] In the chaotic initial arrests of black men found in the streets, several of the Long Bridge Boys ended up in jail first. As the progressing conspiracy investigation happened to uncover, members of this group sometimes referred to themselves also as "the Geneva Club," based on a 1738 caper in which they broke into a tavern to help themselves to jenever (gin), and they talked openly about holding a "Club" or "Meeting" and "Swearing" oaths. (Horsmanden also claimed that they organized themselves as a lodge of black Freemasons, perhaps reading too literally the satirical newspaper item that drew parallels between these black criminals and the town's new Freemason lodge, in a writer's effort to tarnish the latter.)[71] In the early days of the conspiracy scare, one of the leaders of the Long Bridge Boys complained loudly to a cellmate that the "Smith's-Fly Negroes . . . were as much concerned as they . . . [of] the Long Bridge," leading investigators to arrest them too. For an in-group to protect its people, it had to prey on outsiders and rivals.[72]

As the associative politics in New York's taverns and outbuildings shaped the nature and extent of informers' accusations, investigators overlaid a story that made sense within their knowledge of other colonies' experiences. They explained the Long Bridge Boys and the Smith's Fly Boys more as military divisions than as neighborhood identities or even criminal gangs. Primed to expect an officer structure, Horsmanden believed that conspirators divided the town militarily "into two Districts" organized geographically as in a colonial militia, each subdivided "into Companies."[73] Through give-and-take with Sandy, an informant, Horsmanden determined that the enslaved Spanish person of color Juan de la Silva would be "Captain of the Fly Company," Cuffee would be "an Officer in the Fly Company," and Caesar—who had been hanged, and who had been a leader of the Long Bridge Boys—would have been "Captain of the Long-Bridge Company."[74] Horsmanden assumed solidarity between these two associations and did not see that enslaved people focused on survival rather than revenge, and therefore banded into groups with little loyalty to outsiders and only a tentative trust within their own ranks.

Accusing Acquaintances

Through associational politics, enslaved people intended to use cautious social connection to strengthen their survival efforts, but during a conspiracy scare their tentative acquaintanceships became fuel for the investigation. These outer networks that aspired to form larger communities crumbled quickly compared to core communities of immediate family. Informants tried not to mention friends and loved ones. In Antigua, for example, a man named Dick served as a trial witness against several men but specifically protected his father-in-law, Cromwell, by testifying that "I Did not see him Drink" at a particular gathering. He also tried to discredit the prosecution's primary witness against his father-in-law by testifying that he did not see the witness "there that Day." It was only later that the judges learned of his personal loyalty to the man on trial.[75] In New York, similarly but with less subtlety, Quack protected his wife by saying that she "was no Ways concerned, for he never would trust her with it."[76] Fortunately the judges were apt to overlook women's participation anyway.

Informants also shielded loved ones by redirecting suspicion toward others. While some took the judges' hunger for names as an opportunity to ensnare enemies and rivals, most found it expedient to shift suspicion to people they knew only glancingly. By accusing mere acquaintances, they moved the danger away from their own homes and small core communities. The strangers whose names came up most often were those whose social activities most frequently bridged plantations and households, making them widely noticeable and nameable without being known intimately. In Antigua, in fact, the first two "ringleaders" to be tried and executed were Court and Tomboy, two well-known leaders of the island's patron-client networks, and their most well-known associates were drawn in soon after. Investigators tapped into vast networks of acquaintanceship in both the urban landscape of New York and the agricultural landscape of Antigua.

In Antigua, informants tended to accuse men of relatively high social profile. These suspects were social leaders who were known more by reputation than in person. The investigation disproportionately claimed large numbers of people who were assigned to so-called privileged occupations, such as gang drivers, craftsmen, and mobile workers, who struck a higher social profile. Only 10 to 20 percent of the island's enslaved population were "privileged" workers, but they constituted more than 75 percent of the convicted men (at least 122 of 156 men).[77] Contemporary characterizations of these supervisory figures, including gang drivers, hint at their centrality to the community. An old driver, Parham Watty, who was burned at the stake, was understood by the judges to be "one of the Top Negro's in Parham Plantation," with a large family "and much beloved." In a different plantation community, the African-born Quou was a gang driver estimated by one witness to be "as Top a Negro as any in his Masters Plantation." The elderly Minian was also revered; he had a "foot boy" and rode a horse to one of the gatherings. These well-known people were afforded material benefits, longer lives, and some spatial mobility. Many knew them by reputation outside of the gangs of laborers that they oversaw.[78]

Craftsmen, who comprised an even larger proportion of the alleged conspirators, were probably on average younger than the gang drivers. Tradesmen were recruited in their late teenage years, but they were still key figures in their communities by virtue of having some autonomy in their work.[79] They avoided the grueling labor of cane cultivation and processing. Skilled workers, like supervisory workers, received better rations than field workers and better provision grounds, allocated to them to raise their own additional food. They had more of their own time and wider economic opportunity because they plied trades that could earn money on the side. Craftsmen in town labored during less of the day than plantation field hands and rarely had reason to work at night (unlike cane workers). Their lighter and more independent workload provided opportunity to meet with other people from different households and plantations, and to become acquainted with people who could break their trust.[80]

Mobile workers—carters, fishermen, coachmen, and personal waiting men—had even more opportunity than drivers and tradesmen for mobility through this carceral landscape. One Saturday afternoon, for example, an enslaved man was "Carting Sugar Down to the Bay" when he passed a gang driver who was "Digging Caneholes in Royals Plantation." The driver saw him and invited him to come to his house the next day. Another man, Jemmy, came to town to "Do his Master's Business" and allowed himself to be drawn into a breakfast gathering at Scipio's dwelling.[81] Mobile workers, like supervisory figures and skilled workers, had wide social networks of people who knew their names and faces. This left them vulnerable to multiple accusations by people who preferred to protect loved ones by instead implicating these relative strangers whose names they knew. These men in continuous motion posed a special threat to a slave regime that viewed widespread communication as a precursor to insurrection. Mobile workers, once convicted, were twice as likely to be executed as supervisors and four times more likely than stationary craftsmen.[82]

In New York, too, informants protected their home circles by accusing acquaintances further afield. As a result, suspects hailed from all quarters of the compact town. The nature of enslavement in the town gave informants several opportunities to meet these strangers. Enslavers frequently sent enslaved men into public spaces to work. Specialists in skilled trades were integral to enslavers' workshops, sometimes even running them, while other tradesmen such as bricklayers and carpenters went out to job sites. Other enslaved people labored at the docks in this trading entrepôt; 31 percent of enslaved people mentioned in the trial record were owned by either merchants or people in the maritime industry.[83] Enslaved people whom enslavers deemed underutilized were hired out to other white people and served as day laborers on public works projects. Almost everyone ran errands in the streets and, as historian Jill Lepore discovered, many of them filled kegs every day at the few freshwater wells in a town otherwise plagued with brackish water. Jack got to know many people because his enslaver, Gerardus Comfort, had built one such well and pump. At least eight enslaved trial participants mentioned visiting Comfort's well, and Horsmanden commented that Jack had many occasions to meet new people when they went "to his Well every Morning and Evening . . . from all Quarters of the Town for Tea-Water."[84] Comfort's pump did not, as Horsmanden would have it, deliver new recruits into Jack's arms, but rather it connected water-carriers in strings of acquaintanceship, many of which entangled Jack. The water pump helped informants come up with acquaintances' names to implicate in the place of loved ones' when they faced such dire circumstances that they decided this was necessary in order to survive the investigation.

As informants tried to protect loved ones by keeping the danger away from their home quarters, they generally gave evidence against suspects with whom they had no close connection. The years of cautious community-seeking social activities among relative strangers that normally promoted mutual responsibility as a survival strategy occasionally provided fodder for conspiracy accusations. Any acquaintance who was "Present Every Saturday Night," as one informant put it, could then be implicated by the logic of complementary testimony that "every Saturday Night we talked of this Affair."[85] The investigation devoured these chains of relatively weak social links. Enslaved people were, therefore, wise to shun strangers during a conspiracy scare and to close ranks with known allies.

Terror in the Quarter

During a crisis, webs of acquaintanceship among enslaved households in New York and in Antigua carried a supply of vital information. In New

York, enslaved people asked each other "What news?" in the streets and gathering spots. They sought more than an entertaining story. They wanted information by which a vulnerable person could navigate another day of extreme power relations. When a fire consumed a house one night, an enslaved man named Toby was led by his natural curiosity to ask Jack "What news?" of that neighborhood, "for he had heard that there had been a fire at the other End of the Town." Quack also remarked on the unusual frequency of fires within a single week and used "some suspicious words" within hearing of an informant.[86] Such suspicious words were unavoidable when enslaved people discussed fires and rumors of a possible uprising. When they cautiously turned to each other for information that would help them survive, their trust in acquaintances' discretion made them vulnerable to informants who profited from revealing the conversations. As the investigation commenced and word began leaking out about an uncovered insurrectionary conspiracy, a man named Pompey stopped by another man's, Tom's, doorstep to ask "whether he heard any talk of the negroes rising," to which Tom answered, "Not I; why, have you?"[87] As New York descended into a conspiracy scare in April 1741, the question "What news?" became as fraught as it was useful, as investigators incentivized eavesdroppers to repeat these conversations.

To discuss the mysterious fires and the growing conspiracy investigation was, beyond a matter of survival, also an opportunity to quietly express rage at the systems that enslaved them. We know about the conversations betrayed to authorities. During one of the fires that provoked the New York conspiracy scare, for example, two enslaved men, Patrick and Dundee, stood together to watch the governor's house burn at Fort George. Patrick remarked that he had no misgivings that this symbol and seat of imperial power was turning to ash. His only regret, he said, was that he "wished the governor had been burnt in the middle of it." Other enslaved men responded to the town's frequent fires with understandable glee. When the town suffered its sixth fire in just two weeks, a small group of enslaved men walked to church in celebratory laughter and taunts of "Fire, Fire, Scorch, Scorch," catching the ear of a white woman they passed. (They explained it away later as a cheer for Admiral Edward Vernon's expedition to the Caribbean.) For his part, the man named Bill who traveled from Antigua to New York reportedly admitted to Jack that "he would sooner see all the houses burnt down to the ground, before he would lend a hand" to extinguish the fire. At the water pump, a gathering place for mere acquaintances, when Sandy ran into a woman named Sarah, he unwisely commented on the fires by boasting that he too would "set them all on fire" if his own enslaver abused him much more.[88] Ironically, enslaved New Yorkers were now meditating with some seriousness on the feasibility of rebellion precisely because the growing conspiracy investigation forced them to compare notes to survive it. Even when they witnessed a spectacle of execution such as the burning of Cuffee and Quack, they rejected the message of submission that the authorities meant to impart, and instead took inspiration: York turned to Prince and wryly commented that the "the great number of white people present" in this crowd furnished "a fit time for them . . . to rise."[89] Most did not speak so openly about the mechanics of insurrection, but even simple complaints, observations about the investigation itself, and advice for staying safe ironically served as a new basis to brand them rebels and arrest them.

Some individuals managed to learn from their networks that someone was accusing them. They slipped away from New York's investigation, taking advantage of the maritime hub's connections to many other towns on the mainland and in the Caribbean. At least seven black men escaped before they could be arrested. One of them left when his enslaver, Henry Holt, set off for Jamaica as soon as the trouble started.[90] Another was found in Jamaica three years later. Warnings for specific individuals outside of New York also flew along shipping routes. An example that survives in the record is the letter of Joseph Hilton, "a Negro," which washed up in the shipping hub of Bermuda and reached the attention of the governor. It warned its intended black recipients in Bermuda that "the timese were very dead in New York" because white authorities were "hanging six or seven negroes of a day." Hilton warned that informers in New York had mentioned the names of "free Joe and Charles Cuff" and that they "would be taken up if they should come tither" to New York.[91]

As Antigua's conspiracy investigation grew in intensity, chilling information seeped from the courthouse and coursed through enslaved networks. An enslaved man named Delmore was visiting town when Court was arrested as the ringleader, later to be broken on the wheel, and he brought the information home. He announced that "he was Glad he was Come home" because Court could have spotted him at the execution and "Possibly . . . Named him" out of simple acquaintanceship even though he actually "knew Nothing of it." He was safe for the time being. A few weeks later, Jack confided his own fears that, with "Secundi . . . [now] taken up,

I am afraid they will come higher & higher up in the Country," and possibly arrest Jack because the two were "very intimate."[92] When the investigation did reach the plantations where Delmore and Jack were enslaved, an acquaintance named Tom saved himself by turning king's evidence and revealing these two acquaintances' admissions of fear, which the court took to be evidence of their guilt. Delmore was banished, and Jack was burned at the stake.

The pressures of slavery battered the tentative acquaintanceships that the enslaved had been able to create. Conspiracy scares, and other times that informants reported on acquaintances, encouraged the enslaved to remain guarded in their associations. Individuals turned to family and friends whom they believed they could count on, while keeping wary of relative strangers. Unfortunately, even that was not always enough to protect a vulnerable person. When an unidentified enslaved woman learned that her acquaintance Treblin was arrested, she correctly predicted that he would accuse her brother Jacko. She preemptively organized "Some friends to Stand by" Jacko, as he told a friend, but the tribunal decided that both Jacko and his confidant were guilty. One was gibbeted and the other broken with the wheel.[93] Shortly after Christmas, Parham Watty found out that his own name had been mentioned during one of the examinations in the courthouse. He learned about it through an old man who was watering the horses at a pond near Parham plantation, who had been instructed by Cudjoe, a carpenter at a neighboring labor camp, to "tell Watty that he heard that Griggs's Dick had impeached him." For cautiously extending the helpful information, Cudjoe asked only that Watty reciprocate by "not mention[ing] his (Cudjo's) name" if arrested. Within a month, however, someone reported the conversation and both Watty and Cudjoe were sentenced to burn at the stake.[94]

Enslaved men went into hiding when they heard rumors that someone in jail, maybe a neighbor or acquaintance, had mentioned their names. In the daytime, these terrified acquaintances and fugitive suspects delayed arrest by feigning illness. Secundi, for example, "hid himself" by staying with another slave who "Concealed him in his House[,] Pretending to be Sick himself [so] that he might be in his House with him." In a similar situation, Caesar absented himself from his duties as a gang driver by "tell[ing] the Overseer that he was Sick" and then "Sculk[ing] about" out of sight. Periodically he asked around whether anyone had seen "any white People come from St. John's [Town]" that day, and someone usually replied, "no, not that Day." During the nights, Caesar was too terrified to risk sleeping in his own cabin; it seemed safer to hole up in the outbuilding near his enslaver's great house with another fugitive who had already been acquitted "but was afraid of being taken up again." Fugitives were indeed not safe at night. A militia officer reported being awakened by a patroller who learned the nocturnal hiding places of two suspects who "were there together [nearby] and might be taken." The patrol narrowly missed the fugitives that night, but they were ultimately jailed, tried, and convicted— one was banished, the other burned. Caesar, for his part, was right to be careful. Ultimately the constable did come for him, and after a short trial he was burned at the stake.[95] Secundi was also eventually discovered, arrested and tried, and ultimately starved to death in a hanging cage. The friend who harbored him was burned at the stake a few months later.[96]

Even after condemnation, convicted prisoners could send word to their families about what to do after they were gone. In Antigua, Court sent a message by a "Boy on a White Horse" to a plantation seven miles outside of town. Court said that a woman there, Queen, whom he had "very often" visited, and who used to sell provisions supplied by him, should after his death "keep what thing's she had of his."[97] Similarly, in New York, one man, Adam, prepared for his death as soon as he learned that the person testifying against him was a strong witness. When two white men who worked for his enslaver came to visit him, he asked them to give his "Shoe- and Knee-Buckles (being Silver) and some other Things" to his brother Caesar.[98] Conspiracy scares stripped social branches from enslaved people's lives, and death focused them on the relationships that mattered most.

Unraveling

Colonial officials sensed danger in interplantation and interhousehold associational activities, and they policed enslaved people's movements and gatherings out of fear that they were plotting. They failed to notice a more fundamental political activity of attempted reintegration after their social alienation as forced migrants. Alcohol served as more than a social lubri- cant by catalyzing the toasts, healths, and oaths as tentative affiliative bonds, and women hosted suppers in support of these relational political structures. Residents of neighborhoods identified with one another in localized ethnic groups. Patrons and clients joined to form retinues. All of this political activity was largely disguised to enslavers who misinterpreted this activity to be leading to seemingly inevitable vengeful racial violence. They took it as evidence of a slave conspiracy.

Even so, this associational activity informed the resultant conspiracy scare because it provided avenues for informants to think of new names to implicate and to identify regular social venues for alleged conspiratorial activities. The very evidence of conspiracy, which consisted of reported conversations among enslaved people about overturning enslavers' political control, existed only because they were meeting and striving to self-organize. When ascertaining the details of the plot, informants and investigators found common ground in testimony that paired enslavers' expectations about conspiracy with verifiable reports of social activity in the slave quarter. Through the alchemy of the trials, everyday activities like friendly suppers and celebratory toasts morphed into the insidious cabals and treacherous oaths that they had been learning to expect since the seventeenth century. Informants met judges' demands for fresh impeachments by culling the names of acquaintances from prior social gatherings, redirecting the danger away from loved ones.

In slave societies defined by extreme power differentials and perpetual wariness on both sides, a conspiracy scare among white inhabitants pushed already-terrorized enslaved people deeper into their own world of fear. The terror of the proceedings swept beyond the courthouse walls, through the streets of town, and out into slave quarters where unverifiable rumors about newly divulged names inflamed fears. With each new arrest, the possibilities multiplied that the investigation would reach deeper into New York's households and further into Antigua's countryside. Already-off-balance people, stripped of resources, struggled to keep their footing as the conspiracy investigation shook the entire social landscape. It was impossible to know whom to trust when so many were being impeached by rivals and allies alike. Trusting one's neighbor in a slave quarter could be as dangerous as relying on anyone encountered in prison. As investigators arrested ever more suspects, they pulled at threads and caused a social unraveling that began in the courthouse and affected most of the communities around the town of New York and the island of Antigua. Social leaders became implicated by virtue of their visibility in interhousehold and interplantation networks. By executing these social connectors, investigators inadvertently undermined key aspects of the political lives of the enslaved—associational activities across communities, and the building of trust—even though they failed to recognize its value and the true nature of the devastation they wrought.

At the Parham plantation, in Antigua, only one of three gang drivers returned to the estate from the investigation. That man, Attaw, had testified against one of the plantation's other gang drivers, Cuffey, and caused him to be sold to Spanish America. He also provided secret evidence against Parham Watty, a "much beloved" leader with "many . . . relations" there. The judges declined to openly use Attaw's evidence at Watty's trial because they believed that upon releasing the informant "it was a Moral Certainty that Watty's Relations and friends would murder him" for causing his death.[99] The judges rewarded Attaw by sparing his life and releasing him back into slavery after the conspiracy trials. His position of leadership in the slave labor camp had always depended on using violence against other enslaved people, together with rewards, to exploit them on behalf of enslavers. His actions during the conspiracy scare enhanced his access to the power of fear in supervision. He remained at Parham as the plantation's main gang driver for at least the next fourteen years.[100] As with the return of hundreds of released men all across the island, his continued presence at Parham plantation was a living reminder of the dangers of trusting acquaintances. Conspiracy scares such as those in Antigua and New York claimed their victims and passed, but the prospect of another scare was always just beyond the horizon.

CHAPTER 5

The Accountants, the Opportunists,
and the Rebels

Taking Chances in the Era of the Seven Years' War

Around eight o'clock on Monday, October 12, 1761, a group of about seven
black men stood talking outside a house in Bermuda. One of them, a free
person named Natt, mentioned that he and his wife wanted to host a "Frolick" for his friends. He announced that he would slaughter a cow for the
occasion and would not allow any white person to partake. Two other men
boasted that if any white person tried to use any of their hard-won posses-
sions they would "kill him" and "be revenged." At just this moment, an
enslaver named John Vickers walked by and overheard the conversation. A
third, unidentified speaker exclaimed, "There would be a very great Victory
gained here soon, or if not, one half or two thirds of the Negroes will be
hanged in Bermuda." Vickers informed a justice of the peace, who in turn
brought his deposition to Bermuda's council, the small, appointed body
that held responsibility for assisting the governor in protecting the colony.[1]
For the next five months, Bermudians experienced a costly conspiracy
scare.

Events outside of Bermuda heightened white people's acute awareness
of their own vulnerability to slave violence. One year earlier, thousands of
rebels had taken up arms in a series of insurrections across Jamaica. Colonial printers published reams of news about this largest insurrection in
eighteenth-century British America. In one such letter, a resident complained of the mustering required by colonial governors during such
alarms: "We are now all Soldiers: I have been upon duty ever since the first
day," threatening violence against the enslaved people who stayed behind

after revolts. Then, in the months before Bermuda's conspiracy scare, smallpox weakened the colony and French privateers cruised its shipping lanes as part of the Seven Years' War (1754–63), causing food shortages.[2] Meanwhile, early murmurs came from England that Spain would soon enter the conflict on the side of the French.[3]

William Popple, the governor of Bermuda, offered rewards of cash or freedom to anyone with information. Members of the council smugly believed that, as they had technically not engaged in judicial torture, the discoveries provided by terrorized enslaved people were somehow "unextorted Information and Confessions." The circle of suspects expanded geometrically and forced the council to reassign men from each parish to guard the jail because "we have so many in Prison now." The fearful investigators and their coerced informants decided that that free black instigators organized nearly all of the enslaved people to "Massacr[e] the White Inhabitants," "subver[t] the Government," and take control of the island. When five French privateers set out from Saint-Domingue, it also appeared that they were headed for Bermuda to "joi[n] our disaffected Negroes" and to help "the slaves here . . . to rise."[4]

The council took drastic countermeasures once it became convinced of the threat. It mobilized the militia, doubled the watches, and stopped the harbor traffic. Such an embargo was a common but costly move intended to "keep the White Men on the Island" to staff patrols in a place undermanned as a colonial outpost.[5] The port closure hurt Bermuda's business in the carrying trade as a hub roughly equidistant to New England and the Caribbean. The island's merchants clamored against the measure, but with "many slaves . . . in custody and charged with conspiring to murder all the White People," and "our fears every day increasing from fresh discoveries," the government did not entertain their objections.[6] Governor Popple acknowledged that "Great Troubles and great Expences" accumulated to the colony with "business of all sorts . . . interrupted," but he maintained that white people's personal safety demanded it. Patrollers' crops went untended, merchants' ships idled in port, and—"still worse" for business—these interruptions would continue for an indeterminate length of time.[7] Finally, two months into the investigation, the council lifted the embargo to placate merchants who grew anxious as the hurricane season ended and who had an eye on the profits of the winter trading season.[8] This depopulated the island of a white policing force. It also allowed news of the ongoing threat of rebellion to slip into Atlantic trading networks, leading vessels to temporarily shun the port. Many months later, a correspondent in Bermuda finally announced to mainland North American newspapers that the conspiracy had been completely suppressed and the hub was back open for business.[9]

Martial law was the other expensive countermeasure to which Bermuda's assembly assented, as the elected body that controlled the purse, in light of new and seemingly credible revelations. This allowed the governor to bypass the representative government of the assembly and to force residents to muster as a militia and to patrol the island. The assembly expressed its inhabitants' concerns that "the Continuance of Martial Law was very severe on the People," but once again the council's assessment of white people's exposure to perceived danger took priority.[10] For months, additional watches patrolled the region of the island deemed most vulnerable. The high costs of slave conspiracy scares included loss of human life, destroyed property, trial expenses, jail expenses, patrolling expenses, losses in patrollers' untended crops, interrupted commerce, the colony's reputation as a safe harbor, and even the future terms of commercial credit.

Despite these costs, Bermuda's scare also presented opportunities. This was a "useable" fear. The governor did not allow this crisis to pass without attempting to capitalize on it. The conspiracy scare focused the assembly's attention on laws regulating the militia, the watch, and manumission. More boldly, however, Popple seized this opportunity to promote his pet project of establishing a central town as the colony's capital. In this fearful atmosphere, while extra guards still patrolled, he proposed that white inhabitants "live together collected in a Body." He was trying to compensate for the fact that the only town, St. George's, at the end of the elongated island, did not offer a focal point for settlement because residents located wharves at their houses along its entire coastline. Popple reasoned that domestic insurgents or foreign invaders could easily "butche[r] half the Inhabitants" at one end of the island "before the other half . . . kn[ew] any thing of it." He argued so forcefully for the new town that he had to clarify his position: he did not want to *compel* settlers "by force . . . to live in any one single spot," but only to encourage them through inducements. Popple's planned metropolis, however, never became more than a dream.[11]

This chapter explains the opportunities and costs inherent to colonial officials' investigation of possible conspiracies in the eighteenth century. Accounting for these trade-offs exposes the steep price of false alarms. At stake were white people's safety and property, on the one hand, and black people's lives, merchants' economic misfortune, and the colony's constitutional corrosion, on the other. This chapter also elaborates on earlier explanations of how war impinged on slave societies' dynamics of fear by situating the plots of the 1750s and 1760s within the landscape of the Seven Years' War. While particular military setbacks sometimes established flammable conditions, as in Virginia in the 1750s, on balance this war was favorable to the interests of British slavers in the Caribbean. Only Tacky's Rebellion in Jamaica truly shook the confidence of slaveholders and presented new opportunities and dangers for the enslaved. Finally, the chapter takes up the issue introduced by Governor Popple at the conclusion of the Bermuda scare: how best to capitalize on the fears of colonists, even if that meant deliberately creating a conspiracy scare, as costly as that would be for so many people.

Domestic Fronts in the Seven Years' War

A comparison between the War of Jenkins's Ear (1739–48) and the Seven Years' War (1754–63) illustrates how the prosecution of a war, together with the braided dynamics of military presence and rumor, gave rise to climates either of security or fear. The War of Jenkins's Ear quickly became a series of defeats for the British. As a result, nearby colonies became distracted, weakened, and felt more vulnerable to domestic insurrection. On the other hand, the Seven Years' War paradoxically brought circumstances of imperial strength to many areas, generally dampening fears of conspiracy in the Greater Caribbean. To be sure, troubling circumstances in particular places and times gave rise to white people's insurrectionary fears, as when Native Americans flexed their power on the frontiers of Virginia and South Carolina in the 1750s, thousands of rebels roiled Jamaica with insurrections in 1760, and privateers and amphibious invasions hovered offshore in the West Indies. But, in general, enslavers' confidence surged with imperial victories and by hosting unprecedentedly large garrisons and naval deployments. As a result—if one temporarily factors out the eight scares in Jamaica (1760) that were induced by the island's year of insurrections—disproportionately few conspiracy scares occurred in the rest of the colonies in the whole of the Seven Years' War. Instead, island colonists were more apt to credit rumors of insurrection *after* the war, in the late 1760s, when imperial planners reduced the number of soldiers in the region.

Even at the eve of the Seven Years' War, tensions mounted in the Ohio Country on the frontiers of Virginia, Maryland, and Pennsylvania in the early 1750s. French, Chippewa, and Ottawa soldiers attacked the large but poorly defended English-allied Miami Indian settlement of Pickawillany. The town was one of the region's great trading posts, with connections to Pennsylvania and Virginia. To intimidate the English and their allies, members of the French-Indian force took captives, reportedly ate the heart of a wounded English trader, and cooked and ate the town's Miami leader. The Miami alliance with the English suffered, and colonists noted the terror that the French were willing to deploy through their nonwhite allies.[12] With this major setback and geopolitical realignment against English influence in the region, Virginia and Maryland experienced three minor slave conspiracy scares even before the Seven Years' War broke out (1752, 1753, 1753).[13]

In 1754, Virginians sparked the Seven Years' War with their ambitions for the Ohio Country and George Washington's botched attempt to warn the French off the Forks of the Ohio. A year later, Virginia launched another failed enterprise under General Edward Braddock. He carved a path through the wilderness toward Fort Duquesne without the benefit of Native American intelligence, blazing his way directly into a French and Indian ambush. His defeat at the Monongahela River set back the broader war effort and—more to the point—shook the confidence of Virginians on the frontier, "seiz'd with a Panick" in their exposure to enemy Indians.[14] One week after Braddock's defeat, as the astonishing news arrived, enslaved people from several plantations happened to "appea[r] in a Body" at Charles Carter II's plantation near the Potomac River, in a corridor that led from the increasingly volatile frontier. Carter and his father, who built his fortune on the backs of people he enslaved, believed that the large group met to plot an insurrection in which "the Fr[ench] will give them their Freedom." They called out the patrols, asked sheriffs to arrest participants, and prepared for trials and punishments that would make "an Example of one or two" to dissuade others from "enter[in]g into Combinat[ion]s and wicked Designs." Virginia's governor, Robert Dinwiddie, confided that "w[ha]t I always fear'd" was coming true: a slave uprising during a wartime "Emergency." He informed his supervisors at the Board of Trade that he had to keep every county's militia close to home "to protect . . . from the Combinations of the Negro Slaves," especially in light of Braddock's defeat and the likely "Designs of our Enemies."[15]

Colonists in South Carolina also sat exposed to Indian incursions. In Charleston, Robert Raper hectored his correspondents in early 1760 with the progress of the Cherokees in making advances and "coming in our Backs & Cruelly Scalping and Burning all." He took alarm at their proximity "within 150 Miles of this place," and then "within 80 or 90 Miles of Town." Governor James Glen noted white people's growing "fears & Apprehensions" of a more devastating attack from the Cherokee and the Creek. In the meantime, Raper noted that "French Privateers [were] becom[ing] Numerous" at sea.[16] The South Carolina council ordered militia colonels to "strictly observ[e]" and to "pointedly execut[e]" the laws for policing enslaved people. The crackdown sowed additional unease in enslaved society. One enslaved person, Prince, played on white people's fear to accuse his enslaver, a free black man named Philip Jones, of using his position as a preacher to plan a rebellion. Prince claimed that Jones and two other free men of color, John Pendarvis and Humphrey Primus, assured conspirators that God ordained their rebellion. It is unclear whether they meant to imply protection, as when obeah practitioners furnished bulletproof powders, but black preachers generally found no shortage of biblical messages approving of resistance to abuse and enslavement. Investigators arrested three more enslaved people, "ke[pt] them in seperate appartments" in jail, and extracted confessions that Jones, Pendarvis, and Primus coordinated with "the Indians . . . in killing all the Buckraas [white people]" and recruited new plotters by passing around "a written paper . . . to all the negroes." White people were on edge in a war that caught them between inland Indians and the French at sea. Indians had their own geopolitical reasons to play on colonizers' fears, unaware of the potential consequences for enslaved people. They displaced their fear onto the most vulnerable people within their own society, and Prince redirected that suspicion against the man who enslaved him, whose preaching may have advocated resistance of some kind, and whose racial identity certainly exposed him to the charge.[17]

Britain's Caribbean territories were also vulnerable to invasion, but judging from the vantage of three enslavers in Jamaica and Antigua—Samuel Martin, Thomas Thistlewood, and Stephen Blizzard—the Seven Years' War brought at least as much celebration as it did concern. At the beginning of the war, Martin, a sugar grandee, worried that the "internal safety" of Antigua and other sugar islands might be jeopardized if British regulars redeployed to North America (the "vast wilds in a frozen region"). He took the news of the French amassing between four and ten thousand soldiers as an indication "no doubt of an attack upon this Island or Jamaica, or both." He grumbled that the English Caribbean was "exposed to Invasion" because too much of the Royal Navy was tied up, as ever, in a defensive posture in the English Channel.[18] According to his nephew, Josiah Martin, colonists in the Leeward Islands predicted that the French would use the forces "against Jamaica" or "these Islands."[19] The people enslaved in these places probably braced themselves, too, because they were the most valuable and vulnerable property that raiders would want to seize.

However, the Seven Years' War developed differently from the War of Jenkins's Ear.[20] To Samuel Martin's delight, the number of British regiments posted in the Caribbean grew from two in 1755 to eight in 1764, a peak for the period. Within a year of the outbreak of hostilities, Martin no longer worried about the insufficiency of British naval attention and instead praised Britain's "indefatigable" squadrons for protecting West Indian shipping. In Jamaica, Thomas Thistlewood also cheered the "good News" that the English captured the Canadian fortress of Louisbourg "from the French!" and that a massive deployment from England took the island of Guadeloupe in January 1759 and appeared to be making moves against Martinique. Stephen Blizzard of Antigua foresaw the business opportunities that the war's conquests created, and he predicted that "a new Trade [would be] open'd" with Guadeloupe after its surrender.[21] Anglo-Caribbean enslavers' manifest awareness of these positive developments may help explain why they investigated comparatively few slave conspiracies during this war. Perhaps the balance of power also explains why the French community of Cap Français, in what is now Haiti, exhibited insecurity. Residents there suffered a poisoning scare when unexplained illness spread through northern Saint-Domingue (1757) along the paths of spoiled provisions at a time of scarcity. An informant pinned the conspiracy on François Macandal, a self-liberated fugitive from enslavement. A Boston newspaper reported that five hundred conspirators were executed, citing information from one of "no less than 17 English Privateers" who swarmed the waters off Cap Français and surely set the town's free and enslaved inhabitants on edge.[22]

Two major developments dampened British colonists' spirits in the face of these triumphant developments—slave rebellion in Jamaica (1760–61) and Spain's entry into the war (1762). The series of uprisings and the resulting guerrilla war that rocked Jamaica, known collectively as Tacky's Rebellion, opened a major domestic front in the Seven Years' War.[23] Enslaved people who joined the conflict took advantage of their oppressors' attempt to simultaneously fight a global war and to keep them in subjection with a chronically understaffed colonial force. Indeed, Jamaica was surrounded by enemies with Cuba and Saint-Domingue very close. White Jamaicans immediately viewed the uprisings as tentacles of a colony-wide conspiracy. While hundreds of insurgents actively rebelled and defended themselves in different pockets of the island, white people in areas under colonial control grew in their own fear. In a series of conspiracy scares, they terrorized the vast population of people who remained enslaved.

The first insurrection in Tacky's Rebellion occurred April 7–9, 1760, in St. Mary Parish, Jamaica, in the northeastern part of the island. A group of about 110 rebels broke into a fort to arm themselves, marched into the interior, and grew their numbers to about 400. As in many places on the island, mountains near the plantation zone provided a natural refuge to establish a maroon polity to live more autonomously (fig. 15). Colonial forces, including existing Maroons under the terms of the 1739 treaty, skirmished with the rebels for five days.[24] The governor proclaimed martial law and established an embargo.[25] In the aftermath of the St. Mary revolt, white Jamaicans used past conspiracy scares to think through this revolt's possible genesis and to warn each other that it could have been worse for them. A resident of Montego Bay reported that "most people here" thought that the insurrection was supposed to be island-wide, as they had always feared, and the governor was "fully persuaded" of the same.[26] A resident theorized that "each of" the rebellion's original plotters were promised an enslaver's "Estate for his good Service." He supposed that conspirators all around the island had "long been concerting a Rebellion" but that the St. Mary arm rose prematurely when its leader, Tacky, got "Drunk & committed sev[era]l Murders" at the Easter holiday.[27]

The rebels' actions in St. Mary Parish, and the colony's response with island-wide instruments of terror, generated an electric climate in other parts of the island. Colonists in Kingston believed that "since the Account came of the Insurrection in St. Mary's" their own slaves now acted more suspiciously. Indeed, enslaved people may have been looking for some way to seize the moment, or perhaps what white people noticed was that the enslaved proceeded with more caution in these tumultuous times. Certainly, white people were primed to perceive danger, even though they were the less vulnerable of the two populations. They believed they discovered alleged plots in the two major towns. In Kingston, authorities discovered

Figure 15. In Jamaica, the mountains that were visible from many of the slave labor camps attracted rebels and self-liberated fugitives during Tacky's Rebellion (1760) because the terrain provided defensible space for developing new autonomous lives. G. M. Terrenise, *Canna da zucchero Platazione di zucchero.* In *Il gazzettiere Americano* [. . .], vol. 2 (Livorno [Leghorn], 1763), plate following 110. Courtesy of the John Carter Brown Library at Brown University.

that a man possessed a wooden sword, thought to be a Coromantee cere-monial piece, and they arrested and punished at least twelve people, some by execution. In Spanish Town, they tried and executed five people. With these parallel sets of trials, residents came to believe that authorities uncov-ered the other two tentacles of the conspiracy behind the premature St. Mary revolt. In the towns, investigators and informants claimed, the con-spirators would have "set fire . . . in several places at once" and ambushed "all the Whites who C[a]me [to] Extinguish them . . . in the Confusion." This did not ultimately come to pass.[28]

A second major group of rebels rose up on May 25, the Whitsuntide holiday, in Westmoreland Parish. In the course of two days, two hundred insurgents grew their numbers to a thousand and established a fortified

encampment. One day before the violence, Thomas Thistlewood had dinner at a neighbor's house and heard a rumor—accurate this time—that
there would be an "*Insurection . . .* to-Morrow" of "8000 Negroe Men."[29]
Thistlewood returned home. If he slept, it was not for long. After midnight,
four neighbors notified him that the uprising had begun and summoned
him to help guard the town. He rushed out in such a "Fright" that he forgot
to "Secur[e] [his] Keys, writings &c." In the next few days he believed he
observed "a Strange alteration" in the people he enslaved and decided he
was "pretty Certain they were in the Plot." He kept a "Strict Watch" each
night, nervously "passing the Words Alls Well almost Continuously." He
was understandably jumpy and "almost Spent." In the dark, he noted shots
that he heard in the distance and on one occasion "a Noise in the Water
. . . like a Multitude of horsemen in a hurry." When none materialized he
"Conjecture[d] it Must be Cattle."[30] The colony's forces eventually dis-
lodged the rebels from their stronghold but then contended with a guerrilla
war as skirmishes continued around Westmoreland Parish for months. The
violence spread in viral fashion as small contingents of enslaved people
elsewhere on the island saw this as their best opportunity to take the risk
of rising up and going into the woods and mountains. "All over the Island,"
one plantation manager wrote to England, "ther is a Turbulent & Rebellious
Spirit."[31]

In the meantime, white colonists continued to look "in great confusion"
for more conspiracies as they anticipated another wave of uprisings, and by
the middle of July, authorities around the island credited at least six new
alleged conspiracies.[32] In the parishes of Hanover and St. James, magistrates
executed people from "several Estates" when they believed that they discovered plots on "the day before" they would have launched.[33] In St. Thomas-
in-the-East, officers arrested several people based on "a discovery made by
a Negroe Woman."[34] In the parish of St. John, an overseer believed he
discovered a plot, and authorities compelled detainees to name "a Great
many Negroes" as conspirators. They executed "about twenty" people, banished more, and traumatized countless others.[35] Authorities in the parishes
of Clarendon and St. Dorothy discovered more plotters and condemned
them as well.[36] In late July, when restrictions on enslaved people's travel in
Westmoreland Parish were relaxed, Thistlewood immediately thought he
sensed that "Something more [was] a brewing" among the people he
enslaved.[37] Given the military success of earlier insurgents, perhaps he was
right; but with his frayed nerves and distorted lens, he was more likely to

be wrong. As the months of violence continued, colonists discovered "by Accident" another alleged conspiracy in the parish of St. James that involved people from five plantations.[38] Meanwhile, insurgents who remained at large found cover in the mountains and forests. As colonial detachments chased them "Night & Day," cried out one resident, they "Fly Like Deer which gives us Great trouble."[39] It was not until October 1761 that Governor Henry Moore had enough confidence to declare that the colony had finally quashed the insurrections.[40]

To explain the multipart rebellion, Thistlewood and his acquaintances unsurprisingly looked for an outside instigator, with their longstanding disbelief in enslaved people's capacity for self-organization. For this reason, they came to believe their French enemy relished launching nonwhite enemies at them. In the first week of the Westmoreland revolt, Thistlewood noticed a "Suspicious" traveler whom he took to be "a Frenchman in disguise" and indeed "a Jesuit likely" who was "appointed to Stirr the Negroes." One month later, an acquaintance visited Thistlewood and shared his own theories about how Jesuits had infiltrated the island. Perhaps it was "those who pass ffor [sic] Jew distillers," he offered, or maybe there were "Black Jesuits in the Island amonst the Negroes." Whichever way the French had accomplished this, he added, reports arrived from Trinidad that they were "overjoy'd to hear the News" of the uprising and nudging each other that "now is the time to take Jamaica." He used a well-worn theory about insurgents and invaders, but this time instead of a threatened invasion creating a conspiracy scare, the rebellion actually occurred and created a dubious invasion scare.[41] White Jamaicans' concern was allayed in March 1761 with the arrival of five independent companies of soldiers.[42]

Aside from Tacky's Rebellion, the other major development that stoked fear in the hearts of white Jamaicans was Spain's entry into the Seven Years' War in January 1762. A year earlier, before the secret agreement was finalized, Thomas Hall in Jamaica received advice from a merchant in England to "put yourselves in the Best Posture of defence" because Spain coveted the island.[43] Hall expressed dismay that "a Spanish War seems unavoidable, which will distress a great deal on this side of the Island, where we are so much expos'd."[44] Almost immediately after Spain entered, Thistlewood reported "Some Conjecture" based on intelligence from a captured schooner that the French and Spanish were about to combine their forces to "invade this Island." That night he dreamed that a Spanish fleet descended on the town of Savannah la Mar and occupied it, but noted that it was "only a dream[,] I thank god."[45] He "Consult[ed]" with neighbors about the possibility of invasion and admitted that he was "much afraid off the Spaniards."[46] But the invasion never came, because the Spanish meant only to strike fear into Jamaicans. The Spanish sent out a schooner "on purpose to be taken" as a way to spread disinformation "in order to terrify Jamaica," as a merchant correspondent explained a few months later. The real threat posed by the Spanish was to enslaved people who lived near the coasts when raiders "plunder'd & Pillaged by small Parties" to kidnap them. In this traumatic war for black Jamaicans, Spanish raids terrified them in another, far more direct way.[47]

Despite Tacky's Rebellion and Spain's entry into the conflict, disproportionately few conspiracy scares occurred in the remainder of the Seven Years' War. In late 1761 and early 1762, large British deployments continued to fortify the eastern Caribbean from Europe and from North America, leading to the capture of Martinique, Grenada, and Havana. Samuel Martin took heart from news that a British naval force was on its way in August 1761.[48] As garrisons grew and troops, convoys, and naval squadrons gained success, no conspiracy scares occurred after Bermuda's of October 1761 for the remainder of what had become a successful war. In February 1762, planters in Antigua rejoiced at news that the Martinique invasion went well. In April, Thomas Hall and his Jamaican neighbors were "free from . . . Alarms" and were "all . . . easy as to . . . apprehensions of a visit from the Enemy." He wrote to his wife in England about the "very great rejoicings . . . for the Conquest of the Havanah"[49] (fig. 16).

Paradoxically, it was the *end* of the Seven Years' War that most troubled planters because of the discontinuation of large wartime deployments. The West Indian contingent deflated from eight regiments to six in 1765, five in 1772, and three in 1776. In the region, a major slave insurrection that dwarfed Tacky's Rebellion occurred in Dutch Berbice in 1763. The post–Seven Years' War reduction meant that Antigua's garrison shrank from a peak of two regiments to one after the war. Jamaica's garrison was drawn down to two regiments at the same time. The other postwar garrison, at least two regiments, manned the newly acquired Windward Islands. The assemblies of Antigua and Jamaica expressed worry at the diminishing number of soldiers in their colonies and complained about the removal.[50]

During these troop reductions, conspiracy scares occurred in Jamaica and the British Leeward Islands. In St. Mary Parish, Jamaica, enslaved people on a few estates rose up in November 1765. Their attempt in turn

Figure 16. Incredibly, the British captured Havana from the Spanish in one of many victories that gave white Caribbean colonists confidence during the Seven Years' War. Elias Durnford (artist) and Peter Canot (engraver), *A View of the Entrance of the Harbour of the Havana, taken from within the Wrecks*. In *Scenographia Americana: or, A collection of Views in North America and the West Indies* [. . .] *from drawings taken on the spot* [. . .] (London, 1768). Courtesy of the John Carter Brown Library at Brown University.

sparked an investigation into a rumored broader conspiracy. Investigators told some suspects "that if they would impeach any other negroes, they would thereby save their own lives," unleashing a torrent of evidence that included allegations against even the Maroons, who had been the deciding factor in the colonial state's suppression of the rebellions of 1760. The judges had difficulty coming to conclusions from the informants' "great discoveries" on the one hand, and "inconsistency and improbability" on the other.[51]

In the Leeward Islands, colonists believed that they discovered a major plot in Montserrat (1768) and a minor one in St. Christopher (1770), after nearly twenty years without a conspiracy scare. In Montserrat, a white woman who "was much in Liquor," and so almost dismissed ("scarcely credited"), revealed that she overheard two enslaved people arguing about something to do with weapons. The ensuing investigation relied on torture and generated confessions that the insurrection would have occurred on St. Patrick's Day when the white colonists "were engaged in balls." The conspirators would surround each room and, "upon a Signal given," fire their weapons. Informants claimed that they had amassed an arsenal for this in the mountains, but upon inspection, as with other confessed-to weapons caches, there were "none to be found." After the insurrection, informants claimed, conspirators would "cast lots" for which white woman each man would claim, and then they would use the harbor ships to sail to Spanish Puerto Rico and claim freedom as religious refugees. During the trials, colonial officials arrested at least fifty suspects, executed seven alleged ringleaders, and banished about thirty more people. Two suspects killed themselves in jail.[52]

The North American mainland did not exhibit such insecurity during the drawdown of British troops because it relied effectively on its militias. The two postwar conspiracy scares that occurred there correlated instead to the political turmoil of the imperial crisis. Colonists took to the streets to protest British imperial regulation in the Stamp Act in the fall and early winter of 1765. In Charleston, South Carolina, a woman on a balcony overheard a conversation in which two enslaved people "hinted a design of . . . a general insurrection & Massacre of the White People" set for Christmas Eve. When her husband did not believe her, she shared her story more widely and gave "uneasiness to many people," forcing the colony's officials to mobilize one hundred members of the militia, to prepare to issue arms to the "great Number of sailors" in town, and to ask the Catawba Indians to parade to "strike terrour into the Negroes." During the Christmas holidays, a large group of enslaved people marched in town, cried out "Liberty," and 107 of them ran away to join a maroon polity. No conspiracy trials occurred, but the militia kept guard for more than a week.[53]

In 1767, as colonists grappled with how to protest the latest regulation in the Townshend Acts, a minor scare occurred in Alexandria, Virginia. County authorities investigated the apparent poisoning of several overseers and ordered the execution and public display of at least eight enslaved people.[54] In 1769, a large gathering of enslaved people unsettled white residents and brought out the militia. Upon arresting and examining the suspects, however, the militia officers determined that no insurrection was planned.[55] The North American mainland colonies avoided major scares throughout much of the Seven Years' War and immediately after, until the American Revolution brought new levels of political tension and opened a war in colonists' very homes.

The Costs of False Alarms

Just as in Bermuda in 1761, when insurrectionary scares occurred governors used the opportunities to offer various solutions for temporarily enhancing a colony's defenses: martial law and merchant shipping embargoes. Martial law allowed governors to compel militia duty and patrolling, to redeploy colonists' enslaved laborers toward defense, and to streamline decision-making. Although colonial governors routinely declared martial law when attempting to suppress purported conspiracies and actual rebellions, as well as during invasion scares, white inhabitants found many reasons to loathe the measure and criticize its overuse.[56] It was expensive in labor and on ledgers. Planters experienced the miserable burden of mustering as a militia and patrolling. The governor of Virginia acknowledged that compelling extra patrols "occasioned a good deal of Fatigue" and at the wrong time of a growing cycle could cause "some loss in their Crops."[57] Planters regularly commented on the burden. A correspondent in Antigua complained that "the whole island in General [was] under great fatigue" during the investigation there in 1736–37, and as a planter in Jamaica recounted while suppressing both Tacky's Rebellion and a conspiracy scare in 1760, residents were "much fatigued with long and Constant Duty. . . . [while] Martial Law still Continues."[58] After all, martial law was meant to compel men to military service beyond what they wished to perform. Other critics voiced objections to the public expense associated with martial law and conspiracy scares. In Jamaica's investigation of 1776, the government spent £1,870 for incidentals such as provisioning guards and purchased nearly £2,500 of gunpowder on credit from the governor and his merchant group, including a 5 percent commission and 6 percent interest.[59]

Many members of assemblies were inclined to push back against what they regarded as an abridgment of their authority and English liberties. After all, martial law enabled the governor to commandeer private property, particularly in the form of enslaved laborers to work on fortifications, to force men to abandon normal agricultural production at inopportune times, and to subject all colonists to court martial for noncompliant behavior. Some governors used the threat of "a little smarting under martial law" as a cudgel against their colonies' assemblies.[60] Governors did find it useful that martial law made it easier and cheaper to compel private enslavers to redirect their enslaved people's labor toward public works. Governor Nicholas Lawes of Jamaica used a declaration of martial law during an invasion scare in 1719 to catch up on repairing fortifications because, through compulsory labor contributions, the work "can be done with much less charge to the Government in time of Martial Law than otherwise."[61] Jamaica's assembly, however, did not appreciate such heavy-handed governance and asserted in 1751 that "the Love and Affection of his Majesty's Subjects" was a more effective strategy than "the Dread and Fear of Laws made with rigorous Pains and Punishments," in a striking divergence from their view on governing enslaved people.[62]

James Pinnock, a lawyer in Jamaica in the second half of the eighteenth century, took note in his plantation journal whenever the governor declared martial law. He recorded these episodes alongside reminders of the earthquakes, hurricanes, and fires that also temporarily shifted the tone of public life in the colony. In the context of a rumored slave conspiracy, Pinnock scribbled into his journal for December 23, 1769: "Martial Law throughout the Island." During a large-scale conspiracy scare and investigation in the summer of 1776, he recorded: "Martial Law, proclaimed on the Discovery of an intended Rebellion in the Parishes of Hanover & St. James, and the Mischief thought to be much more extensive." But Pinnock was no ordinary observer. He came from a family whose patriarch, Philip Pinnock, briefly served as assembly speaker during some of the alarms. James himself became clerk of the court in 1772 and the king's advocate general in the court of vice admiralty in 1787. Pinnock noted in his journal on September 4, 1778 that "Martial Law [was] proclaimed," but "nobody thinks any good reason for it." A month later he noted with satisfaction that the governor lifted martial law, "it being at last discovered that there was no Occasion for imposing it." During another episode of martial law in August 1779, he grumbled at the flimsy reason for declaring it, on account of "the most absurd Advices of an Intended Invasion [from] Hispaniola."[63]

* * *

The nuisance of being "harrassed with military duties" was only the beginning of the practical drawbacks to martial law, for the economic consequences could be staggering.[64] The first problem was local. Merchants and local creditors loathed martial law because it closed the civil courts that usually ensured debt collection and oversaw other business instruments, playing into the usual delaying tactics of delinquent debtors. Among the obstacles were the fees and bribes creditors had to pay to restart debt collection proceedings and to maintain their place of priority on the list of payees. During Antigua's conspiracy scare of 1736, a plantation manager complained to his brother that "on this negroe affair" a local debtor "has taken the advantage of our forbearance [from debt collection]" by paying nothing during the long period of court closure.[65] In an effort to avoid this problem in the wake of Jamaica's large-scale conspiracy scare in 1776, the governor asked the assembly to meet a week earlier than planned, thus predating the next Kingston assize court, in order to write an act guaranteeing that the recent martial law had not discontinued the civil suits which were in process.[66]

Martial law, if enacted without modification, also made it easier for debtors to flee creditors. Throughout the eighteenth century the assembly of Jamaica regularly renewed a statute that prohibited debtors from leaving the island with their effects during martial law, and it assured creditors that despite any military emergencies they could provisionally seize collateral.[67] During the Maroon conflict of the 1730s, representatives of Kingston's merchants lobbied Jamaica's council not to agree to three months of martial law. They feared that "Persons of dishonest principles" would abdicate their debt obligations by quitting the colony during martial law "with their Effects", "to the great loss and prejudice of their Creditors."[68] They were less concerned with the anguish of enslaved people whom, as moveable property, they wrested from their communities.

These local problems, in turn, tarnished the colony's reputation. Colonial merchants' fickle trading partners continually gathered information from correspondents about changing market conditions in far flung ports, and they shifted their trading networks accordingly.[69] For example, the merchants who petitioned against the imposition of martial law in Jamaica in 1734 claimed that observers would interpret martial law to be a clear signal that Jamaica was now an "unsafe mart or place of trade." They worried that traders would seek partners in other colonies now that they had "sufficient grounds to suspect the unhappy circumstances of the Country to be more precarious and desperate than they are." Edward Trelawny, the governor of Jamaica, noted that it did not help that Jamaican factors of British merchant houses took advantage of martial law "not to send remittances home."[70] Antigua's creditors nearly fell into that very trap during a conspiracy scare of 1736—almost destroying their reputation with commercial contacts. Inhabitants petitioned the assembly to close the courts.[71] A plantation manager there quietly informed his brother of this "scandalous affair" in which the assembly narrowly avoided, by a single vote, extending the two-month court closure to a full year. He asked his brother "not to speak freely of it [lest] it should hurt our credit."[72]

Black insurgency's potential to disrupt white people's property claims could also hurt the economic reputation of a colony. During Tacky's Rebellion (1760), a planter's agent predicted to his employer that "these Rebellions Will hurt the Creditt of this Island," explaining that during a revolt on a plantation "a Mans Whole Interest may thereby be at once destroyed." He proposed that the assembly insure against such individual losses to "greatly Strengthen its Creditt."[73]

Under the umbrella of a colony's reputation, individual lines of credit also seemed to be at stake. Credit was a financial manifestation of calculated risk: when a creditor's own fear of non-repayment increased, such as due to insurrection or martial law, he adjusted the terms of credit accordingly. Local merchants ultimately feared that overseas creditors would reduce their involvement with a colony that seemed on the brink of serious military challenges and whose civil courts tended to close frequently. Colonial governments borrowed on the "publick credit" too and hoped to do so at better terms by improving their political stability.[74] In the 1730s, during the First Maroon War, merchant petitioners in Kingston warned about a "generall Stagnation" not only of trade but also of "Credit."[75] Wealthy whites tangled themselves in webs of debt and credit by receiving loans from British merchants and then offering local credit to other residents.[76] Edward Long saw such credit as the original wellspring of Jamaican prosperity, and he worried that its availability was drying up and at less favorable terms.[77] A Barbadian author similarly saw transatlantic lending as "where our Credit is of the greatest Value to us."[78]

The assembly of Jamaica regularly considered fiscal reforms, currency laws, and changes in corrupt fee structures to build the colony's public credit. In 1737, a committee tasked with "raising the credit of the island" recognized the depressive effect of the Maroon War on Jamaica's reputation. It recommended that "terms should be offered the rebels, and particularly their pardon and freedom," to remove a source of instability from the calculus of potential lenders.[79] Likewise, during Jamaica's conspiracy scare of 1776, a planter and member of the council worried that if news of the

conspiracy scare reached Britain before it was fully investigated, the resulting uncertainty among merchants would "undoubtedly reduce the credit of
this Island, to the lowest Ebb."[80] Edward Long thought keeping the island
"well fortified . . . against domestic and foreign enemies," particularly by
attracting white immigrants, would secure property and raise its value, thus
providing "a firmer basis" for longer lines of credit. This hoped-for "state
of security" from insurrection would inspire "much greater confidence and
alacrity among the merchants and money-holders of Great Britain . . . in
making advancements to the planters." Long wanted Jamaica to outshine
other sugar colonies as the safest and most promising investment for
creditors.[81]

*   *   *

Overseas merchants redirected shipping and adjusted credit only if they
received news about deteriorating conditions in a colony. Colonial governors attempted to manipulate the transmission of news by embargoing
merchant shipping from leaving port. Embargos helped to control the
spread of bad news about the discovery of a conspiracy before there was
good news to replace it by reporting that the potential insurrection was
completely quashed. In the early days of the 1760 rebellions in Jamaica,
Governor Moore attempted to prevent premature and potentially alarmist
reports from getting out. He "detain[ed] the Pacquet [mail-carrying ship]
a few days, as [he] apprehended the Credit of the Island would have been
greatly hurt by any imperfect Accounts carried home of this Disaster."[82] Of
course, he did not yet know that this would become the largest British slave
rebellion of the century. Governor Basil Keith relied on similar reasoning
when deciding to detain the merchant convoy and packet boats during a
1776 conspiracy scare. He may have been successful in softening the economic fallout. Merchants in St. Croix learned from their correspondents
about the Jamaica conspiracy a full six weeks after its first discovery (three
weeks after the embargo was lifted), "with orders not to send any more
goods there till further orders, as they imagined there would soon be a
strange revolution in that island."[83] Embargos were cumbersome for merchants in the short term, but they kept credit networks open in the longer
term.

The other reason to embargo shipping from leaving the port was to
retain a large number of white men for fighting potential insurgents, com-
pensating for the small numbers of free white men resident in the colony

relative to enslaved blacks. Sailors were a far cry from professional soldiers, but at least they were available. In Barbados's scare of 1701, for example, the council arranged a distress signal so that harbor ships would know to send "well armed" men ready to extinguish fires and suppress insurgents.[84] In Jamaica's invasion scare of 1729, the governor had such little regard for a militia composed "mostly of Irish Popish servants" that he used an embargo "to keep their seafaring men at home, in whom, as they apprehended, consisted their greatest safety." In fact, according to a resident of Jamaica during Tacky's Rebellion, not just sailors but all white residents "left their Habitations to go . . . to the Sea."[85] Thus, twenty-five years later in the conspiracy scare of 1776, the Jamaican council closed the port not only to keep news of the conspiracy from escaping but also out of fear of "how greatly the Strength of White People would be diminished" if the convoy were to depart the next day as scheduled.[86]

Although an embargo could control the reputation of the colony and temporarily furnish able white men, merchants debated whether it could potentially backfire and ultimately hurt the credit of the colony. Within a day of the embargo's enforcement in Montego Bay (St. James Parish), at least thirty-six merchants held a meeting at which they organized a petition effort to end the embargo while continuing martial law. The St. James petitioners, and some from the neighboring parish, expressed concern that delaying the merchant convoy would bring "much hurt to the Credit of the Island," because the ships that had sneaked away on the eve of the embargo "sailed at a time when these disturbances were at an alarming Crisis." Detaining the fleet, they complained, would allow those calamitous stories to deflate foreign confidence in trading to Jamaica.[87]

Planters and governors correctly worried that disruption in one colony was a boon to others—as when an Antiguan heard about troubles in Jamaica. Samuel Martin rejoiced in spring 1770 that his sugar promised to bring higher prices because of news of calamities disrupting other suppliers. He heard from a friend in Jamaica that its people were "under arms and Martials Law for more than 3 months; on acct. of the insurrection of [their] negroes, and from the apprehension of an Invasion" by the Spanish. In turn, Martin relayed this news to two of the merchant houses he dealt with, explaining that Jamaica's revolt and expectation of invasion by the Spanish—"and I suppose the French too," he added parenthetically—led him to expect Jamaica, an island with which he competed, to close down its "trade or Sugr making." He professed, "I am sorry to profit by the disasters of our fellow Creatures," but cheered, "Those disasters . . . will probably make our Sugar sell well!" Those who gained financially from conspiracy scares were the planters and merchants who were fortunate enough to be far away from them.[88]

With so much at stake, colonial officials of all levels carefully weighed their decisions to launch investigations and interpret new discoveries. They did not investigate every rumor or entertain every informer's suspicion, and they earnestly tried to avoid false alarms because of the economic consequences and the harm to local creditors and their relationships with the transatlantic merchant houses that backed them. Nevertheless, colonial officials took many threats so seriously as to risk these economic harms—signaling for us the moments when they sincerely believed a slave insurrection was probable and a rumor worth investigating.

Manipulating Fear

Those who best understood colonists' fears and the ways to assuage them—royal governors, colonial assemblies, and even justices of the peace—could also use their facility with fear to promote special projects, just as William Popple did in 1761 for his dream of a metropolis in Bermuda. Conspiracy scares invited colonists to reconsider matters of security and law, and in the realm of formal politics local officials sometimes used this to their advantage. This phenomenon fully matured in the American Revolution, but it also occurred decades earlier when governors capitalized on heightened fears to push their agendas. In the most egregious examples, colonial officials deliberately exacerbated conspiracy scares to achieve their goals, whether personal or professional. In one case, a rogue justice of the peace and the woman whom he enslaved were equally savvy in manipulating the fears of white society to achieve what they wanted.

Governors fulfilled their duty as chief military officers by imploring assemblies to strengthen their militias and to rebuild fortifications. In Virginia, Alexander Spotswood, Hugh Drysdale, and William Gooch each used conspiracy scares (in 1710, 1722, and 1730, respectively) to propose and even to achieve reforms of the militia. In the West Indies, such proposals usually met with sparse enthusiasm from the white men who would need to staff those militias. Instead, island colonies often competed to host a company of soldiers, as in a tug-of-war between Bermuda and the Bahamas in which each pulled harder after their respective scares of 1730 and 1734. The company bounced between the two.[89]

In June 1770, three months after a minor scare in which colonists in St. Christopher "were greatly alarmed" about a threatened revolt that, "upon the strictest examination," was averted, the colony's council requested a garrison of two hundred soldiers, for whom the colony would furnish barracks and provisions. The petitioners cited "apprehensions of Danger . . . from an external Enemy," specifically the French, but noted that their vulnerability was "considerably increased when we reflect upon the Number of Slaves."[90] Clamoring for attention at the same time, however, the colony of Tobago made a similar demand for professional soldiers in the wake of an actual insurrection involving dozens of slaves. Governor Robert Melville argued that the current garrison of two companies was insufficient for "a reasonable Security . . . against their Slaves," and that "Tobago ought not to have less . . . than five or six Companies of Foot Quarter'd in it." In response to this petition, the secretary of state for the colonies regretted that no additional companies would become available until the war against the Black Caribs in St. Vincent was concluded. The empire, in short, was insufficiently manned to prevent the domestic insurrections threatened by its reliance on coerced labor. Enslaved people knew this and sometimes used it to their advantage by launching insurrections or by issuing threats to strike fear into their tormenters.[91]

In Jamaica, Governor William Trelawny (cousin of Edward, the former governor) wanted a stronger militia law so badly that he exaggerated a potential threat to pressure the assembly into taking it up. His opportunity came at Christmas 1769 when, as resident Duncan Macglashan reported to a correspondent, "there are many Informations & Surmises of an Insurrection amongst the Negroes this Holiday time from different Quarters of the Island." When Trelawny spotted his opportunity, he confessed privately that the "Rumours" of a Christmas slave conspiracy spanning several parishes "were too slightly founded to gain much Credit with me," but he made a public show of suppressing the threat in order to move his agenda forward. He rationalized, in a verbal construction as tortured as his conscience, that the need for "an effectual Militia Bill and Articles of War made me think it would not be inexpedient to declare Martial Law, which . . . may be a means to induce the Assembly to establish a serviceable Militia." With Trelawny's declaration of martial law in force, Macglashan grumbled that "we are all military men here at present." Thomas Thistlewood mustered with the militia five of the six days surrounding Christmas, despite having "such a bad cold that I can scarce speak" or "get any sleep." In fact he patrolled until two o'clock Sunday morning, including "thro' thick logwood (where no path)," driving his party to be "much fatigued."[92] Although Trelawny forced sick men to muster and patrol, he wisely did not go so far as to allow an investigation that would potentially identify conspirators and destroy lives and property. Unfortunately for Trelawny, fanning the flames of rumor alone was not pressure enough to get the militia reform he wanted. The assembly considered the bill but failed to pass it.[93]

Even a justice of the peace, James Akin, and an enslaved "mustee" woman named Susana almost got what they wanted by manipulating the governor and council of South Carolina with their fear of rebellion. In January 1749, Akin traveled to Charleston to announce that he had just discovered a rebellion plot. For two decades already, Akin had cultivated profitable connections as part of South Carolina's political community. His neighbors elected him to the provincial assembly eight times, and he had frequent business in Charleston on government contracts. By the time Akin brought his charges to town, he had established himself as a recurring presence among the men who were to evaluate the merits of his story.[94]

In Charleston, Akin produced an enslaved boatman, Agrippa, to perform a pitch-perfect confession and seven more who "all Agreed and Tallied with what Agrippa had said." They identified transient white figures of alleged Catholic faith and ties to St. Augustine as the "first Broacher[s] and Instigator[s]." The conspirators supposedly "pledged . . . by drinking" that they would "fir[e] the Town," "blow up the Magazine," and "murde[r] the White People" to enable their "Escape to the Spaniards." The informants implicated scores of enslaved men from plantations along the Cooper River. Akin credited Susana as the one who first revealed the plot just before the violence would have begun, getting this "Sincible [sensible]"-presenting woman into the legal record in very favorable terms.[95]

The plan sounded convincingly feasible, as the governor pointed out later to account for believing it. He hailed two navy ships to station near Charleston and he made costly decisions to restrict maritime traffic, to double the guard for the town and magazine, and—of particular nuisance—to call out the militia to patrol by boat, horse, and foot. In the course of a week, he issued arrest warrants for twenty-one more enslaved people and seven white people and, in examining them, burned through the Council chamber's budget for candles.[96] When accused conspirators from other plantations began arriving in Charleston to answer the charges of Akin's people, they turned to resources similar to those cultivated by suspects elsewhere including Antigua and New York. In the jail, two men "could speak to one another . . . thro' the Partition that divided the two Rooms," and they discussed a need to "speak out the same thing always and keep the same Mouth." Another advised a companion to let him do the talking because the other man was "a Fool and did not know how to talk before White People." They muddied the picture of the plot with their confused weaving between firm denials and tentative confessions.[97]

The inconsistencies from people enslaved at other plantations went unheeded until the voice from a reputable planter introduced doubt into the council chamber. William Bruce, Akin's neighbor, wrote a letter from his sickbed because he heard about the investigation, thought it sounded amiss, and realized that "a White Mans word would go further than a Negroes" in countering the prevailing narrative. Bruce hypothesized that Akin and Susana orchestrated the whole affair to protect her and her children from court-ordered banishment from the colony for the prior, lesser crime of setting fire to a barn. If they made her a star witness she would be "set free by the Government & . . . receive a Gratuity," as Bruce explained, so that Akin would not need to follow through with transporting her. Perhaps this is why Akin wrote at length about Susana's child for no clear reason in his statement on the conspiracy. Was the child possibly his own?[98]

Now that the governor and council entertained doubts about the conspiracy, the accused were empowered to reassert their denials. The governor privately reexamined the original witnesses, all of whom were enslaved by Akin, and one by one they recanted their confessions. One of them now denied seeing any conspirators "either Black or White" and explained that "at first he did not think it would come to blood and taking away Life, but since he understood it would, he could not sleep or have Peace for what he had done." Another confided that the people he implicated were actually complete strangers.[99] No longer in fear of Akin, the witnesses explained how their enslaver forced them to coordinate their stories before he brought them to Charleston. Akin had assembled everyone and told them that Susana, Kate, and Susie had just revealed "that the Town was to be set on fire, the white People killed &ca." Akin "tye[d] . . . up" one man and threatened to whip others who failed to "say as the Wenches said" that there was a "Negro design to rise &ca." He coached them to implicate the people on neighboring plantations whose names Susana, Kate, and Susie supplied because it "would make their Evidence Stronger if more People besides his Own confessed" through the court's predictable coercion.[100] On the way to town, Akin practiced "the Story" with Agrippa on the boat and went over it again at the council chamber door "before they went in" to report the conspiracy. During the investigation, Akin supervised Agrippa and the other informants when they gave confessions, and he took them back into his own custody at the end of each day so they could discuss the proceedings.[101]

The governor and council realized that this alleged plot was "nothing but a Forgery." Strangely, they decided that Akin was not at fault. They concluded that Susana and Kate duped Akin into believing their story and convinced him to coerce the others into confessing.[102] That might have been true. Their circumstances were the most desperate of anyone's: they faced deportation for the earlier barn burning unless they took drastic measures. Perhaps they played on Akin's fear of an uprising in a bid to gain freedom, and maybe they believed they could direct the investigation's destruction toward other plantations. On the other hand, Akin had his own incentives to initiate the ruse, especially if his sister correctly diagnosed that "of late" he seemed "not right in his Sences."[103] Possibly Bruce was correct about the nature of his enslavement of Susana in unequal affection, or maybe he saw this as a route to appointment to a higher post. Regardless of who proposed the idea, both parties had incentives to collaborate. Once the investigation was underway, those incentives were made stronger with the dangers of being found out, binding Susana and Akin more firmly together. Ultimately, they depended on each other to make these revelations work. Susana and Kate needed Akin for access to legal power, and Akin relied on them to serve as credible witnesses.

The council sentenced Susana, Kate, Susie, and another informant, Robin, to banishment. Akin was far less vulnerable, and the fiasco did not ruin him. He continued to serve as a justice of the peace into the 1750s, but on the other hand his neighbors did not entrust him with a seat in the provincial assembly ever again. Akin died a wealthy man. At the time of his death in 1758, he controlled 845 acres and had more than enough tableware to throw lavish parties. He accumulated these comforts through his violence against countless enslaved people, including the fifty-nine people he owned at the end of his life. Two of his pieces of property were a woman named Kate and her young child named Susannah. Either Akin managed to harbor Kate from the mandated sale out of the colony, or he committed new violence against a woman as a way to remember the departed.[104]

Final Accounting

On top of the traumatically high stakes for the enslaved people who bore the brunt of conspiracy scares, the enslavers who boxed themselves into these circumstances also believed that they faced a risk—to their ledgers—when governors and councils evaluated whether to investigate rumors of insurrection. Resorting to martial law strained ordinary white colonists by disrupting their normal economic activities and making claims on their property, and it burdened enslaved people with compulsory labor for the government and with the psychic toll of increased militarized policing. It interfered with local creditors' ability to collect debts by closing civil courts, and it made transatlantic creditors nervous about lending to people in the colony. From merchants' perspective, martial law could also dim the reputation of a colony as a reliable place to trade. The other emergency tool for suppressing insurrection—embargo—also upset merchants who would rather that their ships did not sit idle. But white people's fear eroded colonial assemblies' usual objections to implementing martial law and embargoes. While in some places, such as Jamaica and the Leeward Islands, conspiracy scares were so common as to warrant rewriting debt laws to lessen the impact, *any* disruption to the economic activity of these colonies was a serious blow to planters' ledgers, their terms of credit, and sometimes the enslaved people whom creditors viewed as collateral. Planters lost thousands of pounds of property and saw their agricultural production interrupted, all of which potentially forced them to sell off more laborers when they could not meet their debt obligations. Atlantic slavery-based economies' emphasized marginal returns and threatened to resell mortgaged slaves. This exacerbated the horrors of the fear's economic fallout.[105]

When governors and members of councils and assemblies chose to act, they debated the appropriate way to suppress the perceived insurrectionary threat to white people. That they paid attention to costs and benefits in their counter-insurgency reveals that they understood that they dealt not with certainties and absolutes, but with probabilities of danger to white people and acceptable costs of suppression, including to enslaved people. Sometimes they struggled to reach stopping points at which they convinced themselves and other settlers that they had terrorized black people enough to restore public safety for white people. With so much at stake, they deemed the lives of enslaved people expendable; colonial officials who lacked proprietary or personal interest regarded them as a threat to the public and an example for striking fear into others. They believed that they needed instead to overcome their feelings of helplessness by demonstrating vigilance, restoring white people's sense of mastery by requiring some enslaved men to fill the roles of "conspirators."

Colonists temporarily overcame their objections to martial law and shipping embargoes when, as with any war, the Seven Years' War brought circumstances that increased fear in particular times and places. Peaks and troughs in the frequency of conspiracy scares are equally instructive. The French and Indian successes on the Virginia and Carolina frontiers in the 1750s, the rebellions of thousands of enslaved people in Jamaica in 1760, and the swarm of French privateers around Bermuda in 1761 all made it easier for colonists to believe they saw conspiracies in those places. At the same time, the Seven Years' War did not generate as many conspiracy scares as in the War of Jenkins's Ear. It produced so many victories in the Caribbean that slaveholders cheered and professed that they felt perfectly safe. When conspiracy scares did occur in wartime, however, they worsened any negative economic impacts already generated by the conflict. Enslaved people already suffered from wartime shortages in provisioning, but now several hundreds of lives were destroyed and families broken apart through conspiracy investigations. Credit became more expensive for merchants as their colonies developed reputations for legal instability and the possibility of social unrest. With enemies pressing from without as well as within, these colonies seemed more vulnerable to invasion, insurrection, or a combination of the two, thereby calling into question for Atlantic merchants the wisdom of trading with them and the security of their debts. War was very expensive, but for colonies with large populations of exploited slaves the outbreak of insurrectionary scares made it even more costly for everyone involved.

Some governors capitalized on the high stakes of conspiracy scares to implore their assemblies to reform militia laws, policing statutes, and other policies for the defense of a colony. Occasionally they abused martial law or allowed conspiracy scares to develop in order to pressure assemblies or prove a point about vulnerability. In at least one case, a planter brazenly abused his power as a justice of the peace to present a manufactured conspiracy to the colonial government in an effort perhaps to retain ownership of a handful of people, at the cost of embargo, martial law, and potentially the lives of the people enslaved by his neighbors. Perhaps others played similar gambits, now covered up, given how often conspiracy scares erupted on the basis of *one* informer or *one* overheard conversation. Certainly, once a conspiracy scare began, many people, free and enslaved, manipulated the proceedings to their own ends unrelated to revealing or discovering the truth of the matter. This would prove no less true when the American Revolution's civil war and political turmoil established perfect conditions for conspiracy scares.

CHAPTER 6

Governing in a World of Fear

Political Mobilization in the American Revolutionary Era

The wisdom of joining the American Revolution was not self-evident in the colonies of the Lower South, even if some of the growing critiques of the imperial arrangement made sense to southern white subjects who had become accustomed to a certain leeway in self-governance. Fundamentally, the Lower South's economic structures and political cultures were more similar to those of the Caribbean archipelago than to those of New England. The Lower South's affinity with the West Indies was particularly evident in this larger region's shared experiences with slave conspiracy scares in the course of the preceding century. Inhabitants of these colonies learned from each other about what to fear and how to respond, even if those lessons were faulty.

At first, in the late 1760s and early 1770s, the imperial crisis resembled a legal argument that promised to be resolved one way or another. Those who wished to reform the imperial arrangement with the British Ministry used a combination of political philosophy and out-of-doors crowd activity. They appointed themselves to extralegal committees to resist the government. This was fitting for people who viewed "conspiracy," for white people, as a standard practice of factional politics within institutions and as a just remedy in seventeenth-century England's crises. Sometimes they coordinated violence, but they did not consider their own conspiracy to be like one of enslaved African American plotters who supposedly lusted after a bloody wave of vengeance. When they rhetorically accused the British Ministry of "enslaving" them, they did not propose killing members of Parliament. Instead, white revolutionaries directed their violence toward the people over whom they wielded the most power.[1]

For a long time, actual war did not seem possible; the lives and property of colonists seemed secure. With the outbreak of hostilities in Massachusetts in April 1775, mainland colonists of all persuasions realized against hope that New Englanders' collective protests and the mainland Provincial and Continental Congresses' organizing activities were becoming a war of rebellion and a civil war. In the conspiracy scares that predictably followed the outbreak of military conflict, leaders in each colony consolidated power, or lost it, through the ways they addressed white people's fear of enslaved black people's potential rebellion. These terrifying events confirmed for white colonists exactly which center of power, provincial or imperial, they could rely on to safeguard their persons and privilege. Conspiracy scares accelerated political affiliation and confirmed partisan structures of power within each colony.

Enslaved people took advantage of the deepening political division and spreading military conflict to press for concessions from enslavers or, if circumstances allowed, to flee enslavement for a chance to live with more autonomy someplace else. Collective insurrection was still risky even in the midst of the civil war that engulfed revolutionary America; many individuals found it more sensible to vanish first and exact revenge later, under one flag or another, rather than to act on any impulses that might leave them without protection. Nevertheless, white men eyed their neighbors' enslaved people warily, believing that they had been lying in wait for this opportunity to exact their just vengeance. They also watched the frontier for signs that the Indian raiding parties that had terrorized them so much ten years earlier would once again descend on their outlying settlements. In the Hudson Valley of New York, for example, an enslaver was in bed when he overheard a conversation between York, whom he enslaved, and Joe, who was visiting. The subsequent investigation brought the arrests of at least twenty enslaved people and concluded that conspirators in several towns would "fire the houses, cry fire, and kill the people as they came out," with the assistance of "five or six hundred Indians." White people throughout the colonies read about this familiar-feeling scene, and black people recognized the dangers that came with it.[2]

In the Caribbean, white colonists were just as concerned. Even if Caribbean colonists avoided civil war within their own colonies, they felt the economic strains of interrupted provisioning after 1775 and the regional military threats of French naval deployments starting in 1778. As with enslaved people on the mainland, those in the Caribbean took advantage of the moment to press their fortunes. In frontier zones such as Tobago and the Windward Islands, collective insurrection was a viable strategy because no colonial state had the power to pursue the fleeing rebels in these areas. Longer-colonized regions such as Jamaica and the Leeward Islands, however, no longer offered potential insurgents the same stateless zones of refuge from pursuers. Nevertheless, white colonists believed that the conditions appeared ripe for insurrection: discontent swelled in the slave quarters as provisions became scarce and hunger deepened, enemy fleets threatened invasions that would occupy colonists with a war on two fronts, and political turmoil was dividing and distracting the ruling class. Colonists in the islands and in South Carolina alike considered conspiracy scares a "danger which we are always exposed to," but "more especially at this time."[3]

The outbreak of hostilities in 1775 primed colonists in the Caribbean and the southern mainland to investigate rumors that might otherwise have been dismissed in a time of peace. With unprecedented frequency in 1775, colonists believed that they discovered conspiracies in New York, Virginia, the Carolinas, Jamaica, and the Leeward Islands. "Great apprehensions prevail," one Scottish newspaper reported, "thro' the whole continent with regard to the negroes."[4]

If there were slave conspiracies, as experience taught white people, then outside instigators and coordinated invaders were probably involved. Prior to 1763, Anglo-American colonists believed for good reason that Spanish and especially French liaisons armed and directed Indians in devastating and terroristic assaults. They also believed, on the shakier foundation of conspiracy scare findings, that provocateurs from those Catholic powers attempted to topple Anglo-American colonies by coordinating uprisings from below. After ousting the French from North America at the conclusion of the Seven Years' War in 1763, colonists there expanded their view of who might organize Indians and African Americans against them. In the decade leading up to 1775, a significant minority of them came to suspect that agents of the British Ministry might attempt to use those same devices to foist on them a political enslavement, which they called popery and associated with Roman Catholicism, essentially the same as in the authoritarian-seeming Bourbon regimes.

Whereas prior to 1765 it was unfathomable to mainland North Americans that professional soldiers would do anything other than defend His Majesty's subjects at frontiers and port towns, a series of poorly handled imperial crises from 1765 to 1775 convinced many that the British Ministry was trying to enslave them politically. The supposed threat of popery extended beyond the possibility of political enthrallment: it was also a threat of violence. With the expulsion of colonial squatters from fertile western lands, the consolidation of the Indian trade and its political alliances in the vast new province of Quebec—Catholic and Francophone, no less!—and the policing of colonists' political protests with professional soldiers, colonists saw much evidence for the ministry's sympathy and collusion with Indians whom they considered an enemy. By the time they declared independence in 1776 they expressed conviction that the king was inciting Indians and black people against them. As historian Robert Parkinson has put it, the Revolution involved a great deal of destruction of "the public's affection for their ancestors."[5] In this they departed from their Caribbean counterparts.

For mainland colonists, the exchange of gunfire between professional soldiers and Massachusetts farmers at Lexington and Concord in April 1775 confirmed that George III could no longer be trusted to protect them and that he was willing to act against his own subjects. Rebel newspapers in New England propagated the radical but understandable conclusion that these new popish agents directed their minions to attack colonists on the frontiers and in their households, threatening the liberties and the lives of freeborn Englishmen. Now they worried that the popish-acting British Ministry might do the same, but to greater effect, armed with intimate knowledge of colonial weaknesses. One hundred years of accumulated experience in discovering slave conspiracies, and of reading about similar discoveries in other colonies, made this guiding framework seem more solid than it really was—but it felt useful. A series of apparent conspiracies from New York to South Carolina brought to life the vaguer rumors that circulated about the ministry's contemplation of arming enslaved populations, Canadian Catholics, and Indians.[6]

In both mainland North America and the West Indies, fear of insurrection occupied colonists, and yet most enslavers in each region chose divergent political paths. The difference between the regions was not whether conspiracies would be detected, for they surely would, but rather who took the lead in quashing them. Royal governors in Jamaica and the Leeward Islands acted quickly on suspicions, partly because the possibility of catastrophic insurrection was much more palpable among such large numbers of enslaved people. Royal governors in Virginia, South Carolina, and North Carolina, by comparison, left the aggressive investigation of possible conspiracies to the revolutionary committees that had been organizing themselves for at least five or six years. As two governments, royal and revolutionary, vied for slaveholders' allegiance, it was the self-appointed Committees of Safety that investigated the mushrooming rumors of insurrectionary conspiracy with an eagerness shared only by other men on the make from earlier times, such as Robert Arbuthnot and Daniel Horsmanden. Whether the committee members truly believed that a threat existed is almost beside the point. They channeled the popular demands of a large segment of the free white population.

The conspiracy scares of the American Revolution accelerated political tendencies peculiar to each region by focusing property holders' attention on instruments of protection against this particular internal vulnerability. For the colonists of the British West Indies, this experience of the American Revolution renewed their appreciation for how the imperial relationship maintained a tenuous stability within societies of such extreme exploitation and potential explosiveness; conspiracy scares highlighted the islands' dependence on the imperial state's military and, especially, its navy. On the mainland, reliance on self-defense organizations was demographically possible and had matured beyond many of their archipelagic counterparts. These conspiracy scares were tests that fundamentally demonstrated that committees of safety, and the militias that they inherited, were capable of defending white colonists from the enemies within their households. The stable continuation of this exploitative system seemed to depend on the imperial embrace in the West Indies, while it appeared to many enslavers in the Lower South to require political independence.

Virginia

In late April 1775, the apparent likelihood of a plot for royal agents to arm enslaved people against colonists received a tremendous boost from the actions of John Murray, Earl of Dunmore and governor of Virginia. In two counties along the James River, white colonists were already acting on rumors of slave rebellion. Residents of Chesterfield County were "alarm'd for an Insurrection of the Slaves . . . —a dreadful enemy," according to one correspondent, and in Surry County another "alarm . . . at first seem'd too well founded," according to another, " 'tho it afterwards proved Groundless."[7] In these days of heightened concern, Dunmore accidentally played into northern newspapers' reports of suspected ministerial plans to unleash slaves and natives on white colonists when he seized the municipal gunpowder, arms, and ammunition from a magazine at Williamsburg in the dead of night. When townspeople learned of the removal of the powder, they assembled as a crowd and demanded its return. Whether out of genuine fear, political usefulness, or a mixture of the two, they petitioned the governor that they needed the powder on hand because of the possibility of slave rebellion: "from various reports . . . in different parts of the country, we have too much reason to believe that some wicked and designing persons have instilled the most diabolical notions into the minds of our slaves." Dunmore responded with a brief speech that relied on a similar rationale to explain his actions. He said that "hearing of an insurrection in a neighboring county," and noticing enslaved people gathering in "large numbers, in the nighttime, about the magazine" in Williamsburg, he "removed the powder from the magazine, where he did not think it secure." Although revolutionaries maintained that this particular powder house "had never yet been attempted by the negroes," Dunmore's explanation was in keeping with purported conspiracies discovered elsewhere in previous decades when slaves said they would, for example, "set the magazine afire and in the confusion kill the white people."[8] In Williamsburg, at least one resident found Dunmore's concern credible and reported to a correspondent "some disturbances in the City, by the Slaves."[9]

Immediately after the confrontation over the removal of gunpowder in Williamsburg, Governor Dunmore played on those fears and tried to manipulate them to keep revolutionaries from making an attempt against his government. He sent a back-channel message through William Pasteur, a medical doctor who was attending a patient at the royal palace, that if patriots assaulted any high-level officials, "he would declare Freedom to the Slaves, and reduce the City of Williamsburg to Ashes." He also predicted that if he "se[t] up the Royal Standard, . . . he should have a Majority of white People and all the Slaves on the side of Government," with whom he would "depopulate the whole Country" of its patriot population. On the following day, Dunmore imprudently reiterated his threat and said that if armed militiamen marched near Williamsburg, "he would immediately enlarge his plan, and carry it into Execution" using "two hundred Muskets loaded in the Palace."[10] Dunmore's posturing played on ideas about the roles of agitators in insurrections that had been developing for a century, giving it potency, but colonists in Virginia received it with greater alarm than perhaps he anticipated. Some inhabitants of Williamsburg "sent their

Wives and Children into the Country." In the countryside, not everyone believed the news, but it became a rallying cry for those who did. In Louisa County, on the frontier, the threat "greatly inflamed the Minds of those who believed it." Settlers in other counties said that the prospect "was not generally believed, but as far as it gained Credit, it tended greatly to inflame the People." Newspapers throughout the colonies soon ensured widespread knowledge of the powder's seizure, the revolutionaries' complaint, and the governor's self-defense.[11]

Dunmore's threats to incite insurrection exacerbated the concerns of colonists along the James River who already believed that they had just detected conspiracies in Chesterfield and Surry Counties. One person observed that the already existing "alarm concerning the Slaves . . . was greatly increased" by the governor's threat.[12] Within days the white colonists of Norfolk suspected "the Negroes [of] having formed a new conspiracy," and town authorities ordered the execution of two "principals" for "conspiracy to raise an insurrection."[13] One of the suspects was Emanuel de Antonio, who claimed unsuccessfully to be a free subject of Spain, and whose time in Spanish America Virginians found perhaps as threatening as New Yorkers had in the conspiracy scare of 1741.[14] Enough colonists decided that the risk was real, prompting one correspondent to report that "the planters are distressed beyond measure" about the growing possibility of insurrection, which was made even more probable as trade restrictions worsened the living conditions for enslaved people who were "almost naked" and might make "desperate attempts." All of these conspiracy scares—the "insurrections having been attempted at different places"—and Dunmore's threats together brought Virginia's colonists to the costly decision of increasing their policing presence. A resident of Yorktown reported that "a strict patrole is kept every night" to arrest any enslaved people who attempted to visit each other, and "the like cautions are observed in other towns."[15]

In the summer of 1775, revolutionaries' newspapers linked loyalists and ministry officials to new conspiracies that continued to be discovered. An essayist in the *Virginia Gazette* reflected this tendency later in an open letter of explanation to the people of England: all of these "various reports," he wrote, amounted to a combined "threatened insurrection." "Whether this was general" throughout the colony, he wrote, "or who were the instigators, remains as yet secret," but he guessed that an officer of a naval vessel stationed on the James River had probably attempted to coordinate this failed uprising.[16] Based on these rumors and investigations, historians Woody Holton and Michael McDonnell argue that enslaved blacks formed actual plans to rise in April, thereby "ma[king] the first bid for independence" and forcing confrontation between Dunmore and the patriots.[17] But it would be more accurate to say that colonists' *fear* of slave rebellion, more than anything else, informed the political moment. Revolutionaries and loyalists both maneuvered politically by referring to a shared assumption that white colonists feared slave rebellion; partisans on both sides understood the potency of fears of rebellion and commanded fluency in the language of how slaves formed conspiracies and rebelled. Aspiring rulers seized on these fears and events, regardless of enslaved people's actual intentions, and played on assumptions of outside agitation.

With the bloodshed at Lexington in April 1775, and the formation of the Continental Army in June, the Continental Congress was at war with Britain and the southern colonies risked invasion. White colonists' fear of Dunmore's ability to instigate insurrection was growing, and it began inspiring them to participate with their communities in military bodies. Virginians formed thirty-two new volunteer companies, in whole or in part as a response to Dunmore's threat to raise a slave rebellion. The slaveholding residents of Chesterfield County "were greatly alarmed and exasperated at the Governor's Declaration," and they reported that they now practiced "uncommon diligence . . . in training the independent Company and the Militia to Arms."[18] Along with people of Chesterfield County, residents in Hanover County explained their formation of a company as a necessary response "his threatening to enfranchise the slaves." Albemarle County's company voted to march on Williamsburg "to demand satisfaction of Dunmore for the powder, and his threatening to fix his standard and call over the Negroes." When the Virginia Convention met in July and August 1775, at the same time that the Southampton County Court tried two enslaved men "on suspicion of a conspiracy," the delegates organized the colony into military districts to support a regular force of professional soldiers. If the royal government could no longer keep the peace and assure domestic tranquility, the Virginia Convention saw its opportunity to attempt to do so itself.[19]

As colonist Benjamin Waller explained to the governor at a chance encounter, Dunmore "had lost the Confidence of the People not so much for having taken the Powder as for the declaration he made of raising and freeing the Slaves" in April.[20] Dunmore made only more trouble for himself when he tried to assure revolutionaries, again and again, that he would "not carry these plans into execution unless he was attacked"—implicitly admitting each time that he was capable of enacting such a plan. In repeatedly defending his original words against patriots' misrepresentations, he only fanned the flames of fear. By midsummer, the rumors surrounding Dunmore had taken on more classic elements of slave conspiracy. A Maryland clergyman cited Dunmore's indiscretions as proof of the British Ministry's intention to unleash against the colonists the familiar multipronged threat of Indians, foreign Catholics, and enslaved Africans and African Americans. He wrote that "The ministerial agents are endeavouring to rouse the Indians against us, . . . using every method to embody the Canadians to fall upon us, . . . [and forcing] His Majesty's conquered Roman Catholick vassals to cut the throats of his natural-born Protestant subjects." With these Indian, Canadian (Francophone), and Catholic threats, he added, "To complete the horrid scene," Dunmore and his officers held "nightly meetings" with slaves to "entic[e] them to cut their masters' throats while they are asleep."[21] In fact they were not entirely wrong: as the American conflict grew, impatient members of the political and military establishment in London contemplated implementing the very strategy that colonists feared most. One suggested that General Sir Henry Clinton "bring them upon their knees" by orchestrating "a Revolt of the Virginian Slaves, the Indians in Force upon their Backs, & a large Diversion from the Side of Canada."[22] For his part, Governor Dunmore did not begin with the intention of introducing such inflammatory maneuvers. He expressed exasperation that his threats "stirred up fears in [whites] which cannot easily subside as they know how vulnerable they are in that particular."[23] In mishandling the issue of slave rebellion, he alienated himself from Virginians. Only later did Dunmore reluctantly issue a proclamation welcoming those of revolutionary masters, after enslaved people began assembling at his standard because they decided that these rumors presented a possible path toward autonomy.[24] In North Carolina and South Carolina the governors did not make such clumsy threats, but revolutionaries' movements there also galvanized around the threat of rebellion when they discovered apparent conspiracies and attributed them to loyalists and British officials.

South Carolina

The revolutionary committees of Charleston appointed themselves as the protectors of the white people by terrorizing vulnerable black people with

militarized policing that introduced additional possibilities for new violence. The familiar problem of insurrection took on new urgency in
May 1775 when a rumor came from London that the British Ministry was
considering a plan to "encourage our Slaves to act against us!"[25] The
suggestion—a false one at this point—disturbed white settlers who were
sensitive that Carolina was "a weak Colony from the Number of Negroes
we have amongst us." Enslaved people made up more than 50 percent of
Charleston's eleven-thousand-person population, and as much as 80 to 90
percent in the rice growing districts.[26] This weakness, a revolutionary leader
theorized, "therefore exposed [us] to . . . formid[able] ministerial Tricks"
in the form of a coordinated invasion by a foreign European power, in this
case the imperial adminstration and its Indian allies.[27]

The Provincial Congress, a self-appointed representative body for the
colony, established a special five-member committee to police any anticipated slave insurrection, as well as a thirteen-member Committee of Safety.
Revolutionaries tried to demonstrate that the king's agents could no longer
safeguard white colonial subjects.[28] The militia, which had been mustering
aimlessly since the outbreak of war in April, now oriented itself vigorously
against a concrete threat. "Massacres and Instigated Insurrections," a loyalist wryly recalled, "were Words in the mouth of every Child." The threat of
some kind of uprising was familiar and exercising. Under the leadership of
revolutionary committees, the town's militia mobilized against the enemy
within by performing nightly patrol duties in numbers estimated at "100
men every evening," surely reminding enslaved Charlestonians of past
trauma experienced in the same public spaces.[29]

In May 1775, revolutionary leaders used "this Bugbear of instigated
insurrections," as one loyalist put it, to draw the white population into
political participation in two ways.[30] One was through participating in martial displays. This militarized civic duty drew on a long tradition of white
men mobilizing in conspiracy scares to defend lives and properties, to perform community, and to support the slaveholding regime. Even though
many of Charleston's white inhabitants were still ambivalent about contra-
dicting the king's government, they could at least rally together against the
familiar and immediate threat of slave rebellion.[31]

This force, in turn, could "intimidate" the rest of Charleston's white
inhabitants and "terrif[y] the weak," as two loyalists characterized it, into a
second form of civic participation: signing a new association agreement
proffered by the Provincial Congress. Previous subscription lists often were

vows of nonimportation or nonconsumption in protest of imperial policies. The Association of 1775 centered on "the dread of instigated Insurrections in the Colonies" and secured its subscribers' promises to "unite . . . as a band in . . . defence against every foe."[32] Loyalist critics noted the political symbiosis between the association and the alleged insurrectionary threat: the militia musters and the language in the association agreement conjured the very fears that they were meant to answer. A former colonial official remarked that the revolutionaries adroitly manipulated the "fears of the [white] People" by convincing them that "His Majesty's Ministers . . . instigated their Slaves to rebel against their Masters and to cut their throats."[33] The new provincial government increasingly staked its claim for legitimacy on its ability to protect colonists from rebel enslaved people, Indians, and their alleged ministerial coordinators.

In the estimation of white Carolinians, the slave threat depended on coordinated invasion by another enemy. Revolutionaries whispered that the chief British official for Indian diplomacy, John Stuart, was rumored to have "tampered with the Indians" to instigate them to attack the white colonists of the Carolinas and Georgia.[34] A posse's attempt to arrest Stuart for coordinating "Horrid Cruel Schemes" of "insurrection from our Slaves & Invasions from our Neighbors" drove him to the safety of St. Augustine, now a loyalist stronghold in British hands.[35] His flight was taken as confirmation of his guilt, and his absence left him powerless to defend against the "falshoods . . . industriously propogated in order to inflame the People against me" and the British Ministry. William Campbell, the royal governor of South Carolina, had to admit that this specter was "well calculated to alarm & terrify."[36] Revolutionaries aimed their quills at Campbell and Stuart by publishing accusations that they plotted "to set the Indians on us."[37]

After white people's inchoate fear of insurrection developed, the General Committee believed it discovered a conspiracy in the middle of June 1775, enabling it to signal its new role safeguarding colonists by terrorizing the enslaved population. The committee interrogated two loyalist residents, identified as Catholics, about possibly "exciting an insurrection."[38] Within the week, the committee learned from an enslaver that he overheard two people whom he enslaved discussing a plot "to destroy the white people, and take both town and country." To form a convoluted plot would have been an enormous risk for enslaved people. It was far more likely that they observed the militia displays and then "naturally conversed amongst themselves on the reasons for it," as Governor Campbell astutely perceived. When "one of those conversations was . . . overheard," he suggested, the committee arrested the participants and "easily induced [them] to accuse themselves & others to escape punishment," as so many powerless people before them had done. One critic of the investigation postulated that some suspects agreed to turn informant because they believed that whipping was "the only punishment" that would befall whomever they accused. Perhaps some did. The governor pointed out, however, that the most powerful inducement was terror: they were "terrified at the recollection of former cruelties" against suspects who did not satisfy judges with an abundance of information. Indeed, the investigating committee "repeatedly told" them that confessing "was the only chance they had for life."[39] Consequently, the informants declared that they knew about plans for an uprising in coordination with the king's troops: when the soldiers arrived, the slaves would "set the town on fire, and fall on the inhabitants," "burning the Town, &c.," in an insurrection that was supposed to be "general throughout the province."[40]

These enslaved informants came under a great deal of pressure in captivity to name new suspects and they had limited paths to survival. The committee, expecting a loyalist agitator, encouraged them to "mention names" of white people "let their Rank or station be what it would."[41] It ultimately arrested several enslaved black people and "two or three White people."[42] After the committee examined everyone, it decided that it had "Strong . . . Evidence" against two people, one white, one black.[43] The alleged white financier and supplier of arms was "one Bishop, a Dutchman, [who] was to have been their leader," and whose fate went unrecorded.[44] The alleged black leader was Thomas Jeremiah, perhaps the wealthiest man of African descent in colonial North America, holding £1,000 in property, including several people whom he held in bondage to work on his fishing vessel. He served as a firefighter and harbor pilot and reportedly held the respect of many white colonists. In other words, he had far too much to lose to involve himself in an uprising; as the governor put it, the "improbability" was overwhelming that "a fellow in such affluent circumstances, . . . possessed of slaves of his own, [would] ente[r] into so wild a scheme." Far more likely, and in keeping with the patterns of earlier conspiracy scares, is that his "thriving situation" may have made him a high-profile target for any enslaved informants looking to implicate a man whom they knew by reputation only. On top of that, some enslaved people may have resented his enslavement of others, material wealth, and straddling of white and black communities. White people may have found little reason to protect him because he tested racial boundaries. Henry Laurens, a chief enslaver and a leading revolutionary, scoffed that Jeremiah was "puffed up by prosperity, ruined by Luxury & . . . grown to an amazing pitch of vanity & ambition."[45]

Thousands of enslaved people in town faced increasing terror as the Committee of Safety mobilized white colonists in renewed patrols against the threat that they perceived in the people whom they exploited.[46] Partisans celebrated white participants' patriotic spirit as they swelled the ranks of the militia, without concern that that this near unanimity was achieved by stoking racial fear. "Even the boys," they marveled, "form themselves into companies."[47] A resident surveyed this military mobilization and described the town as a place that looked more like a "garrison town than a mart for trade," which would have made merchants and politicians of an earlier generation shudder, but which made eminent sense in a revolutionary moment that emerged by way of boycotts and self-appointed governing committees.[48] Within two weeks, this militarization of Charleston life temporarily restored white residents' confidence in their control and security. Laurens announced that "I am sure we have nothing to fear," now that the militia shifted the burden of fear onto black people's bodies and psyches.[49]

Thomas Jeremiah and other black Charlestonians faced greater danger as the General Committee compelled enslaved people to turn informant before this frightening militarized backdrop. One witness recounted Jeremiah's assessment that "a great War is coming soon"—he wasn't wrong—and his hope that perhaps "the War was come to help the Poor Negroes." Just as Governor Campbell surmised, black people seemed to be discussing the news that was also on white people's minds that summer.[50] The committee waited two months to try him in hopes that "more evidence" of other conspirators would come to light. The most damning evidence against Jeremiah in the eyes of his judges—that he wanted guns and boasted that he would "have the Chief Command of the . . . Negroes"—came from his brother-in-law, Jemmy, who made the harrowing decision to prioritize his own survival. Strangely, Jeremiah "positively denied" knowing his brother-in-law at first, perhaps in a panic. Jemmy gave evidence against Jeremiah in exchange for a pardon.[51]

In early July, enslaved people just south of Charleston, in St. Bartholomew's Parish, contended with another conspiracy scare that revolutionaries

enabled with their drumbeat of warnings for white people and encouragement of violence against black people. The local Committee of Safety
arrested several people for planning "a General Insurrection." Facing the
certainty of pain or death, some of them attempted to save themselves by
implicating a Scottish preacher, John Burnet, whose itinerancy already
made him suspicious to some authorities. They accused him of convening
illegal assemblies in the woods at which they planned "to take the Country
by Killing [all] the Whites" except him. They said that he taught them that
in the past George II had ignored a divine book that ordered him to eman-
cipate them, and so was sent to hell, but that George III would enact God's
will and "set the Negroes Free." This message would have held strong
appeal to the enslaved. Burnet admitted that he ministered to "those poor
ignorant Creatures," but he denied saying anything like that. He did not
need to; such rumors already circulated regularly among enslaved people.
Burnet was banished from the area, protected from greater punishment by
his whiteness in a way that Thomas Jeremiah, although free, was not when
defending himself against a similar charge. The enslaved people who
accused Burnet of leading them, on the other hand, suffered physical punishment. The alleged ringleaders were sent to the gallows. The informants'
terror-induced allegations ended up costing people their lives and spreading the terror more widely among enslaved people, all coordinated by white
people as a way to manage their feelings of vulnerability to "horrible butch-
eries of Innocent Women & Children."[52]

In Charleston, under a dubious interpretation of existing law, a court
of two justices of the peace and five freeholders used the testimony of
enslaved people to convict Thomas Jeremiah on August 11.[53] Jemmy, Jeremiah's brother-in-law, introduced more doubt to the legality of hanging
Jeremiah when he retracted his testimony after the sentencing. He "volun-
tarily declared his perfect innocence." His vacillation is understandable
given the terrible choices he faced.[54] The revolutionary committee did not
consider this a material change in the case against Jeremiah and prepared
to put him to death. When Governor Campbell made noises about inter-
vening to save his life, Charlestonians took it as another sign of the British
Ministry's involvement in the conspiracy. Campbell refrained from stepping in because it was clear to him that he had lost control of this particular
judicial realm, predicting that if he lifted a finger "they would hang [Jere-
miah] at my door," in a demonstration of the new legal order.[55] Laurens
agreed that white people would have become "enraged" in the event of a

pardon and would have done things that "fill me with horror."[56] Jeremiah was hanged and burned on August 18. The execution completed white Charleston's cycle of anxiety and release around the possibility of slave insurrection—a correspondent confirmed that "our Negroes are quite quiet since the execution"—and the process had transformed the politics of the city.[57]

Throughout the summer, the revolutionary committees enflamed white people's fears and heightened black people's experiences of terror, all of which they then capitalized on by identifying themselves—in extralegal committees—as a force for stability and keeping the peace. Governor Campbell dryly noted that more than civic duty must have inspired their zeal because there was no evidence, beyond retracted hearsay, of the conspiracy that "they pretended to fear." But Campbell recognized the role of the white populace's awakened fear, commenting that the conspiracy scare "raised such a Clamor amongst the people as is incredible." Revolutionary voices in the South Carolina assembly took advantage of this pressure from below, shrugging that it was "not in our power to prescribe limits to Popular Fury." They harnessed the various forms of fear that they stoked toward directing the discovery of a familiar-looking conspiracy.[58]

If state authorities considered public executions to be political theater, in revolutionary Charleston the long performance began months earlier than the killing of Thomas Jeremiah, and it relied heavily on audience participation. This theater of governance enveloped Charleston when it demanded many white men's participation as performers by mustering them for slave patrols. They joined in on the basis of racial fear rather than partisan sympathies, but the revolutionary committees encouraged them to transform whiteness into patriotism by emphasizing the possibility that the loyalist agitators had organized a slave conspiracy. Their findings rhymed with decades of experience in thinking about the roles of cunning outsiders in purported plots, and it led to a politically useful conclusion.[59] The resulting popular mobilization proved astoundingly successful by the time of Jeremiah's execution, when a resident observed that "Every thing here is suspended but warlike preparations. It is said that there are scarce two hundred men in town not enrolled. The country is unanimous."[60] Troops of white men in the streets of Charleston were the performers of act one of this drama. The execution of Thomas Jeremiah in act two appeared to confirm to other white people their heroic status, prompting Henry Laurens to reveal more than he knew by crying out, "The Scene is closed!

Justice is satisfied!"[61] Revolutionaries appeared to have delivered their promise to keep the public peace. This argument paid off ten days after the execution, when Charleston elected its representatives for the next Provincial Congress of South Carolina.[62]

Simultaneous to the sentencing and execution of Jeremiah, revolutionaries also aggressively intimidated the town's remaining loyalist population. On August 12, a crowd seized a gunner who served at the fort and tarred and feathered him "ten or twelve" times over five hours. "The populace of this Town," Laurens regretted, "acted upon the whole like an ungovernable Mob." They wheeled him through the streets of town in a "circumcartation," and they paused at the houses of several of the leading loyalists to perform the ritual punishment. At the end of August, revolutionaries delivered an "absolute order" to disarm. By September, they banished leading loyalists who refused to sign the association agreement. Governor Campbell withdrew, too, for his own safety. After a month of violence and intimidation, all facilitated by concrete fears of slave rebellion, revolutionaries had consolidated their hold on governing Charleston. Only by "discovering" a slave conspiracy—a threat from below, instigated by a loyalist threat from within, and compounded by British and Indian allies without—could they accomplish all of this so efficiently. The price was that they "now dipped their hands in blood," as Governor Campbell wrote, and violently racialized the Revolution.[63]

North Carolina

In North Carolina, fear of insurrection grew in late June and early July 1775 in Wilmington and its neighboring counties with large black populations. Despite a popular outcry, Royal Governor Josiah Martin declined to investigate the rumors because he believed they were calculated by revolutionaries to unsettle the population. He may have been correct. The colony's delegation to the Continental Congress in Philadelphia wrote home in June 1775 with a warning that the British were ready "to raise the hand of the servant against the master" and to unleash Indians and Catholics from the vast new province of Quebec on North Carolina's frontiers.[64] They also misrepresented a British proclamation. The false version supposedly "promis[ed] every Negro that would murder his Master and family that he should have his Master's plantation," using the familiar and plausible scenario of instigated insurrection to forge a more useful fiction. In reality the actual proclamation promised clemency for the wayward colonists.[65]

These were potent rumors in North Carolina. Governor Martin recognized that enslavers in the southern colonies were "very sensible of their weakness" with regard to the number of potentially rebellious enslaved blacks, a perspective enhanced by his relation as nephew to one of the investigating judges in Antigua's conspiracy scare of 1736. He worried that the persistent rumors in North Carolina were all too believable that he "had formed a design of Arming the Negroes . . . and proclaiming freedom to all such as should resort to the King's Standard." These "false reports," he noticed by the middle of July, "operate most fatally upon the people here."[66] But Martin inadvertently breathed life into these rumors, as Dunmore did in Virginia, when his denial included a proviso that he would use slaves against their enslavers only in the unlikely case of "the failure of all other means to maintain the King's Government." This afterthought in a letter to another imperial officer was his undoing. When a Committee of Safety intercepted that letter, it seized on his admission that he considered inciting insurrection to be plausible policy, and it published an "alarm to the people" that Martin was considering "a crime of so horrid and truly black a complexion."[67] Henry Laurens, hearing in South Carolina about this new evidence of ministerial misconduct, wrote to his son that yet another royal governor contemplated the "expediency of exciting the Negroes to butcher their Masters" in the event of the revolutionaries' political rebellion.[68]

North Carolina's revolutionaries capitalized on Governor Martin's implied threat. They believed that they were on the best constitutional ground, as did their counterparts in South Carolina, when they could demonstrate that a monarch and his direct representatives failed to protect his subjects. With the governor possibly plotting with slaves against the public peace, Joseph Hewes, a representative to the Continental Congress, asserted that the "powers of Government must soon be superseded and taken into the hands of the People." Governor Martin responded in a published defense that *he* was the public officer working "for the maintenance of peace and good order throughout the province," but he watched with dismay as his colony's Committees of Safety used what he regarded as "pretended apprehensions" to get inhabitants to sign papers promising they would defend the colony and "array themselves in companies" as a military body prepared for "any violence."[69] Two new militia companies formed in Wilmington through the compulsory service of every arms-bearing white person, and new slave patrols for "disarming & keeping the negroes in order" signaled to white and black residents that something was afoot.[70]

A conspiracy scare in North Carolina in July 1775 occasioned the peak of community military mobilization, as similar circumstances did in Virginia and South Carolina. When two enslaved men in Beaufort County revealed "an intended insurrection of the negroes against the whole people" to be ignited "that night," the county's Committee of Safety alerted neighboring towns and counties.[71] Upon this alarm, the Pitt County Committee of Safety sent out at least one hundred men on patrol and arrested around forty accused conspirators by the end of the night. On the following day, a Sunday, the committee took responsibility for the investigation, performing a duty that once fell to the royal governor. It produced evidence from enslaved informants of an alleged "deep laid" conspiracy for "destroying the inhabitants of this province without respect of persons, age or sex," led by an instigator named "Capt —— Johnson," who sailed a brig based in "Whitehaven," and his liaison, an enslaved pilot based around Pimlico Sound. For the next week, the committee continued "taking up, examining and scouring more or less every day," finding what seemed to be evidence of a widespread plot.

Perhaps too quick to see what they wanted, and unaware of how suspects shared rumors in jail and took cues from their questioners, the committee members marveled that "from whichever part of the County they come they all confess nearly the same thing." According to the committee's report, informants warned that "one and all" enslaved persons would massacre their masters' families and burn their houses in the dead of night, and then march into the backcountry to meet "a number of Persons there appointed and armed by Government." After the planned insurrection, the committee reported, the British Ministry would reward rebel slaves with "a free government of their own" and would compensate the chief instigator, Johnson, with his "choice of the Plantations upon this River." The Committee of Safety demonstrated its vigilance to white North Carolinians by punishing the conspirators "in presence of the Committee and a great number of spectators." Although the committee claimed authority to exercise justice, it did so with whipping rather than execution, to avoid alienating enslavers with the financial loss of people they claimed to own. This was traumatic in itself for the victims and terrorizing for people in the area.

We cannot know the extent to which enslaved North Carolinians actually conspired or truly intended to rebel, but we do know that revolutionary leaders took advantage of the most exaggerated findings to claim judicial authority and to appear to keep the colonists in peace and security. Janet

Schaw, a traveler with loyalist sympathies, assessed this conspiracy scare as a "farce" by revolutionaries whose "sinister purpose" was to whip up support. She confidently attributed her "sleepless night" more to "the musquetoes . . . than my fears of the Negroes." She found her skepticism shared by the captain of a patrol, who confided in her that he believed this was all "a trick intended in the first place to inflame the minds of the populace, and in the next place to get those who had not before taken up arms to do it now and form an association for the safety of the town."[72]

The conspiracy scare mobilized many white North Carolinians to arms under the auspices of the Committee of Safety. Schaw recorded in her diary that "every man is in arms and the patroles going thro' all the town, and searching every Negro's house, to see they are all at home by nine at night."[73] A week after North Carolina's conspiracy scare, the revolutionary movement pinned the threat to public peace directly on Governor Martin and John Collet, a senior military commander at Fort Johnston. Relying on accusations of "exciting . . . insurrection," revolutionaries mobilized "a great many Volunteers" from neighboring counties, numbering at least five hundred, to assault Fort Johnston, recover fugitive slaves who were harbored there, burn its buildings, and demolish part of the fortification.[74] In August, the Committees of Safety leveraged their new authority by sending armed revolutionaries to drum loyalists out of the community. James Cotton, a loyalist and a justice of the peace, later described how an armed company dragged him from his bedchamber and berated him for supporting a royal government that was guilty of organizing a slave uprising. When one of the men whom he enslaved tried to flee the scene, a member of the company trained his weapon on him out of concern that he would warn the neighborhood. "Now you see Gentlemen," the captain remarked as he turned to his company, "Governor Martin and his damned officers will set the Negroes on to kill us." Any hint of black criminality was woven into the allegations of ministerial instigation.[75] Schaw observed that "all parties are now united against the common enemies," extending to royal government and loyalist neighbors. "Every mouth male and female," she wrote, "is opened against Britain."[76]

Revolutionaries successfully mobilized many North Carolinians because they painted a picture of slave conspiracy that emphasized two familiar elements—outside instigation and a coordinated invasion by foreign armies. The British Ministry's increasingly popish-seeming attempts at firmer administration of the American colonies enabled revolutionaries to complete a familiar picture of organizing traditional bogeymen—Indians and French Catholic settlers—to invade in conjunction with an uprising. A North Carolinian loyalist refugee later deposed that a representative of the Committee of Safety called Lord North, Prime Minister of Great Britain, "a Roman Catholick" and cited the Quebec Act (1774) as evidence that he intended to "establish Popery on all the Continent of America."[77] By the end of July, John Stuart, the British agent for Indian affairs in the region, reported with dismay that the patriots' plan for mobilizing the general populace had been successful: because "nothing can be more alarming to the Carolinas than the Idea of an attack from Indians and Negroes, the Leaders of the [patriots] easily carried into execution their plan of arming the People."[78]

The revolutionary message, put simply, was that they preserved the public peace. They cast the governor and his officers as agents of disruption and disorder, claiming that officials of the British Ministry were trying to threaten the populace into submission and political slavery. In June 1776, James Iredell wrote a long manuscript essay on the imperial crisis in North Carolina. He proudly declared that he had not been "intimidated" by the ministry's "diabolical [plan] of exciting our own Domestics . . . to cut our throats, and involve Men, Women, and Children in one universal Massacre." He maintained that his concern about insurrection did not reduce him to submission but rather inspired him to action. "Resentment for such cruel usage," he affirmed, "added spurs to our Patriotism." The instigated insurrection—or at least his fear of it—was what "initiated our Minds, and compelled us to renounce you, [the king.]"[79]

Jamaica

In the British West Indies, by comparison, enslaved people's terror-induced contributions to conspiracy scares facilitated white people's dependence on empire rather than dreams of independence. When the Revolutionary War came to the Caribbean, major conspiracy scares predictably followed. Indeed, actual insurrections were occurring in the frontier regions of the southeastern Caribbean, spurring the vigilance of enslavers in older colonies to look for slave conspiracies. Jamaica's occurred in July and August 1776, when the Continental Congress's assertion of independence confirmed and worsened the political crisis in the American empire. The escalating war demanded redeployment of the soldiers who usually garrisoned the islands away to the northern theater. "Without this strength we are very insecure," an enslaver complained. "How impolitic then to take from us the very few soldiers we had!"[80] Jamaicans "Look'd with uneasy and jealous dread," another confided, "on every addition of Naval or Military strength on the Neighbouring Islands of France or Spain." Indeed, when France later entered the war its amphibious assaults made inroads into the British Caribbean (fig. 17).[81] In the struggle to survive, enslaved people's position was already precarious. It was made more unsteady in 1776 with unusually dry weather that left "the very face of the Country . . . Burnt off," as an overseer put it. The drought wiped out enslaved people's efforts to plant their own food. "God knows," he sighed, "what will be the Consequence" of this "great Scarcity." Another enslaver joined him in observing that the "dry weather has brought on a scarcity of Provisions" that only worsened enslaved people's conditions. The Revolutionary War compounded this problem. Business between merchants of the regions slowed under the Prohibitory Act of 1776, and North American privateers threatened other supplies that entered the British West Indies. A plantation overseer repeatedly expressed consternation that he was "Cut off from supplies usually sent from North America," leaving enslavers with "no Market to fly to in Case of necessity" to feed Jamaica's enslaved population.[82]

Under these circumstances, West Indian colonists considered past experiences and calculated that they were at considerable risk of rebellion. A conspiracy was discovered on a plantation in the northwestern Jamaica parish of Hanover in 1776. White enslavers' concern began developing in late June, when parochial magistrates tried to manage a swirl of rumors by arresting enslaved people. They decided at first that this was not so much a conspiracy as it was "crudely formed" idle talk. Accordingly, the colony's governor and council thought it perfectly safe to send away the regiment of regulars, as planned, for the war effort on the North American mainland.[83] However, an unidentified elderly enslaved driver reignited the parish's fear two weeks later when he reported "very serious conversations" among a group of enslaved people who "put a sudden stop to their business" when he approached. From their perspective, regardless of what they were discussing, distrust of him was a natural and understandable impulse. The enslaving regime criminalized many strategies for survival and acts of self-claiming, large and small, and it incentivized enslaved people to surveil each other. What's more, as a gang driver, he wielded a whip to torture them on behalf of their enslaver. He informed his overseer that there

Figure 17. When France entered the American Revolution to assist the United States, white colonists of the British Caribbean recognized their sudden vulnerability to amphibious invasions such as that of Grenada shown here. Roger Fils, *Prise de l'isle de la Grenade* [. . .], Paris, 1782. Courtesy of the John Carter Brown Library at Brown University.

seemed "something not right amongst the Negroes." When the overseer began arming himself, he came under the impression that the charges in his pistols had been replaced with dust, and the powder with black sand. Perhaps enslaved people planned some kind of personal violence against him or his family, but little evidence exists that they intended the extensive slave conspiracy to which informers later confessed.[84]

As with other conspiracy scares, white people's coercive questioning of enslaved people shaped the early discoveries. According to a letter written soon after, the overseer "interrogated" his own personal servant and observed in his behavior that he "show'd a guiltiness by shifting the Enquery" to another man. The enslaver, Edward Chambers, happened to be a parish magistrate and invited neighboring enslavers for what was probably intended to be an inquiry or trial. When an enslaved attendant brought the guests wine and punch, he spilled the bowl and revealed what Chambers took to be "a Quantity of Arsnic which he had mix'd with the cup." Whatever was in the bowl may have been a form of poison—in the African sense of a magical charm, or a pharmacological substance—but it was almost certainly not arsenic, which would have dissolved on contact. The enslavers located the man's source vial and connected these dots to form familiar and eminently warranted suspicions of an insurrectionary conspiracy.[85]

In the production of knowledge about the vial and its uses, the gentlemen now wielded extraordinary power over the poisoner. They knew he "had nothing to hope for, but by clear confession," as a resident explained in his letter. On July 17, the unidentified prisoner told the gentlemen about a far-reaching insurrectionary plot so that he could earn reprieve for the poisoning attempt by preventing the greater purported crime. He explained that "he had combined with many hundreds from the Neighbouring Estates to effect a General Massacre of Whites throughout the Island."[86] On July 19, another man, Coromantee Sam, added sweeping statements that engaged directly with the conventional expectations of white colonists. He spoke of "put[ting] to death all the White people they could" and elaborated that the conspirators were organized as "Captains and Officers, each to Act in their separate districts." Each diasporic African ethnic group, Coromantee, Igbo, and Creole, had plans to install a king of its own after the insurrection, and he claimed to be king of the Coromantees. In addition to these conventional elements of slave conspiracies, he also named thirty-eight coconspirators from distant labor camps across most of the parish. In short, he furnished information that both reflected conventional conspiracies and suggested wide geographic involvement around the parish of Hanover.[87]

During these revelations by terrified black informants, Simon Clarke wrote a letter that dripped with white people's feelings of vulnerability and visions of their own victimhood. Clarke resided in Hanover's port town of Lucea, where the trials now commenced, and he owned several labor camps around the parish. The weight of family history informed his experience; his late father had been a member of the council and had alerted the island about a threatened conspiracy in 1744. "Last night we had no less than three alarms," the younger Clarke now wrote. In the darkness he had listened with anguish to the "cries and squawling" of the "Women and Children, who resort here from every quarter, as the only place of safety." It is difficult to know whether they were comforted or provoked by "the sound of Trumpets, and drums beating to arms" in the night. When the sun rose the next morning, the fears of the preceding hours did not dissipate.[88]

Enslaved people experienced this terror both night and day. The person whom Clarke enslaved as a cook was arrested "while he was dressing dinner." The man was "tried, condemned, and executed the day after," suggesting the disorienting suddenness with which these events could change the lives of enslaved people. In fact, Clarke interjected into his own letter that, "since writing the above, fresh discoveries [have been] made" in the fast-moving investigation. The enslaved people in his household learned that at least twenty or thirty more people had just been arrested, each threatening to ensnare them. Clarke ignored how this news and the cook's jarring exit traumatized the other people whom he enslaved. He chose instead to dwell on his own surprise that someone he trusted implicitly was a conspirator. Danger to him, he believed, dwelled within his home, unseen even in plain daylight. He did not perceive, or did not care, that danger to enslaved people was pervasive.

Clarke learned also that the details of the plot matched the general expectations learned from conspiracy scares past. Allegedly, plotters kept a secret weapons cache. The place was searched, "but the Guns and Ammunition were removed"—and absence became evidence. They appeared to organize themselves with officer titles, such as "Captains and Lieutenants." They seemed to recruit mostly gang drivers and skilled tradesmen, whom enslavers generally trusted. An overseer from the other end of the island heard similar reports and marveled that most of the accused conspirators were creoles "who were never known before to have been concerned in any thing of this sort." It appeared that their outward obedience had been only a mask.[89]

Governor Basil Keith, as the primary representative of the king, attempted to assuage white colonists' fears by using the power of the state to strike fear into enslaved people. He ordered a man-of-war to anchor at Lucea, fly the Union Jack, and "fire Morning and Evening Guns." He and the colony's council, also royally appointed, remained apprised of the situation through almost two dozen "expresses" that parochial magistrates and military officers sent across the island to Spanish Town. The confession of Coromantee Sam proved decisive for Governor Keith when he received it on July 23. He decided within "half an hour after it came to my hand" to declare martial law and to embargo ships from leaving, so as to keep up the number of white people, despite the burden to residents and merchants.[90] Thus the governor involved local colonists in securing the island, as revolutionaries were doing in the Lower South, by declaring martial law and forcing free white men to patrol.[91] An overseer wrote from the countryside near Kingston that "we are all in arms, on account of a Conspiracy" and he hoped that the exercises of militiamen during martial law would "sho[w] such a Damp" that enslaved people would not attempt any "machinations" for the foreseeable future.[92] The governor and council reached these decisions as they monitored the situation on paper, from afar, but with the keen interest and active involvement that Jamaican colonists expected from the royal government.[93]

Two revelations encouraged white subjects in Jamaica to embrace the king's protection. One was the political arithmetic of conspiracy. George Spence, the senior magistrate in Hanover Parish, offered a thought experiment to help "perceive more clearly the latent and the Degree of Danger attending this Conspiracy." He estimated with false precision—feeding a need for an illusion of certainty during chaos—that 8,618 potential insurgents were involved in the conspiracy. He arrived at this figure by cross-referencing the parish tithable records against the list of estates containing at least one accused conspirator, based on the obviously extreme assumption that each conspirator could garner the support of everyone at his home plantation. Spence observed that this initial estimate numbered almost half of the parish's enslaved population, and he added that it was easy to imagine that the number would grow when neighboring estates decided to join in the heat of the moment. Although he already risked overselling the threat, he also pointed out that the rebellious estates formed "an uninterrupted line or Chain" from one end of the parish to the other, enabling them to revolt "decisively, . . . jointly and uniformly." In reality, the formidable-looking map reflected the associational networks that formed at night and on Sundays in neighborhoods of contiguous estates. Unaware that the chain of accusations was actually a chain of acquaintanceship, Spence used this arithmetic reasoning to advocate for stronger imperial measures, particularly the continuation of an embargo that was unpopular with the merchant community. The phantasm of solid blocs of people of African descent tipped political calculations toward allowing the royal governor and the imperial state greater powers.[94]

Dependence on the British professional army and the Royal Navy became even more pronounced when it temporarily appeared that the Maroons, who were usually allies of the colonial state after 1739, perhaps had authored the conspiracy and recruited slaves. The perceived threat from Jamaica's mountainous frontier in the island's interior, particularly as allies of enslaved people, resembled concerns that mainland colonists harbored about Indians in the backcountry whom colonists sometimes accused of planning to coordinate frontier violence with enslaved peoples' domestic insurrection. An enslaved man named Pontack claimed that he "saw two of Cudjoe's Negroes [Maroons]," Billy and Asherry, at a supper on a neighboring plantation and—in yet another overheard fragment of conversation—"heard them recommend it to [their host] to make haste, take the Country themselves, and drive the white people entirely out of it." In addition to instigating the conspiracy, they allegedly promised to furnish arms and ammunition for the slaves of the region. Pontack also indicated that the two instigators acted as emissaries on behalf of the Maroons: he claimed to see Asherry "str[ike] the ground with great violence" and complain that he could not wait any longer for "the negroes of their Town [to do] what they said they would." Pontack explained that the Maroons planned to coordinate the uprising by "send[ing] down at a certain time (Pontack knows not when) to know if the Estates Negroes were ready."

White residents dreaded reopening hostilities with the Maroons. They remembered how Maroons, in their resistance against the colonial state, terrorized Jamaica's residents in the frontier of the island's interior just as much as American Indians did with their own "skulking way of war" in the Eastern Woodlands of North America.[95] Decades of the Maroons' military success resulted in forcing colonists to temporarily abandon several plantations. Since the peace of 1739, by which Maroons promised to assist in recapturing fugitive slaves and quelling rebellions, white Jamaicans harbored anxieties about whether these proven freedom fighters really would use their military prowess on behalf of the enslaving regime. In this way, too, Maroons were similar to the Indian powers of mainland North America who had even more latitude to shift their diplomatic posture with profound consequences. White settlers understood that their security depended on Maroon pacification, but they also lacked confidence in their ability to discern Maroon intentions. Governor Keith observed that if the Maroons were involved in the conspiracy they were "very capable of doing us the greatest Mischief: from their situation in the very heart of the Country, their manner of Life, and the very high Idea the Slaves entertain of them." Keith recommended that his correspondents read Edward Long's *History of Jamaica* to better understand this background.[96]

Pontack described the Maroons' conspiracy to be an odd formulation of the familiar arson plot. He said that the insurrection would begin when the Maroons led enslaved people away from their labor camps while the "white People [came] after them into the woods," not as an escape but as a gambit. As their white pursuers were busy bushwhacking, the Maroons and slaves would return to the plantation district to "burn all the cane-pieces of all the Estates, and during the general fire, whilst the white people were employed in extinguishing it, . . . instantly to repair to the Towns, break open the Stores, and houses, and from thence supply themselves plentifully." In the course of this examination, Pontack named forty more men as conspirators.[97] A day later, the informant Charles, enslaved at the same estate as Pontack, tentatively corroborated some of these revelations. General James Palmer went to the Maroon settlement of Trelawny Town to gauge the group's posture. He wrote to the governor that he was satisfied with the town's "fidelity" to the government.[98]

The Maroons were also cleared when Pontack abruptly recanted his confession in the heat of the trials, possibly knowing that this would throw the cases into disarray. The Hanover magistrates suddenly became "embarrassed in our trials." The judges now found themselves compelled to acquit several suspects "whom we are certain deserved capital Punishment." The judges decided that "after several proofs of [Pontack's] prevarication" they could not use him as a trial witness. Instead they relied on the informant Charles, because he had originally corroborated Pontack's accusations. Charles, whose evidence had never matched Pontack's in specificity, "gave so weak and equivocal an evidence that nothing was further proved . . .

[except] a few indiscreet expressions," which indeed is the most apt characterization of the snippets of conversation that touched off this entire conspiracy scare. With this abrupt reversal in the assessment of Pontack's character, the parochial magistrates no longer entertained their nightmare scenario of Maroon instigation.[99]

After convicting seventy-three enslaved men and terrorizing thousands more, Hanover's parochial magistrates and Jamaica's royal governor and council decided to end the investigation. The governor's speech to the assembly, which appeared in the newspaper for an audience of common white colonists, credited "the Admiral's ready assistance" and the "martial and active spirit" of the militia in shifting the onus of fear even more firmly onto enslaved people. He promised that the island could expect to be soon "re-inforced with . . . troops . . . for our protection." Edward East, an overseer, reported to his absentee employer that the royal government was to be commended for acting so swiftly to protect white subjects.[100] The imperial state had served one of its primary purposes in visibly protecting them, and they reaffirmed their decision to embrace imperial dependence. They took confidence in the imperial demonstrations of power in the deployment of soldiers, presence of naval vessels, compulsion of patrolling through martial law, and—not least—the spectacle of the trial and execution of suspected conspirators.

As local militias faltered, especially in the Caribbean where white men were relatively scarce, governors pointed to averted slave plots to convince the Board of Trade to send professional soldiers to garrison. Nathaniel Phillips wrote to his London creditors with news of the conspiracy scare. He suggested that greater involvement by the colonial state, and indeed His Majesty's forces, was necessary, offering his estimation that "2,000 soldiers distributed in different parts of the Island would always keep the Negroes in good order, and prevent their entering into such diabolical plots."[101] As historian Andrew O'Shaughnessy has demonstrated, by the time of the American Revolution, the colonies in the West Indies relied heavily on the British Empire's naval prowess and military might to stave off the coupled threat of invasion and insurrection. In the wake of averted insurrections, colonial governments often petitioned the monarch for improved garrisons.[102]

Yet while Jamaicans' concern about insurrection sprouted from a configuration of historical circumstances shared with the mainland—war and political turmoil—the absence of revolutionary committees in Jamaica left the enthusiastic royal government to investigate. The parochial magistrates pushed enslaved people to describe a familiar plot, and the government terrorized black people across the island with military displays. This built on a foundation of Jamaican politics that did not regard the relationship with Parliament with as much suspicion as mainlanders did.[103] The governor may have believed he had little choice because of white people's fears in the moment, but by embracing the investigation he solidified colonists' recognition of the value of royal rule. As a result, white Jamaicans welcomed the imperial state with a warmth that grew as the imperial crisis increased the likelihood of slave insurrection. The political and economic structures of the Caribbean's sugar colonies encouraged colonists there to look to imperial officials for protection rather than to look within. It was the very experience of conspiracy scares—growing from a century of memory and informational circuits—that made these fears of insurrection relevant in the revolutionary period and drove the island's colonists into the imperial embrace at a critical juncture.

St. Christopher

British Caribbean colonists experienced heightened fear, with grave consequences for enslaved people, when France entered the war on the side of the United States. This turned the Caribbean into a theater of interimperial conflict and the British islands into prime targets. As early as 1776, white colonists predicted this development and noted the gathering French fleets. In the Leeward Islands, which included St. Christopher, Antigua, Nevis, and Montserrat, Samuel Martin shared his "fears that these Islands might be invaded by France by being left destitute of Regular Troops." He caught wind of troubling rumors that thousands of soldiers and several frigates were amassing at nearby Martinique and Guadeloupe.[104] Just as it became clear at the beginning of April 1778 that France was about to enter the war, Alice Carroll, a white resident of St. Christopher, displaced her fear onto enslaved people. She alerted a justice of the peace of conversations that made her uneasy because of the "manner in which they were Delivered," even though she was interpreting them across a cultural divide and in a climate of wartime fear.[105]

Especially at this juncture, enslaved people had to be more guarded in their conversations with white people, who had direct access to legal power,

Figure 18. Alice Carroll felt threatened by her conversation with Jingo and Basseterre Peter as she supervised them in a boiling house such as the one shown here. William Clark, *Interior of a Boiling House*. Hand-colored lithograph. In Clark, *Ten Views of the Island of Antigua* (London, 1823). Courtesy of the John Carter Brown Library at Brown University.

than they were with acquaintances. Basseterre Peter and Jingo, two enslaved sugar boilers, engaged Carroll in one such dangerous discussion. Late one night, Carroll was "watching" on behalf of her husband, an overseer, in the hot, stinking boiling house (fig. 18) when she asked Basseterre Peter "if he had got a Wife yet." He replied, "No Mistress I have got no Wife yet," according to her later deposition. At that point, Jingo accidentally endangered himself when he "Whispered . . . something [to Basseterre Peter] which [Carroll] did not Articulately hear," eliciting Basseterre Peter's response, "Damn my Blood, do I mind that?" The caution with which the men spoke to one another was necessary for surviving a system of enslavement in which some speech was criminalized and potential informers lurked everywhere. However, the wary men's secrecy also invited white people's suspicion. In Carroll's case, she interpreted their remarks as sexual threats against her when Jingo added, "How sweet Bacara's [a white person's] Mouth is." Basseterre Peter agreed and said, "My Skin trembles till the Night comes, I wish tonight was the night," in obvious reference to some kind of assignation. Perhaps Carroll was primed to perceive the threat of rape both because she continually faced the possibility, especially from white men, and because the idea of black men's supposed lust for white women was well established both in slave conspiracy discourse and in literary representations of insurrection.[106]

Other black people's later conversations seemed to take on a sinister aura when Carroll reflected on them in light of the remarks at the boiling house. One exchange she overheard while resting near an open window during the day, and another at night while sitting "at the Chamber Door." When she thought back on them during her deposition, she managed only to muster recollections of maddeningly imprecise remarks, most of them idiomatic turns of speech. For example, she assessed an inaudible "Whispe[r]" in terms of the uproarious response it elicited. Most of the imprecision and space for interpretation in these overheard snippets was in the unclear signification of pronouns. Without having heard the rest of the conversation, what was one to make of an enslaved man saying "When it does Come, Are We going to leave any?" or, in a different conversation, "Eigh Eigh, them Ready I believe Dem be tonight"? Carroll acknowledged this problem when deposing that she heard a man say, out of context, "Are you not going to give *them* a Broad Side first?" She felt compelled to explain to the justice of the peace that "by *them* this Deponent understood they meant the White Inhabitants." In essence, the depositions documented a loose string of vague pronouns such as "it," "them," and "we"—all cinched together in whites' anxious minds into a clear announcement of looming disaster.

Carroll and her family brought her suspicions to a justice of the peace, who began weaving the snippets of conversation together into a threatening composite. By and large, when white people overheard enslaved people's conversations, they nearly always recalled phrasings of tantalizing suspense, in the future tense, however vague the intended action. Consider some of the suggestively sinister action phrases that Carroll and other white people on the island of St. Christopher reported hearing: "When it does Come," "Are you going to leave any," "What do you intend to do," "When we come . . . We shall Share in two." In the end, perhaps the imprecision of this speech is precisely what made it seem so ominous to anxious whites. Not only were these words chimeras, but veiled speech might also suggest that a speaker had something to hide. Surely white listeners were capable of imagining alternative meanings for an isolated statement such as, "I

tremble the time is not come about." But when they swore it into an affi-
davit and framed it alongside another statement from a different conversation, such as "When we come to Bakers Plantation We shall Share in two,"
they in effect constructed an artificial new conversation that suggested the
most disturbing interpretation. Obviously, white inhabitants of slave societies relied heavily on interpretive categories of their own construction
related to race, slavery, and deviance. Although some magistrates and planters made efforts to discern a few trusted slaves from the threatening multitude, in doing so they proved the rule that they assumed most slaves,
especially Africans, had criminal inclinations and conspiratorial intentions.
They could draw on a century of apparently averted conspiracies and
quashed revolts throughout the British Atlantic to convince themselves of
this.

Along a road that served as an artery of communication, two other
enslaved people inadvertently contributed to white people's idea that a conspiracy was afoot with their conversation. As the nameless men rattled past
with a cart, James Warrington sat at his window preparing his firearms,
because he had already "heard a Rumor of an intended Insurrection," likely
through the governor's emergency arrival at the scene. It did not occur to
Warrington that these men were discussing the news of the day because of
the terror it threatened for them and their loved ones. Similarly, Carroll's
sister probably did not consider this ramification when she deposed that
she "frequently heard her intimate Acquaintances Express their Fears and
apprehensions lest any Insurrection should happen from among the Negro
Slaves in this Island." For her, the rumor among her peers was further
evidence of a probable conspiracy; but historians should consider that
rumor has often begot rumor and that white people's expressions of concern may have inspired terrified conversations among the enslaved.

The governor worked through the night to arrest all of the enslaved
people implicated by the depositions of white eavesdroppers. At first the
suspects "would not confess a Single Syllable" and continued in confinement. On April 18, the day before Easter, a jailed man agreed to break his
silence on the provision that, as the governor put it, "I myself would come
to the Jail" to take the confession. For a moment, the prisoner could force
the most powerful man in the colony to answer his summons. The informant revealed that the uprising was scheduled for that very night, on
account of the Easter holiday, and he identified the first intended victims to
be the white people whose names had been introduced through the original

depositions: Baker, Calhoun, and Carroll. Surely those names had been on everyone's lips in jail that week. Only after the governor extracted coerced confessions did he get more suspects to become informants and induce them to furnish details that conformed to stereotypes about slave conspiracy. With these later confessions he finally generated information about the alleged plot that historians usually identify as the key elements: that there was an island-wide massacre scheduled for Easter Sunday, that the conspirators intended to deliver the island to French invaders, and that if they failed to control the island they would flee to Spanish Puerto Rico. With these findings in hand, the governor ordered the alarm canon to be fired and the militia to muster. He believed that the guard's "Activity & Spirit . . . procured Ease to the [white] Inhabitants," exceeding his royally appointed role of protecting them by attempting to make them feel safe. He did not remark upon the trauma that this inflicted upon enslaved people.[107]

Rebellion

In the southern mainland colonies, by the end of 1775 the British really *did* invite people enslaved by revolutionaries to take up arms against them, although not in the way colonists had learned to fear. Throughout 1775, African Americans in Virginia and South Carolina seized on the revolutionary moment to flee their captors. Hearing rumors of even a limited form of royal intervention on their behalf, and sensing a new national boundary forming that they could profitably cross, they presented themselves as volunteers at governors' encampments. In early November, Governor Dunmore of Virginia reluctantly incorporated the growing number of African American refugees into his plans for counterinsurgency against the revolutionaries. He established a policy, expanded a few years later in the Philipsburg Proclamation, that welcomed the military service of men formerly enslaved by revolutionaries (while promising to return those enslaved by loyalists). The *Virginia Gazette* dubbed him "king of the blacks," branded him as more of a rebel than they for "having armed our slaves against us," and misleadingly portrayed him as an abolitionist who supposedly issued sashes declaring "Liberty to Slaves."[108] In December, Henry Laurens and Charleston's Committee of Safety took heart in the news that Dunmore's first foray into battle with liberated black soldiers was inconclusive against the revolutionary Virginians. But they nervously watched the "alarming evil" of fugitives in South Carolina flocking to Governor Campbell's encampment.[109] George Washington warned that as Dunmore's army grew "like a snow Ball in rolling," it was shifting the calculus of fear by which enslaved people were supposedly controlled by enslavers. They would no longer be "affraid" to take the risk of leaving their enslavers, he cautioned, and instead would join Dunmore "through Fear" of his reprisals against those who stayed with revolutionaries. Indeed, enslaved people faced significant risks in this situation whether they took action or not.[110]

The fear of slave rebellion that exploded in 1775 accelerated the revolutionary consolidation of the coastal regions of the southern mainland colonies and it confirmed the value of royal rule to enslavers in the West Indies. In the Lower South, revolutionary leaders responded to the tumultuous period's threat of insurrection by mustering white men into militia companies and patrols. Focusing on the familiar bogeyman of "slave conspirators" helped them to convince neighbors to take up arms. In doing so, they mobilized men into a form of civic participation that implicitly bolstered the authority of local committees and expanded their powers. The significance of civic military participation grew as soon as revolutionary leaders spelled out connections between slave rebellion and the machinations of British Ministry officials and loyalists. Colonists already understood, from long experience, that slave conspiracies typically required secret instigators, coordinated invasions, and unholy alliances with a range of ethnic, religious, and national outsiders, and revolutionary leaders sounded the alarm. Several actions by the ministry helped revolutionaries to slot it neatly into this picture. No wonder these charges of incited insurrections were foundational to the Declaration of Independence.[111]

These political moves and partisan manipulations were possible because of how conspiracy scares had always leant themselves to crafting performances and shaping narratives. Conspiracy was a crime of speech, planning, and intention; and evidence about conspiracy relied on the recollections and explanations of enslaved informants in environments of fear and coercion. Investigations of conspiracy synthesized these fragments of coerced evidence to produce official narratives. Those narratives resonated powerfully with audiences when they echoed and elaborated on what they already believed from more than one hundred years of experience with conspiracy scares. White people imagined themselves as potential victims who saved themselves through their participation in a governing structure and gained political identities. At a fundamental level, in addition to becoming a revolutionary citizen or confirming their status as a subject of the king, the political identity that they developed was whiteness.

White people's mechanisms for suppressing conspiracy, too, had always been collective performances in which militias patrolled to demonstrate their readiness to themselves and other whites, as much as to the ostensible audience of enslaved people. Royal and revolutionary governments that took seriously the fears of white people, in whom a great deal of political power dwelled, could use these public demonstrations of vigilance to claim authority. The governments that thrived during the American Revolution were those that strived to "keep the peace" by stabilizing the status quo with which white people kept black people in fear and claimed to possess them. In the Lower South, where revolutionaries had to clear a higher bar, they credibly cast their opponents as disturbers of the public peace. For all its radical tactics, the revolutionary movement in the southern mainland colonies was a defense of property rights and a slavery-based hierarchical social order, uneasily bound in fear. On these principles, white American citizens and their colonist cousins in the British West Indies could still agree.[112]

The Transforming Fires of
the Haitian Revolution

In August 1791, enslaved rebels set fire to plantations in the countryside surrounding Cap Français and slayed hundreds of their French oppressors in the colony of Saint-Domingue, in what is now Haiti. This was the massive, unstoppable insurrection that Anglo-American slaveholders had been predicting for 150 years. Black and white Americans in the United States and British West Indies were mesmerized as the rebels achieved remarkable military victories and compelled the French state to confirm their legal freedom. White horror grew at the stories of atrocities, many exaggerated, and the elevation of black leaders to rule the French colony. In the fiery heat of the Haitian Revolution, these black leaders forged an independence movement that successfully established a new nation of formerly enslaved people.

The Haitian Revolution (1791–1804) transformed more than the island; it also changed Anglo-American fears of slave insurrection and racial rebellion. Even though enslavers had been anticipating cataclysmic insurrections for a long time, they also believed that their conspiracy investigations had detected the largest ones before alleged conspirators converted them from plan to action. When large insurrections did occur, as in St. John (1733), Jamaica (1760), and Berbice (1763), colonial powers regained control of the territories in less than a year. Even after smaller revolts, in which rebels successfully achieved freedom in inaccessible zones away from colonial rule, enslavers congratulated themselves that they had prevented the rebels from achieving "true" success in toppling the colonial order. At first Anglo-American enslavers viewed the rebellion in northern Saint-Domingue as another revolt in this tradition, but when the flames of insurrection catalyzed black leadership and national independence, they knew that they had something new to fear.

As it catapulted black revolutionaries to new heights of power, the Haitian Revolution forced white people to see a new dimension of danger in slave insurrection. This is evident in the several large-scale conspiracy scares that they believed they discovered in the United States and British Caribbean in the final years of the revolution and in the decades that followed. They expressed newly racialized fear of free African Americans, anticipated racial atrocities similar to those reported in Saint-Domingue, and reminded each other not to run the risk of "another Saint-Domingo." Anglo-American enslavers' intensified and broadened fear of black people inspired them to expand their brutal crackdowns to terrorize free people of color in addition to enslaved people. The Haitian Revolution ended one era of American fear, and it sparked another.

The Spreading Flames

The great cataclysm began as the enslavers had predicted it would, with the Saint-Domingue insurrection of 1791–93. Thousands of enslaved people took up arms in August 1791. They successfully struck at the economic heart of the sugar regime in the plantations of the Northern Plain that surrounded the city of Cap Français. They killed hundreds of white people and drove refugees into the city, clearing former plantations for farming by self-liberated people focused on survival. Finally, in June 1793, the insurgents secured their first widespread emancipation when the colony's white civil administrators, internally embattled by dissident white colonists, strengthened their claim to authority by enlisting the military assistance of the black rebels in surrounding encampments. As compensation, they offered to legally confirm the rebels' status as freed people. The new army of thousands of formerly enslaved people, including some of the original insurgents from the Northern Plain, sacked Cap Français in June 1793 and drove enslavers to evacuate the city, some taking refuge in the United States (fig. 19).[1]

With the sack of Cap Français in the second year of the rebellion, enslavers in the United States and the British West Indies worried that the flames of rebellion would spread. Southern legislatures attempted to establish a firewall by blocking the admission of refugees of color and the importation of enslaved people from Saint-Domingue, and some white residents worried that black refugees spoke "so much about the insurrections at *St.*

Figure 19. When enslaver-occupied Cap Français fell to an insurgent army in
1793, some evacuees took refuge in Jamaica and the United States and brought
news that appeared to confirm white people's worst fears. *Incendie du Cap.
Révolte générale des Nègres. Massacre des Blanca*, [1820]. Engraving. In *Saint-
Domingue, ou Histoire de ses révolutions* [. . .] (Paris, [1820]). Courtesy of the
John Carter Brown Library at Brown University.

Domingo that we have every reason to apprehend one here."[2] They tried to
comfort themselves by applying eighteenth-century theories to dismiss the
agency of enslaved people, claiming that the Saint-Domingue rebels were
overexploited by cruel French masters, and that outside instigators were
responsible for the success of the revolt. But in the decade's climate of
interimperial war and political turmoil, enslavers also believed they discovered conspiracies throughout the region, including in the British colonies
of Jamaica, Tobago, and the Bahamas, and in the states of South Carolina,
North Carolina, Virginia, and New York.[3]

Many enslavers in Anglo-America took the horrifying stories from
Saint-Domingue to confirm their eighteenth-century theories of slave
inability and black vengefulness and savagery. They heard of a banner
emblazoned with the words "Death to All Whites!" and, more dubiously, a
battlefield standard created by holding aloft a spike with the lifeless body

of a white child. Perhaps this image struck enslavers because it reflected back to them their own willingness to harm enslaved children and their own language of violent spectacle. They emphasized the most exceptional bloody atrocities, such as the dismemberment of white men and the rape of white women atop the corpses of their husbands. They described the rebels as "unchained tigers" who "thirst[ed] after blood" and left bite marks on white bodies. Such scenes, once scarcely imagined by eighteenth-century enslavers, established newly realized and more violent reference points for the manufacture of white fear in the nineteenth century.[4]

The complete transformation of whites' fear occurred only with the consolidation of black leadership over the colony of Saint-Domingue (1798) and the emergence of the independent black state of Haiti (1804). Leading up to 1798, François-Dominique Toussaint Louverture, a formerly enslaved man, directed the insurrection toward forcing a general emancipation, plotted deft diplomatic maneuvers, and warded off colonizers as French Republicans, Britain, and Spain each sought to control the "pearl of the Antilles." By 1798, Toussaint took leadership of the French colony of black citizens. With Napoléon Bonaparte's rise, Toussaint issued a new constitution for Saint-Domingue and led a military defense of the island's bid for independence. In 1804, Jean-Jacques Dessalines, his successor after his arrest, finally declared independence for the new nation of Haiti and established dictatorial rule.[5]

A focus on fear reveals the Haitian Revolution to be an inflection point for white and black fear in the arc of the history of slavery. For decades, scholars have already considered whether the Haitian Revolution was a point of transition between different styles of slave rebelliousness.[6] What is equally clear, and readily documentable, is that the world's perception of slave rebellion changed. Before this time, an independent state of formerly enslaved people was "unthinkable" to white people, as the scholar Michel-Rolph Trouillot put it. After this moment, the Haitian Revolution itself expanded the realm of possibility in white people's fears, now that a self-authored independent black state existed.[7] What was once unthinkable to white people now became impossible for them to dismiss. The Haitian Revolution showed that an entire enslaved population could free itself and author its own political change under black leaders. White people could no longer rest on their eighteenth-century confidence that they could routinely discover plots and beat back the few insurrections that slipped through. Instead, they had to worry about new levels of destruction of white lives and property and the irretrievable loss of white dominance in a racialized political culture. Everyone seemed aware that enslavers had more to fear in these times of self-emancipation and black citizenship.[8]

Reports, however inaccurate, of racial atrocities reinforced the danger that white Americans perceived in the creation of this new black nation. Soon after Haiti's independence, Dessalines traveled the country to compel reluctant Haitians to fulfill his command to kill any white French people who remained. White Americans commented on this "cruel massacre of *all 'the whites'* in retaliation" as a confirmation of their stereotypes of the savagery of unfettered slaves and vengeful Africans.[9] Even though atrocities did occur, white commentators greatly exaggerated them and used inflammatory language. Bryan Edwards, a Jamaican planter and historian, published an account of the Saint-Domingue rebellion after briefly visiting the war zone at the beginning of the insurrection. With fear and contempt, he portrayed self-liberated Haitians as a "savage people" with "fierce and unbridled passions." He dismissed their political rebellion as bloodlust, compared them to "famished tygers thirsting for human blood," and he howled that their uncontrollable violence reduced the once-flourishing colony to "a wilderness of desolation!"[10] These images affected white people for decades (fig. 20). In this surreal storyscape, a resident of New Orleans regularly went to bed "with the most sinister thoughts creeping into mind . . . [from] the dreadful calamities of Saint-Domingue." Sleepless, he devised "the tactics [he] would pursu[e]" to defend his family "if we were attacked."[11] The example of Haiti launched frantic policy debates among Anglo-American enslavers about how to avert their own "repetition of the horrors of Saint-Domingo."[12] Tragically, they exorcised their own fears by inducing terror in free and enslaved black people with preemptive crackdowns.

Shadows Cast by Haitian Fires

In the United States, Haiti's example of black leadership burned brightly and cast frightening shadows among whites. With European affairs also looming on the horizon, white Americans reevaluated their internal security and believed that they found conspiracies of their own. In Virginia, the politician John Randolph noted in 1812 that over the "last ten years" he experienced "repeated alarms of insurrection among the slaves—some of

Revenge taken by the Black Army for the Cruelties practised on them by the French.

Figure 20. The reversal of racial violence depicted here represented the fulfillment of "Revenge . . . for . . . Cruelties" in the Haitian Revolution that white Anglo-Americans had been predicting for more than a century. J. Barlow, *Revenge taken by the Black Army for the Cruelties practised on them by the French*, 1805. Engraving. In Marcus Rainsford, *An Historical Account of the Black Empire of Hayti* [. . .] (London, 1805). Courtesy of the John Carter Brown Library at Brown University.

them awful indeed."[13] This series began with a conspiracy scare in Richmond in 1800, later called Gabriel's Conspiracy, that led to the trial of seventy-one men.[14] Some aspects of this conspiracy scare resembled its eighteenth-century counterparts, but white people's engagement with it connected the scare directly to the Haitian Revolution. As with eighteenth-century scares, this one occurred as the United States prepared for war, in this case with France, just a year after Napoléon seized power.[15]

The scare started when a town council responded to a rumor of insurrection by increasing its policing, which gave enslaved people much more to talk about as they strategized for self-preservation. Two enslaved men, confident of their own innocence, alerted a member of the militia, perhaps believing there really was a plot, or perhaps seeking to get ahead of the trouble.[16] As with eighteenth-century scares, trial evidence in Gabriel's Conspiracy would center on identifying male conspirators by name and proving that they supported the plot. And as with earlier scares, the jail provided excellent opportunities for the thirty initial suspects to collect information and compare notes. Informants found power in familiar eighteenth-century tropes, and investigators cultivated their own false sense of understanding. Informants referred to lists of recruits (which they never found), officer titles, decoy fires to draw firefighters into an ambush, racial massacre, and claiming the best houses of Richmond for themselves. Investigators ignored evidence that women participated in the same behaviors that criminalized men as conspirators.[17]

While many particulars of conspiracy scares' narratives remained the same, the Haitian Revolution introduced new characters as villains and novel stratagems inspired by the island nation's history. The familiar figure of the outside instigator was now "two white Frenchmen," as initial newspaper accounts emphasized, and enslavers worried that they recruited conspirators by instructing them in the "French principles of Liberty and Equality." According to one version of the plot, the rebels intended to kidnap Governor James Monroe and other hostages to negotiate for the abolition of slavery, a new tactic now that Haitian rebels had bargained their own way into liberty.[18] After the conspiracy scare, lessons from the "dreadful scenes . . . realized in the rich cities and fertile plains of St. Domingo," as one essayist put it, loomed in Virginia's debates about how to strengthen enslavers' grip. After Richmond's wake-up call, white Virginians scrutinized their free black neighbors both because of their increased numbers after the American Revolution and because free people of color contributed to destabilizing the Saint-Domingue regime, providing rebels their opening. Virginians entertained proposals to curtail the rights of free blacks, expel them from towns or even the entire state, and slow the growth of the free black population by restricting manumission and by barring free blacks from moving to Virginia. Memory of the conspiracy scare lingered for decades.[19]

In light of the Haitian Revolution, the War of 1812 also alarmed white Americans in ways beyond the theorized connection between enemies "foreign and domestic" of the eighteenth century. Toussaint had used attempted invasions by Spain and Great Britain to strengthen insurgents' influence over revolutionary France's abolition policy and to consolidate his own authority within the colony. Americans recognized the destabilizing influence of the swarm of imperial rivals' invasion forces around the desirable island in the 1790s. When British warships entered the Chesapeake Bay one year into the War of 1812, conspiracy scares occurred twice in 1813 and again in 1814 amid cries that "a Saint Domingo Scene will be exhibited." In reality, enslaved people liberated themselves not by breaking away as a new black nation by but slipping off as families to take refuge with the British navy. Some white Americans expressed relief when the war ended in 1815 because of rumors that the West India Regiments, consisting of black soldiers recruited in the Caribbean, were about to invade to "excite insurrection" and to bring "all the horrors of a St. Domingo revolution."[20]

The echoes of Haiti still reverberated when white people in Charleston, South Carolina, believed they discovered a conspiracy led by Denmark Vesey, a free black preacher. Once again lessons from the Haitian Revolution infused familiar patterns from the eighteenth century. The investigation began when a vessel arrived from Cap-Haïtien (formerly Cap Français) and sparked a conversation between William and Peter, two enslaved men, about the possibility of fleeing to Haiti. Perhaps they were inspired by President Jean-Pierre Boyer's standing invitation to black Americans. Peter turned in William and, upon interrogation, William revealed a "very extensive" plot that involved "an indiscriminate massacre of the whites." He accused two more people as conspirators, one of whom later accused ten more. Eventually investigators executed or banished seventy-seven people, and city officials estimated that nine thousand enslaved people had at least some exposure to the plot.[21] As with eighteenth-century scares, skilled tradesmen dominated the ranks of accused conspirators. Informants claimed that they took an oath when joining the plot, and held meetings under the guise of religious classes in the home of Denmark Vesey.[22] They planned to use a decoy fire to draw out white people into a racial massacre in which, it was said, "the children were to have been spiked murdered & ca" as allegedly occurred in Saint-Domingue. As in the colonial period, and as with reports from the Saint-Domingue insurrection, the conspirators supposedly planned to rape young white women, "reserved *for worse than death,*" as a resident wrote. The idea seemed entirely believable to one white woman who informed her correspondent that "we poor divils were to have been reserved to fill their—Harams—horrible," and relayed a rumor that her "very beautiful cousin . . . was set apart for the wife . . . of one of their chiefs."[23]

White Americans viewed Vesey's alleged conspiracy as a direct consequence of the Haitian Revolution. Enslavers in the United States faced greater danger from the people they exploited, wrote one essayist, now that "the example of St. Domingo [was within] . . . ten days sail of Charleston."[24] Thomas Pinckney, the former governor of South Carolina and diplomat, lamented that the "influence of the example of St. Domingo" would continue to inspire enslaved Americans to rebel, "so long as it retains its condition" as an independent black nation.[25] Informants convinced investigators that Vesey read aloud Haitian newspaper accounts to other conspirators and rallied his followers by referring to the "unanimous and courageous" example of "the St. Domingo people." Some claimed that he planned to lead an exodus from liberated Charleston to Haiti, bringing money from the city's bank vaults. Or, as one white woman heard, the rebels would "carry *us* & the common negroes to St D there to be sold as slaves" in a feared reversal that subjected white American women to domination by Haitians.[26]

White Americans measured the conjectured violence of the averted rebellion against the new touchstone of the age, the Haitian Revolution. As the coercive investigation and trials generated more alarming accusations, a resident of Charleston wrote two weeks later that she narrowly averted "horrors equal if not superior to the scenes acted in St. Domingo." When she looked upon the faces of white people in the streets of Charleston, she wrote, she discerned "a look of horror in every countenance." Another correspondent compared the findings of the Charleston investigation, with its "Scene of Guilt, and murder, to be intended," to the Haitian Revolution, "unparalleled even exceeding if possible, the *Demons,* of St. Domingo!!!"[27] Some white people worried that talking about the Denmark Vesey affair at all would inspire another rebellion attempt, and asked whether "we are prepared to rehearse that direful tragedy" of the "sanguinary and memorable catastrophe of St. Domingo."[28]

White Americans regularly referred to Haiti in the aftermath of conspiracy scares when debating how to bolster slavery against rebellion. Some northerners suggested ending slavery, identifying it as the root cause of insurrection. According to one essayist, "the vengeful hand of the slaves" existed only because the Saint-Domingue enslavers "taught [them] to be cruel" by example. He suggested that each of the hemisphere's enslaving powers, in time, would "go thro' the same fiery trial with Hayti."[29] Southern enslavers rejected emancipation as too dangerous, not to mention too financially inconvenient and ideologically uncomfortable, and pointed also to the example of Saint-Domingue. Recalling that French abolitionism and the colony's large population of free people of color had catalyzed "the extermination of the whites [and] the utter destruction of that fine colony," they warned that "such would be the case in the southern states" if northern calls for emancipation succeeded.[30] The fires of the Haitian revolution burned so brightly as to cast monstrous shadows in neighboring slave societies.

Torchbearers of Revolution

Sparks from the Haitian Revolution did land in the United States and other parts of the Caribbean. Free and enslaved black people in the Anglo-American world did use the Haitian Revolution as a rallying cry for political action, if not in the violent ways that whites imagined. During the revolution, some wore ribbons and cockades to express support for the cause of liberty, and others celebrated it by singing songs with lyrics such as "black, white, brown, all the same." They connected themselves to the black revolutionary tradition by naming children after Toussaint and christening organizations with his name. They commemorated Haitian independence among their holidays. The completion of the Haitian Revolution provided an example for black people of the feasibility of self-emancipation and the possibility of self-rule. Consequently, free people of color in the United States, Jamaica, and Barbados agitated for rights with new vigor, as their counterparts had done in Saint-Domingue, and they sometimes cited Haiti by name. In the British West Indies, for instance, some black activists held out hope that they could curry favor with imperial authorities, as in Saint-Domingue, to achieve concessions from colonial authorities.[31]

Enslaved people did rise up in the decades after the Haitian Revolution. They used its lessons to chart relatively nonviolent courses for massive rebellions in Barbados (1816), Demerara (1823), and Jamaica (1831), uprisings occasioned by rumors that colonial officials were ignoring edicts of emancipation.[32] In Barbados, rebels set fire to the equipment and buildings of the island's seventy largest estates at the height of sugar harvest season. Amazingly, they killed only one white civilian and one British soldier.[33] In Demerara, ten to twelve thousand enslaved people rose on sixty plantations to loot and burn buildings, but they killed only three white people. In Jamaica, sixty thousand enslaved people burned hundreds of plantation buildings in protest but killed only fourteen white people. They limited their violence perhaps to initiate negotiations with colonial authorities along the lines of the Haitian Revolution.

Nevertheless, white people viewed these rebellions through the prism of accounts of the Haitian Revolution and eighteenth-century slave conspiracies, expecting outside instigation, racial massacres, and rapes where none occurred. In the aftermath of the uprisings, military authorities captured rebels and interrogated them to learn their intentions. They decided through coercive questioning that missionaries organized the rebellions in Demerara and Jamaica, with special assistance from enslaved craftsmen such as carpenters, to install a new emperor, king, or governor. Colonial authorities in Jamaica also came to believe that leaders recruited rebels at special dinners, administered oaths, and took officer titles such as colonel and captain.[34] They decided that the rebels in Barbados and Demerara had intended to massacre "all the white men" and save the "white women, who were to be reserved for their own purpose" in sexual slavery. In reality, the white counterinsurgents committed the massacres: They killed 1,000 rebels in the struggle in Barbados, including many who surrendered, and executed or banished 300 prisoners.[35] In Demerara, they killed 255 rebels and executed 33 more prisoners. In Jamaica, they killed 540 rebels in the heat of conflict and executed 344 people in later trials.[36] Ironically, white people's exaggerated stories of black protesters' violence in the British West Indies in the 1810s and 1820s accelerated Parliament's embrace of emancipation.[37]

A comparison with Nat Turner's uprising in Virginia (1831) underscores the political savvy of enslaved people's violence against buildings rather than persons in Barbados, Demerara, and Jamaica. Turner deliberately provoked racial massacre to fulfill his millennial visions that leading a war between "white spirits and black spirits" would hasten the second coming of Christ. His small band murdered almost sixty white people, mostly women and children. In contrast, tens of thousands of insurgents in Jamaica killed just fourteen white people, because they had a political message for an imperial audience. Some white Americans obscured Turner's peculiar religious motive by explaining the unusually bloody insurrection as his attempt at another Haitian Revolution. In reality, his violence was religious. Undeterred, white commentators drew connections between the massacres in Saint-Domingue and Virginia and reminded readers that they "nearly depopulated the once flourishing island of St. Domingue of its white inhabitants." In the end, white people killed one hundred rebels and tried and convicted thirty more people. They also expelled three hundred free black Americans to Liberia, in keeping with the expanded scope of fear to include formerly enslaved people after the Haitian Revolution.[38] Contrary to Nat Turner's attempt to fulfill his millennial visions, most rebels pursued the Haitian-influenced strategy of forcing colonial powers to begin negotiating, as in Barbados in 1816, Demerara in 1823, and Jamaica in 1831.

White people reduced these sophisticated political protests and this religious movement to stereotypes of bloodlust borrowed from salacious reports about Saint-Domingue. The Haitian Revolution issued sparks that lit fires of black political activity; but through the smoke, white people were unable or unwilling to see those protest movements clearly. In reality, those African American activists demanded more than legal freedom, personal autonomy, and physical security—they longed to live free of the terror that white people inflicted with systemic, sanctioned violence. Their struggle continues to this day.

APPENDIX

Table 1. Known Slave Conspiracy Scares in Anglo-America, 1655–1786

Year	Location
1656	Bermuda
1659	Barbados
1661	Bermuda
1673	Bermuda
1675	**Barbados**
1682	Bermuda
1683	Jamaica
	Barbados
1685	Jamaica
1686	**Barbados**
1687	Antigua
	Virginia
	Jamaica
1692	**Barbados**
1700	South Carolina
1701	Barbados
1710	**Virginia**
1713	South Carolina
1720	South Carolina
1721	New York
1722	**Virginia**
1723	Massachusetts
1725	**Nevis**
1729	**Antigua**
1730	**Bermuda**
	Virginia
	South Carolina
1734	South Carolina
	New Jersey
	Pennsylvania
	Bahamas

Table 1. (Continued)

Year	Location
1736	**Antigua**
1737	South Carolina
1738	St. Christopher
1739	**South Carolina**
1740	Maryland
	South Carolina
	South Carolina
1741	South Carolina
	New York
	New Jersey
	South Carolina
1742	New York
1744	Jamaica
1745	**Jamaica**
1747	Virginia
1749	**South Carolina**
1752	Virginia
	Bermuda
1753	North Carolina
	Virginia
	Maryland
1755	Jamaica
	Maryland
	Virginia
1759	South Carolina
1760	Jamaica (Kingston & Spanish Town)
	Jamaica (Hanover)
	Jamaica (St. James)
	Jamaica (St. Thomas in the East)
	Jamaica (St. John)
	Jamaica (Clarendon)
	Jamaica (St. Dorothy)
	Jamaica (St. James)
1761	New York
	Nevis
	Bermuda
1764	Jamaica
1765	**Jamaica**
	South Carolina
1767	Virginia
1768	**Montserrat**

Table 1. (Continued)

Year	Location
1769	{ Virginia
	Jamaica
1770	St. Christopher
1775	New York (Ulster)
	New York (Long Island)
	Massachusetts
	Virginia (Chesterfield)
	Virginia (Surry)
	Virginia (Prince Edward)
	New York (White Plains)
	New York (Long Island)
	South Carolina
	Virginia (Norfolk)
	North Carolina
1776	**Jamaica**
	Pennsylvania
	Antigua
	St. Christopher
1778	Barbados
	St. Christopher
1779	New Jersey
1780	New York
1784	Jamaica
1786	Virginia

Notes: When more than one scare occurred in a calendar year in a given colony, each incident is indicated by a town, parish, or county name. For major scares, the location name appears in bold. For the difference between major and minor scares, and for a discussion of the nature of the archival documentation behind this table, see pages 15–19.

Table 2. Annual Transatlantic Arrivals of Enslaved Africans in Barbados, Expressed as Proportions of Five-Year and Ten-Year Rolling Averages, 1670–1703

Year	% of 10-Year Avg.	% of 5-Year Avg.
1670	34%	29%
1671	75%	78%
1672	77%	83%
1673	90%	95%
1674	72%	111%
1675	120%	158%
1676	121%	128%
1677	63%	64%
1678	160%	164%
1679	82%	69%
1680	124%	106%
1681	197%	185%
1682	139%	127%
1683	224%	190%
1684	102%	85%
1685	92%	74%
1686	79%	63%
1687	113%	100%
1688	69%	65%
1689	45%	51%
1690	18%	22%
1691	62%	90%
1692	83%	117%
1693	52%	80%
1694	101%	146%
1695	103%	130%
1696	157%	161%
1697	238%	223%
1698	119%	96%
1699	132%	99%
1700	158%	120%
1701	190%	148%
1702	224%	176%
1703	63%	52%

Notes: A white colonist's estimation of a "normal" number of enslaved Africans arriving in port can be approximated by a five-year average and a ten-year average. This table represents a given year's number of African arrivals as a proportion of that five-year or ten-year norm to indicate whether the year's arrivals seemed to the white observer to be higher or lower than usual. A year in which a conspiracy scare occurred is indicated in bold. Source: Voyages: The Trans-Atlantic Slave Trade, Estimates Database, accessed December 30, 2018, https://www.slavevoyages.org/estimates/.

Table 3. Annual Transatlantic Arrivals of Enslaved Africans in the Chesapeake Bay
Region, Expressed as Proportions of Five-Year and Ten-Year
Rolling Averages, 1702–32

Year	% of 10-Year Avg.	% of 5-Year Avg.
1702	29%	97%
1703	33%	23%
1704	207%	167%
1705	285%	232%
1706	194%	154%
1707	148%	124%
1708	181%	155%
1709	66%	48%
1710	75%	58%
1711	0%	0%
1712	0%	0%
1713	47%	65%
1714	18%	42%
1715	26%	78%
1716	34%	144%
1717	92%	248%
1718	313%	486%
1719	493%	426%
1720	349%	226%
1721	466%	262%
1722	23%	13%
1723	75%	44%
1724	55%	36%
1725	125%	103%
1726	237%	236%
1727	253%	322%
1728	87%	84%
1729	45%	41%
1730	62%	51%
1731	87%	70%
1732	124%	104%

Notes: A white colonist's estimation of a "normal" number of enslaved Africans arriving in port can be approximated by a five-year average and a ten-year average. This table represents a given year's number of African arrivals as a proportion of that five-year or ten-year norm to indicate whether the year's arrivals seemed to the white observer to be higher or lower than usual. A year in which a conspiracy scare occurred is indicated in bold. Source: Voyages: The Trans-Atlantic Slave Trade, Estimates Database, accessed December 30, 2018, https://www.slavevoyages.org/estimates/.

Table 4. Annual Transatlantic Arrivals of Enslaved Africans in the Leeward Islands, Expressed as Proportions of Five-Year and Ten-Year Rolling Averages, 1720–39

Year	% of 10-Year Avg.	% of 5-Year Avg.
1720	14%	13%
1721	139%	156%
1722	105%	121%
1723	105%	129%
1724	148%	148%
1725	198%	205%
1726	238%	190%
1727	184%	140%
1728	155%	111%
1729	203%	149%
1730	205%	144%
1731	97%	73%
1732	38%	31%
1733	50%4	5%
1734	54%	54%
1735	74%	90%
1736	144%	223%
1737	249%	344%
1738	123%	122%
1739	167%	149%

Notes: The Leeward Islands included Antigua, Nevis, St. Christopher, and Montserrat. A white colonist's estimation of a "normal" number of enslaved Africans arriving in port can be approximated by a five-year average and a ten-year average. This table represents a given year's number of African arrivals as a proportion of that five-year or ten-year norm to indicate whether the year's arrivals seemed to the white observer to be higher or lower than usual. A year in which a conspiracy scare occurred is indicated in bold. Source: Voyages: The Trans-Atlantic Slave Trade, Estimates Database, accessed December 30, 2018, https://www.slavevoyages.org/estimates/.

NOTES

Introduction

1. Peter C. Hoffer, *Cry Liberty: The Great Stono River Slave Rebellion of 1739* (New York: Oxford University Press, 2010); Peter H. Wood, *Black Majority: Negroes in South Carolina from 1670 Through the Stono Rebellion* (New York: Alfred A. Knopf, 1974), 308–30; Jane Landers, *Black Society in Spanish Florida* (Champaign: University of Illinois Press, 1999), 35–45.

2. Charles Fanshaw, report, aboard the *Phoenix*, Cooper River, South Carolina, October 4, 1739, Admiralty Office series (hereafter ADM), 1/1780, no fol., National Archives of the United Kingdom, Kew, London. Throughout this book, I have tried to use terminology that avoids reinscribing the chattel principle. Unlike "slaveowner," "slaveholder," or "master," the term "enslaver" more explicitly labels a person's elective, continual violence against another human being. For a similar reason, I avoid identifying enslaved individuals by their enslavers' surnames, except when relevant to my discussion or necessary to differentiate between two people with the same given name. For "slave labor camp," see Edward E. Baptist, *The Half Has Never Been Told: Slavery and the Making of American Capitalism* (New York: Basic Books, 2014), xxiv.

3. Philip D. Morgan and George D. Terry, "Slavery in Microcosm: A Conspiracy Scare in Colonial South Carolina," *Southern Studies* (Summer 1982): 121–45.

4. Confession of Agrippa, Evidence of Sambo, and Report of Governor James Glen, January 23, January 27, and February 7, 1749, South Carolina Council Journal no. 17, pp. 48, 64, 67–68, 69–70, 167, South Carolina Department of Archives and History (hereafter SCDAH), Columbia. For dates prior to 1752, this book aids comprehension by converting all Old Style (Julian) years to New Style (Gregorian) years, as if each year commenced on January 1 rather than March 25. Thus January 1748 (Old Style) is rendered as January 1749. For days of the month, letters that correspondents originally marked with a single date, such as "November 3," retain that date to ease retrieval. When correspondents dated their letters with both the Julian and Gregorian days of the month, as with "October 3/13," this book's references silently drop the Julian signifier and retain the Gregorian, making it "October 13."

5. Tobias Frere, Richard Scott, Thomas Morris, and John Duboys, Report on the Conspiracy, encl. in James Kendall to Lords of Trade, November 3, 1692, Colonial Office series (hereafter CO), 28/1, 200–205, National Archives of the United Kingdom, Kew, London.

6. Deposition of Mary Burton, in *A Journal of the Proceedings in the Detection of the Conspiracy* [. . .], ed. and comp. Daniel Horsmanden (New York, 1744), 15.

7. "Extract of a Letter from Jamaica," *New-York Weekly Journal*, April 8, 1745.

8. "Advices from Ulster County, February 22," *New York Journal*, March 2, 1775.

9. Evidence Document B, Records of the General Assembly, November 28, 1822, quoted in Michael P. Johnson, "Denmark Vesey and His Co-Conspirators," *William and Mary Quarterly*, 3rd ser. (hereafter *WMQ*), 58, no. 4 (October 2001): 957.

10. Richard Dunn, *Sugar and Slaves: The Rise of the Planter Class in the English West Indies, 1624–1713* (Chapel Hill: University of North Carolina Press, 1972), 259–61; John K. Thornton, *Warfare in Atlantic Africa, 1500–1800* (London: University College London Press, 1999), 56–65, 90, 131–39.

11. Whereas enslavers used the term "plot" (well-schematized plans) or "conspiracy" (secret, treasonous agreements, often to commit murder) to refer to a real plan for insurrection, thus sometimes retroactively explaining a rebellion as having been preceded by an undiscovered conspiracy, I prefer the more neutral term "plan" for actual intentions of violence. The strictly legal definition of conspiracy as "the verbal agreement itself" is helpful only in interpreting standards of evidence in slave trials. OED Online, s.vv. "conspiracy," "conspire," "plot (*n.*)," "plot (*v.*)," accessed July 4, 2019, https://www.oed.com; cf. Thomas J. Davis, "Conspiracy and Credibility: Look Who's Talking, About What: Law Talk and Loose Talk," *WMQ* 59, no. 1 (2002): 168.

12. Bryan Edwards, *The History Civil and Commercial of the British Colonies in the West Indies* [. . .] (London, 1793), 2:58–59; Baptist, *Half Has Never Been Told*, chap. 4; David Buisseret, ed., *Jamaica in 1687: The Taylor Manuscript at the National Library of Jamaica* (Kingston: University of the West Indies, 2010), 269–72, 277; Sowande' M. Mustakeem, *Slavery at Sea: Terror, Sex, and Sickness in the Middle Passage* (Champaign: University of Illinois Press, 2016); Trevor Burnard, *Mastery, Tyranny, and Desire: Thomas Thistlewood and His Slaves in the Anglo-Jamaican World* (Chapel Hill: University of North Carolina Press, 2004), chap. 5; Trevor Burnard, *Planters, Merchants, and Slaves: Plantation Societies in British America* (Chicago: University of Chicago Press, 2015), 105–7; Wilma King, "'Prematurely Knowing of Evil Things': The Sexual Abuse of African American Girls and Young Women in Slavery and Freedom," *Journal of African American History* 99, no. 3 (2014): 173–96; Sasha Turner, *Contested Bodies: Pregnancy, Childrearing, and Slavery in Jamaica* (Philadelphia: University of Pennsylvania Press, 2017), 63–64, 168–69, 215–18; Walter Johnson, ed., *The Chattel Principle: Internal Slave Trades in the Americas* (New Haven, CT: Yale University Press, 2005).

13. A periodically updated treatment of this historiography is available in Jason T. Sharples, "Slavery and Fear," in *Oxford Bibliographies* in Atlantic History, ed. Trevor Burnard, last modified November 29, 2018, http://www.doi.org/10.1093/OBO/9780199730414-0308.

14. Vincent Brown, "Spiritual Terror and Sacred Authority: Supernatural Power in Jamaican Slave Society," in *New Studies in the History of American Slavery*, ed. Edward E. Baptist and Stephanie M. H. Camp (Athens: University of Georgia Press, 2006), 179–210.

15. Marisa J. Fuentes, *Dispossessed Lives: Enslaved Women, Violence, and the Archive* (Philadelphia: University of Pennsylvania Press, 2016), 37–39.

16. John Hamilton to Robert Hamilton, June 12, 1760, AA/DC/17/113, Ayrshire Record Office, Ayr, Scotland; Ronald Schechter, *A Genealogy of Terror in Eighteenth-Century France* (Chicago: University of Chicago Press, 2018), chap. 3.

17. Saidiya Hartman, *Scenes of Subjection: Terror, Slavery, and Self-Making in Nineteenth-Century America* (New York: Oxford University Press, 1997); Alex Bontemps, *The Punished Self: Surviving Slavery in the Colonial South* (Ithaca, NY: Cornell University Press, 2001); Nell Irvin Painter, "Soul Murder and Slavery: Toward a Fully Loaded Cost Accounting," in *Southern History Across the Color Line*, ed. Nell Irvin Painter (Chapel Hill: University of North

Carolina Press, 2002), 15–39; Wendy Warren, "'The Cause of Her Grief': The Rape of a Slave in Early New England," *Journal of American History* 93, no. 4 (March 2007): 1031–49; Baptist, *Half Has Never Been Told*; Marcus Rediker, *The Slave Ship: A Human History* (New York: Viking, 2007); Stephanie E. Smallwood, *Saltwater Slavery: A Middle Passage from Africa to American Diaspora* (Cambridge, MA: Harvard University Press, 2007); Heather Andrea Williams, *Help Me to Find My People: The African American Search for Family Lost in Slavery* (Chapel Hill: University of North Carolina Press, 2012); Burnard, *Planters, Merchants, and Slaves*; Mustakeem, *Slavery at Sea*; Fuentes, *Dispossessed Lives*.

18. Eugene D. Genovese, *Roll, Jordan, Roll: The World the Slaves Made* (New York: Vintage, 1976); Mechal Sobel, *The World They Made Together: Black and White Values in Eighteenth-Century Virginia* (Princeton, NJ: Princeton University Press, 1987).

19. Randy M. Browne, *Surviving Slavery in the British Caribbean* (Philadelphia: University of Pennsylvania Press, 2017).

20. Raymond A. Bauer and Alice H. Bauer, "Day to Day Resistance to Slavery," *Journal of Negro History* 27, no. 4 (1942): 399–419; Gerald W. Mullin, *Flight and Rebellion: Slave Resistance in Eighteenth-Century Virginia* (Oxford: Oxford University Press, 1972); Hilary McD. Beckles, *Black Rebellion in Barbados: The Struggle Against Slavery, 1627–1838* (Bridgetown, Barbados: Caribbean Research and Publications, 1987), 30–36, 63–72; David Barry Gaspar, *Bondmen and Rebels: A Study of Master-Slave Relations in Antigua* (Baltimore: Johns Hopkins University Press, 1985), chap. 9; Morgan, *Slave Counterpoint*, chaps. 8–10.

21. Stephanie M. H. Camp, "The Pleasures of Resistance: Enslaved Women and Body Politics in the Plantation South, 1830–1861," in Baptist and Camp, *New Studies*, 87–124; Vincent Brown, *The Reaper's Garden: Death and Power in the World of Atlantic Slavery* (Cambridge, MA: Harvard University Press, 2010), 63–77, 113–28; Calvin Schermerhorn, *Money over Mastery, Family over Freedom: Slavery in the Antebellum Upper South* (Baltimore: Johns Hopkins University Press, 2011).

22. For temporary absenteeism revealed in work logs, diaries, and the careful reading of fugitive advertisements, see Justin Roberts, *Slavery and the Enlightenment in the British Atlantic, 1750–1807* (Cambridge: Cambridge University Press, 2013), 265–75; Rhys Isaac, *Landon Carter's Uneasy Kingdom: Revolution and Rebellion on a Virginia Plantation* (Oxford: Oxford University Press, 2004), 199–201, 208–9, 227–28; Philip D. Morgan, *Slave Counterpoint: Black Culture in the Eighteenth-Century Chesapeake and Lowcountry* (Chapel Hill: University of North Carolina Press, 1998), 151–54, 525–30.

23. Neil Roberts, *Freedom as Marronage* (Chicago: University of Chicago Press, 2015), 39–49, 71–80.

24. For the early period in anglophone colonies, see Herbert Aptheker, *American Negro Slave Revolts* (New York: International Publishers, 1944); Anthony S. Parent Jr., *Foul Means: The Formation of a Slave Society in Virginia, 1660–1740* (Chapel Hill: University of North Carolina Press, 2003); Walter C. Rucker, *The River Flows On: Black Resistance, Culture, and Identity Formation in Early America* (Baton Rouge: Louisiana State University Press, 2006); Michael Craton, *Testing the Chains: Resistance to Slavery in the British West Indies* (Ithaca, NY: Cornell University Press, 1982); Vincent Brown, Slave Revolt in Jamaica, 1760–1761: A Cartographic Narrative, accessed November 1, 2018, http://revolt.axismaps.com/; Vincent Brown, *Tacky's Revolt: The Story of an Atlantic Slave War* (Cambridge, MA: Harvard University Press, forthcoming).

25. David Brion Davis, *Inhuman Bondage: The Rise and Fall of Slavery in the New World* (New York: Oxford University Press, 2006), 210. For a related perspectival shift from sociology's emphasis on resistance against mastery to history's centering of the human strategies pursued by enslavers and enslaved persons, see Joseph C. Miller, *The Problem of Slavery as History: A Global Approach* (New Haven, CT: Yale University Press, 2012).

26. Alvin O. Thompson, *Flight to Freedom: African Runaways and Maroons in the Americas* (Kingston, Jamaica: University of the West Indies Press, 2006); Craton, *Testing the Chains*, 81–92; Mavis Campbell, *The Maroons of Jamaica, 1655–1796: A History of Resistance, Collaboration, and Betrayal* (Trenton, NJ: Africa World Press, 1990); Sylviane A. Diouf, *Slavery's Exiles: The Story of the American Maroons* (New York: New York University Press, 2014); Tim Lockley and David Doddington, "Maroon and Slave Communities in South Carolina Before 1865," *South Carolina Historical Magazine* 113, no. 2 (April 2012): 125–44; Tim Lockley, *Maroon Communities in South Carolina: A Documentary Record* (Columbia: University of South Carolina Press, 2009); Daniel O. Sayers, *A Desolate Place for a Defiant People: The Archaeology of Maroons, Indigenous Americans, and Enslaved Laborers in the Great Dismal Swamp* (Gainesville: University Press of Florida, 2014); Kevin Mulroy, *The Seminole Freedmen: A History* (Norman: University of Oklahoma Press, 2007); Antonio T. Bly, ed., *Escaping Bondage: A Documentary History of Runaway Slaves in Eighteenth-Century New England, 1700–1789* (Lanham, MD: Lexington Books, 2012); Erica Armstrong Dunbar, *Never Caught: The Washingtons' Relentless Pursuit of their Runaway Slave Ona Judge* (New York: 37ink / Atria, 2017); Eric Foner, *Gateway to Freedom: The Hidden History of the Underground Railroad* (New York: W. W. Norton, 2016); David Waldstreicher, *Runaway America: Benjamin Franklin, Slavery, and the American Revolution* (New York: Hill and Wang, 2004). One group that traces its roots to maroon activity, the Maroons of Jamaica, adopted the general term as their ethnonym.

27. Sylvia Frey, *Water from the Rock: Black Resistance in a Revolutionary Age* (Princeton, NJ: Princeton University Press, 1991); Gary B. Nash, *The Forgotten Fifth: African Americans in the Age of Revolution* (Cambridge, MA: Harvard University Press, 2006); Alan Taylor, *The Internal Enemy: Slavery and War in Virginia, 1772–1832* (New York: W. W. Norton, 2013), 23–30, 245–73; Landers, *Black Society in Spanish Florida*, 35–45.

28. Corey Robin, *Fear: The History of a Political Idea* (New York: Oxford University Press, 2006); Joshua Cohen, *The Arc of the Moral Universe and Other Essays* (Cambridge, MA: Harvard University Press, 2011), chap. 1; Laura Ann Stoler, *Along the Archival Grain: Epistemic Anxieties and Colonial Common Sense* (Princeton, NJ: Princeton University Press, 2009), 4.

29. Linda Colley, *Captives: Britain, Empire, and the World* (New York: Anchor Books, 2004), 43–47.

30. Fanshaw, report, aboard the *Phoenix*, ADM 1/1780, no fol.

31. "Extract of a Letter from S. Carolina, dated October 2," *Gentleman's Magazine* 10 (1740): 127–29.

32. George Gamble to Christopher Codrington, December 29, 1701, encl. in Codrington to Board of Trade, December 30, 1701, CO 152/4, 205–7; Gaspar, *Bondmen and Rebels*, 185–89.

33. Bryan Edwards, *The History Civil and Commercial, of the British Colonies in the West Indies. To which is added, an Historical Survey of the French Colony in the Island of St. Domingo* (London, 1798), 154.

34. Thomas Tryon, *Friendly Advice to the Gentlemen-Planters of the East and West Indies* [. . .] (London, [1684]), 206–8.

35. Tryon, *Friendly Advice*, 127, 206–8, 215, 216.

36. Winthrop Jordan, *White over Black: American Attitudes Toward the Negro, 1550–1812* (Chapel Hill: University of North Carolina Press, 1968).

37. Vincent Brown, "A Vapor of Dread: Observations on Racial Terror and Vengeance in the Age of Revolution," in *Revolution! The Atlantic World Reborn*, ed. Richard Rabinowitz, Laurent Dubois, and Thomas Bender (New York: D. Giles, 2011), 178–98.

38. A precise comparison of the number of conspiracy scares in this period and that of revolts is not possible due to inconsistent documentation of small-scale uprisings, especially in the Caribbean. A rough estimate, including an allowance for undocumented revolts, is that scares occurred perhaps twice as often as domestic insurrections. (Note that certain military conflicts, such as those waged by former slaves in the British Army, constituted resistance and rebellion but not domestic revolt. See pages 25–27 and 67–70.)

39. Some of the most important works here are C. L. R. James, *The Black Jacobins: Toussaint L'Ouverture and the San Domingo Revolution* (New York: Secker and Warburg, 1938); Aptheker, *American Negro Slave Revolts*; Eugene D. Genovese, *From Rebellion to Revolution: Afro-American Slave Revolts in the Making of the Modern World* (Baton Rouge: Louisiana State University Press, 1979); Craton, *Testing the Chains*; Gaspar, *Bondmen and Rebels*; Thomas J. Davis, *A Rumor of Revolt: The "Great Negro Plot" in Colonial New York* (New York: Macmillan, 1985); David Patrick Geggus, "The French and Haitian Revolutions, and Resistance to Slavery in the Americas: An Overview," *Revue française d'histoire d'outre-mer* 76, no. 282–83 (1989): 107–24; Michael Mullin, *Africa in America: Slave Acculturation and Resistance in the American South and the British Caribbean, 1736–1831* (Urbana: University of Illinois Press,1992); Douglas R. Egerton, *Gabriel's Rebellion: The Virginia Slave Conspiracies of 1800 and 1802* (Chapel Hill: University of North Carolina Press, 1993).

40. Richard C. Wade, "The Vesey Plot: A Reconsideration," *Journal of Southern History* 30, no. 2 (1964): 143–61; Bertram Wyatt-Brown, *Southern Honor: Ethics and Behavior in the Old South* (New York: Oxford University Press, 1982), chap. 15; Winthrop D. Jordan, *Tumult and Silence at Second Creek: An Inquiry into a Civil War Slave Conspiracy* (Baton Rouge: University of Louisiana Press, 1993); Johnson, "Denmark Vesey and His Co-Conspirators."

41. Robert A. Gross, ed. "Forum: The Making of a Slave Conspiracy," *WMQ* 58, no. 4 (October 2001): 913–14, continued in *WMQ* 59, no. 1 (January 2002): 135–202; Robert L. Paquette, "From Rebellion to Revisionism: The Continuing Debate About the Denmark Vesey Affair," *Journal of the Historical Society* 4, no. 3 (2004): 291–334; James O'Neil Spady, "Power and Confession: On the Credibility of the Earliest Reports of the Denmark Vesey Slave Conspiracy," *WMQ* 68, no. 2 (2011): 287–304; Michael L. Nicholls, *Whispers of Rebellion: Narrating Gabriel's Conspiracy* (Charlottesville: University of Virginia Press, 2012); Douglas R. Egerton and Robert L. Paquette, introduction to *The Denmark Vesey Affair: A Documentary History*, ed. Douglas R. Egerton and Robert L. Paquette (Gainesville: University Press of Florida, 2017).

42. Fuentes, *Dispossessed Lives*, 5.

43. On colonizers' "uncertainty and doubt" in the creation of the archive, see Stoler, *Along the Archival Grain*. On fear as a historical force, see Georges Lefebvre, *The Great Fear of 1789: Rural Panic in Revolutionary France*, trans. Joan White (New York: Vintage, 1973); Timothy Tackett, *When the King Took Flight* (Cambridge, MA: Harvard University Press, 2003); Peter Silver, *Our Savage Neighbors: How Indian War Transformed Early America* (New York: W. W. Norton, 2008); Gregory Evans Dowd, "The Panic of 1751: The Significance of Rumors on the South Carolina-Cherokee Frontier," *WMQ* 53, no. 3 (1996): 527–60. For analytical precision in discussing fear, see Lauric Henneton, "Introduction: Adjusting to Fear in

Early America," in *Fear and the Shaping of Early American Societies*, ed. Lauric Henneton and L. H. Roper (Leiden: Brill, 2016), 1–37; Joanna Bourke, *Fear: A Cultural History* (Emeryville, CA: Shoemaker and Hoard, 2006). For the history of emotions, a different intellectual project that traces changes in norms of emotional expression, see Barbara H. Rosenwein and Riccardo Cristiani, *What Is the History of Emotions?* (Cambridge: Polity, 2018); Barbara H. Rosenwein, *Generations of Feeling: A History of Emotions, 600–1700* (Cambridge: Cambridge University Press, 2016); William M. Reddy, *The Navigation of Feeling: A Framework for the History of Emotions* (Cambridge: Cambridge University Press, 2001); Joanna Bourke, *Fear: A Cultural History* (London: Virago, 2005); Nicole Eustace, *Passion Is the Gale: Emotion, Power, and the Coming of the American Revolution* (Chapel Hill: University of North Carolina Press, 2008).

44. For more on using conspiracy trials against the grain, James Sidbury, "Plausible Stories and Varnished Truths," *WMQ* 59, no. 1 (2002): 182; Philip D. Morgan and George D. Terry, "Slavery in Microcosm: A Conspiracy Scare in Colonial South Carolina," *Southern Studies* 21, no. 2 (1982): 121–45; João José Reis, *Slave Rebellion in Brazil: The Muslim Uprising of 1835 in Bahia*, trans. Arthur Brakel (Baltimore: Johns Hopkins University Press, 1993); James Sidbury, *Ploughshares into Swords: Race, Rebellion, and Identity in Gabriel's Virginia, 1730–1810* (Cambridge: Cambridge University Press, 1997), chap. 2; Jill Lepore, *New York Burning: Liberty, Slavery, and Conspiracy in Eighteenth-Century Manhattan* (New York: Alfred A. Knopf, 2005), chap. 5; Serena R. Zabin, *Dangerous Economies: Status and Commerce in Imperial New York* (Philadelphia: University of Pennsylvania Press, 2009); J. William Harris, *The Hanging of Thomas Jeremiah: A Free Black Man's Encounter with Liberty* (New Haven, CT: Yale University Press, 2009); Justin Pope, "Inventing an Indian Slave Conspiracy on Nantucket, 1738," *Early American Studies: An Interdisciplinary Journal* 15, no. 3 (2017): 505–38. For cultural values refracted through expressions of fear, see María Elena Martínez, "The Black Blood of New Spain: Limpieza de Sangre, Racial Violence, and Gendered Power in Early Colonial Mexico," *WMQ* 61, no. 3 (2004): 479–520; Joshua Rothman, *Flush Times and Fever Dreams: A Story of Capitalism and Slavery in the Age of Jackson* (Athens: University of Georgia Press, 2012).

45. Mary Beth Norton, *In the Devil's Snare: The Salem Witchcraft Crisis of 1692* (New York: Vintage, 2002); James L. Given, *Inquisition and Medieval Society: Power, Discipline, and Resistance in Languedoc* (Ithaca: Cornell University Press, 1997); Stuart Clark, "Inversion, Misrule, and the Meaning of Witchcraft," in *The Witchcraft Reader*, ed. Darren Oldridge (New York: Routledge, 2002), 149–60; Stuart Clark, ed., *Languages of Witchcraft: Narrative, Ideology, and Meaning in Early Modern Culture* (New York: St. Martin's Press, 2001); Malcom Gaskill, *Witchfinders: A Seventeenth-Century English Tragedy* (Cambridge, MA: Harvard University Press, 2007); John Demos, *The Enemy Within: A Short History of Witch-Hunting* (New York: Penguin, 2008).

46. Matthew Mulcahy, *Hubs of Empire: The Southeastern Lowcountry and the British Caribbean* (Baltimore: Johns Hopkins University Press, 2014); April Lee Hatfield, *Atlantic Virginia: Intercolonial Relations in the Seventeenth Century* (Philadelphia: University of Pennsylvania Press, 2007).

47. South Carolina Council, minutes, January 31, 1749, South Carolina Council Journal no. 17, p. 50, SCDAH.

48. Thomas Collins, deposition, Trial of Vernon's Cudjoe, January 26, 1737, CO 9/11, 16.

Chapter 1

1. Tobias Frere et al., Report on the Conspiracy, encl. in James Kendall to Lords of Trade, November 3, 1692, Colonial Office series (hereafter CO), 28/1, 200–205, National Archives of

the United Kingdom, Kew, London; Payment to Alice Mills, Barbados Council, minutes, January 24, 1693, CO 31/4, 397; Edmund Bohun, *A Brief, But Most True Relation of the Late Barbarous and Bloody Plot* [. . .] (London, 1693); Jerome S. Handler, "Slave Revolts and Conspiracies in Seventeenth-Century Barbados," *New West Indian Guide* 56, no. 1 (1982): 5–42; Hilary McD. Beckles, *Black Rebellion in Barbados: The Struggle Against Slavery, 1627–1838* (Bridgetown, Barbados: Caribbean Research and Publications, 1987), 47.

2. Michael Jarvis, *In the Eye of All Trade: Bermuda, Bermudians, and the Maritime Atlantic World, 1680–1783* (Chapel Hill: University of North Carolina Press, 2010), 26–29, 56–57; Robin Blackburn, *The Making of New World Slavery: From the Baroque to the Modern, 1492–1800* (London: Verso, 1997), 229–56, 258–61; Robert V. Wells, *The Population of British Colonies in America Before 1776* (Princeton, NJ: Princeton University Press, 1975), 196, table VI-8; 209, table VI-13; 238, table VI-25; 240, 251; Jennifer Morgan, *Laboring Women: Reproduction and Gender in New World Slavery* (Philadelphia: University of Pennsylvania Press, 2004), 96; Richard S. Dunn, *Sugar and Slaves: The Rise of the Planter Class in the English West Indies, 1624–1713* (Chapel Hill: University of North Carolina Press, 1972), 87–88, table 4; 122–23; 127, table 12; 131; 155, table 16; 168–76; Trevor Burnard, *Planters, Merchants, and Slaves: Plantation Societies in British America, 1650–1820* (Chicago: University of Chicago Press, 2015), 66–71; John C. Coombs, "The Phases of Conversion: A New Chronology for the Rise of Slavery in Early Virginia," *William and Mary Quarterly*, 3rd ser. (hereafter *WMQ*), 68, no. 3 (July 2011): 332–60.

3. Sowande' M. Mustakeem, *Slavery at Sea: Terror, Sex, and Sickness in the Middle Passage* (Champaign: University of Illinois Press, 2016); Marcus Rediker, *The Slave Ship: A Human History* (New York: Viking, 2007); John Paige to [William Clarke], June 1, 1654, in *The Letters of John Paige, London Merchant, 1648–1658*, ed. George F. Steckley (London: London Record Society, 1984), 106; Eric Robert Taylor, *If We Must Die: Shipboard Insurrections in the Era of the Atlantic Slave Trade* (Baton Rouge: Louisiana State University Press, 2006), 180–81; Slave Voyages: The Trans-Atlantic Slave Trade—Database, accessed September 15, 2018, https://slavevoyages.org/voyage/database.

4. Barbados Council, minutes, March 6, 1655, and September 3, 1657, Lucas Transcript, microfilm, reel 2:160–62, 364, Barbados National Library Service (hereafter BNLS), Bridgetown, Barbados; Richard Ligon, *A True and Exact History of the Island of Barbados*, ed. Karen Ordahl Kupperman (Indianapolis: Hackett Publishing Company, 2011), 75; William Waller Hening, ed., *The Statutes at Large: Being a Collection of All the Laws of Virginia* [. . .] (New York, 1823), 2:277, 299–300, 3:86–88.

5. "History of the Revolted Negroes," n.d., British Library, London (hereafter BL), Additional Manuscripts (hereafter Add. MSS), 12,431; Jonathan Atkins to Robert Southwell, February 20, 1675, CO 1/36, 51; Jamaica Council, minutes, January 23, 1676, and February 17, 1676, CO 140/3, 449–57.

6. Henry Barham, "The Civil History of Jamaica to the Year 1722," n.d., BL, Add. MSS 12,422:150–51; James Knight, "The Natural, Moral, and Political History of Jamaica [. . .] to the Year 1746," n.d., BL, Add. MSS 12,418–19:114, 141–42; *Account of the British Colonies in the Islands of America, Commonly Called the West Indies* [. . .] (n.p., 1759), 135, National Library of Jamaica (hereafter NLJ), Kingston; David Buisseret, ed., *Jamaica in 1687: The Taylor Manuscript at the National Library of Jamaica* (Kingston, Jamaica: University of the West Indies, 2010), 276.

7. Bermuda Council, minutes, August 18, 24, 25, 1682, in *Bermuda Under the Sommer Islands Company, 1612–1684, Civil Records*, ed. A. C. H. Hallett (Pembroke, Bermuda: Juniper-hill Press, 2005), 2:461–62.

8. Dunn, *Sugar and Slaves*, 48, 57, 96–100; Morgan, *Laboring Women*, 96; Gary A. Puckrein, *Little England: Plantation Society and Anglo-Barbadian Politics, 1627–1700* (New York: New York University Press, 1987), 154–55; Hilary McD. Beckles, *White Servitude and Black Slavery in Barbados, 1627–1715* (Knoxville: University of Tennessee Press, 1989), 126, table 5.3.

9. Bermuda Council, minutes, December 24, 1673, in Hallett, *Somer Island Company*, 2:185–87.

10. Stephanie E. Smallwood, *Saltwater Slavery: A Middle Passage from Africa to American Diaspora* (Cambridge, MA: Harvard University Press, 2008), 101–21.

11. John K. Thornton, *Africa and Africans in the Making of the Atlantic World, 1400–1800*, 2nd ed. (Cambridge: Cambridge University Press, 1998); Philip D. Morgan, "The Cultural Implications of the Atlantic Slave Trade: African Regional Origins, American Destinations, and New World Developments," *Slavery and Abolition* 18, no. 1 (1997): 122–45.

12. Ligon, *History of the Island of Barbados*, 97; An Act for the Better Ordering and Governing of Negroes, September 27, 1661, CO 30/2, 16–22; An Act for the Good Governing of Servants, and Ordaining the Rights between Masters and Servants, September 27, 1661, in *Acts Passed in the Island of Barbados from 1643 to 1762* [. . .], ed. Richard Hall (London, 1764), 35–42.

13. William Willoughby to Lords of Council, July 9, 1668, in *Calendar of State Papers, Colonial Series: America and West Indies, 1574–1739* (hereafter *CSPCS*), 45 vols. (London, 1860–1994), 5:586–88; Buisseret, *Jamaica in 1687*, 274.

14. Hallett, *Sommer Islands Company*, 1:404–5; Bermuda Council, minutes, November 2, 1656, in *Memorials of the Discovery and Early Settlement of the Bermudas or Somers Islands, 1511–1687: Compiled from the Colonial Records and Other Original Sources*, ed. J. H. Lefroy (London, 1879), 2:94–95; Virginia Bernhard, *Slaves and Slaveholders in Bermuda, 1616–1782* (Columbia: University of Missouri Press, 1999), 84–88.

15. Bernhard, *Slaves and Slaveholders in Bermuda*, 84–88, 161–62.

16. "Management of Slaves," in *Virginia Magazine of History and Biography* 7 (1899): 314; Bermuda Council, minutes, December 24, 1673, in Hallett, *Somer Islands Company*, 2:185–87; Proclamation by Governor Sir John Heydon, January 10, 1674, in Hallett, *Somer Islands Company*, 2:185–87; and Governor and Council General Letter to Company, February 20, 1675, in Hallett, *Somer Islands Company*, 2:233.

17. Jamaica Council, minutes, January 8 and 23, 1673, CO 140/3, 334–36, 449–55; Address of Governor to Assembly, in Jamaica Council, minutes, December 15, 1675, CO 140/3, 448.

18. Atkins to Lords of Trade, October 13, 1675, CO 1/35, 231; Barbados Assembly, minutes, July 6 and 7, August 4, 1675, CO 31/2, 184–89.

19. Ligon, *History of the Island of Barbados*, 95.

20. Barbados Assembly Journal, November 25, 1675, CO 31/2, 201; *Great Newes from the Barbadoes* [. . .] (London, 1676), 9–13; [Nathaniel Saltonstall] *A Continuation of the State of New-England Being a Farther Account of the Indian Warr*, [. . .] *Together with an Account of the Intended Rebellion of the Negroes in the Barbadoes* (London, 1676), 19; John K. Thornton, "War, the State, and Religious Norms in 'Coromantee' Thought: The Ideology of an African American Nation," in *Possible Pasts: Becoming Colonial in Early America*, ed. Robert Blair St. George (Ithaca, NY: Cornell University Press, 2000), 195.

21. Journal of Lords of Trade and Plantations, October 8, 1680, in *CSPCS*, 10:611–12; Morgan Godwyn, *The Negro's and Indians Advocate* [. . .] (London, 1680), 65, 111–12, 131–32.

22. Beckles, *White Servitude and Black Slavery*, 135.

23. A Supplemental Act [. . .] For the Better Ordering and Governing of Negroes, 1676, CO 30/2, 65v–71.

24. Alan Marshall, *Intelligence and Espionage in the Reign of Charles II, 1660–1685* (Cambridge: Cambridge University Press, 1994), 147–49.

25. Anonymous Note, discovered November 29, 1683, encl. in Anonymous Letter, December 18, 1683, CO 1/53, 265. Sic.

26. Anonymous Letter, December 18, 1683, CO 1/53, 264–66.

27. Antigua Council, minutes, February 14, 1687, and March 9, 17, 24, and 31, 1687, CO 155/1, 58–68, 95–96; John K. Thornton, "The Coromantees: An African Cultural Group in Colonial North America and the Caribbean," *Journal of Caribbean History* 32 (1998): 161–78; Thornton, "War, the State, and Religious Norms," 194–96.

28. Virginia Council, minutes, October 24, 1687, in *Executive Journals of the Council of Colonial Virginia*, ed. H. R. McIlwaine (Richmond: Virginia State Library, 1925), 1:86–87; Governor's Proclamation, November 5, 1687, in *Executive Journals of the Council*, 1:511; Virginia Assembly, minutes, October 28, 1686, in *Journals of the House of Burgesses of Virginia, 1659/ 60–1693*, ed. H. R. McIlwaine (Richmond: n.p., 1914), 266; Virginia Assembly, minutes, November 3, 1686, in McIlwaine, *Journals of the House*, 271.

29. Unless otherwise noted, information in this section is from Frere et al., Report on the Conspiracy, encl. in Kendall to Lords of Trade, November 3, 1692, CO 28/1, 200–205.

30. List of Persons Recommended by Governor Kendall, June 10, 1692, in *CSPCS*, 13:649; Order of Queen in Council, January 3, 1706, *CSPCS*, 23:2; Vere Langford Oliver, ed., *Caribbeana: Being Miscellaneous Papers Relating to the History, Genealogy, Topography, and Antiquities of the British West Indies*, 6 vols. (London: Mitchell, Hughes and Clarke, 1916), 4:220; A List of the Most Eminent Planters in Barbados, May 28, 1673, in *CSPCS*, 7:495–97; Information of the Earl of Bridgewater, June 29, 1698, in *CSPCS*, 16:298–99; Dunn, *Sugar and Slaves*, 58, 95–96; Order of the King in Council, January 21, 1687, in *CSPCS*, 12:311; Council of Trade and Plantations to the Lords Justices of England, October 28, 1697, in *CSPCS*, 16:2; Council of Trade and Plantations to Secretary Hedges, July 3, 1705, in *CSPCS*, 22:554; Oliver, *Caribbeana*, 5:181; Deposition of Thomas Morris, August 20, 1688, in *CSPCS*, 12:594–96; Barbados Assembly Journal, November 25–27, 1679, in *CSPCS*, 10:446; Barbados Assembly Journal, August 3, 1686, in *CSPCS*, 12:224–25; Barbados Assembly Journal, April 15, 1691, in *CSPCS*, 13:411; Payments to Mary Stowe, in Barbados Council, minutes, October 11 and 25, November 22, 1692, CO 31/4, 377, 378, 379, 388.

31. Thomas L. Morris, *Southern Slavery and the Law, 1619–860* (Chapel Hill: University of North Carolina Press, 1996), 211–15, 229–35.

32. Payment to Latimer Richards, Barbados Council, minutes, October 11, 1692, CO 31/4, 377; Bohun, *Brief, But Most True Relation*; Vincent Brown, *The Reaper's Garden: Death and Power in the World of Atlantic Slavery* (Cambridge, MA: Harvard University Press, 2009), 129–56.

33. Winthrop Jordan, *Tumult and Silence at Second Creek: An Inquiry into a Civil War Slave Conspiracy* (Baton Rouge: Louisiana State University Press, 1993), 90–94; Peter Brooks, *Troubling Confessions: Speaking Guilt in Law and Literature* (Chicago: Chicago University

Press, 2000), 20–25; Lisa Silverman, *Tortured Subjects: Pain, Truth, and the Body in Early Modern France* (Chicago: Chicago University Press, 2001); John H. Arnold, *Inquisition and Power: Catharism and the Confessing Subject in Medieval Languedoc* (Philadelphia: University of Pennsylvania Press, 2001), 74–115; Jenny Shaw, *Everyday Life in the English Caribbean: Irish, Africans, and the Construction of Difference* (Athens: University of Georgia Press, 2013), 131–32.

34. Bohun, *Brief, But Most True Relation*; An Act for the Encouragement of All Negroes and Slaves That Shall Discover Any Conspiracy, November 3, 1692, CO 31/3, 317.

35. James Kendall to Lords of Trade, November 3, 1692, CO 28/1, 200–205; Beckles, *Black Rebellion in Barbados*, 47.

36. Frere et al., Report on the Conspiracy, encl. in Kendall to Lords of Trade, November 3, 1692, CO 28/1, 200–205; Barbados Assembly Journal, November 25, 1675, CO 31/2, 201; *Great Newes from the Barbadoes*; [Saltonstall], *Continuation of the State of New-England*, 19; Marisa J. Fuentes, *Dispossessed Lives: Enslaved Women, Violence, and the Archive* (Philadelphia: University of Pennsylvania Press, 2016), 117–19.

37. Barbara J. Baines, "Effacing Rape in Early Modern Representation," *English Literary History* 65, no. 1 (1998): 70–79; W. S. Holdsworth, *A History of English Law*, 3rd ed. (Boston: Little, Brown, 1923), 3:319, 4:504; Hilary McD. Beckles, "A 'Riotous and Unruly Lot': Irish Indentured Servants and Freemen in the English West Indies, 1644–1713," *WMQ*, 47, no. 4 (1990): 503–22; Shaw, *Everyday Life*, 150–51; Jerome S. Handler, "Escaping Slavery in a Caribbean Plantation Society: Marronage in Barbados, 1650s–1830s," *New West Indian Guide* 71, no. 3/4 (1997): 187–89; Richard Bloome, *Present State of His Majesties Isles and Territories in America* [. . .] (London, 1687), 37; James C. Scott, *Weapons of the Weak: Everyday Forms of Peasant Resistance* (New Haven, CT: Yale University Press, 1985).

38. Robin Law, *The Slave Coast of West Africa, 1550–1750: The Impact of the Atlantic Slave Trade on an African Society* (Oxford: Clarendon Press, 1991), 145, 187, 225–27, 238, 242–43; Sandra E. Greene, *Gender, Ethnicity, and Social Change on the Upper Slave Coast: History of the Anlo-Ewe* (Portsmouth, NH: Heinemann, 1996); Slave Voyages: The Trans-Atlantic Slave Trade—Estimates, accessed September 17, 2018, https://slavevoyages.org/assessment/estimates.

39. Deposition of Thomas Smith, March 19, 1687, Antigua Council, minutes, March 24, 1687, CO 155/1, 62, 64.

40. John K. Thornton, *Warfare in Atlantic Africa, 1500–1800* (London: University College London Press, 1999), 56–65, 75–97; Robin Law, *The Oyo Empire, c. 1600–c. 1836: A West African Imperialism in the Era of the Atlantic Slave Trade* (Oxford: Clarendon Press, 1977).

41. Caroline Winterer, "From Royal to Republican: The Classical Image in Early America," *Journal of American History* 91, no. 4 (March 2005): 1265–66; Meyer Reinhold, *Classica Americana: The Greek and Roman Heritage in the United States* (Detroit: Wayne State University Press, 1984), 31–32, 37, 39; Daniel Woolf, *The Idea of History in Early Stuart England: Erudition, Ideology, and the "Light of Truth" from the Accession of James I to the Civil War* (Toronto: University of Toronto Press, 1990), 170–73, 197–98; Nuala Zahedieh, "London and the Colonial Consumer in the Late Seventeenth Century," *Economic History Review* 47, no. 2 (May 1994), 250–52, tables 9–11; 254, table 12; James Raven, "Importation of Books in the Eighteenth Century," in *A History of the Book in America*, ed. David D. Hall, vol. 1, *The Colonial Book in the Atlantic World*, ed. Hugh Amory and David D. Hall (Cambridge: Cambridge University Press, 2000), 186, 514, graph 7a; Daniel Woolf, *Reading History in Early Modern England* (Cambridge: Cambridge University Press, 2000), 145–50, table 3.7; Peter

Burke, "A Survey of the Popularity of Ancient Historians, 1450–1700," *History and Theory* 5, no. 2 (1966): 137, table 2; Roderick Cave, "Thomas Craddock's Books: A West India Merchant's Stock," *Book Collector* 25 (1976): 481–90; *Barbadoes. A Catalogue of Books, to be Sold by Mr. Zouch* [. . .] (Barbados, n.d. [1716?]), 13, 16, 20–21; David McKitterick, "Books for Barbados and the British Atlantic Colonies in the Early Eighteenth Century: 'A Catalogue of Books to be Sold by Mr. Zouch,'" *Proceedings of the American Antiquarian Society*, 118, pt. 2 (2009): 407–66; Victoria Pagan, *Conspiracy Narratives in Roman History* (Austin, TX: University of Texas Press, 2004); Victoria Pagan, "Toward a Model of Conspiracy Theory for Ancient Rome," *New German Critique* 35, no. 1 (2008): 27–49.

42. [Livy], *The Romane Historie Written by T. Livius of Padua* [. . .], trans. Philemon Holland (London, 1600; repr. 1659), 168, 844; Costanzo Felice, *The Conspiracie of Catiline* [. . .], trans. Alexander Barcklaye (London, 1557), 47; Ben Jonson, *Catiline His Conspiracy* (London, 1611), act 3, scene 8; Rob Hardy, "'A Mirror of the Times': The Catilanarian Conspiracy in Eighteenth-Century British and American Political Thought," *International Journal of the Classical Tradition* 14, no. 3/4 (2007): 431–54.

43. Jason T. Sharples, "Discovering Slave Conspiracies: New Fears of Rebellion and Old Paradigms of Plotting in Seventeenth-Century Barbados," *American Historical Review* 120, no. 3 (June 2015): 831–33.

44. William Fulbecke, *An Historical Collection of the Continual Factions, Tumults, and Massacres of the Romans* [. . .] (London, 1601), 79–82.

45. Ligon, *History of the Island of Barbados*, 96; Beckles, *White Servitude and Black Slavery*, 111.

46. Harry Finestone, ed., *Bacon's Rebellion: The Contemporary News Sheets* (Charlottesville: University of Virginia Press, 1956), 15–17; Edmund Morgan, *American Slavery, American Freedom: The Ordeal of Colonial Virginia* (1975; repr., New York: W. W. Norton, 1995), 261, 268–69; Simon P. Newman, *A New World of Labor: The Development of Plantation Slavery in the British Atlantic* (Philadelphia: University of Pennsylvania Press, 2013), chap. 1.

47. Information of Roger Hyett, May 10, 1679, Henry Coventry Papers, Osborn fb153, Beinecke Rare Book and Manuscript Library, Yale University, New Haven, CT; Henry Coventry to Colonel Jefferies, December 5, 1678, BL, Add. MSS 25,120:136, accessed on microfilm compiled as the Virginia Colonial Records Project (hereafter VCRP) at the John D. Rockefeller Jr. Library, Colonial Williamsburg Foundation, Williamsburg, VA; John Jeffreys to [Philip Ludwell?], November 29, 1678, Lee Family Papers, Mss1 L51 f1, Virginia Historical Society, Richmond; Henry Barham, "Civil History of Jamaica," BL, Add. MSS 12,422:99; *The Character of a Popish Successor* [. . .] (London, 1681), 1; Owen Stanwood, *The Empire Reformed: English America in the Age of the Glorious Revolution* (Philadelphia: University of Pennsylvania Press, 2011), 17–19.

48. Titus Oates, *A True Narrative of the Horrid Plot* [. . .] (London, 1679); J. P. Kenyon, *The Popish Plot* (London: William Heinemann, 1972); Alan Marshall, *The Strange Death of Edmund Godfrey: Plots and Politics in Restoration London* (London: History Press, 1999); Eight of clubs, Popish Plot Playing Cards (London: Robert Walton at the Globe, 1679), New-York Historical Society, New York; W. C. Abbott, "The Origin of Titus Oates' Story," *English Historical Review* 25 (1910): 126–29; *A Brief Account of the Several Plots, Conspiracies, and Hellish Attempts of the Bloody-minded Papists* [. . .] (London, 1679).

49. John Miller, *Popery and Politics in England, 1660–1688* (Cambridge: Cambridge University Press, 1973), chap. 5; T[homas] V[incent], *God's Terrible Voice in the City* ([London?],

1667), 55; Adrian Tinniswood, *By Permission of Heaven: The True Story of the Great Fire of London* (London: Jonathan Cape, 2003), 153, 155, 163–65; John Stewart, information, in *Cobbett's Complete Collection of State Trials* [. . .], ed. Thomas Bayly Howell (London, 1810), 6:850; Frances E. Dolan, "Ashes and 'the Archive': The London Fire of 1666, Partisanship, and Proof," *Journal of Medieval and Early Modern Studies* 31, no. 2 (Spring 2001): 391–94.

50. Oates, *True Narrative*, 190, 194–97, 206, 220–21; Andrew Marvell, *An Account of Growth of Popery and Arbitrary Government in England* (Amsterdam, 1677), 10–11; Bernard Capp, "Arson, Threats of Arson, and Incivility in Early Modern England," in *Civil Histories: Essays Presented to Sir Keith Thomas*, ed. Peter Burke, Brian Harrison, and Paul Slack (Oxford: Oxford University Press, 2000), 197–213; Miller, *Popery and Politics in England*, 91–107; Tinniswood, *By Permission of Heaven*, 143–66, 264–74; Dolan, "Ashes and 'the Archive,'" 383.

51. Oates, *True Narrative*, 211, 222–23; *A Scheme of Popish Cruelties or A Prospect of What Wee Must Expect Under a Popish Successor* (London, 1681).

52. Larry Gragg, *The Quaker Community on Barbados: Challenging the Culture of the Planter Class* (Columbia: University of Missouri Press, 2009), 52–53; Barry Reay, *Quakers and the English Revolution* (London: Temple Smith, 1985), 42, 59–60, 91–99; James Kendall to Lords of Trade, July 10, 1693, in *CSPCS*, 14:124–26; Francis Nicholson to Lords of Trade, June 10, 1691, CO 5/1358, 79–82, accessed on VCRP microfilm.

53. Act to Prevent the People Called Quakers From Bringing Negroes to Their Meeting, April 21, 1676, CO 30/2, 62v–64; Atkins to Lords of Trade, September 16, 1677, in *CSPCS*, 10:150–52; Atkins to Lords of Trade, January 31, 1678, in *CSPCS*, 10:213–14; Proposals to Governor, March 21, 1676, Barbados Assembly, minutes, CO 31/2, 207–8; Atkins to Lords of Trade, January 31, 1678, CO 29/2, 114v; George Fox, *To the Ministers, Teachers, and Priests* [. . .] (London, 1672), quoted in Kenneth Carroll, "George Fox and Slavery," *Quaker History* 86, no. 2 (1997): 16–25; Harriet Froer Durham, *Caribbean Quakers* (n.p., 1972), 16; Gragg, *Quaker Community on Barbados*, 38–55; Beckles, *White Servitude and Black Slavery*, 54; Kristen Block, *Ordinary Lives in the Early Caribbean: Religion, Colonial Competition, and the Politics of Profit* (Athens: University of Georgia Press, 2012), 161–63; Katharine Gerbner, *Christian Slavery: Conversion and Race in the Protestant Atlantic World* (Philadelphia: University of Pennsylvania Press, 2018), 66–68.

54. Gerbner, *Christian Slavery*, 42–46, 83–90; George M. Fredrickson, *Racism: A Short History* (Princeton, NJ: Princeton University Press, 2002), 15–48.

55. Joseph Mead to Martin Stuteville, July 13, 1622, reproduced in "The Indian Massacre of 1622: Some Correspondence of the Reverend Joseph Mead," edited by Robert C. Johnson, *Virginia Magazine of History and Biography* 71, no. 4 (October 1963): 408–10; "Two Tragical Events," *WMQ*, 1st ser., 9, no. 4 (April 1901): 212–14; Edward Waterhouse, *A Declaration of the State of the Colony and Affaires in Virginia* [. . .] (London, 1622).

56. Stanwood, *Empire Reformed*, 63–76.

57. William Stapleton to William Blathwayt, March 20, 1683, CO 1/51, 169; Willoughby to Arlington, February 11, 1668, in *CSPCS*, 5:547–48; Stapleton to Lords of Trade, April 26, 1676, CO 1/36, 89–106; A Remonstrance of the Inhabitants of the Island of Antigua [. . .], [April 1676], CO 1/36, 107–8; Summary of Recent History of Leeward Islands, [1680], in *CSPCS*, 10:642.

58. Ian K. Steele, *The English Atlantic, 1675–1740: An Exploration of Communication and Community* (New York: Oxford University Press, 1986), 284–85, tables 2.2 and 2.3; Atkins to

Secretary Joseph Williamson, October 13, 1675, CO 1/35, 231; Atkins to Williamson, November 14, 1675, CO 1/35, letter no. 41; Atkins to Williamson, April 13, 1676, CO 1/36, 70; Barbados Assembly, minutes, June 13 and 14, 1676, CO 31/2, 222–23; N[athaniel] S[altonstall], *A New and Further Narrative of the State of New England* [. . .] (London, 1676), 14; Patrick M. Malone, *The Skulking Way of War: Technology and Tactics among the New England Indians* (Lanham, MD: Madison Books, 1991), 80–82.

59. *Continuation of the State of New-England*, 4, 8, 17–18, 20.

60. Jill Lepore, *The Name of War: King Philip's War and the Origins of American Identity* (New York: Alfred A. Knopf, 1998), 150–70; Wendy Warren, *New England Bound: Slavery and Colonization in Early America* (New York: W. W. Norton, 2016), 91–100; Atkins to Williamson, April 13, 1676; Governor Josiah Winslow to Captain Thomas Smith, Approval for Transportation of 110 Enslaved New England Indians on the *Seaflower*, April 9, 1676, MS 1695, no. 1, NLJ; and Governor John Leavitt to Smith, Certificate for Transporting 70 Enslaved New England Indians on the *Seaflower*, September 12, 1676, MS 1695, no. 2, NLJ.

61. Barbados Assembly, minutes, June 13 and 14, 1676, CO 31/2, 222–24; Atkins to Lords of Trade, March 26, 1680, CO 1/44, 134–39; Atkins to Williamson, April 13, 1676; Linford D. Fisher, " 'Dangerous Designes': The 1676 Barbados Act to Prohibit New England Indian Slave Importation," *WMQ*, 71, no. 1 (January 2014): 114; Jamaica Council, minutes, December 12, 1676, CO 140/3, 535–36; John Eliot to Robert Boyle, November 27, 1683, *Collections of the Massachusetts Historical Society* 1 (1794): 183.

62. Sir John Temple, *The Irish Rebellion* [. . .] (London, 1646); Toby Barnard, "1641: A Bibliographical Essay," in *Ulster 1641: Aspects of the Rising*, ed. Brian Mac Cuarta (Belfast: Queen's University of Belfast, 1993), 178–79; Kathleen Noonan, "Martyrs in Flames: Sir John Temple and the Conception of the Irish in English Martyrologies," *Albion* 36, no. 2 (2004): 223–55.

63. Temple, *The Irish Rebellion*, 6, 31, 40, 66, 68, 84, 87, 91, 93, 94, 103; Nicholas Canny, *Kingdom and Colony: Ireland in the Atlantic World, 1560–1800* (Baltimore: Johns Hopkins University Press, 1988), 64–65; Nicholas Canny, "What Really Happened in Ireland in 1641?" in *Ireland from Independence to Occupation, 1641–1660*, ed. Jane H. Ohlmeyer (New York: Cambridge University Press, 1995), 24–42.

64. Barbados Council, minutes, September 1, 1657, Lucas Transcript, microfilm, reel 2:366–67, BNLS; Beckles, "A 'Riotous and Unruly Lot' "; Newman, *New World of Labor*, 79–82.

65. Governor's Proclamation, Barbados Council, minutes, September 22, 1657, Lucas Transcript, microfilm, reel 2:368, BNLS.

66. Barbados Council, minutes, June 11 and 26, 1660, August 1, 1660, CO 31/1, 810, 1012, 1830; Petition of the Inhabitants of Montserrat to the Governor of Barbados, [January] 1668, CO 1/22, 31; Francis Sampson to John Sampson, June 6, 1666, CO 1/20, 165–66; Henry Willoughby to Secretary Arlington, February 2, 1667, CO 1/21, 24–25; William Willoughby to the King, February 11, 1668, CO 1/22, 62–63; William Willoughby to Williamson, April 3, 1668, CO 1/22, 101–2; Charles Wheler to the Committee Examining the Security of St. Christopher, July 7, 1675, CO 1/34, 225–26; Oliver, *Caribbeana*, 2:69–77.

67. Barbados Council, minutes, February 16, 1686, and March 16, 1686, Lucas Transcript, microfilm, reel 2:157–58, 160, BNLS; Beckles, *White Servitude and Black Slavery*, 112.

68. Stanwood, *Empire Reformed*, 90–96; Steele, *English Atlantic*, 95–97; Shona Johnston, "Papists in a Protestant World: The Catholic Anglo-Atlantic in the Seventeenth Century" (PhD diss., Georgetown University, 2011); Shaw, *Everyday Life*, 140–46.

69. Edwyn Stede to Earl of Shrewsbury, May 30, 1689, in *CSPCS*, 13:48–56; Copy of Andrew Lynche to Sir Thomas Montgomery, February 10, 1689, CO 28/37, 21; Evidences in Behalf of the King Examined Against James Hanley Accused of Speaking Dangerous Words, March 4, 1689, CO 28/37, 37; Deposition of Caesar Crawford, n.d., CO 28/37, 38; Deposition of Willin Legal, March 11, 1689, CO 28/37, 64; Memorandum as to the Appointment of Captain Edward Bourke to the Council of Barbados, June 29, 1698, in *CSPCS*, 16:298–99; Susan Dwyer Amussen, *Caribbean Exchanges: Slavery and the Transformation of English Society, 1640–1700* (Chapel Hill: University of North Carolina Press, 2007), 166; Barbados Council, minutes, March 11, 1689, Lucas Transcript, microfilm, reel 2:497, BNLS.

70. An Act for the Better Ordering and Governing of Negroes, September 27, 1661, CO 30/2, 16–22.

71. Jamaica Assembly, minutes, May 7, 1731, and March 11 and 17, 1736, *Journals of the Assembly of Jamaica* (Spanish Town, Jamaica, 1797), 3:7, 332, 335.

Chapter 2

1. Hugh Drysdale to Board of Trade (hereafter BT), June 29, 1723, Colonial Office series (hereafter CO) 5/1319, 114v, National Archives of the United Kingdom, Kew, London, accessed on microfilm compiled as the Virginia Colonial Records Project (hereafter VCRP) at the John D. Rockefeller Jr. Library, Colonial Williamsburg Foundation, Williamsburg, VA.

2. Jonathan Atkins to Joseph Williamson, April 13, 1676, in *Calendar of State Papers, Colonial Series: America and West Indies, 1574–1739* (hereafter *CSPCS*), 45 vols.(London, 1860–1994), 9:368; Barbados Assembly, minutes, June 13 and 14, 1676, CO 31/2, 222–23; Jamaica Council, minutes, September 3, 1675, and December 12, 1676, CO 140/3, 436–38, 535–36; Gregory E. O'Malley, "Beyond the Middle Passage: Slave Migration from the Caribbean to North America, 1619–1807," *William and Mary Quarterly*, 3rd ser. (hereafter *WMQ*), 66, no. 1 (January 2009), 131–37.

3. Jamaica Council, minutes, December 12, 15, and 19, 1692, CO 140/5, 228–30.

4. Jill Lepore, *The Name of War: King Philip's War and the Origins of American Identity* (New York: Vintage Books, 1999), 173–90; Sandra M. Gustafson, *Eloquence Is Power: Oratory and Performance in Early America* (Chapel Hill: University of North Carolina Press, 2000), 40–74.

5. Valentine Morris, memorandum, January 31, 1737, CO 9/10, 120–29; Earl of Londonderry to BT, January 30 and April 5, 1729, CO 152/17, 47–48, 69–70; Antigua Assembly, minutes, January 20, 24, and 28, 1729, CO 9/6, no fol.

6. [Nathaniel Crouch], *The English Empire in America* [. . .] (London, 1685), 201; Richard Bloome, *Present State of His Majesties Isles* [. . .] (London, 1687), 40. Claims of cheap print and mass audience are based on the quality of *English Empire in America* in five editions at the John Carter Brown Library at Brown University, Providence, RI.

7. John Oldmixon, *The British Empire in America* [. . .] (London, 1708), 2:14–15; cf. Richard Ligon, *A True & Exact History of the Island of Barbados* [. . .] (London, 1657), 45–46; [Crouch], *English Empire in America*, 73.

8. Oldmixon, *British Empire*, 2:38, 47; *Great Newes From the Barbadoes* [. . .] (London, 1676); [Nathaniel Saltonstall], *A Continuation of the State of New-England Being a Farther Account of the Indian Warr*, [. . .] *Together with an Account of the Intended Rebellion of the Negroes in the Barbadoes* (London, 1676).

9. Abbé Prévost, *Histoire Générale des Voyages* [. . .] (Paris, 1746), 15:598; "A Short Account of [. . .] the West-Indies," *London Magazine, or, Gentleman's Monthly Intelligencer Vol. XXVII For the Year 1758* (London, [1758]), 167; George Frere, *A Short History of Barbados* [. . .] (London, 1768), 36; *Atlas Geographus: or, a Compleat System of Geography, Ancient and Modern* [. . .] (London, 1711) 5:478, 481–82; John Pointer, *A Chronological History of England* [. . .] (Oxford, 1714), 1:392, 410.

10. Oldmixon, *British Empire*, 2:38, 47, 56, 58–59, 60–61.

11. Oldmixon, *British Empire*, 2:72, 118–19, 126.

12. Thomas Tryon, *Friendly Advice to the Gentlemen-Planters of the East and West Indies* [. . .] ([London], 1684), 131, 206–8; Robert Robertson, *A Detection of the State and Situation of the Present Sugar Planters* [. . .] (London, 1732), 26; *The World Displayed; or, a Curious Collection of Voyages and Travels, Selected from the Writers of All Nations* [. . .] (London, 1759), 4:157.

13. John Stewart to Charles Wager, July 3, 1730, in *CSPCS*, 37:158–59; "Tuesday the 14," Captain Christopher Allen's Journal to Molly's Town, March 1732, MST 440, National Library of Jamaica, Kingston (hereafter NLJ); Richard Beckford, speech, November 24, 1752, in *Journal of the Assembly of Jamaica* (hereafter *JAJ*) (Spanish Town, 1797), 4:387; Michael Craton, *Testing the Chains: Resistance to Slavery in the British West Indies* (Ithaca, NY: Cornell University Press, 1982), 81–92; Mavis Christine Campbell, *The Maroons of Jamaica, 1655–1796: A History of Resistance, Collaboration, and Betrayal* (Trenton, NJ: Africa World Press, 1990); Kenneth M. Bilby, *True-Born Maroons* (Gainesville: University Press of Florida, 2005). For an important reading of blackness and Maroons, see Kathleen Wilson, "The Performance of Freedom: Maroons and the Colonial Order in Eighteenth-Century Jamaica and the Atlantic Sound," *WMQ* 66, no. 1 (January 2009): 45–86.

14. Randy M. Browne, *Surviving Slavery in the British Caribbean* (Philadelphia: University of Pennsylvania Press, 2017), 157–89; Neil Roberts, *Freedom as Marronage* (Chicago: University of Chicago Press, 2015), 43–49, 71–85; Stephanie M. H. Camp, *Closer to Freedom: Enslaved Women and Everyday Resistance in the Plantation South* (Chapel Hill: University of North Carolina Press, 2004), 60–116; Vincent Brown, *The Reaper's Garden: Death and Power in the World of Atlantic Slavery* (Cambridge, MA: Harvard University Press, 2008), 63–81; Albert J. Raboteau, *Slave Religion: The "Invisible Institution" in the Antebellum South* (Oxford: Oxford University Press, 2004); Steven Hahn, *A Nation Under Our Feet: Black Political Struggles in the Rural South, from Slavery to the Great Migration* (Cambridge, MA: Belknap Press of Harvard University Press, 2003); Justin Roberts, *Slavery and the Enlightenment in the British Atlantic, 1750–1807* (Cambridge: Cambridge University Press, 2013), 266–73; Philip D. Morgan, *Slave Counterpoint: Black Culture in the Eighteenth-Century Chesapeake and Lowcountry* (Chapel Hill: University of North Carolina Press, 1998), 525–30. For a comparative perspective on the hemisphere's other exploitative labor regimes, see Jason T. Sharples, "Weapons of the Weak," in *The Princeton Companion to Atlantic History*, ed. Joseph C. Miller (Princeton, NJ: Princeton University Press, 2015), 491–95.

15. Jamaica Assembly, minutes, March 27, April 5, 8, and 16, 1746, in *JAJ*, 4:8, 11–12, 19.

16. Edward Hyde [Cornbury] to BT, February 10, 1708, in *Documents Relative to the Colonial History of the State of New York* [. . .], ed. E. B. O'Callaghan (Albany: Weed, Parsons, and Co., 1855), 5:39.

17. Kenneth Scott, "The Slave Insurrection in New York in 1712," *New-York Historical Society Quarterly* 45, no. 1 (January 1961): 43–74; Thelma Wills Foote, " 'Some Hard Usage':

The New York City Slave Revolt of 1712," *New York Folklore* 18, nos. 1–4 (1992): 147–59; John Sharpe to the Society of the Propagation of the Gospel in Foreign Parts, June 23, 1712, in "The Negro Plot of 1712," ed. Roswell R. Hoes, *New York Genealogical and Biographical Record* 21 (October 1890): 162–63; William Smith, *The History of the Province of New-York* [. . .] (New York, 1757), 133; Robert Hunter to BT, June 23, 1712, in O'Callaghan, *Documents Relative*, 5:341–42.

18. Virginia Council, minutes, April 22, 1713, in *Executive Journals of the Council of Colonial Virginia*, ed. H. R. McIlwaine (Richmond, VA: Superintendent of Public Printing, 1928), 3:336–37.

19. Ray A. Kea, " 'When I Die, I Shall Return to My Own Land': An 'Amina' Slave Rebellion in the Danish West Indies, 1733–1734," in *The Cloth of Many Colored Silks: Papers on History and Society, Ghanaian and Islamic, in Honor of Ivor Wilks*, ed. John Hunwick and Nancy Lawler (Evanston, IL: Northwestern University Press, 1996), 169, 187; Jon F. Sensbach, *Rebecca's Revival: Creating Black Christianity in the Atlantic World* (Cambridge, MA: Harvard University Press, 2005), 8–27.

20. William Byrd to John Perceval, Earl of Egmont, July 12, 1736, in *The Correspondence of the Three William Byrds of Westover, 1684–1776*, ed. Marion Tinling (Charlottesville: University Press of Virginia, 1977), 2:487–88.

21. Jennifer L. Morgan, *Laboring Women: Reproduction and Gender in New World Slavery* (Philadelphia: University of Pennsylvania Press, 2004), 173.

22. *An Essay Concerning Slavery, and the Danger Jamaica is Expos'd To* [. . .] (London, 1746), 46, 51.

23. Sowande' M. Mustakeem, *Slavery at Sea: Terror, Sex, and Sickness in the Middle Passage* (Champaign: University of Illinois Press, 2016); Marcus Rediker, *The Slave Ship: A Human History* (New York: Viking, 2007); Stephanie E. Smallwood, *Saltwater Slavery: A Middle Passage from Africa to American Diaspora* (Cambridge, MA: Harvard University Press, 2007).

24. Voyages: The Trans-Atlantic Slave Trade, Estimates Database, accessed December 30, 2018, https://www.slavevoyages.org/estimates/. As of now, the Trans-Atlantic Slave Trade Database does not incorporate transshipment estimates—for example, from Barbados to Virginia—from the intercolonial slave trade outlined in Gregory E. O'Malley, *Final Passages: The Intercolonial Slave Trade of British America, 1619–1807* (Chapel Hill: University of North Carolina Press, 2014). Alex Borucki and Gregory E. O'Malley, "Final Passages: The Intra-American Slave Trade Database," paper, American Historical Association Annual Meeting, Washington, DC, January 4, 2018).

25. Susan B. Carter et al., eds. *Historical Statistics of the United States: Millennial Edition* (Cambridge: Cambridge University Press, 2006), 5:653, table Eg53.

26. Virginia Council, minutes, March 21, April 18, 27, 1710, in McIlwaine, *Executive Journals*, 3:234–35, 236, 242–43; Edmund Jenings to BT, April 24, June 10, 1710, CO 5/1316, 141–42, 144–45, accessed on microfilm, VCRP; Philip Meadows to Alexander Spotswood, August 28, 1710, CO 5/1363, 200; Virginia Assembly, minutes, October 26, 1710, in *Journals of the House of Burgesses of Virginia* [. . .] *1710–1712*, ed. H. R. McIlwaine (Richmond: [The Colonial Press], 1912), 240. O'Malley's estimates for the intercolonial slave trade to the Chesapeake region are quintennial and cannot be combined with the annual data in Appendix, table 3. Nevertheless, O'Malley's data's only meaningful amendment to table 3 is to suggest an increased pace of

arrivals of enslaved Africans during 1711–15 and 1716–20. If anything, this signals even greater among white Virginians. O'Malley, *Final Passages*, 175, table 8; 177, table 10.

27. Hugh Drysdale to BT, December 20, 1722, CO 5/1319, 83, accessed on microfilm, VCRP; Judgment, 1722, and Order, 1723, Mss3 V8b 142–144, Virginia Historical Society, Richmond.

28. Morgan, *Slave Counterpoint*, 61, table 10; An Additional Act to an Act Entitled an Act for the Better Ordering and Governing of Negroes and All Other Slaves, December 18, 1714, in *The Statutes at Large of South Carolina*, ed. David J. McCord (Columbia, SC, 1840), 7:367.

29. David Eltis, "The British Transatlantic Slave Trade Before 1714: Annual Estimates of Volume and Direction," in *The Lesser Antilles in the Age of European Expansion*, ed. Robert L. Paquette and Stanley L. Engerman (Gainesville: University Press of Florida, 1996), 182–205; Robert V. Wells, *The Population of the British Colonies in America Before 1776* (Princeton, NJ: Princeton University Press, 1975), 209–12, tables VI-13 and VI-14.

30. Voyages: The Trans-Atlantic Slave Trade, Estimates Database, accessed December 29, 2018, https://slavevoyages.org/estimates.

31. Bermuda Assembly, minutes, February 5 and August 5, 1729, June 22 and 23, 1730, CO 40/3; Bermuda Council, minutes, May 21, 1730, CO 40/4; Ralph Noden, Petition of the Merchants of London Trading to Bermuda and Other American Colonies, in BT, minutes, November 23, 1731, CO 37/12, 76–77; John Pitt to BT, January 27, 1731, CO 37/12, 81–82; BT, Report to Privy Council, December 8, 1731, CO 38/8, 163–65; Clarence V. Maxwell, "The Horrid Villainy: Sarah Bassett and the Poisoning Conspiracies in Bermuda, 1727–30," *Slavery and Abolition* 21, no. 3 (December 2000): 48–74; Wells, *Population of the British Colonies*, 173–74, table VI-1. For French colonists possibly mistaking spoiled food for a poison conspiracy attributed to François Macandal in Saint-Domingue (1757), see Trevor Burnard and John Garrigus, *The Plantation Machine: Atlantic Capitalism in French Saint-Domingue and British Jamaica* (Philadelphia: University of Pennsylvania Press, 2016), 113–19.

32. Bahamas Legislative Council, minutes, August 30, 1734, January 3, 1735, CO 26/2A, 90, 103; Richard Fitzwilliam to Henry Lascelles, September 5, 1734, CO 23/3, 100; Richard Fitzwilliam to BT, September 6, 1734, CO 23/3, 98–99; Fitzwilliam to Duke of Newcastle, March 11, 1735, CO 23/14, 239.

33. [James Knight], "The Natural, Moral, and Political History of Jamaica [. . .] to the year 1742," 2 vols. (unpublished book manuscript), 2:79v–80, 83v–84, British Library, London (hereafter BL), Additional Manuscripts (hereafter Add. MSS) 12,418–19; Edward Long, *The History of Jamaica* [. . .] (London, 1774), 2:405, 415.

34. Archibald Campbell, Memorandum Relative to the Island of Jamaica, 1782, MS 16, 6v, NLJ; Maria Alessandra Bollettino, " 'Of equal or of more service': Black Soldiers and the British Empire in the Mid-Eighteenth-Century Caribbean," *Slavery and Abolition* 38, no. 3 (September 2017): 510–33; Philip D. Morgan and Andrew Jackson O'Shaughnessy, "Arming Slaves in the American Revolution," in *Arming Slaves from Classical Times to the Modern Age*, eds. Christopher Leslie Brown and Philip D. Morgan (New Haven, CT: Yale University Press, 2006), 184–86.

35. [Knight], "History of Jamaica," 2:84–84v; Trevor Burnard, *Mastery, Tyranny, and Desire: Thomas Thistlewood and His Slaves in the Anglo-Jamaican World* (Chapel Hill: University of North Carolina Press, 2004), 172–73; Long, *History of Jamaica*, 1:135, 2:452.

36. Council and Assembly of Jamaica, representation to BT, March 11, 1734, in *CSPCS*, 41:48–52; Oldmixon, *British Empire*, 2:14; Robert Pringle to Nathaniel French, August 20, 1739,

in *The Letterbook of Robert Pringle*, ed. Walter Edgar, (Columbia: University of South Carolina Press, 1972), 1:122.

37. Walter Tullideph to Thomas Tullideph, October 3, 1737, Walter Tullideph Letter Book, GD205/53/8, 67, National Archives of Scotland, Edinburgh; John Lindsay to William Robertson, August 6, 1776, MS 3942, fols. 259–63, National Library of Scotland, Edinburgh.

38. Hilary Beckles, *Black Rebellion in Barbados: The Struggle Against Slavery, 1627–1838* (Bridgetown, Barbados: Antilles Publications, 1984); Morgan, *Laboring Women*, chap. 6.

39. Morgan, *Laboring Women*, 187.

40. Wells, *Population of the British Colonies*, 240.

41. Morgan, *Slave Counterpoint*, 61, table 10.

42. Camp, *Closer to Freedom*, 12–28; Sally Hadden, *Slave Patrols: Law and Violence in Virginia and the Carolinas* (Cambridge, MA: Harvard University Press, 2001).

43. [Knight], "History of Jamaica," 1:224, 227, 2:77–78; Henry Barham, "The Civil History of Jamaica to the Year 1722," Add. MSS 12,422:135, BL; Proposals for Increasing the Number of White Inhabitants and for Promoting the Further Settlement of the Island of Jamaica, n.d., BL, Add. MSS 22,676:141–42; *Weekly Jamaica Courant*, March 25 and June 24, 1730; John Stewart to Charles Wager, July 3, 1730, in *CSPCS*, 37:158–59; Trevor Burnard, *Planters, Merchants, and Slaves: Plantation Societies in British America, 1650–1820* (Chicago: University of Chicago Press, 2015), 63–64; Richard Pares, *War and Trade in the West Indies, 1739–1763* (London: Frank Cass, 1963), 229–30; "An Account of White People come to Jamaica by Virtue of Several Acts for the Introducing and Encouragement of White Setlers Pas'd the 15th of May 1736 the 21st May 1743 the 2 July 1747 and the October 1750 with the Expence attending them & the Quantity of Land Granted to them," copy of CO 137/28, MS 2074, NLJ.

44. [Knight], "History of Jamaica," 2:79v.

45. Pares, *War and Trade in the West Indies*, 228–29, 234–37; Burnard, *Planters, Merchants, and Slaves*, 64–65; Frederick G. Spurdle, *Early West Indian Government: Showing the Progress of Government in Barbados, Jamaica and the Leeward Islands, 1660–1783* (New Zealand: self-pub., 1964), 61; Long, *History of Jamaica*, 1:123–55, 178; Alexander Dirom, *Thoughts on the State of the Militia of Jamaica* (Jamaica, 1783), 7; Archibald Campbell, quoted in Andrew Jackson O'Shaughnessy, *An Empire Divided: The American Revolution and the British Caribbean* (Philadelphia: University of Pennsylvania Press, 2000), 49.

46. [William Wood], *Occasional Papers on the Assiento and the Affairs of Jamaica* (London, 1716), 33; Jamaica Assembly, minutes, May 12, 1731, in *JAJ*, 3:6; [Knight], "History of Jamaica," 1:272v, 2:79v.

47. "Narrative of the Maroons," Papers Relating to Jamaica, BL, Add. MSS 12,431:69–75; Ayscough to BT, May 15, 1735, in *CSPCS*, 41:423–28; William Mathew to BT, January 17, 1737, in *CSPCS*, 43:10–13; Thomas Thistlewood, diary, December 25, 1765, OSB176, folder 16, p. 283, Thomas Thistlewood Papers, James Marshall and Marie-Louise Osborn Collection, Beinecke Rare Book and Manuscript Library, Yale University, accessed February 15, 2019, http://hdl .handle.net/10079/fa/beinecke.thistle; O'Shaughnessy, *Empire Divided*, 43–53; [Knight], "History of Jamaica," 2:79.

48. Jerome Handler, "Freedmen and Slaves in the Barbados Militia," *Journal of Caribbean History* 19, no. 1 (May 1984): 1–3, 8, 17; P. F. Campbell, "The Barbados Militia 1627–1815," *Journal of the Barbados Museum and Historical Society* 35 (1976), 112–15; Beckles, *Black Rebellion in Barbados*, 49–50; Morgan, *Laboring Women*, 43–48.

49. Virginia Assembly, minutes, October 26, 1710, in McIlwaine, *House of Burgesses of Virginia* [. . .] *1710–1712*, 240; Alexander Spotswood to BT, October 15, 1712, CO 5/1316, 385, accessed on microfilm, VCRP; Hugh Drysdale to BT, December 20, 1722, CO 5/1319, 83, accessed on microfilm, VCRP; Drysdale, address to Virginia Assembly, May 10, 1723, in *Journals of the House of Burgesses of Virginia* [. . .] *1720–1722, 1723–1726*, ed. H. R. McIlwaine (Richmond: [The Colonial Press], 1912), 360.

50. William Gooch to BT, June 29, 1729, and Gooch to Andrew Stone, November 6, 1743, William Gooch Official Correspondence, TR 16.1 and TR 16.3, John D. Rockefeller Jr. Library, Colonial Williamsburg Foundation, Williamsburg, VA; Hadden, *Slave Patrols*, 28–31, 96; Gooch to BT, September 14, 1730, February 12, 1731, CO 5/1322, 158–59, 161–63, accessed on microfilm, VCRP; Gooch to Bishop of London, May 28, 1731, Fulham Palace Papers 15, no. 111, accessed on microfilm, VCRP.

51. Hadden, *Slave Patrols*, 19–24; Peter H. Wood, *Black Majority: Negroes in Colonial South Carolina from 1670 Through the Stono Rebellion* (New York: W. W. Norton, 1974), 275–76; *South Carolina Gazette*, June 14–26, 1740.

52. Edward Trelawny to Jamaica Council and Assembly, February 14, 1745, in Jamaica Council, minutes, CO 140/31; Walter Tullideph to Thomas Tullideph, June 11, 1737, GD 205/53/8, 59–61, National Archives of Scotland, Edinburgh.

53. Bryan Edwards, marginalia, 1779, in Long, *History of Jamaica*, 2:383, accessed at the West Indies Collection, University of the West Indies at Mona. Emphasis in the original.

54. "The Speech of Moses Bon Saam [. . .]," *Gentleman's Magazine* 4 (September 1734): 510; [George Clarke] to BT, June 20, 1741, CO 5/1094, 188–89.

55. William Berkeley to Charles II and the Privy Council, July 1673, in *The Papers of Sir William Berkeley, 1605–1677*, ed. Warren M. Billings (Richmond: Library of Virginia, 2007), 423.

56. "The Petition of the Inhabitants of New Inverness, to Gen. Oglethorpe, Jan. 3, 1739," *Gentleman's Magazine* 11 (January 1741): 30; July 13, 1747, *Detailed Reports on the Salzburger Emigrants* [. . .] *Edited by Samuel Urlsperger*, ed. George Fenwick Jones, trans. Eva Pulgram (Athens: University of Georgia Press, 1989), 11:85.

57. Edward Long, memorandum, n.d. [1782?], Papers Relating to Jamaica, BL, Add. MSS 12,431:8, 15; Alan Taylor, *The Internal Enemy: Slavery and War in Virginia, 1772–1832* (New York: W. W. Norton, 2014).

58. Owen Stanwood, *The Empire Reformed: English American in the Age of the Glorious Revolution* (Philadelphia: University of Pennsylvania Press, 2013); Michael Graham, "Popish Plots: Protestant Fears in Early Maryland, 1676–1689," *The Catholic Historical Review* 79, no. 2 (April 1993): 197–216; Smith, *History of the Province of New-York*, 133; Petition, [Feb. 1765], Charles Garth Letter Book, fols. 150v–51, William L. Clements Library, University of Michigan, Ann Arbor.

59. Jamaica Council, minutes, February 15, 21, and 23, 1734, CO 140/25, no fol.; [Knight], "History of Jamaica," 1:270; William Revolution [pseud.], *The Real Crisis* [. . . .] (London, 1735); Letter to James Knight, n.d., Papers Relating to Jamaica, BL, Add. MSS 12,431:75–77.

60. R. P., *The Case of the Negroes in Our American Plantations* ([Kingston, Jamaica?], 1745), 2, 4.

61. Alejandra Dubcovsky, *Informed Power: Communication in the Early American South* (Cambridge, MA: Harvard University Press, 2016); Elena A. Schneider, *The Occupation of*

Havana: War, Trade, and Slavery in the Atlantic World (Chapel Hill: University of North Carolina Press, 2018).

62. Anon. to Mr. Boone in London, June 24, 1720, quoted in Herbert Aptheker, *American Negro Slave Revolts* (New York: Columbia University Press, 1943), 175; Copy of a Representation of the BT, September 8, 1721, in O'Callaghan, *Documents Relative*, 5:610; Jonathan Shrine to Samuel Wragg, March 3, 1720, in *CSPCS*, 32:4; Daniel Bell to William Wragg, March 4, 1720, in *CSPCS*, 32:5.

63. James Kendall to Lords of Trade, November 3, 1692, CO 28/1, 206.

64. Barbados Council, minutes, December 16 and 28, 1701, CO 31/6, 91–94, 94–98; Barbados Council, minutes, January 6, 1702, CO 31/6, 108–9, 112–13, 132–34v; Barbados Council, minutes, January 13, 1702, CO 31/6, 115–17; Barbados Council, minutes, January 20 and 25, 1702, CO 31/6, 121–26; Barbados Council, minutes, February 6, 1702, CO 31/6, 145–46; Barbados Council, minutes, February 10, 1702, CO 31/6, 156–57; Barbados Assembly, minutes, December 23, 1701, CO 31/6, 443–44; Barbados Assembly, minutes, January 13 and 14, 1702, CO 31/6, 444–46; David Marley, *Wars of the Americas: A Chronology of Armed Conflict in the New World, 1492 to the Present* (Santa Barbara, CA: ABC-CLIO, 1998), 220–21.

65. Christian Lilly, notebook, BL, Add. MSS 12,427:44v, 99, 130; Letter of James Glen, February 3, 1748, quoted in Wood, *Black Majority*, 303–4; *South Carolina Gazette*, December 9, 1732, and July 7, 1733.

66. Gooch to BT, June 8, 1728, CO 5/132, 44–46, accessed on microfilm, VCRP; Gooch to brother, April 4, 1728, and June 28, 1729, Sir William Gooch's Letters to His Brother, 1727–1750, TR 17, Colonial Williamsburg Foundation, Williamsburg, Virginia.

67. Commons House of Assembly to the King, March 2, 1734, House Journal for November 14, 1733–May 31, 1734, transcript, pp. 141–48, South Carolina Department of Archives and History (hereafter SCDAH), Columbia; *South Carolina Gazette*, June 15, 1734.

68. *The New-York Gazette*, March 25, 1734, in *Documents Relating to the Colonial History of the State of New Jersey*, ed. William Nelson (Patterson, NJ, 1894), 11:335–37; *The Weekly Rehearsal*, February 11, 1734, in *Documents Relating to the Colonial History*, 11:333; "Extract of a Letter from Antigua," *Boston News-Letter*, February 28, 1734; South Carolina Council, minutes, February 26, 1733, Council Journal no. 5, pt. 2, pp. 571–73, SCDAH; South Carolina Assembly, minutes, February 26 and March 2, 1733, Commons House Journal no. 8, pp. 32–34, 44, SCDAH; William Gooch to Bishop of London, September 20, 1735, Fulham Papers (Papers of the Bishops of London) 15, no. 46, Lambeth Palace Library, London, UK, accessed on microfilm, VCRP.

69. Wood, *Black Majority*, 314; Robert Pringle to Andrew Pringle, December 27, 1739, in Edgar, *Letterbook of Robert Pringle*, 1:163.

70. William Stephens, journal entry, June 11, 1740, in *Colonial Records of the State of Georgia*, ed. Allen D. Candler (Atlanta: Franklin, 1906), 4:592; Robert Pringle to Andrew Pringle, July 14, 1740, in Edgar, *Letterbook of Robert Pringle*, 1:230; Benjamin Martin, "An Impartial Inquiry into the State and Utility of the Province of Georgia" (London, 1741) in *Collections of the Georgia Historical Society* (Savannah, 1840), 1:173; Robert Pringle to Andrew Pringle, November 22, 1740, in Edgar, *Letterbook of Robert Pringle*, 1:273.

71. *Pennsylvania Gazette*, March 25, 1742. For the scare of 1741, see Chapter 3.

72. *South Carolina Gazette*, August 15, 1741; South Carolina Assembly, minutes, January 25, 1742, in *Journal of the Commons House of Assembly, September 14, 1742–January 27, 1744*,

ed. J. H. Easterby (Columbia, SC: SCDAH, 1954), 344; Grand Jury Presentment, March 17, 1742, in Easterby, *Journal of the Commons House*, 72; *South Carolina Gazette*, March 27 and April 24, 1742, quoted in Leigh Eric Schmidt, " 'The Grand Prophet,' Hugh Bryan: Early Evangelicalism's Challenge to the Establishment and Slavery in the Colonial South," *South Carolina Historical Magazine* 87 (October 1986): 239–50; Elizabeth Lucas Pinckney, memoranda, July 2 and September 8, 1742, in *The Letterbook of Eliza Lucas Pinckney, 1739–1762*, ed. Elise Pinckney (Columbia: University of South Carolina Press, 1972), 54, 55; South Carolina Council, minutes, August 10, September 3–4, November 24, 1742, Council Journal no. 8, pp. 189, 233–45, 358, SCDAH; Captain Pepper, letter to the governor, December 31, 1742, in Council Journal no. 8, pp. 406–7, SCDAH; Hill and Guerard to James Pierce, June 16, 1743, quoted in Hadden, *Slave Patrols*, 153.

73. Letters of J. Knight and Others Relating to Jamaica, December 12, 1740, BL, Add. MSS 22,677:44; J. A. Houlding, *Fit for Service: The Training of the British Army, 1715–1795* (New York: Oxford University Press, 1981), 410–13; Marley, *Wars of the Americas*, 260–63.

74. Governor to Jamaica Assembly, addresses, October 31, 1744, and February 14, 1745, CO 140/31; Jamaica Legislative Council, minutes, December 20–21, 1744, CO 140/31; Letters of J. Knight and Others Relating to Jamaica, August 10, 1745, and September 6, 1745, BL, Add. MSS 22,677:61–62; O'Shaughnessy, *Empire Divided*, 44–47.

75. J[ohn] V[ernon], A[shton] W[arner], N[athaniel] G[ilbert], R[obert] A[rbuthnot], *A Genuine Narrative of the Intended Conspiracy of the Negroes at Antigua* [. . .] (Dublin, Ireland, 1737); *Boston News-Letter*, February 24, 1737; *Pennsylvania Gazette*, March 17 and 24, 1737; *New-York Weekly Journal*, March 28, and April 4, 18, and 25, 1737.

76. "By a Letter Dated Dec. 13," *American Weekly Mercury*, March 8, 1737; "By a Ship just arrived from Barbados," *Daily Gazetteer*, March 16, 1737.

77. Josiah Martin to Robert Freeman, December 10, 1736, and Martin to Barry Anderson, August 19, 1737, Martin Family Papers, BL, Add. MSS 41,352:112, 126, 128v; Vere Langford Oliver, comp., *History of the Island of Antigua* [. . .] (London: Mitchell and Hughes, 1896), 2:248.

78. Oliver, *Antigua*, 1:107; State of Council of Antigua, encl. in John Yeamans to Thomas Hill, February 2, 1739, in *CSPCS*, 45:21.

79. Ian K. Steele, *The English Atlantic 1675–1740: An Exploration of Communication and Community* (New York: Oxford University Press, 1986), 153–54, 163–64; James G. Basker, " 'The Next Insurrection': Johnson, Race, and Rebellion," *The Age of Johnson: A Scholarly Annual* 11 (2000): 39; Pierre Eugène Du Simitière, "Negroes Conspiracies in Several Parts of the West Indies and of North America," Papers Relating to the West Indies, 1749–73, box 4, Du Simitière Collection, Library Company of Philadelphia.

80. The conclusions that follow are drawn from consulting the following databases and reference materials: America's Historical Newspapers (EBSCO/Newsbank); *British Periodicals Online*; Burney Collection, BL; *South Carolina Gazette*, microfilm, Library of Congress; *Weekly Jamaica Courant*, microfilm, NLJ; Caribbean newspapers at American Antiquarian Society; Clarence Saunders Brigham, *History and Bibliography of American Newspapers, 1690–1820* (Worcester, MA: American Antiquarian Society, 1947–61), esp. 2; Howard S. Pactor, *Colonial British Caribbean Newspapers: A Bibliography and Directory* (New York: Greenwood Press, 1990).

81. Adam Fox, *Oral and Literate Culture in England, 1500–1700* (Oxford: Clarendon Press, 2000), 5–19, 37, 50. See also Margaret Spufford, *Small Books and Pleasant Histories: Popular*

Fiction and Its Readership in Seventeenth-Century England (Athens: University of Georgia Press, 1982), 11, 68; Walter Ong, "Orality and Literacy: Writing Restructures Consciousness," in *The Book History Reader*, ed. David Finkelstein and Alistair McCleery (New York: Routledge, 2002): 105–17.

82. Douglas Hay et al., *Albion's Fatal Tree: Crime and Society in Eighteenth-Century England* (New York: Pantheon Books, 1975); David D. Hall, *Worlds of Wonder, Days of Judgment: Popular Religious Belief in Early New England*, (New York: Alfred A. Knopf, 1989), 21, 83, 183; Frank Lambert, *Inventing The "Great Awakening"* (Princeton, NJ: Princeton University Press, 1999).

83. "Extract of a Letter from Antigua," *Boston News-Letter*, February 28, 1734. This incident has not been categorized as a conspiracy scare because no evidence indicates that it rose above the level of a rumor.

84. Jill Lepore, *New York Burning: Liberty, Slavery, and Conspiracy in Eighteenth-Century Manhattan* (New York: Vintage Books, 2006), 53.

85. *New-York Weekly Journal*, June 15, 1741; *Pennsylvania Gazette*, June 18, 1741.

86. *American National Biography Online*, s.v. "Parker, James," by Jean Ashton, accessed September 23, 2018, https://doi.org/10.1093/anb/9780198606697.article.0100697; David Waldstreicher, *Runaway America: Benjamin Franklin, Slavery, and the American Revolution* (New York: Hill and Wang, 2004), 121, 155–56; Lepore, *New York Burning*, 214–15; Daniel Horsmanden, *A Journal of the Proceedings in the Detection of the Conspiracy Formed by Some White People, in Conjunction with Negro and Other Slaves* [. . .] (New York, 1744), vi; *Pennsylvania Gazette*, June 28, July 12 and 19, 1744; *New-York Gazette or Weekly Post-Boy*, January 18, and October 10 and 17, 1748.

87. *The Annals of Europe for the Year 1741* [. . .] (London, 1743), 429–31.

88. *The Life and Adventures of Bampfylde-Moore Carew* (London, 1745; many reprints); Robert Goadby, *An Apology for the Life of Mr. Bampfylde-Moore Carew* (London, 1749; nine editions), 33; *Oxford Dictionary of National Biography*, s.v. "Carew, Bampfylde Moore," by John Ashton, rev. Heather Shore, accessed October 3, 2018, https://doi-org/10.1093/ref:odnb/4623.

89. Smith, *History of the Province of New-York*, 133, 188; *The American Gazetteer* (London, 1762), 3:[321]; *The North-American and the West-Indian Gazetteer* (London, 1776), [240].

90. William Douglass, *A Summary, Historical and Political* [. . .] *of the British Settlements in North-America* (Boston, 1752), 2:256.

91. New York City Council Minutes, July 10, 1745, in *Minutes of the Common Council of the City of New York, 1675–1776*, ed. Herbert L. Osgood et al. (New York: Dodd, Mead, 1905), 5:151.

92. *American Weekly Mercury*, February 20, 1745.

93. "Extract of a Letter from Jamaica," *Boston Evening Post*, April 1, 1745; Samuel Boyse, *An Historical Review of the Transactions of Europe, from the Commencement of the War with Spain in 1739* [. . .] (London, 1748), 2:171; Richard Rolt, *An Impartial Representation of the Conduct of the Several Powers of Europe, Engaged in the Late General War* [. . .] (London, 1750), 4:33; *The British Chronologist; Comprehending Every Material Occurrence* [. . .] (London, 1775), 2:345.

94. Jamaica Legislative Council, minutes, December 21, 1744, CO 140/31, no fol.; Jamaica Assembly, minutes, *JAJ*, 3:672; "Petition of Thomas Edwards, Late Slave to Thomas Fuller Esquire of Jamaica," 1744, CO 137/48, 92.

95. Jonathan Atkins to Joseph Williamson, October 3, 1675, CO 1/35, 231.

Chapter 3

1. Daniel Horsmanden, *A Journal of the Proceedings in the Detection of the Conspiracy Formed by Some White People, in Conjunction with Negro and Other Slaves* [. . .] (New York, 1744), 147.

2. John Vernon et al., Report on the Proceedings, December 30, 1736, Colonial Office series (hereafter CO), 9/10, 105, National Archives of the United Kingdom, Kew, London; Trial of Langford's Robin, November 13, 1736, CO 9/11, 57.

3. Walter Tullideph to David Tullideph, January 15, 1737, in Walter Tullideph Letter Book, Ogilvy Papers, GD 205/53/8, 52–54, National Archives of Scotland, Edinburgh; Antigua Council, minutes, October 1736 to March 1737, CO 9/10, 49–91, and CO 9/11, 35–44; David Barry Gaspar, *Bondmen and Rebels: A Study of Master-Slave Relations in Antigua* (Durham, NC: Duke University Press, 1985).

4. Josiah Martin to Robert Freeman, December 10, 1736, and Martin to Barry Anderson, August 19, 1737, Martin Family Papers, British Library, London (hereafter BL), Additional Manuscripts (hereafter Add. MSS), 41,352:112, 126, 128v; Vere Langford Oliver, comp., *History of the Island of Antigua* [. . .] (London: Mitchell and Hughes, 1896), 2:248. For the similar example of Edward Byam Jr., see Oliver, *Antigua*, 1:107, and State of Council of Antigua, encl. in John Yeamans to Thomas Hill, February 2, 1739, in *Calendar of State Papers, Colonial Series: America and West Indies, 1574–1739* (hereafter *CSPCS*), 45 vols. (London, 1860–1994), 45:21.

5. Antigua Council, minutes, March 16, 1738, CO 9/11, 104; Jill Lepore, *New York Burning: Liberty, Slavery, and Conspiracy in Eighteenth-Century Manhattan* (New York: Vintage, 2006), 159; Horsmanden, *Journal*, 32–33, 49, 69, 87, 90, 194.

6. Confession of Pedro, in John Schultz, deposition, July 1, 1741, in Horsmanden, *Journal*, 119; The King v. Ward's Will, July 2, 1741, in Horsmanden, *Journal*, 119; Confession of Will, July 4, 1741, in Horsmanden, *Journal*, 125.

7. Confession of Pedro, June 29, 1741, in Horsmanden, *Journal*, 113–14; John Williams, information, March 19, 1742, in Horsmanden, *Journal*, appendix, p. 9; Confession of Will, July 4, 1741, in Horsmanden, *Journal*, 125.

8. John Schultz, deposition, July 1, 1741, in Horsmanden, *Journal*, 119; Confession of Will, July 4, 1741, in Horsmanden, *Journal*, 125; Serena Zabin, *Dangerous Economies: Status and Commerce in Imperial New York* (Philadelphia: University of Pennsylvania Press, 2009), 1, 132; Gregory E. O'Malley, *Final Passages: The Intercolonial Slave Trade of British America, 1619–1807* (Chapel Hill: University of North Carolina Press, 2014), 219–63.

9. Oliver, *Antigua*, 1:xcviii, cxiii; Robert V. Wells, *The Population of the British Colonies in America before 1776* (Princeton, NJ: Princeton University Press, 1975), 209, table VI-13, and 212, table VI-14; Elsa V. Goveia, *Slave Society in the British Leeward Islands at the End of the Eighteenth Century* (New Haven, CT: Yale University Press, 1965), 169, 176, 182–84; Philip J. Schwarz, *Twice Condemned: Slaves and the Criminal Laws of Virginia, 1705–1865* (Baton Rouge: Louisiana State University Press, 1988), 30; Thomas L. Morris, *Southern Slavery and the Law, 1619–1860* (Chapel Hill: University of North Carolina Press, 1996), 211–15; Robert Olwell, *Masters, Slaves and Subjects: The Culture of Power in the South Carolina Low Country* (Ithaca, NY: Cornell University Press, 1998), 63, 75–76.

10. Information here and in the next three paragraphs all drawn from Robert Arbuthnot, information to Antigua Council, October 15, 1736, CO 9/10, 41–50.

11. Antigua Assembly, minutes, October 15 and 19, 1736, CO 9/12, 13v, 14; Antigua Legislative Council, minutes, October 15 and 19, 1736, CO 9/9, 60, 62.

12. Gaspar, *Bondmen and Rebels*, 22–29. When the members of the first court became overwhelmed in late December by the cascading accusations, arrests, and trial, the assembly relieved them with a five-man board that served for the remainder of the investigation.

13. Susan B. Carter et al., eds. *Historical Statistics of the United States: Millennial Edition* (Cambridge: Cambridge University Press, 2006), 5:655, table Eg62; Graham Russel Hodges, *Root and Branch: African Americans in New York and East Jersey, 1613–1863* (Chapel Hill: University of North Carolina Press, 1999), 273, table 1.

14. James Alexander to David Provoost, April 22, 1741, James Alexander Papers, box 2, microfilm, New-York Historical Society (hereafter NYHS); Horsmanden, *Journal*, 8.

15. Governor George Clarke to Duke of Newcastle, June 20, 1741, CO 5/1094, 183–85; Clarke, speech, April 15, 1741, Parish Transcripts, folder 162, fol. 3, NYHS; Clarke to Board of Trade (hereafter BT), June 20, 1741, CO 5/1094, 187v; Zabin, *Dangerous Economies*, 147; New York City (hereafter NYC) Council, minutes, April 11, 1741, in *Minutes of the Common Council of the City of New York, 1675–1776* (New York: Dodd, Mead, 1905), 5:17.

16. Horsmanden, *Journal*, 4; Anne Kannady, deposition, April 13, 1741, in Horsmanden, *Journal*, appendix, p. 1.

17. New York Council, minutes, April 9 and 10, 1742, Parish Transcripts, folder 162, fols. 10–11, NYHS; NYC Council, minutes, May 8, 1742, in *Minutes of the Common Council*, 5:52–53, 60–61; Lepore, *New York Burning*, 211–14.

18. Peter Charles Hoffer, *The Great New York Conspiracy of 1741: Slavery, Crime, and Colonial Law* (Lawrence: University Press of Kansas, 2003), 43, 77–79; Horsmanden, *Journal*, 13, 27, 28; An Act for the More Effectual Preventing and Punishing the Conspiracy and Insurrection of Negro and other Slaves [. . .], in *Colonial Laws of New York from the Year 1664 to the Revolution*, ed. Charles Z. Lincoln, William H. Johnson, and A. Judd Northrop (Albany, NY: J. B. Lyon, 1894), 2:679–88.

19. Londonderry to BT, April 5, 1729, CO 152/17, 69–70; Antigua Legislative Council, minutes, March 29, 1729, CO 9/6, no fol.; Vincent Brown, *The Reaper's Garden: Death and Power in the World of Atlantic Slavery* (Cambridge, MA: Harvard University Press, 2008), 129–56; James Scott, address to the governor, August 30, 1734, CO 26/2B, 227v; Thomas [Baten?] to Robert Hamilton, postscript June 12, 1760, letter of April 20, 1760, Hamilton Papers, box 17, bundle 113, Ayrshire Archives, Ayr, Scotland; Ronald Schechter, *A Genealogy of Terror in Eighteenth-Century France* (Chicago: University of Chicago Press, 2018), ch. 3.

20. "Extract of a Letter from Antigua," *Virginia Gazette*, May 20, 1737; Gaspar, *Bondmen and Rebels*, 22–23; Marisa J. Fuentes, *Dispossessed Lives: Enslaved Women, Violence, and the Archive* (Philadelphia: University of Pennsylvania Press, 2016), 110.

21. Winthrop D. Jordan, *Tumult and Silence at Second Creek: An Inquiry into a Civil War Slave Conspiracy* (Baton Rouge: Louisiana State University Press, 1993), 90–94; James L. Given, *Inquisition and Medieval Society: Power, Discipline, and Resistance in Languedoc* (Ithaca, NY: Cornell University Press, 1997), 54; Peter Brooks, *Troubling Confessions: Speaking Guilt in Law and Literature* (Chicago: University of Chicago Press, 2000), 20–25; Lisa Silverman, *Tortured Subjects: Pain, Truth, and the Body in Early Modern France* (Chicago: University of Chicago Press, 2001), 11, 86–88.

22. Morris, *Southern Slavery and the Law*, 238; Hoffer, *Great New York Conspiracy*, 28; Lepore, *New York Burning*, 91–92; Antigua Assembly, minutes, October 22 and 23, 1736, CO

9/12, 14v–17; Judges to Governor, messages, November 6 and 11, 1736, CO 9/10, 2–3, 10; Letter from Boston, March 15, 1737, *Virginia Gazette*, May 20, 1737.

23. Vernon et al., Report on the Proceedings, December 30, 1736, CO 9/10, 105; Walter Tullideph to David Tullideph, January 15, 1737, Tullideph Letter Book, 54; Gaspar, *Bondmen and Rebels*, 29–35.

24. Horsmanden, *Journal*, ii, 25.

25. Margaret Salinburgh [Peg Kerry], voluntary confession, May 7, 1741, in Horsmanden, *Journal*, 20, 21; Examination of Margaret Salinburgh, May 9, 1741, in Horsmanden, *Journal*, 24.

26. Examination of Sandy, May 22 and 24, 1741, in Horsmanden, *Journal*, 32–33, 35; Horsmanden, sentencing statement, in *Journal*, 76.

27. Execution of Quack and Cuffee, May 30, 1741, in Horsmanden, *Journal*, 45, 47; Horsmanden, commentary, in *Journal*, 48; Quack, confession, May 30, 1741, CO 5/1094, 197.

28. Execution of Quack and Cuffee, May 30, 1741, in Horsmanden, *Journal*, 47; Fuentes, *Dispossessed Lives*, 103.

29. Jack, confession, June 8–10, 1741, CO 5/1094, 199–20; Examination and Confession of Will alias Tickle, June 12, 1741, in Horsmanden, *Journal*, 71–72.

30. New York Council, minutes, June 14, 1741, Parish Transcripts, folder 162, fol. 7v, NYHS; Horsmanden, commentary, in *Journal*, 86, 107; Clarke to BT, June 20, 1741, CO 5/1094, 188.

31. Report, January 26, 1737, CO 9/10, 116; Robert W. Gordon, "Paradoxical Property," in *Early Modern Conceptions of Property*, ed. John Brewer and Susan Staves (New York: Routledge, 1996), 95–110.

32. Lincoln, Johnson, and Northrop, *Colonial Laws of New York*, 1:519–521, 631; Hoffer, *Great New York Conspiracy*, 26; L. H. Roper, "The 1701 'Act for the better ordering of Slaves': Reconsidering the History of Slavery in Proprietary South Carolina," *William and Mary Quarterly*, 3rd ser., 64, no. 2 (April 2007): 409–10.

33. Trial of Cuffey, December 13, 1736, CO 9/10, 90, 90a; Trial of Primus, CO 9/11, 23–24; Trial of Vigo, December 10, 1736, CO 9/10, 86; Trial of Ned Chester, November 26, 1736, CO 9/10, 68–69; Trial of Cromwell, November 30, 1736, CO 9/10, 75; Trial of Sydserf's Robin, November 15, 1736, CO 9/10, 58.

34. Oliver, *Antigua*, 1:118; Evidence against Johnno, January 21, 1737, CO 9/11, 11; Trial of Monk's Mingo, November 15, 1736, CO 9/10, 59, 60; Trial of Langford's Robin, November 13, 1736, CO 9/10, 57; Trial of Tom, December 8, 1736, CO 9/10, 83; Trial of Ocoo, December 11, 1736, CO 9/10, 88; Evidence against Royal's Hector, January 26, 1737, CO 9/11, 19.

35. Hugh Drysdale to BT, June 29, 1723, CO 5/1319, 112–17; "Bill for Transportation of Dick," Mss3 V8b 69–131, items 93–95, Virginia Historical Society, Richmond; Hoffer, *Great New York Conspiracy*, 27.

36. Judges' Note, January 20, 1737, CO 9/11, 39–40; Antigua Council, minutes, February 24, 1737, CO 9/11, 44; Antigua Council, minutes, March 9, 1737, CO 9/11, 51; Antigua Council, minutes, March 17, 1737, CO 9/11, 56–59; Antigua Council, minutes, March 16, 1738, CO 9/11, 103–4; Gaspar, *Bondmen and Rebels*, 37–38.

37. Hoffer, *Great New York Conspiracy*, 78–79, 100.

38. Examination of Jack, June 6, 1741, in Horsmanden, *Journal*, 63; Hoffer, *Great New York Conspiracy*, 123.

39. Horsmanden, commentary, in *Journal*, 62, 68, 87, 142.

40. Horsmanden, commentary, in *Journal*, 57, 81, 133; J[ohn] V[ernon], A[shton] W[arner], N[athaniel] G[ilbert], R[obert] A[rbuthnot], *A Genuine Narrative of the Intended Conspiracy of the Negroes at Antigua* [. . .] (Dublin, 1737).

41. Trial of Quack and Cuffee, May 29, 1741, in Horsmanden, *Journal*, 42.

42. Horsmanden, commentary, in *Journal*, 81–82.

43. Horsmanden, commentary, in *Journal*, 63, 74, 85–86, 133; Confession of Jack, June 8–10, 1741, CO 5/1094, 199–201v.

44. Horsmanden, commentary, in *Journal*, 133.

45. Robert Delap, Petition to Assembly, November 29, 1736, CO 9/10, 18; Philip Darby, petition, January 31, 1737, CO 9/10, 132; Oliver, *Antigua*, 1:xcix, cii, 195–97; 2:305–8; 3:404, 419.

46. Trial of Vernon's Cudjoe, January 26, 1737; Evidence against Parham Watty, January 14, 1737, CO 9/11, 9, 16–19.

47. Evidence against Parham Watty, January 14, 1737, CO 9/11, 9.

48. Evidence against Oliver's Quou, n.d., CO 9/11, 13; Evidence against Cusack's Yorke, December 12, 1736, CO 9/11, 36; Evidence against Barton's Joe, January 20, 1737, CO 9/11, 38; Evidence against Parham Watty, January 14, 1737, CO 9/11, 9; Trial of Budinot's Dick, November 19, 1736, CO 9/10, 64–65.

49. Trial of Vigo, December 10, 1736, CO 9/10, 86; Trial of Vernon's Cudjoe, January 26, 1737, CO 9/11, 16; Evidence against Parham Watty, January 14, 1737, CO 9/11, 37; Evidence against Parham Cuffey, December 15, 1736, CO 9/11, 9.

50. Trial of George, December 11, 1736, CO 9/10, 66; Chester's Frank [spy], Trial of Budinot's Dick, December 18, 1736, CO 9/10, 88–89.

51. Judges' report, December 30, 1736, CO 9/10, 99; Weatherill's Booty [spy], Evidence against Barton's Joe, January 20, 1737, CO 9/11, 40.

52. Antigua Assembly, minutes, October 22, 1736, CO 9/12, 15v–16; Valentine Morris et al., report on allegations of false testimony, February 14, 1737, CO 9/11, 23–24, 29–30; Antigua Council, minutes, March 10, 1737, and March 16, 1738, CO 9/11, 55, 104; Thomas Collins, deposition, Trial of Vernon's Cudjoe, January 26, 1737, CO 9/11, 16.

53. Trial of Vernon's Cudjoe, January 26, 1737, CO 9/11, 17; Chester's Frank [spy], Evidence against Parham Watty, January 14, 1737, CO 9/11, 9.

54. Judges to Antigua Council, reports, January 25 and 31, 1737, CO 9/10, 116, 119.

55. Lepore, *New York Burning*, 86; NYC Council, order, May 6, 1741, in *Minutes of the Common Council*, 5:20; Horsmanden, commentary, in *Journal*, ii, 107–8, 124.

56. Message from Council to Assembly, May 16, 1723, in *Journals of the House of Burgesses of Virginia* [. . .] *1720–1722, 1723–1726*, ed. H. R. McIlwaine (Richmond: [The Colonial Press], 1912), 367.

57. Daniel Horsmanden to Cadwallader Colden, August 7, 1741, in *The Letters and Papers of Cadwallader Colden* (New York: Printed for the New-York Historical Society, 1919), 2:226; Deposition of Mary Burton, April 22, 1741, in Horsmanden, *Journal*, 12–14.

58. Horsmanden, commentary, in Examination and Confession of Bastian, May 11, 1741, in Horsmanden, *Journal*, 105.

59. Horsmanden, commentary, in *Journal*, 20, 48, 72.

60. Horsmanden, commentary, in *Journal*, 17, 31, 73.

61. Deposition of Arthur Price, May 7, 1741, in Horsmanden, *Journal*, 19.

62. Horsmanden, commentary, in *Journal*, 26, 29, 32–33; Trial of Cuffee Philipse, May 29, 1741, in Horsmanden, *Journal*, 38.

63. Horsmanden, commentary, in *Journal*, 32; Examination of Sawney [Sandy], May 22, 1741, in Horsmanden, *Journal*, 32; Deposition of John Schultz, July 10, 1741, in Horsmanden, *Journal*, 133.

64. Examination of Margaret Salinburgh [Peg Kerry], May 9, 1741, in Horsmanden, *Journal*, 23.

65. Confession of York, June 20, 1741, CO 5/1094, 204a; Horsmanden, commentary, in *Journal*, 69.

66. Zabin, *Dangerous Economies*, 134–35; Lepore, *New York Burning*, 62; Arbuthnot, information to Antigua Council, October 15, 1736, CO 9/10, 41–47; Trial of Morgan's Newport, November 9, 1736, CO 9/10, 55.

67. Barbara J. Shapiro, *A Culture of Fact: England, 1550–1720* (Ithaca, NY: Cornell University Press, 2000), 15; Shapiro, *"Beyond Reasonable Doubt" and "Probable Cause": Historical Perspectives on the Anglo-American Law of Evidence* (Oakland: University of California Press, 1991), 128–38 (quoting Richard Bolton, *A Justice of the Peace for Ireland* [. . .] [Dublin, 1683], 95), 164–68; Evidence against Barton's Joe, January 20, 1737, CO 9/11, 39–40.

68. Trial of Delap's Tom, December 8, 1736, CO 9/10, 83; Trial of John Sabby, December 10, 1736, CO 9/10, 86.

69. Shapiro, *Beyond Reasonable Doubt*, 129; Arbuthnot, information to Antigua Council, October 15, 1736, CO 9/10, 41–50.

70. William Hawkins, *A Treatise of the Pleas of the Crown* [. . .] (London, 1739), 2:400; Hoffer, *Great New York Conspiracy*, 90–91; Arbuthnot, information to Antigua Council, October 15, 1736, CO 9/10, 41–50.

71. Trial of Vernon's Cudjoe, January 26, 1737, CO 9/11, 13, 15; Gaspar, *Bondmen and Rebels*, 103.

72. Zabin, *Dangerous Economies*, 152–53; Horsmanden to Colden, August 7, 1741, in *Letters and Papers of Cadwallader Colden*, 2:226.

73. Horsmanden to Colden, August 7, 1741, in *Letters and Papers of Cadwallader Colden*, 2:226–27; Confession of Sandy, May 22, 1741, in Horsmanden, *Journal*, 32; Trial of Augustine Gutierrez, June 17, 1741, in Horsmanden, *Journal*, 81.

74. Horsmanden, commentary, in *Journal*, 3, 24.

75. Horsmanden to Colden, August 7, 1741, in *Letters and Papers of Cadwallader Colden*, 2:226–27; Horsmanden, commentary, in *Journal*, 48.

76. Shapiro, *Culture of Fact*, 19; Horsmanden to Colden, August 7, 1741, in *Letters and Papers of Cadwallader Colden*, 2:224–28; James Oglethorpe to Clarke, May 16, 1741, encl. in Clarke to BT, June 20, 1741, CO 5/1094, 207; Horsmanden, commentary, in *Journal*, 94.

77. Confession of Tom, June 18, 1741, in Horsmanden, *Journal*, 84; Deposition of Mary Burton, June 25, 1741, in Horsmanden, *Journal*, 95–96; Examination and Confession of Adam Murray, June 27, 1741, in Horsmanden, *Journal*, 103; Clarke to BT, June 20, 1741, CO 5/1094, 189; Horsmanden, commentary, in *Journal*, 94.

78. Examination of Bastian, July 13, 1741, in Horsmanden, *Journal*, 138; James Favieres to Daniel Horsmanden, n.d., in Horsmanden, *Journal*, appendix, pp. 6–7; Clarke to BT, August 24, 1741, CO 5/1094, 211.

79. Trial of Tomlinson's Barryman, n.d., CO 9/10, 62; Trial of Skerret's Billy, November 19, 1736, CO 9/10, 62; Trial of Budinot's Dick, November 19, 1736, CO 9/10, 64; Trial of Ned Chester, November 26, 1736, CO 9/10, 70; Trial of Natty, n.d., CO 9/10, 90a.

80. Trial of Delap's Tom, December 8, 1736, CO 9/10, 83; Trial of Delap's Robin, December 8, 1736, CO 9/10, 83; Trial of Codrington's Sackey, December 8, 1736, CO 9/10, 83–84; Trial of Sanderson's Toney, December 8, 1736, CO 9/10, 84; Trial of Pare's Quawcoo, December 9, 1736, CO 9/10, 84–85; Trial of John Sabby, December 10, 1736, CO 9/10, 85–86; Trial of Pare's Vigo, December 10, 1736, CO 9/10, 86; Trial of Pare's Caesar alias Geddon, December 10, 1736, CO 9/10, 87; Trial of Ash's George, December 11, 1736, CO 9/10, 88; Trial of Lyndsey's Quashee, December 13, 1736, CO 9/10, 91; Evidence against Billy Sabby, n.d., CO 9/11, 41; Evidence against Pare's Cudjoe, n.d., CO 9/11, 42.

81. Arbuthnot, information to Antigua Council, October 15, 1736, CO 9/10, 47–48; Judges' report, November 6, 1736, CO 9/10, 3.

82. Walter Tullideph to David Tullideph, January 15, 1737, Tullideph Letter Book, 53; Judges' report, November 15, 1736, CO 9/10, 14; Trial of Budinot's Dick, November 19, 1736, CO 9/10, 64.

83. Trial of Sydserf's Robin alias Baggo, CO 9/10, 57–58.

84. Trial of Monk's Mingo, November 15, 1736, CO 9/10, 58–60; Trial of Lavington's Sampson, November 17, CO 9/10, 60–61; Trial of Tomlinson's Barryman, n.d., CO 9/10, 61–62; Trial of Budinot's Dick, November 19, CO 9/10, 63–65; Trial of Tom, November 24, CO 9/10, 66–68; Trial of Hanson's Quashee, November 24, CO 9/10, 66–[67a]; Trial of Ned Chester, November 26, CO 9/10, [67a]–70; Trial of Tilgarth Penezar alias Targut, November 26, CO 9/10, 71–72.

85. Trial of Budinot's Dick, November 19, 1736, CO 9/10, 63.

86. Trial of Budinot's Dick, November 19, 1736, CO 9/10, 63; Judges' report, November 11, 1736, CO 9/10, 9.

87. Trial of Tilgarth Penezar alias Targut, November 26, 1736, CO 9/10, 72.

88. Trial of Ned Chester, November 26, 1736, CO 9/10, 69.

89. Antigua Assembly to Governor and Council, March 31, 1737, CO 9/11, 63, 64; Mathew to BT, June 21, 1738, in *CSPCS*, 44:149.

90. [Charles Dunbar], "Some Reasons Humbly Offered to Consideration for Stopping the Farther Execution of Slaves Concern'd in the Barbarous Conspiracy," January 17, 1737, CO 9/10, 97–98; John Vernon, response to "Some Reasons for Stopping," January 24, 1737, CO 9/10, 131.

91. Valentine Morris and John Vernon, responses to "Some Reasons for Stopping," January 24, 1737, CO 9/10, 120–32; Antigua Council, message to Assembly, January 31, 1737, CO 9/10, 133–34; Antigua Council, minutes, January 24, 1729, CO 9/6; Londonderry to BT, April 5, 1729, CO 152/17, 69–70.

92. Antigua Assembly, minutes, January 24, 1737, CO 9/12, 61; Valentine Morris et al., report on allegations of false testimony, February 14, 1737, CO 9/11, 21–34.

93. Antigua Council, minutes, January 8 and 31, 1737, CO 9/10, 39–40, 119; Antigua Assembly, minutes, January 25, 1737, CO 9/12, 62; Messages between Antigua Assembly and Council, February 1, 1737, CO 9/11, 31–33.

94. Antigua Council, minutes, February 28, CO 9/11, 46; March 7, 1737, CO 9/11, 47; March 9, 1737, CO 9/11, 51; March 10, 1737, CO 9/11, 55; March 31, 1737, CO 9/11, 63; April 25, 1737, CO 9/11, 81–82; March 16, 1738, CO 9/11, 103–4; Walter Tullideph to David Tullideph, January 15, 1737, Tullideph Letter Book, 56–58.

95. [Josiah Cotton] to Cadwallader Colden, [July] 1741, copy encl. in Colden to Clarke, [August 1741], in *Letters and Papers of Cadwallader Colden*, 8:270–72; Lepore, *New York Burning*, 208–10 and notes 10–12.

96. Horsmanden to Colden, August 7, 1741, in *Letters and Papers of Cadwallader Colden*, 2:226–27.

97. New York Shipping Register, July 9–August 15, 1741, CO 5/1226, 177–80; "A List of Negroes Committed on Account of the Conspiracy," and Deposition of Elias Rice, March 19, 1742, in Horsmanden, *Journal*, appendix, pp. 8, 12–15.

Chapter 4

1. John Vernon et al., Report on the Proceedings, December 30, 1736, Colonial Office series (hereafter CO), 9/10, 104, National Archives of the United Kingdom, Kew, London.

2. Stephanie Smallwood, *Saltwater Slavery: A Middle Passage from Africa to American Diaspora* (Cambridge, MA: Harvard University Press, 2007); 101–21; James Sweet, *Recreating Africa: Culture, Kinship, and Religion in the Afro-Portuguese World, 1441–1770* (Chapel Hill: University of North Carolina Press, 2003); Herman Bennett, *Africans in Colonial Mexico: Absolutism, Christianity, and Afro-Creole Consciousness, 1570–1640* (Bloomington: Indiana University Press, 2003); Richard S. Dunn, *A Tale of Two Plantations: Slave Life and Labor in Jamaica and Virginia* (Cambridge, MA: Harvard University Press, 2014), 74–130; Michael A. Gomez, *Exchanging Our Country Marks: The Transformation of African Identities in the Colonial and Antebellum South* (Chapel Hill: University of North Carolina Press, 1998); Dylan Penningroth, *The Claims of Kinfolk: African American Property and Community in the Nineteenth-Century South* (Chapel Hill: University of North Carolina Press, 2003), 79–109; Anthony Kaye, *Joining Places: Slave Neighborhoods in the Old South* (Chapel Hill: University of North Carolina Press, 2009); Stephanie M. H. Camp, *Closer to Freedom: Enslaved Women and Everyday Resistance in the Plantation South* (Chapel Hill: University of North Carolina Press, 2004), 60–78; Vincent Brown, *The Reaper's Garden: Death and Power in the World of Atlantic Slavery* (Cambridge, MA: Harvard University Press, 2008), 63–77, 113–28.

3. Camp, *Closer to Freedom*, 60–78; Neil Roberts, *Freedom as Marronage* (Chicago: University of Chicago Press, 2015), 39–49, 71–80.

4. Jeff Forret, *Slave Against Slave: Plantation Violence in the Old South* (Baton Rouge: Louisiana State University Press, 2015), 2–8, 25, 75–79; Randy M. Browne, *Surviving Slavery in the British Caribbean* (Philadelphia: University of Pennsylvania Press, 2017), 3–4, 176–78, 193; Marjoleine Kars, "Dodging Rebellion: Politics and Gender in the Berbice Slave Uprising of 1763," *American Historical Review* 121, no. 1 (February 2016): 39–69; Vernon et al., Report on the Proceedings, December 30, 1736, CO 9/10, 109.

5. Joseph C. Miller, "Retention, Re-Invention, and Remembering: Restoring Identities Through Enslavement in Africa and Under Slavery in Brazil," in *Enslaving Connections: Changing Cultures of Africa and Brazil During the Era of Slavery*, ed. José C. Curto and Paul E. Lovejoy (Amherst, NY: Prometheus/Humanity Books, 2003), 81–121; Vincent Brown, "Social Death and Political Life in the Study of Slavery," *American Historical Review* 114, no. 5 (December 2009): 1246.

6. Smallwood, *Saltwater Slavery*, 195–96; Dunn, *Tale of Two Plantations*, 74–130; Robin Law, "Ethnicity and the Slave Trade: 'Lucumi' and 'Nago' as Ethnonyms in West Africa," *History in Africa* 24 (1997): 205–19.

7. Kaye, *Joining Places*; Philip D. Morgan, *Slave Counterpoint: Black Culture in the Eighteenth-Century Chesapeake and Lowcountry* (Chapel Hill: University of North Carolina Press, 1997), 441–77.

8. Walter Johnson, *River of Dark Dreams: Slavery and Empire in the Cotton Kingdom* (Cambridge, MA: Belknap, 2013), 209–43.

9. [James Knight], "The Natural, Moral, and Political History of Jamaica [. . .] to the year 1742," 2 vols. (unpublished book manuscript), 2:79–79v, 81v–82v, British Library, London (hereafter BL), Additional Manuscripts (hereafter Add. MSS), 12,418–19.

10. Evidence against Vernon's Cudjoe, January 26, 1737, CO 9/11, 15; Robert Holloway to Charles Tudway, July 19, 1759, Tudway of Wells Antiguan Estate Papers (East Ardsley, UK: Microform Academic Publishers, 1998–99), microfilm, reel 16, Columbia University Library; Jeffery Bryan Taylor, information to Valentine Morris, Evidence against Cochran's Green, n.d., CO 9/11, 20.

11. Trial of Lavington's Sampson, November 17, 1736, CO 9/10, 60–61; Evidence against Buckhorne's Sampson, December 6, 1736, CO 9/11, 35; Chester's Frank [spy], report, December 18, 1736, CO 9/10, 65; Evidence against Lyons's Minan, n.d., CO 9/11, 20.

12. Trial of Budinot's Dick, November 19, 1736, CO 9/10, 64; Trial of Tilgarth Penezar alias Targut, November 26, 1736, CO 9/10, 71; Trial of Royal's Hector, January 6, 1737, CO 9/11, 18.

13. Trial of Tilgarth Penezar alias Targut, November 26, 1736, CO 9/10, 71, 72, 74; Trial of Jack, December 7, 1736, CO 9/10, 78–79; Trial of George, December 11, 1736, CO 9/10, 88; Trial of Cubbinah, December 8, 1736, CO 9/10, 81–82; Trial of Delap's Robin, December 8, 1736, CO 9/10, 83.

14. Evidence against Barton's Joe, January 20, 1737, CO 9/11, 40; Trial of Primus, December 13, 1736, CO 9/10, 90; Valentine Morris et al., report on allegations of false testimony, February 14, 1737, CO 9/11, 25–28; Browne, *Surviving Slavery*, 103, 119, 130, 176–79.

15. E. B. O'Callaghan, *The Documentary History of the State of New-York* (Albany, 1851), 4:186.

16. Peter Charles Hoffer, *The Great New York Conspiracy of 1741: Slavery, Crime, and Criminal Law* (Lawrence: University Press of Kansas, 2003), 63–65, 77, 91; Jill Lepore, *New York Burning: Liberty, Slavery, and Conspiracy in Eighteenth-Century Manhattan* (New York: Vintage, 2006), 130, 147, 149, 151; Confession of Caesar, June 20, 1741, in Daniel Horsmanden, *A Journal of the Proceedings in the Detection of the Conspiracy Formed by Some White People, in Conjunction with Negro and Other Slaves* [. . .] (New York, 1744), 89.

17. Confession of Cato, June 20, 1741, in Horsmanden, *Journal*, 90; Examination of Sandy, June 1, 1741, in Horsmanden, *Journal*, 49; Confession of Cajoe alias Africa, June 28, 1741, in Horsmanden, *Journal*, 111; Confession of Braveboy, June 30, 1741, in Horsmanden, *Journal*, 114; Examination and Confession of Jack, June 8, 1741, CO 5/1094, 200.

18. Trevor Burnard and Emma Hart, "Kingston, Jamaica, and Charleston, South Carolina: A New Look at Comparative Urbanization in Plantation Colonial British America," *Journal of Urban History* 39 (2013): 214–34; Trial of Tom, November 24, 1736, CO 9/10, 65; Trial of Cubbinah, December 8, 1736, CO 9/10, 80; Trial of Targut, November 26, 1736, CO 9/10, 73; Evidence against Parham Cuffey, December 15, 1736, CO 9/11, 37; Evidence against Parham Cuffey, December 15, 1736, CO 9/11, 36–38; Evidence against Parham Watty, January 14, 1737, CO 9/11, 6; Trial of Natty, January 12, 1737, CO 9/10, 92–93.

19. Trial of Caesar alias Geddon, December 10, 1736, CO 9/10, 87.

20. Evidence against Johnno, January 21, 1737, CO 9/11, 11; Trial of Monk's Mingo, n.d., CO 9/10, 58, 59; see also Evidence against Pare's Cudjoe, January 20, 1737, CO 9/11, 42.

21. Sasha Turner, *Contested Bodies: Pregnancy, Childrearing, and Slavery in Jamaica* (Philadelphia: University of Pennsylvania Press, 2017), 63–64, 168–69, 215–18; Browne, *Surviving Slavery*, 103, 130; Wilma King, "'Prematurely Knowing of Evil Things': The Sexual Abuse of African American Girls and Young Women in Slavery and Freedom," *Journal of African American History* 99, no. 3 (2014): 173–96.

22. Justices' report, January 24, 1737, CO 9/10, 99.

23. [Knight], "History of Jamaica," 2:79–79v; "Narrative of the Maroons," n.d., Papers Relating to Jamaica, BL, Add. MSS. 12,431:69–75.

24. Leeward Islands Council, minutes, December 5, 1729, CO 155/7, no fol.; Jamaica Council, minutes, December 15, 1744, and February 14, 1745, CO 140/31, no fol.

25. Trial of Hanson's Quashee, November 24, 1736, CO 9/10, 67a; Trial of Monk's Mingo, n.d., 1736, CO 9/10, 59; Trial of Ned Chester, November 26, 1736, CO 9/10, 68.

26. David Barry Gaspar, "From 'The Sense of Their Slavery': Slave Women and Resistance in Antigua, 1632–1763," in *More Than Chattel: Black Women and Slavery in the Americas* (Bloomington: Indiana University Press, 1996), 218–38; Hilary McD. Beckles, *Centering Woman: Gender Discourses in Caribbean Slavery* (Kingston, Jamaica: Ian Randle Publishers, 1999); Jennifer L. Morgan, *Laboring Women: Reproduction and Gender in New World Slavery* (Philadelphia: University of Pennsylvania Press, 2004), 64; Betty Wood, *Gender, Race, and Rank in a Revolutionary Age: The Georgia Lowcountry, 1750–1820* (Athens: University of Georgia Press, 2000); Betty Wood, *Women's Work, Men's Work: The Informal Slave Economies of Lowcountry Georgia* (Athens: University of Georgia Press, 1995); Jacqueline Jones, *Labor of Love, Labor of Sorrow: Black Women, Work, and the Family, from Slavery to the Present* (New York: Basic Books, 1985); Marietta Morrissey, *Slave Women in the New World: Gender Stratification in the Caribbean* (Lawrence: University Press of Kansas, 1989), chaps. 4–5; C. G. A. Oldendorp, *History of the Mission* [. . .] *of St. Thomas, St. Croix, and St. John*, ed. Johann Jakob Bossart, trans. Arnold R. Highfield and Vladimir Barac (Ann Arbor, MI: Karoma Publishers, 1987), 185, 264; Edna G. Bay, *Wives of the Leopard: Gender, Politics, and Culture in the Kingdom of Dahomey* (Charlottesville: University of Virginia Press, 1998).

27. Deposition of Arthur Price, May 12, 1741, in Horsmanden, *Journal*, 26; Examination of Fortune, May 22, 1741, in Horsmanden, *Journal*, 33; Lepore, *New York Burning*, 149.

28. Quack, Confession at the Stake, May 30, 1741, in Horsmanden, *Journal*, 46.

29. Lepore, *New York Burning*, 151–52; Kars, "Dodging Rebellion."

30. David Barry Gaspar, *Bondmen and Rebels: A Study of Master-Slave Relations in Antigua* (Durham, NC: Duke University Press, 1985), 248.

31. Trial of Budinot's Dick, November 19, 1736, CO 9/10, 63; Trial of Hanson's Quashee, November 24, 1736, CO 9/10, 67a; Evidence against Caesar, January 20, 1737, CO 9/11, 10; Trial of Sydserf's Robin, November 15, 1736, CO 9/10, 58; Evidence against Parham Watty, January 14, 1737, CO 9/11, 8; see also Evidence against Vernon's Cudjoe, January 26, 1737, CO 9/11, 13; Trial of Morgan's Newport, November 9, 1736, CO 9/10, 55; Horsmanden, commentary, in *Journal*, 25, 51.

32. Joseph C. Miller, "The Value of Material Goods and People in African Political Economies," in *Way of Death: Merchant Capitalism and the Angolan Slave Trade, 1730–1830* (Madison: University of Wisconsin Press, 1988), chap. 2.

33. Robert Arbuthnot, information to Antigua Council, October 15, 1736, CO 9/10, 41–47; Trial of Ned Chester, November 26, 1736, CO 9/10, 69.

34. Trial of Monk's Mingo, n.d., CO 9/10, 59–61; Trial of Natty, December [13], 1736, CO 9/10, 90; Trial of Langford's Robin, November 13, 1736, CO 9/10, 56–57; Trial of Ned Chester, November 26, 1736, CO 9/10, 67–70; Trial of Tom Hanson's Quashee, November 24, 1736, CO 9/10, 66–68.

35. Trial of Ned Chester, November 26, 1736, CO 9/10, 69–70.

36. Trial of Langford's Robin, November 13, 1736, CO 9/10, 57–58.

37. Evidence against Lyons's Minian, n.d., CO 9/11, 19; Trial of Otto's Tom, November 24, 1736, CO 9/10, 65.

38. Sandra E. Greene, *Gender, Ethnicity, and Social Change on the Upper Slave Coast: History of the Anlo-Ewe* (Portsmouth, NH: Heinemann, 1996); Law, "Ethnicity and the Slave Trade," 205–19; Mieko Nishida, *Slavery and Identity: Ethnicity, Gender, and Race in Salvador, Brazil, 1808–1888* (Bloomington: Indiana University Press, 2003).

39. Trial of Tilgarth Penezar alias Targut, November 26, 1736, CO 9/10, 71, 72; Trial of Cochran's Jack, December 3, 1736, CO 9/10, 77; Evidence against Oliver's Quou, January 21, 1737, CO 9/11, 12–13; Trial of Ned Chester, November 26, 1736, CO 9/10, 69–70; see also various examples in CO 9/10, 67, 84, 87, 91.

40. Trial of Ned Chester, November 26, 1736, CO 9/10, 69.

41. Evidence against Cusack's Yorke, December 12, 1736, CO 9/11, 36; Trial of Caesar alias Geddon, December 10, 1736, CO 9/10, 87; see also various examples at CO 9/10, 78, 68, 89–90.

42. Examination of Emanuel, October 12, 1736, CO 9/10, 50–53; Trial of Quawcoo, December 11, 1736, CO 9/10, 89; John K. Thornton, "War, the State, and Religious Norms in 'Coromantee' Thought: The Ideology of an African American Nation," in *Possible Pasts: Becoming Colonial in Early America*, ed. Robert Blair St. George (Ithaca, NY: Cornell University Press, 2000), 195–96.

43. Confession of London, June 20, 1741, CO 5/1094, 205; Examination and Confession of Bastian alias Tom Peal, June 11, 1741, in Horsmanden, *Journal*, 70.

44. Quack's Confession at the Stake, May 30, 1741, in Horsmanden, *Journal*, 46; cf. King v. Quack and Cuffee, CO 5/1094, 197v; Confession of Jack, June 8–10, 1741, CO 5/1094, 199; King v. Ben et al., June 15, 1741, in Horsmanden, *Journal*, 76.

45. Examination of Sawney [Sandy], May 22, 1741, in Horsmanden, *Journal*, 32, 33; Trial of Cook, June 12, 1741, in Horsmanden, *Journal*, 62; Deposition of Mary Burton, April 22, 1741, in Horsmanden, *Journal*, 13.

46. Shane White, " 'It Was a Proud Day': African Americans, Festivals, and Parades in the North, 1741–1834," *Journal of American History* 81 (1994): 13–50; Robert Dirks, *Black Saturnalia: Conflict and Its Ritual Expression on British West Indian Slave Plantations* (Gainesville: University of Florida Press, 1987); Walter C. Rucker, *The River Flows On: Black Resistance, Culture, and Identity Formation in Early America* (Baton Rouge: Louisiana State University Press, 2006), 56–57.

47. Confession of Bastian Upon Sentencing, June 11, 1741, in Horsmanden, *Journal*, 69; Deposition of Mary Burton, April 22, 1741, in Horsmanden, *Journal*, 13; Confession of London, June 25, 1741, in Horsmanden, *Journal*, 96–97.

48. Evidence against Lucas's Caesar, January 20, 1737, CO 9/11, 10; Evidence against Cusack's Yorke, December 12, 1736, CO 9/11, 36; Evidence against Lyons's Minian, n.d. [January 26, 1737], CO 9/11, 20; Trial of Quawcoo, December 9, 1736, CO 9/10, 84–85.

49. Deposition of Margaret Salingburgh [Peg Kerry], May 9, 1741, in Horsmanden, *Journal*, 22–23. Response of Elizabeth Romme, May 9, 1741, in Horsmanden, *Journal*, 23–24; Confession of Jack, June 8–10, 1741, CO 5/1094, 200v; Confession of Sleydall's Jack, June 12, 1741, in Horsmanden, *Journal*, 72–73; Lepore, *New York Burning*, 148.

50. Confession of London, June 25, 1741, in Horsmanden, *Journal*, 96–97; Evidence of Sawney alias Sandy, May 25, 1741, in Horsmanden, *Journal*, 35; Examination of Burk's Sarah, June 1, 1741, in Horsmanden, *Journal*, 50–52.

51. Charles Leslie, *A New and Exact Account of Jamaica* (London, 1740), 324; Edward Long, *History of Jamaica* (London, 1774), 2:422–23; Robin Law, *The Slave Coast of West Africa, 1550–1750: The Impact of the Atlantic Slave Trade on an African Society* (Oxford: Clarendon Press, 1991), 114–15, 155; John K. Thornton, *Warfare in Atlantic Africa, 1500–1800* (London: University College London Press, 1999), 90; Gaspar, *Bondmen and Rebels*, 244–47; Thornton, "War, the State, and Religious Norms," 192–93; Brown, *Reaper's Garden*, 149–50; Anne Gilbert to Rev. Richard Park, June 1, 1801, quoted in Vincent Brown, "Slavery and the Spirits of the Dead: Mortuary Politics in Jamaica, 1740–1834" (PhD diss., Duke University, 2002), 183; Diana Paton, *The Cultural Politics of Obeah* (Cambridge: Cambridge University Press, 2015); Kenneth Bilby, "Swearing by the Past, Swearing to the Future: Sacred Oaths, Alliances, and Treaties Among the Guianese and Jamaica Maroons," *Ethnohistory* 44, no. 4 (1997): 655–89.

52. Evidence against Parham Watty, January 14, 1737, CO 9/11, 8; Trial of Budinot's Dick, November 19, 1736, CO 9/10, 64; Trial of Ned Chester, November 26, 1736, CO 9/10, 70; Trial of Quashee, November 24, 1736, CO 9/10, 66.

53. Trial of Sydserf's Robin alias Boggo, November 15, 1736, CO 9/10, 57; Trial of Budinot's Dick, November 19, 1736, CO 9/10, 64; Information of Chester's Frank [spy], revealed December 18, 1736, appended to Trial of Buduinot's Dick, November 19, 1736, CO 9/10, 65; Trial of Ned Chester, November 26, 1736, CO 9/10, 70; Trial of Tilgarth Penezar alias Targut, November 26, 1736, CO 9/10, 73–74.

54. John Spurr, "A Profane History of Early Modern Oaths," *Transactions of the Royal Historical Society*, ser. 6, 11 (2001): 37–63.

55. Evidence against Parham Watty, January 14, 1737, CO 9/11, 7.

56. Vernon et al., Report on the Proceedings, December 30, 1736, CO 9/10, 106.

57. George Clark to Board of Trade, August 24, 1741, CO 5/1094, 211v; Confession of Tom Peal alias Bastian, June 11, 1741, CO 5/1094, 203.

58. Confession of Cuffee, May 9, 1741, in Arthur Price [jailer], deposition, May 26, 1741, in Horsmanden, *Journal*, 38; Sawney [Sandy], May 25, 1741, in Horsmanden, *Journal*, 35.

59. Confession of Tom Peal alias Bastian, June 11, 1741, CO 5/1094, 202v.

60. Confessions of Marschalk's York, June 20, 1741, CO 5/1094, 204a; Examination and Confession of Will alias Tickle or Ticklepitcher, June 12, 1741, in Horsmanden, *Journal*, 71, 75–76, 83.

61. Spurr, "Profane History," 49, 55, 62; Paul Kléber Monod, *Jacobitism and the English People, 1688–1788* (Cambridge: Cambridge University Press, 1989), 236–60.

62. Will alias Tickle or Ticklepitcher, June 12, 1741, in Horsmanden, *Journal*, 71–72; Confession of Caesar, June 22, 1741, in Horsmanden, *Journal*, 89; Confession of Wan, June 18, 1741, CO 5/1094, 204; Spurr, "Profane History," 46; Confession of Marschalk's London, June 20, CO 5/1094, 205; Confession of Sleydall's Jack, June 12, 1741, in Horsmanden, *Journal*, 72.

63. Confession of Tom Peal alias Bastian, June 11, 1741, CO 5/1094, 202v–203; Marschalk's York and Marschalk's London, confessions, June 20, 1741, in Horsmanden, *Journal*, 87–88.

64. Trial of London, December 3, 1736, CO 9/10, 78; Trial of Jack, December 7, 1736, CO 9/10, 78; Trial of Quamina, December 7, 1736, CO 9/10, 79; Trial of Delmore, December 13, 1736, CO 9/10, 91.

65. Trial of Quashee, November 24, 1736, CO 9/10, 66; Trial of Cubbinah, December 8, 1736, CO 9/10, 81–82; Evidence against Parham Watty, January 14, 1737, CO 9/11, 6; Evidence against Royall's Hector, January 26, 1737, CO 9/11, 17. For neighborhood identification in the United States, see Anthony E. Kaye, "Neighbourhoods and Solidarity in the Natchez District of Mississippi: Rethinking the Antebellum Slave Community," *Slavery and Abolition* 23 (April 2002): 2–16.

66. Trial of Jack, December 7, 1736, CO 9/10, 78.

67. Trial of London, December 7, 1736, CO 9/10, 77.

68. Brown, *Reaper's Garden*, 120–23; Smallwood, *Saltwater Slavery*, 111–12.

69. Bilby, "Swearing by the Past," 659–62; Brown, "Slavery and the Spirits of the Dead," 119; Greene, *Gender, Ethnicity, and Social Change*; Leroy Vail, ed., *The Creation of Tribalism in Southern Africa* (Los Angeles: University of California Press, 1989), esp. the essays by Leroy Vail, Robert Papstein, and Terence Ranger.

70. Horsmanden, commentary, in *Journal*, 194.

71. Deposition of Arthur Price, May 12, 1741, in Horsmanden, *Journal*, 26; Hoffer, *Great New York Conspiracy*, 63; Lepore, *New York Burning*, 99–101; Examination and Confession of Adam, June 27, 1741, in Horsmanden, *Journal*, 104.

72. Deposition of Arthur Price, May 12, 1741, in Horsmanden, *Journal*, 26–27; Hoffer, *Great New York Conspiracy*, 63.

73. Horsmanden, commentary, *Journal*, 33n, 193.

74. Examination of Sawney [Sandy], May 22, 1741, in Horsmanden, *Journal*, 32–33.

75. Trial of Cromwell, November 30, 1736, CO 9/10, 75.

76. Dying Confession of Quack, May 30, 1741, in Horsmanden, *Journal*, 46.

77. Inventory of Parham Estate, 1737, cited in Gaspar, *Bondmen and Rebels*, 105; Richard S. Dunn, "'Dreadful Idlers' in the Cane Fields: The Slave Labor Pattern on a Jamaican Sugar Estate, 1762–1831," *Journal of Interdisciplinary History* 17, no. 4 (Spring 1987): 806, table 2; B. W. Higman, *Slave Populations of the British Caribbean, 1807–1834* (Baltimore: Johns Hopkins University Press, 1984), 159–61, 170, 228, 585–86, tables 6.1, 6.2, 7.1, S7.9, S7.10; Oldendorp, *History of the Mission*, 225. The roster of field hands includes six people identified as such in the record and up to fifty-one more whose occupations were not recorded. In all likelihood, however, only thirty-four of those fifty-one were probably field workers because the other twenty-three served as informants and witnesses, a judicial role that correlated strongly throughout the record to holding more specialized positions in the labor structure.

78. Evidence against Parham Watty, January 14, 1737, CO 9/11, 8–9; Evidence against Oliver's Quou, January 21, 1737, CO 9/11, 12–13; Evidence against Lyons's Minan, n.d. [after January 26, 1737], CO 9/11, 20; Browne, *Surviving Slavery*, 73–74; Justin Roberts, *Slavery and the Enlightenment in the British Atlantic, 1750–1807* (Cambridge: Cambridge University Press, 2013), 213–14, 259–61.

79. Higman, *Slave Populations*, 189; Dunn, "Dreadful Idlers," 809, table 4.

80. Higman, *Slave Populations*, 171, 218, 246, 250, 259; Elsa V. Goveia, *Slave Society in the British Leeward Islands at the End of the Eighteenth Century* (New Haven, CT: Yale University Press, 1965), 146, 231, 250. John Blassingame, "Status and Social Structure in the Slave Community," in *Perspectives and Irony in American Slavery*, ed. Harry P. Owens (Jackson: University Press of Mississippi, 1976), 137–51.

81. Evidence against Royal's Hector, January 26, 1737, CO 9/11, 18; Trial of Tilgarth Penezar alias Targut, November 26, 1736, CO 9/10, 73.

82. Higman, *Slave Populations*, 94, 175.

83. Calculated from Jill Lepore, "Replication Data for: New York Burning: Liberty, Slavery, and Conspiracy in Eighteenth-Century Manhattan," version 2, Harvard Dataverse, 2011, http://hdl.handle.net/1902.1/16862.

84. Lepore, *New York Burning*, 135–36, 144, 148.

85. Trial of Skerret's Billy, November 19, 1736, CO 9/10, 62.

86. Confession of Comfort's Jack, Monday, June 8, 1741, CO 5/1094, 201v; Execution of Ward's Will, July 4, 1741, in Horsmanden, *Journal*, 125.

87. Confession of Soumain's Tom, June 26, 1741, in Horsmanden, *Journal*, 99.

88. Horsmanden, commentary, in *Journal*, 6–7; Confession of Todd's Dundee, June 24, 1741, in Horsmanden, *Journal*, 93–94; Confession of Tiebout's Jack, June 24, 1741, in Horsmanden, *Journal*, 94; Examination of Sarah Burk, May 25, 1741, in Horsmanden, *Journal*, 35.

89. Confession of Prince, June 13, 1741, in Horsmanden, *Journal*, 75.

90. Deposition of Arthur Price, in Horsmanden, *Journal*, 20.

91. Bermuda Council, minutes, September 1, 1741, *Bermuda Historical Quarterly* 27, no. 1 (1970): 1–6.

92. Trial of Lynch's Delmore, n.d. [December 1736], CO 9/10, 91; Trial of Elmes's Jack, December 3, 1736, CO 9/10, 78–79.

93. Confession of Martin's Tony, November 15, 1736, in Trial of Monk's Mingo, n.d., CO 9/10, 59–60.

94. Trial of Vernon's Cudjoe, January 26, 1737, CO 9/11, 13; Evidence against Parham Cuffey, December 15, 1736, CO 9/11, 36–37; Evidence against Parham Watty, January 14, 1737, CO 9/11, 6–10.

95. Evidence against Lucas's Caesar, January 20, 1737, CO 9/11, 10. This incident occurred sometime before December 7, 1736, when the witness began testifying.

96. Evidence against Barton's Joe, January 20, 1737, CO 9/11, 19; Evidence against Lyons's Minian, January 27, 1737, CO 9/11, 40–41.

97. Trial of Quawcoo, December 9, 1736, CO 9/10, 85.

98. Examination and Confession of Adam, in Horsmanden, *Journal*, 106.

99. Godsell's Ionian [spy], Evidence against Parham Cuffey, December 15, 1736, CO 9/11, 37; Evidence against Parham Watty, January 14, 1737, CO 9/11, 8–9.

100. Browne, *Surviving Slavery*, 74–75, 101; Gaspar, *Bondmen and Rebels*, 103.

Chapter 5

1. William Popple to Board of Trade (hereafter BT), February 28, 1762, Colonial Office series (hereafter CO), 37/19, 54v, National Archives of the United Kingdom, Kew, London; John Vickars, deposition, October 16, 1761, CO 40/11, 25–26.

2. "A Gentleman on the island of Jamaica, [. . .] dated Montego Bay, May 10," *Boston Evening Post*, July 28, 1760; Popple to BT, August 5, 1761, CO 37/19, 46–49; Michael J. Jarvis,

In the Eye of All Trade: Bermuda, Bermudians, and the Maritime Atlantic World, 1680–1783 (Chapel Hill: University of North Carolina Press, 2010), 382.

3. Stephen Fuller to Thomas Hall, January 2, 1761, MS 0220, box 1, folder 56, microfilm, Hall Family Papers and Sugar Plantation Records, Mandeville Special Collections Library, Geisel Library, University of California, San Diego (hereafter Hall Family Papers, UCSD).

4. "Part of a Letter from Bermuda dated December 3, 1761," *New York Mercury*, January 11, 1762; Bermuda Council, minutes, November 30, 1761, CO 40/11, no fol.; Bermuda Legislative Council, minutes, March 11, 1762, CO 40/10, no fol.; Legislative Council to Governor, October 21, 1761, CO 40/10, no fol.; Bermuda Legislative Council, address to Popple, March 25, 1762, CO 37/19, 64; Popple to Egremont, February 28, 1762, CO 37/19, 58; Bermuda Council, minutes, March 9, 1762, CO 40/11, no fol.

5. Bermuda Council Minutes, November 5, 1761, CO 40/11; Linda Colley, *Captives* [. . .] (New York: Pantheon Books, 2002), 8–10.

6. Bermuda Council, minutes, October 29 and November 5, 1761, CO 40/11, 30, 32; Popple to BT, February 28, 1762, CO 37/19, 54–57v.

7. Bermuda Council, minutes, October 16 and 17, 1761, CO 40/11, 25–27; Popple to BT, February 28, 1762, CO 37/19, 55v; Governor's Message, December 2, 1761, CO 40/10, 39.

8. Bermuda Council, minutes, November 13, 1761, CO 40/11, 33.

9. *New-York Mercury*, December 21, 1761, and January 8, 11, and 18, 1762; *Boston Evening-Post*, January 4 and 18, 1762, and June 14, 1762; *New York Gazette*, December 21, 1761; *Pennsylvania Journal*, December 24, 1761; *New-Hampshire Gazette*, January 8, 1762.

10. Popple to BT, February 28, 1762, CO 37/19, 54v–56; Bermuda Legislative Council Journal, March 9, 1762, CO 40/10, 4.

11. Popple, Address to Bermuda Assembly and Council, April 10, 1762, CO 40/10, no fol.; Popple to BT, November 3, 1762, CO 37/19, 108–109v; Jarvis, *Eye of All Trade*, 97.

12. Fred Anderson, *The Crucible of War: The Seven Years' War and the Fate of Empire in British North America, 1754–1766* (New York: Alfred A. Knopf, 2000), 28–29; Richard White, *The Middle Ground: Indians, Empires, and Republics in the Great Lakes Region, 1650–1815* (Cambridge: Cambridge University Press, 1991), 230–35; Matthew C. Ward, *Breaking the Backcountry: The Seven Years' War in Virginia and Pennsylvania, 1754–1765* (Pittsburgh: University of Pittsburgh Press, 2003); B. Scott Crawford, "A Frontier of Fear: Terrorism and Social Tension Along Virginia's Western Waters, 1742–1775," *West Virginia History: A Journal of Regional Studies*, n.s., 2, no. 2 (Fall 2008): 1–29; Peter Silver, *Our Savage Neighbors: How Indian War Transformed Early America* (New York: W. W. Norton, 2007).

13. Trials of Will and Abraham, August 4, 1752, Surry County Criminal Court Proceedings, 29–32, Library of Virginia, Richmond; Minutes of the Proceedings of the York County Court, April 4, 1753, York County Record Project; *Boston Post-Boy*, May 21, 1753.

14. Robert Dinwiddie to David Stewart, July 16, [1755], and Dinwiddie to Colonel Patton, July 16, 1755, in *The Official Records of Robert Dinwiddie* [. . .], ed. R. A. Brock (Richmond, VA: The [Virginia Historical] Society, 1883–84), 2:100–101.

15. Dinwiddie to Charles Carter, July 18, 1755, and Dinwiddie to Earl of Halifax, July 23, 1755, in Brock, *Records of Robert Dinwiddie*, 2:102–3, 114; W. Robert Higgins, "The Ambivalence of Freedom: Whites, Blacks, and the Coming of the Revolution in the South," in *The Revolutionary War in the South: Power, Conflict, and Leadership*, ed. W. Robert Higgins (Durham, NC: Duke University Press, 1979). Genealogical determination of younger Carter's identity

(Charles of Ludlowe) from Stella Pickett Hardy, *Colonial Families of the Southern States of America* [. . .] (New York: Tobias A. Wright, 1911), 111, 117–18.

16. Robert Raper, letters, February 9, March 4, March 19, March 23, May 31, and July 12, 1760, Robert Raper Letter Book, 34/0511, fols. 26–26v, 27v–28, 30–30v, 31–31v, 38, 42, South Carolina Historical Society, Charleston; William Henry Lyttelton to Paul Demere, August 15, 1759, fol. 384, Letter Book, August 1757–October 1759, Lyttelton Papers, Clements Library, University of Michigan; Lyttelton to Henry Ellis, August 18, 1759, fol. 388; Lyttelton to Captain Fairchild, August 28, 1759, fol. 391; and Lyttelton to Board of Trade, September 1, 1759, fols. 397–402.

17. South Carolina Council, minutes, June 20 and July 9, 1759, Council Journal no. 28, pp. 105–11, South Carolina Department of Archives and History (hereafter SCDAH), Columbia.

18. Samuel Martin to Samuel Martin Jr., August 6, 1754, British Library, London (hereafter BL), Additional Manuscripts (hereafter Add. MSS), 41,346:114; N. A. M. Rodger, "Sea-Power and Empire, 1688–1793," in *The Oxford History of the British Empire, Volume II: The Eighteenth Century*, ed. P. J. Marshall and Alaine Low (Oxford: Oxford University Press, 2001), 169.

19. Samuel Martin to Samuel Martin Jr., January 15, 1757, BL, Add. MSS 41,346:183; Josiah Martin to Samuel Martin Jr., February 2, 1757, BL, Add. MSS 41,361:9.

20. For the war's progress in the Caribbean, see Trevor Burnard and John Garrigus, *The Plantation Machine: Atlantic Capitalism in French Saint-Domingue and British Jamaica* (Philadelphia: University of Pennsylvania Press, 2016), 85–93.

21. Samuel Martin to Daniel Mathew, July 5, 1758, BL, Add. MSS 41,349:49v; Thomas Thistlewood, diary (hereafter Thistlewood Diary), March 23, 1756, box 2, folder 7, p. 52, accessed July 8, 2019, https://brbl-dl.library.yale.edu/vufind/Record/3971633, Thomas Thistlewood papers, OSB MSS 176, James Marshall and Marie-Louise Osborn Collection, Beinecke Rare Book and Manuscript Library, Yale University; Thistlewood Diary, March 26, 1757, box 2, folder 8, p. 63, accessed July 8, 2019, https://brbl-dl.library.yale.edu/vufind/Record/4079872; Thistlewood Diary, August 1, 1758, box 2, folder 9, p. 81, accessed July 9, 2019, https://brbl-dl .library.yale.edu/vufind/Record/4079873; Thistlewood Diary, April 8, 1759, box 2, folder 10, p. 73, accessed July 9, 2019, https://brbl-dl.library.yale.edu/vufind/Record/4079874; Stephen Blizzard, letter, June 10, 1759, Tudway of Wells Papers, microfilm, reel 16, Columbia University Library.

22. *Boston Gazette and Country Journal*, May 8, 1758; Burnard and Garrigus, *Plantation Machine*, 101–22. News of this "great Rebellion" arrived to Thistlewood in Jamaica on August 23, 1760, and he recorded that the number of insurgents was "6000" on December 20, 1760, Thistlewood Diary, box 2, folder 11, pp. 150, 232, accessed July 9, 2019, https://brbl-dl.library .yale.edu/vufind/Record/4079875.

23. Maria Alessandra Bollettino, "Slavery, War, and Britain's Atlantic Empire: Black Soldiers, Sailors, and Rebels in the Seven Years' War" (PhD diss., University of Texas at Austin, 2009); Vincent Brown, Slave Revolt in Jamaica, 1760–1761: A Cartographic Narrative, accessed July 9, 2012, http://revolt.axismaps.com/; Natalie A. Zacek, "Reading the Rebels and Mining the Maps: Digital Humanities and Cartographic Narratives," *American Historical Review* 121, no. 1 (February 2016): 167–75; Vincent Brown, *The Reaper's Garden: Death and Power in the World of Atlantic Slavery* (Cambridge, MA: Harvard University Press, 2010), 129–56; Michael Craton, *Testing the Chains: Resistance to Slavery in the British West Indies* (Ithaca, NY: Cornell

University Press, 1982), chap. 11; Burnard and Garrigus, *Plantation Machine*, 122–36; Trevor Burnard, *Mastery, Tyranny, and Desire: Thomas Thistlewood and His Slaves in the Anglo-Jamaica World* (Chapel Hill: University of North Carolina Press, 2012), 170–74; David Geggus, "The Causation of Slave Rebellions: An Overview," repr. in *Haitian Revolutionary Studies*, ed. David Patrick Geggus (Bloomington: Indiana University Press, 2002), 55–68.

24. Thomas [Baten?] to Robert Hamilton, April 20, 1760, Hamilton Papers, AA/DC/17/113, Ayrshire Archives, Ayr, Scotland; Craton, *Testing the Chains*, 136–37.

25. Jamaica Council, minutes, April 10 and 17, 1760, CO 137/32, 3–6.

26. Henry Moore, letter, April 24, 1760, CO 137/60, 300.

27. Francis Treble to Caleb Dickinson, June 2, 1760, quoted in Brown, Slave Revolt in Jamaica.

28. *Pennsylvania Gazette*, June 5, 1760, and July 24, 1760; Extract of a Letter from Jamaica, May 8 and 21, 1760, *Annual Register for the Year 1760* (London: J. Dodsley, 1789), 123–24; Thistlewood Diary, June 7, 1760, box 2, folder 11, p. 108, accessed July 9, 2019, https://brbl-dl.library.yale.edu/vufind/Record/4079875; *Pennsylvania Gazette*, September 4, 1760.

29. Thistlewood Diary, May 24, 1760, box 2, folder 11, p. 97, accessed July 9, 2019, https://brbl-dl.library.yale.edu/vufind/Record/4079875.

30. Thistlewood Diary, May 28, May 30, June 4, July 2, and October 1, 1760, box 2, folder 11, pp. 100, 102, 106, 120, 171, accessed July 9, 2019, https://brbl-dl.library.yale.edu/vufind/Record/4079875; Craton, *Testing the Chains*, 134.

31. Samuel Cleland to Thomas Hall, June 10, 1760, Thomas Hall Correspondence and Accounts, MS 1069, National Library of Jamaica, Kingston (hereafter NLJ).

32. John Hamilton to Robert Hamilton, June 1760, Hamilton Papers, AA/DC/17/113, Ayrshire Archives, Ayr, Scotland.

33. Jamaica Council, minutes, July 14, 1760, CO 137/32, 21–24.

34. Thistlewood Diary, July 12, 1760, box 2, folder 11, p. 126, accessed July 9, 2019, https://brbl-dl.library.yale.edu/vufind/Record/4079875; Brown, Slave Revolt in Jamaica.

35. Cleland to Hall, July 21 and 31, 1760, MS 1069, NLJ.

36. Jamaica Council, minutes, July 14, 1760, CO 137/32, 21–24.

37. Thistlewood Diary, July 27, 1760, box 2, folder 11, p. 133, accessed July 9, 2019, accessed July 9, 2019, https://brbl-dl.library.yale.edu/vufind/Record/4079875.

38. Thistlewood Diary, January 2, 1761, box 2, folder 12, p. 4, accessed July 9, 2019, https://brbl-dl.library.yale.edu/vufind/Record/3974262.

39. George Ricketts to Hall, August 30, 1760, box 1, folder 54, Hall Family Papers, UCSD.

40. Craton, *Testing the Chains*, 137.

41. Thistlewood Diary, June 6 and July 12, 1760, box 2, folder 11, pp. 107, 125, accessed July 9, 2019, https://brbl-dl.library.yale.edu/vufind/Record/4079875.

42. Moore to BT, March 7, 1761, CO 137/32, 62.

43. Stephen Fuller to Thomas Hall, January 2, 1761, box 1, folder 56, Hall Family Papers, UCSD.

44. Thomas Hall to Molly Hall, February 20, 1762, box 1, folder 63, Hall Family Papers, UCSD.

45. Thistlewood Diary, January 29, 1762, box 3, folder 13, p. 19, accessed July 9, 2019, https://brbl-dl.library.yale.edu/vufind/Record/3971634.

46. Thistlewood Diary, November 27 and November 29, 1762, box 3, folder 13, pp. 213, 214, accessed July 9, 2019, https://brbl-dl.library.yale.edu/vufind/Record/3971634.

47. Fuller to Hall, April 27, 1762, box 1, folder 65, Hall Family Papers, UCSD.

48. Samuel Martin to Samuel Martin [son], August 1761, BL, Add. MSS 41,347:100–101.

49. Correspondence of February 2, 1762, Tudway of Wells Papers, microfilm, reel 16, Columbia University Library; Fuller to Hall, April 27, 1762, box 1, folder 65, Hall Family Papers, UCSD; Fuller to Hall, August 4, 1762, box 1, folder 66, Hall Family Papers, UCSD; Thomas Hall to Molly Hall, October 14, 1762, box 1, folder 68, Hall Family Papers, UCSD.

50. J. A. Houlding, *Fit for Service: The Training of the British Army, 1715–1795* (New York: Clarendon Press, 1981), 410–13; Andrew Jackson O'Shaughnessy, *An Empire Divided: The American Revolution and the British Caribbean* (Philadelphia: University of Pennsylvania Press, 2000), 44–47, 50–51; Marjoleine Kars, "Dodging Rebellion: Politics and Gender in the Berbice Slave Uprising of 1763," *American Historical Review* 121, no. 1 (February 2016): 39–69.

51. William Lewis to William Henry Lyttelton, December 5, 1765, Lyttelton Papers, Clements Library, University of Michigan; Zachary Bayly to Lyttelton, December 1765, Lyttelton Papers; Long, *Jamaica*, 2:468–71.

52. Woodley to Secretary of State, March 22, 1768, CO 152/48, 7–8v; Extract of a Letter from Montserrat, March 21, 1768, *Georgia Gazette*, May 18, 1768; Extract of a Letter from Montserrat, March 22, 1768, *Virginia Gazette*, May 5, 1768.

53. South Carolina Council, minutes, December 17, 1765, Council Journal no. 32 (1765–66), pp. 680–83, SCDAH; William Bull, message to South Carolina Assembly, Commons House Journal no. 37, pt. 1 (1765–67), 34–43, SCDAH; Bull to BT, December 17, 1765, in Records in the British Public Record Office Relating to South Carolina, 1663–1782, transcript, comp. W. Noel Sainsbury, microfilm; Henry Laurens to John Lewis Gervais, January 29, 1766, in *The Papers of Henry Laurens*, ed. David R. Chesnutt et al. (Columbia: University of South Carolina Press, 1985), 5:51–56.

54. "Philadelphia," *Pennsylvania Chronicle, and Universal Advertiser*, December 28, 1767; *Boston Chronicle*, January 11–18, 1768; *The Annual Register* [. . .] *for the Year 1767* (London, 1768), 69–70.

55. Journal of the House of Burgesses, November 7–December 21, 1769, CO 5/1436, 187.

56. Jamaica Council, minutes, July 21, 1692, in *Calendar of State Papers, Colonial Series: America and West Indies, 1574–1739* (hereafter *CSPCS*), 45 vols. (London, 1860–1994), 13:676; William Beeston to BT, April 5, 1694, in *CSPCS*, 14:279; Mr. Mackenzie to BT, October 8, 1712, in *CSPCS*, 27:59–60; Nicholas Lawes to BT, July 30, 1719, in *CSPCS*, 31:180–83; Robert Hunter to Duke of Newcastle, September 6, 1729, in *CSPCS*, 36:478; Hunter to BT, March 11, 1734, in *CSPCS*, 41:48–52; John Ayscough to Newcastle, December 6, 1734, in *CSPCS*, 41:321–22; Ayscough to the BT, April 16, 1735, in *CSPCS*, 41:407–9; Ayscough to the BT, May 15, 1735, in *CSPCS*, 41:423–28; Frederick G. Spurdle, *Early West Indian Government: Showing the Progress of Government in Barbados, Jamaica, and the Leeward Islands, 1660–1783* (New Zealand: published by the author, 1964), 57–62.

57. William Gooch to BT, September 14, 1730, CO 5/1322, 158–59, accessed on microfilm compiled as the Virginia Colonial Records Project at the John D. Rockefeller Jr. Library, Colonial Williamsburg Foundation, Williamsburg, VA.

58. Martin to Robert Freeman, December 10, 1736, BL, Add. MSS 41,352:113; Petition of Assembly to Governor in Antigua, February 2, 1737, CO 9/11, 2–3; Samuel Cleland to Thomas Hall, July 31, 1760, MS 1069, NLJ.

59. Public Money Accounts, *Index to Sixth Volume of Journals of the Assembly of Jamaica* [. . .] (Jamaica: Alexander Aikman, 1803), 20; Jamaica Assembly Minutes, November 6, 1776, in *Journals of the Assembly of Jamaica* (Jamaica: Alexander Aikman, 1795–1829), 6:639.

60. Hender Molesworth to William Blathwayt, September 28, 1686, in *CSPCS*, 12:251–52; Petition of Inhabitants of Jamaica to the King, July 26, 1689, in *CSPCS*, 13:107.

61. Nicholas Lawes to BT, July 30, 1719, in *CSPCS*, 31:180–83.

62. An Act for Explaining [. . .] An Act for settling the Militia, no. 177, 1751, in *Acts of Assembly, Passed in the Island of Jamaica* (St. Jago de la Vega, Jamaica: Lowry and Sherlock, 1769–71), 1:331.

63. James Pinnock Plantation Journal, December 23, 1769, July 19, 1776, September 4 and November 1, 1778, and August 7, 1779, BL, Add. MSS 33,316:3v, 4v, 7v, 8v, 9; Jonathan Spain, "Dalling, Sir John, first baronet (c. 1731–1798), army officer and colonial governor," in Oxford Dictionary of National Biography, modified January 3, 2008, https://doi-org /10.1093/ref:odnb/ 53621; Vere Langford Oliver, *Caribbeana Being Miscellaneous Papers* [. . .] (London: Mitchell, Hughes, and Clarke, 1912), 2:118, 290–91.

64. Long, *Jamaica*, 1:383.

65. Walter Tullideph to David Tullideph, May 25, 1737, "finished" June 5, 1737, GD 205/ 53/8, pp. 56–58, National Archives of Scotland, Edinburgh.

66. Petition of Kingston Merchants (Nathaniel Lloyd, James Woodcock, Anthony Danvers, Edward Manning, and John Stevens) against the Imposition of Martial Law, Edward Long Papers, BL, Add. MSS 12,431:80–81; Jamaica Council, minutes, March 6, 1734, CO 140/ 25, no fol.; Gentlemen's Private Advice to Governor [in lieu of a Council meeting], September 19, 1776, CO 137/71, 386–88; Jamaica Legislative Council Minutes, October 25, 1776, CO 140/ 54, no fol.

67. An Act for the Prevention of Indebted Persons from Departing this Island in the Time of Martial Law, in *Acts of Assembly*, 2:126–28. This law was first enacted in 1693 and renewed several times.

68. Merchants of Kingston, petition to Jamaica Council, March 6, 1734, CO 140/25, no fol.

69. David Hancock, *Citizens of the World: London Merchants and the Integration of the British Atlantic Community, 1735–1785* (New York: Cambridge University Press, 1995), 115–92.

70. Merchants of Kingston, petition to Jamaica Council, March 6, 1734, CO 140/25, no fol.; Edward Trelawny to Newcastle, September 20, 1739, and Trelawny to Andrew Stone, September 22, in *CSPCS*, 45:189–90.

71. Antigua Assembly, message to Council, April 11, 1737, CO 9/11, 75–76.

72. Walter Tullideph to David Tullideph, May 25, 1737, "finished" June 5, 1737, GD 205/ 53/8, pp. 56–58, National Archives of Scotland, Edinburgh.

73. Cleland to Hall, July 31, 1760, MS 1069, NLJ.

74. Governor Hunter to BT, August 3, 1728, in *CSPCS* 36:167–69.

75. Merchants of Kingston, petition to Jamaica Council, March 6, 1734, CO 140/25, no fol.

76. Richard Sheridan, *Sugar and Slavery: An Economic History of the British West Indies, 1623–1775* (Baltimore: Johns Hopkins University Press, 1973), 294, 305; Alan Karras, *Sojourners in the Sun: Scottish Migrants in Jamaica and the Chesapeake, 1740–1800* (Ithaca, NY: Cornell University Press, 1992), 51–52, 60, 75; Serena R. Zabin, *Dangerous Economies: Status and Commerce in Imperial New York* (Philadelphia: University of Pennsylvania Press, 2009), 11, 14.

77. Long, *Jamaica*, 1:383, 518.

78. George Frere, *A Short History of Barbados* [. . .] (London, 1768), 44.

79. Jamaica Assembly, minutes, February 11, 1737, *Journals of the Assembly of Jamaica*, 3:406.

80. Simon Clark to Benjamin Lyon, July 23, 1776, CO 137/71, 256–57.

81. Long, *Jamaica*, 1:384–85.

82. Moore to BT, June 9, 1760, CO 137/32, 7–8.

83. *Royal Danish American Gazette* (St. Croix), vol. 7, no. 910, September 7, 1776.

84. Barbados Council Minutes, December 23, 1701, CO 31/6, 97.

85. George Ricketts to Hall, August 30, 1760, box 1, folder 54, Hall Family Papers, UCSD.

86. Basil Keith, August 6, 1776, CO 137/71; Jamaica Council, minutes, July 23 and 25, 1776, CO 140/55; Jamaica Council of War, minutes, July 24, 1776, CO 137/71, 300–318v.

87. James Palmer to Keith, July 30, 1776, CO 137/71, 280–81; Petition of Gentlemen, Planters, Merchants, and Others in the Parish of Hanover, n.d., CO 137/71, 282–83; Petition of Planters and Merchants of St. James to the Governor, July 28, 1776, CO 137/71, 284–85; George Spence to Keith, July 28, 1776, CO 137/71, 268–69v.

88. Samuel Martin to Warner and Johnson, April 28, 1770, BL, Add. MSS 41,350:118v; Martin to George Thomas, April 28, 1770, BL, Add. MSS 41,350:119v.

89. Bermuda Assembly, minutes, February 5 and August 5, 1729, and June 22 and 23, 1730, CO 40/3; Bermuda Council, minutes, May 21, 1730, CO 40/4; Petition of the Merchants of London [. . .], in BT, minutes, November 23, 1731, CO 37/12, 76–77v; John Pitt to BT, January 27, 1731, CO 37/12, 81–82; BT, report to Privy Council, December 8, 1731, CO 38/8, 163–65; Bahamas Council, address to King, January 3, 1735, CO 26/2A, 103v. For the Virginia governors, see Chapter 2.

90. William Woodley to Earl of Hillsborough, April 20, 1770, CO 152/31, 38–38v; St. Christopher Council, petition to King, June 29, 1770, St. Christopher Council, minutes, CO 241/12.

91. Robert Melville to Hillsborough, December 3, 1770, CO 101/15, 58–59; Earl of Dartmouth to William Pulteney, August 20, 1772, CO 101/16, 143.

92. Thistlewood Diary, December 22–31, 1769, box 4, folder 20, pp. 231–37, accessed July 9, 2019, https://brbl-dl.library.yale.edu/vufind/Record/4079830.

93. Duncan Macglashan to Roger Hope Elletson, December 23, 1769, Brydges Correspondence, ST 14, vol. 1, Huntington Library, San Marino, CA; Gov. William Trelawny to BT, December 31, 1769, CO 137/65, 49–50; Jamaica Assembly, minutes, December 20, 22, and 23, 1769, *Journals of the Assembly of Jamaica*, 5:234–37.

94. Walter B. Edgar and N. Louise Bailey, eds., *Biographical Directory of the South Carolina House of Representatives* (Columbia: University of South Carolina Press, 1989), 2:27–28.

95. Confession of Agrippa, January 24, 1749, Council Journal no. 17, pp. 48–51, SCDAH; Examination of Sambo, January 27, 1749, Council Journal no. 17, pp. 63–64, SCDAH; Confession of Susana, January 27, 1749, Council Journal no. 17, p. 101, SCDAH; Examination of George, February 1, 1749, Council Journal no. 17, pp. 120–23, SCDAH; Narrative of James Akin, February 6, 1749, Council Journal no. 17, p. 164, SCDAH; Report of James Glen, February 7, 1749, Council Journal no. 17, p. 167, SCDAH.

96. Philip D. Morgan and George D. Terry, "Slavery in Microcosm: A Conspiracy Scare in Colonial South Carolina," *Southern Studies* (Summer 1982): 122–45; South Carolina Assembly, minutes, *Journal of the Commons House of Assembly: March 28, 1749–March 19, 1750*, ed. J. H. Easterby and Ruth S. Green (Columbia: South Carolina Archives Department, 1962), 145.

97. Examination of Scipio, January 27, 1749, Council Journal no. 17, p. 61, SCDAH; Testimony of Warden of the Workhouse, February 1, 1749, Council Journal no. 17, pp. 98–99, SCDAH.

98. William Bruce to Mr. Drake, January 30, 1749, Council Journal no. 17, pp. 95–96, SCDAH; and Narrative of James Akin, February 6, 1749, Council Journal no. 17, pp. 140, 144, SCDAH. Bruce misidentified Kate as the woman in whom Akin had special interest in continuing to hold in sexual slavery, as evident in Akin's differing characterizations of the two women and behavior toward them.

99. Examination of George, February 1, 1749, Council Journal no. 17, p. 100, SCDAH.

100. Examination of George, February 1, 1749, Council Journal no. 17, p. 101, SCDAH; James Glen, report, February 7, 1749, Council Journal no. 17, pp. 164, 167, SCDAH.

101. Examinations of George, January 30 and February 1, 1749, Council Journal no. 17, pp. 83–84, 101, SCDAH; Examination of Agrippa, February 6, 1749, Council Journal no. 17, pp. 147–49; Judges' notes, January 27, 1749, Council Journal no. 17, p. 67.

102. South Carolina Council, minutes, February 7, 1749, Council Journal no. 17, pp. 164–65, SCDAH.

103. Mary Russell, deposition, February 3, 1749, Council Journal no. 17, p. 118, SCDAH.

104. South Carolina Council, minutes, February 6, 1749, Council Journal no. 17, p. 165, SCDAH; Inventory of James Akin, December 8, 1758, Inventory Book T, 118–23.

105. Edward E. Baptist, *The Half Has Never Been Told: Slavery and the Making of American Capitalism* (New York: Basic Books, 2014), 91–94.

Chapter 6

1. Gordon S. Wood, "Conspiracy and the Paranoid Style: Causality and Deceit in the Eighteenth Century," *William and Mary Quarterly*, 3rd ser. (hereafter *WMQ*), 39, no. 3 (July 1982): 401–41; Rob Hardy, "'A Mirror of the Times': The Catilanarian Conspiracy in Eighteenth-Century British and American Political Thought," *International Journal of the Classical Tradition* 14, no. 3/4 (December 2007): 431–54.

2. *The New-York Journal*, March 2, 1775; *Dunlap's Pennsylvania Packet or, the General Advertiser*, March 6, 1775; *New-London Gazette*, March 10, 1775; *Virginia Gazette*, March 17, 1775; *Virginia Gazette*, March 18, 1775.

3. Henry Laurens to the South Carolina Delegates to Congress, September 8, 1775, in "Papers of the First Council of Safety," *South Carolina Historical and Genealogical Magazine* (hereafter *SCHM*) 1, no. 4 (October 1900): 288.

4. *The Weekly Magazine, or Edinburgh Amusement*, June 1, 1775.

5. Robert Parkinson, *The Common Cause: Creating Race and Nation in the American Revolution* (Chapel Hill: University of North Carolina Press, 2016), 21, 249–63.

6. Parkinson, *Common Cause*; Peter Silver, *Our Savage Neighbors: How Indian War Transformed North America* (New York: W. W. Norton, 2007), 227–60.

7. Robert Donald to Patrick Hunter, April 18, 1775, quoted in Woody Holton, *Forced Founders: Indians, Debtors, Slaves, and the Making of the American Revolution in Virginia* (Chapel Hill: University of North Carolina Press, 1999), 141; Report of the Committee Appointed to Inquire into the Causes of the Late Disturbances and Commotions, June 14, 1775, *Journals of the House of Burgesses of Virginia 1773–1776* [. . .], ed. John Pendleton Kennedy (Richmond: [E. Waddy], 1905), 231–37 (hereafter *JHB 1773–76*).

8. Municipal Common Hall to Dunmore, April 21, 1775, and Dunmore to Common Hall, April 21, in *Revolutionary Virginia: The Road to Independence*, ed. Robert L. Scribner and Brent Tarter (Charlottesville: University Press of Virginia, 1977), 3:55; Dunmore, proclamation, in *Virginia Gazette*, May 5, 1775; *Virginia Gazette*, June 16, 1775.

9. Edmund Pendleton to George Washington, April 21, 1775, in *The Letters and Papers of Edmund Pendleton, 1734–1803*, ed. David John Mays (Charlottesville: University Press of Virginia, 1967), 1:102.

10. "Deposition of Dr. William Pasteur, In Regard to the Removal of Powder from the Williamsburg Magazine," *Virginia Magazine of History and Biography* 13, no. 1 (July 1905): 49.

11. *Virginia Gazette*, May 4, 5, and 6, 1775; *Connecticut Journal*, May 10, 1775; *New England Chronicle*, May 12, 1775; *Connecticut Courant*, May 15, 1775; *Pennsylvania Packet*, May 18 and 22, 1775; *Story & Humphrey's Pennsylvania Mercury*, May 19, 1775.

12. Causes of the Late Disturbances, *JHB 1773–76*, 231–32, 234–35.

13. Replies to Questions, in Archibald Cary to James Lyle et al., June 12, 1775, Colonial Office Series (hereafter CO) 5/1353, 401, National Archives of the United Kingdom, Kew, London.

14. *Virginia Gazette*, April 28 and 29, 1775, supplement; *Maryland Journal*, May 10, 1775.

15. *The Weekly Magazine, or Edinburgh Amusement*, June 1, 1775.

16. *Virginia Gazette*, June 16, 1775.

17. McDonnell, *The Politics of War: Race, Class, and Conflict in Revolutionary Virginia* (Chapel Hill: University of North Carolina Press, 2007), 49; Holton, *Forced Founders*, 141–43.

18. Causes of the Late Disturbances, *JHB 1773–76*, 231–32, 234–35.

19. McDonnell, *Politics of War*, 54–56, 61–62, 93.

20. Causes of the Late Disturbances, *JHB 1773–76*, 232.

21. Extract of a Letter from a Clergyman in Maryland to his Friend in England, "T.T.", August 2, 1775, in *American Archives*, ed. Peter Force (Washington, 1775), 3:10.

22. Charles Rainsford to Sir Henry Clinton, July 29, 1775, Henry Clinton Papers, William L. Clements Library, University of Michigan (hereafter CL).

23. McDonnell, *Politics of War*, 61; Dunmore to Earl of Dartmouth [Secretary of State], June 25, 1775, in *Documents of the American Revolution, 1770–1783: Colonial Office Series*, ed. K. G. Davies (Shannon, Ireland: Irish University Press, 1972–81), 9:204.

24. James Corbett David, *Dunmore's New World: The Extraordinary Life of a Royal Governor in Revolutionary America* [. . .] (Charlottesville: University of Virginia Press, 2013).

25. General Committee [Charleston] to General Committee at Philadelphia, May 8, 1775, *The Papers of Henry Laurens*, ed. David R. Chesnutt et al., vol. 10, *Dec. 12, 1774–Jan. 4, 1776* (Columbia: University of South Carolina Press, 1968), 113–14.

26. Philip D. Morgan, *Slave Counterpoint: Black Culture in the Eighteenth-Century Chesapeake and Lowcountry* (Chapel Hill: University of North Carolina Press, 1998), 97, 663; Philip D. Morgan, "Black Life in Eighteenth-Century Charleston," *Perspectives in American History*, n.s., 1 (1984): 188–89.

27. Christopher Gadsden to Samuel Adams, [Charleston], May 23, 1774, in *The Writings of Christopher Gadsden, 1746–1805*, ed. Richard Walsh (Columbia: University of South Carolina Press, 1966), 92–94.

28. J. William Harris, *The Hanging of Thomas Jeremiah: A Free Black Man's Encounter with Liberty* (New Haven, CT: Yale University Press, 2011), 89–90; Eva B. Poythress, "Revolution By Committee: An Administrative History of the Extralegal Committees in South Carolina, 1774–1776," (PhD diss., University of North Carolina at Chapel Hill, 1975), 192, 239.

29. George Milligen, Report of September 15, 1775, CO 5/396, 209–11; William Campbell to Dartmouth, May 1, 1775, in Records in the British Public Record Office Relating to South

Carolina, 1663–1782, transcript, comp. W. Noel Sainsbury, microfilm (hereafter Sainsbury Transcript); John Drayton and William Henry Drayton, *Memoirs of the American Revolution* (Charleston, 1821), 1:258; Anecdote March 76 [document], reproduced in John Richard Alden, "John Stuart Accuses William Bull," *WMQ* 2, no. 3 (July 1945): 318.

30. George Milligen, Report of September 15, 1775, CO 5/396, 209–11.

31. Henry Laurens, quoted in William R. Ryan, *The World of Thomas Jeremiah: Charles Town on the Eve of the American Revolution* (New York: Oxford University Press, 2010), 42.

32. Alexander Innes to Dartmouth, May 16, 1775, in "Charles Town Loyalism in 1775: The Secret Reports of Alexander Innes," ed. B. D. Bargar, *SCHM* 63, no. 3 (July 1962): 128; George Milligen, Report of September 15, 1775, CO 5/396, 209–11; Thomas Knox Gordon et al. to Campbell, September 1, 1775, Sainsbury Transcript.

33. George Milligen, Report of September 15, 1775, CO 5/396, 209–11.

34. John Stuart to Thomas Gage, Extract of Letter, July 9, 1775, Henry Clinton Papers, CL.

35. *Pennsylvania Evening Post*, July 18, 1775; John Lewis Gervais to Alexander Cameron, abstract of letter, June 27, 1775, Henry Clinton Papers, CL.

36. John Stuart to Thomas Gage, Extract of Letter, July 9, 1775, Henry Clinton Papers, CL; Campbell to Dartmouth, August 31, 1775, CO 5/396, 225v.

37. "Extract of a Letter from Charlestown, June 29, 1775," *Pennsylvania Evening Post*, July 18, 1775; *Pennsylvania Gazette*, July 19, 1775; *Virginia Gazette*, August 4, 1775.

38. "To the Honourable Members of the Committee of Correspondence at Charlestown, the humble petition of Michael Hubart," in Drayton and Drayton, *Memoirs*, 1:302; "Charles-Town, June 13," *South Carolina Gazette and Country Journal*, June 13, 1775; *South Carolina American General Gazette*, June 2–9, 1775; Laughlin Martin, apology, *South Carolina Gazette and Country Journal*, June 13, 1775.

39. Campbell to Dartmouth, August 31, 1775, CO 5/396, 226v.

40. "Letter from Charlestown, South Carolina," June 18, 1775, and postscript, June 20, *Newport Mercury*, July 31, 1775; "Extract of Letter to a Gentleman in Philadelphia, Dated Charlestown, South-Carolina, August 20, 1775," in Force, *American Archives*, 3:180; Drayton and Drayton, *Memoirs*, 2:24.

41. Henry Laurens to John Laurens, June 23, 1775, in Chesnutt, *Papers of Henry Laurens*, 10:191.

42. Wood, "'Taking Care of Business' in Revolutionary South Carolina: Republicanism and the Slave Society," in *The Southern Experience in the American Revolution*, ed. Jeffrey J. Crow and Larry E. Tise (Chapel Hill: University of North Carolina Press, 1978), 269–94, 83–86; Henry Laurens to John Laurens, June 18, 1775, in Chesnutt, *Papers of Henry Laurens*, 10:184–85.

43. George Milligen, Report of September 15, 1775, CO 5/396, 209–11.

44. *Newport Mercury*, July 31, 1775.

45. Ryan, *World of Thomas Jeremiah*, 7n10; Henry Laurens to John Laurens, August 20, 1775, in Chesnutt, *Papers of Henry Laurens*, 10:320; Campbell to Dartmouth, August 31, 1775, Sainsbury Transcript.

46. Extract of a Letter from Charlestown, June 29, 1775, *Pennsylvania Evening Post*, July 18, 1775; Letter from Charlestown, June 18, 1775, *Newport Mercury*, July 31, 1775.

47. *Virginia Gazette*, July 6, 1775; *Newport Mercury*, July 17, 1775.

48. Extract of a Letter from Charlestown, June 29, 1775, *Pennsylvania Evening Post*, July 18, 1775; *Pennsylvania Gazette*, July 19, 1775; *Virginia Gazette*, August 4, 1775.

49. Henry Laurens to John Laurens, July 2, 1775, in Chesnutt, *Papers of Henry Laurens*, 10:202.

50. John Coram, [justice of the peace for Charleston], record of slave testimony, June 16, 1775, in Campbell to Dartmouth, August 31, 1775, CO 5/396, 237.

51. Evidence Declared before John Coram, [justice of the peace for Charleston], June 16, 1775, in Campbell to Dartmouth, August 31, CO 5/396, 237; Ryan, *World of Thomas Jeremiah*, 62, 64, image 3.1; Henry Laurens to John Laurens, August 20, 1775, in Chesnutt, *Papers of Henry Laurens* 10:321; George Milligen, report, September 15, 1775, CO 5/396, 209–11.

52. Thomas Hutchinson to Council of Safety, July 5, 1775, in Chesnutt, *Papers of Henry Laurens*, 10:206–8; Laurens to Thomas Fletchall, July 14, 1775, in Chesnutt, *Papers of Henry Laurens*, 10:214–18; Council of Safety to St. Bartholomew Committee, July 18, 1775, in Chesnutt, *Papers of Henry Laurens*, 10:231; Henry Laurens to John Laurens, July 30, 1775, in Chesnutt, *Papers of Henry Laurens*, 10:256–61; Wim Klooster, "Slave Revolts, Royal Justice, and a Ubiquitous Rumor in the Age of Revolutions," *WMQ* 71, no. 3 (July 2014): 401–24.

53. Report of the Judges and Attorney General on the Case of Jerry [Thomas Jeremiah] [. . .], August 17, 1775, in Campbell to Dartmouth, August 31, 1775, CO 5/396, 231–32; Henry Laurens to John Laurens, August 20, 1775, in Chesnutt, *Papers of Henry Laurens*, 10:320. For a full discussion of the legal debate, see Ryan, *World of Thomas Jeremiah*, 53–68, 169–73.

54. Campbell to Dartmouth, August 31, 1775, CO 5/396, 226.

55. Henry Laurens to John Laurens, August 20, 1775, in Chesnutt, *Papers of Henry Laurens*, 10:329–30; Enclosure in Laurens to Campbell, August 17, 1775, in Chesnutt, *Papers of Henry Laurens*, 10:321–22; Campbell to Dartmouth, August 31, 1775, CO 5/396, 226; Harris, *Hanging*, 148.

56. Henry Laurens to John Laurens, August 20, 1775, in Chesnutt, *Papers of Henry Laurens*, 10:321.

57. Extract of Letter from Charlestown, September 12, 1775, *Dunlap's Pennsylvania Packet or, the General Advertiser*, October 16, 1775.

58. Campbell to Dartmouth, August 31, 1775, CO 5/396, 226; South Carolina Assembly, message to Governor, August 18, 1775, House Assembly Journal no. 39, p. 311, South Carolina Department of Archives and History, Columbia.

59. Council of Safety [Charleston] to South Carolina Delegates in Congress, September 18, 1775, in Chesnutt, *Papers of Henry Laurens*, 10:397–403.

60. "Extract of Letter to a Gentleman in Philadelphia, Dated Charlestown, South-Carolina, August 20, 1775," in Force, *American Archives*, 3:180. The same letter reported on Jeremiah's execution that "Yesterday a negro was hanged and burnt for intended sedition, and burning the Town, &c."

61. Laurens to James Brisbane, April 24, 1775, in Chesnutt, *Papers of Henry Laurens*, 10:333–34.

62. Harris, *Hanging*, 148.

63. Henry Laurens to John Laurens, August 20, 1775, in Chesnutt, *Papers of Henry Laurens*, 10:323; Henry Laurens to John Laurens, September 18, 1775, in Chesnutt, *Papers of Henry Laurens*, 10:396–97; Campbell to Dartmouth, August 19, 1775, Sainsbury Transcript; Thomas Knox Gordon et al. to Campbell, September 1, 1775, Sainsbury Transcript; Andrew

Marvell [Arthur Middleton] to William Henry Drayton, August 12, 1775, in "Correspondence of Hon. Arthur Middleton," ed. Joseph W. Barnwell, *SCHM* 27, no. 3 (July 1926): 125–28; Peter Timothy to William Henry Drayton, August 13, 1775, in Barnwell, "Middleton," 128–31; Charles Drayton to William Henry Drayton, September 16, 1775, in Barnwell, "Middleton," 136–37; Mr. Milligen's Report of the State of South Carolina, quoted in *Colonial South Carolina: Two Contemporary Descriptions* [. . .], ed. Chapman J. Milling (Columbia: University of South Carolina Press, 1951), xix–xxi.

64. Address of the North Carolina Delegates [. . .] to the Committees of the Several Towns and Counties [. . .], June 19, 1775, in *The Colonial Records of North Carolina*, ed. Stephen B. Weeks and William Laurence (Raleigh, NC: P. M. Hale, 1886–90), 10:20–23.

65. Joseph Hewes to James Iredell, Philadelphia, July 8, 1775, in *The Papers of James Iredell*, ed. Don Higginbotham (Raleigh, NC: North Carolina Division of Archives and History, Department of Cultural Resources, 1976), 1:313; Janet Schaw, *Journal of a Lady of Quality*, ed. Evangeline Walker Andrews (New Haven, CT: Yale University Press, 1921), 199, 200; By his excellency the Hon. Thomas Gage, Esq [. . .]. A proclamation [. . .], June 12, 1775 (New York, 1775), accessed November 20, 2018, https://www.loc.gov/item/rbpe.03801700/, Library of Congress.

66. Martin to Dartmouth, June 30, 1775, in Weeks and Laurence, *Colonial Records*, 10:41–46; Martin to Dartmouth, July 6, 1775, in Weeks and Laurence, *Colonial Records*, 10:96.

67. Proceedings of the New Bern Committee of Safety, August 2, 1775, containing copy of Martin to Lewis H. DeRossett, June 24, 1775, in Weeks and Laurence, *Colonial Records*, 10:137–38a; *Virginia Gazette*, August 31, 1775; *Pennsylvania Evening Post*, September 12, 1775.

68. Henry Laurens to John Laurens, July 30, 1775, in Chesnutt, *Papers of Henry Laurens*, 10:256–61.

69. Proclamation of Governor Martin, June 16, 1775, in Weeks and Laurence, *Colonial Records*, 10:16–19.

70. Wilmington Committee of Safety, proceedings, June 21, 1775, in *Wilmington-New Hanover Safety Committee Minutes, 1774–1776*, ed. Leora H. McEachern and Isabel M. Williams (Wilmington, NC: Bicentennial Association, 1974), 30–31; Proceedings of the Wilmington Committee of Safety, July 7, 1775, in Weeks and Laurence, *Colonial Records*, 10:72.

71. Information and quotes in this paragraph and the next are from Letter from Pitt County Committee of Safety to Craven County Committee of Safety, July 15, 1775, in Weeks and Laurence, *Colonial Records*, 10:94–95.

72. Schaw, *Journal of a Lady of Quality*, 199–201.

73. Schaw, 199–201.

74. Wilmington and New Hanover Committee of Safety, minutes, July 20 and 21, 1775, in McEachern and Williams, *Wilmington-New Hanover*, 45–47; *Virginia Gazette*, August 11, 1775; *Pennsylvania Ledger*, August 19, 1775; *Pennsylvania Evening Post*, August 19, 1775; *New York Gazette and Weekly Mercury*, August 21, 1775; *Boston News-Letter*, September 7, 1775.

75. Depositions of Jacob Williams and James Cotton, aboard HMS *Cruizer* in Cape Fear River, August 13 and 18, 1775, in Weeks and Laurence, *Colonial Records*, 10:126–28.

76. Schaw, *Journal of a Lady of Quality*, 199–201.

77. Deposition of Jacob Williams, aboard HMS *Cruizer* in Cape Fear River, August 13 and 18, 1775, in Weeks and Laurence, *Colonial Records*, 10:126–28.

78. Stuart to Dartmouth, July 21, 1775, in Weeks and Laurence, *Colonial Records*, 10:118.

79. James Iredell, [*Causes of the American Revolution*], June 1776, in Higginbotham, *Papers of James Iredell*, 1:409; Iredell, *To His Majesty George the Third, King of Great Britain*, February 1777, in Higginbotham, *Papers of James Iredell*, 1:441.

80. Trevor Burnard and John Garrigus, *The Plantation Machine: Atlantic Capitalism in French Saint-Domingue and British Jamaica* (Philadelphia: University of Pennsylvania Press, 2016), 204; Nathaniel Phillips to Mssrs. Hibbert, Purrier, and Horton, October 7, 1776, Letter Book of Nathaniel Phillips (1766–89), Slebech Papers, MS 1965, n.p., National Library of Jamaica, Kingston (hereafter NLJ).

81. John Lindsay to William Robertson, August 6, 1776, Robertson-Macdonald Papers, MS 3942, fols. 259–63, National Library of Scotland, Edinburgh (hereafter NLS).

82. Edward East to Anna Eliza Elletson, May 11, June 5, and July 22, 1776, Roger Hope Elletson Letter Book, MS 29a, no fol., NLJ; Phillips to Hibbert, Purrier, and Horton, October 7, 1776, MS 1965, n.p., NLJ; Burnard and Garrigus, *Plantation Machine*, 205.

83. Keith to George Germain, July 1, 1776, CO 137/71, 201–4.

84. George Scott [Hanover magistrate] to John Allen, July 21, 1776, CO 137/71, 254–55; Hanover Magistrates to Keith, July 17, 1776, CO 137/71, 232; Palmer [Montego Bay commander] to Keith, July 20, 1776, CO 137/71, 236–37; Keith to Board of Trade (hereafter BT), August 6, 1776, CO 137/71, 230; Jamaica Council Minutes, July 22, 1776, CO 140/55 and CO 137/71, 300–318v.

85. Lindsay to Robertson, August 6, 1776, Robertson-Macdonald Papers, MS 3942, fols. 259–63, NLS.

86. Lindsay to Robertson, August 6, 1776, Robertson-Macdonald Papers, MS 3942, fols. 259–63, NLS.

87. Examination of Coromantee Sam, July 19, 1776, CO 137/71, 252–53v; John Grizzell and James Lawrence to Keith, July 19, 1776, CO 137/71, 238; Hanover Magistrates to Keith, July 20, 1776, CO 137/71, 250.

88. This paragraph and the next two are supported by Simon Clarke to Benjamin Lyon, July 23, 1776, CO 137/71, 256–57.

89. East to Elletson, September 3, 1776, MS 29a, no fol., NLJ.

90. Keith to BT, August 6, 1776, CO 137/71, 230; Jamaica Council, minutes, July 22–25, 1776, CO 140/55, 36–44; Jamaica Council of War, minutes, 1776, CO 137/71, 300–318v; George Scott [Hanover magistrate] to John Allen, July 21, 1776, CO 137/71, 254–55; Hanover Magistrates to Keith, July 17, 1776, CO 137/71, 232; Palmer [Montego Bay commander] to Keith, July 20, 1776, CO 137/71, 236–37.

91. James Pinnock Plantation Journal, July 19, 1776, British Library, London (hereafter BL), Additional Manuscripts (hereafter Add. MSS) 33,316:7.

92. East to Elletson, September 3, 1776, MS 29a, no fol., NLJ.

93. Keith to BT, August 6, 1776, CO 137/71, 230; Jamaica Council, minutes, July 23 and 25, 1776, CO 140/55, 39–44; Jamaica Council of War, minutes, July 24, 1776, CO 137/71, 300–318v.

94. George Spence to Keith, July 28, 1776, CO 137/71, 268–69v.

95. Patrick M. Malone, *The Skulking Way of War: Technology and Tactics Among the New England Indians* (Lanham, MD: Madison Books, 1991); Silver, *Our Savage Neighbors*.

96. Edward Long, *History of Jamaica* (London, 1774), 2:338–50; Keith to BT, August 6, 1776, CO 137/71, 230.

97. Palmer to Keith, July 30, 1776, CO 137/71, 280–81; Examination of Pontack, July 26, 1776, CO 137/71, 276–78, 280–81.

98. Examination of Charles, July 29, 1776, CO 137/71, 288; Hanover Magistrates to Keith, July 29, 1776, CO 137/71, 274–75v; Palmer to Keith, July 30, 1776, CO 137/71, 280–81; Palmer to Keith, August 1, 1776, CO 137/71, 292–93.

99. George Spence and George Scott to Keith, August 4, 1776, CO 137/71, 340–41; Extract of Letter from the Magistrates of Hanover, August 16, 1776, CO 137/71, 350–51.

100. Governor to the Assembly, October 26, 1776, *Supplement to the Kingston Journal and Jamaica Universal Museum*, October 26, 1776; East to Elletson, July 31, 1776, MS 29a, no fol., NLJ.

101. Philips to Hibbert, Purrier, and Horton, October 7, 1776, MS 1965, n.p., NLJ.

102. Andrew Jackson O'Shaughnessy, *An Empire Divided: The American Revolution and the British Caribbean* (Philadelphia: University of Pennsylvania Press, 2000).

103. Trevor Burnard, *Planters, Merchants, and Slaves: Plantation Societies in British America, 1650–1820* (Chicago: University of Chicago Press, 2015), 242–44.

104. Burnard and Garrigus, *Plantation Machine*, 205–6; Samuel Martin to Christopher Baldwin, April 16, 1776, BL, Add. MSS 41,351:76.

105. Depositions recorded by Samuel Okes Taylor, April 10 and 11, 1778, encl. in Burt to Germain, April 18, 1778, CO 152/58, 34–41. All quotations in the next several paragraphs come from these depositions. Emphasis in the original.

106. Edward Kimber, *The History of the Life and Adventures of Mr. Anderson* (New York: Garland, 1975; repr. of 1754 ed.), 135–38, 144.

107. Burt to George Germain, April 18, 1778, CO 152/58, 32–34.

108. *Virginia Gazette*, November 16, 1775; *Virginia Gazette*, December 2 and December 8, 1775.

109. Council of Safety to Richard Richardson, December 19, 1775, in Chesnutt, *Papers of Henry Laurens*, 10:575–77.

110. "From George Washington to Lieutenant Colonel Joseph Reed, 15 December 1775," Founders Online, National Archives of the United States, accessed June 13, 2018, https://founders.archives.gov/documents/Washington/03-02-02-0508.

111. Parkinson, *Common Cause*, 249–63.

112. Laura Edwards, *The People and Their Peace: Legal Culture and the Transformation of Inequality in the Post-Revolutionary South*, new ed. (Chapel Hill: University of North Carolina Press, 2009).

Epilogue

1. Laurent Dubois, *Avengers of the New World: The Story of the Haitian Revolution* (Cambridge, MA: Harvard University Press, 2004), 91–193.

2. Alfred N. Hunt, *Haiti's Influence on Antebellum America: Slumbering Volcano in the Caribbean* (Baton Rouge: Louisiana State University Press, 1988), 107–10; Ashli White, *Encountering Revolution: Haiti and the Making of the Early Republic* (Baltimore: Johns Hopkins University Press, 2010), 2, 125, 139–52.

3. James Alexander Dun, *Dangerous Neighbors: Making the Haitian Revolution in Early America* (Philadelphia: University of Pennsylvania Press, 2016), 61–67; David P. Geggus, ed., *The Impact of the Haitian Revolution in the Atlantic World* (Columbia: University of South Carolina Press, 2001), xii; David Brion Davis, *Inhuman Bondage: The Rise and Fall of Slavery in the New World* (Oxford: Oxford University Press, 2006), 210–11; David P. Geggus, "Slavery, War, and Revolution in the Greater Caribbean, 1789–1815," in *A Turbulent Time: The French*

Revolution and the Greater Caribbean, ed. David Barry Gaspar and David P. Geggus (Bloomington: Indiana University Press, 1997), 47–49; David P. Geggus, "Jamaica and the Saint-Domingue Slave Revolt, 1791–93," *The Americas* 38 (1981): 219–31; White, *Encountering Revolution*, 139, 142–43; James Sidbury, *Ploughshares into Swords: Race, Rebellion, and Identity in Gabriel's Virginia, 1730–1810* (Cambridge: Cambridge University Press, 1997), 39–43; Olwyn M. Blouet, "Bryan Edwards and the Haitian Revolution," in Geggus, *Impact of the Haitian Revolution*, 46; Robert Alderson, "Charleston's Rumored Slave Revolt of 1793," in Geggus, *Impact of the Haitian Revolution*, 93–100.

4. Dun, *Dangerous Neighbors*, 18, 21–25, 56, 59, 60–67; White, *Encountering Revolution*, 4–5, 56–57; Matthew J. Clavin, *Toussaint Louverture and the American Civil War: The Promise and Peril of a Second Haitian Revolution* (Philadelphia: University of Pennsylvania Press, 2010), 13.

5. Dubois, *Avengers of the New World*, 231–50, 292–300.

6. Eugene D. Genovese, *From Rebellion to Revolution: Afro-American Slave Revolts in the Making of the Modern World* (Baton Rouge: Louisiana State University Press, 1979), xviii–xxi; cf. David Geggus, "The French and Haitian Revolutions, and Resistance to Slavery in the Americas: An Overview," *Rev. franc. d'hist. d'outre-mer* 76, no. 282–83 (1989): 107–24.

7. Dubois, *Avengers of the New World*, 304–6; Michel-Rolph Trouillot, *Silencing the Past: Power and the Production of History* (Boston: Beacon Press, 1995), 70–107.

8. Douglas R. Egerton, *He Shall Go Out Free: The Lives of Denmark Vesey* (Madison, WI: Madison House, 1999), 167.

9. Dun, *Dangerous Neighbors*, 236.

10. Blouet, "Bryan Edwards," 46, 50; Clavin, *Toussaint Louverture*, 11–12, 18.

11. Clavin, *Toussaint Louverture*, 4, 10, 18; Brian Gabrial, "From Haiti to Nat Turner: Racial Panic Discourse During the Nineteenth Century Partisan Press Era," *American Journalism* 30 (2013): 336–64; White, *Encountering Revolution*, 205.

12. Alan Taylor, *The Internal Enemy: Slavery and War in Virginia, 1772–1832* (New York: W. W. Norton, 2013), 100–104; White, *Encountering Revolution*, 205; Hunt, *Haiti's Influence*, 122–26; *Newburyport Herald*, July 12, 1822, in *The Denmark Vesey Affair: A Documentary History*, ed. Douglas R. Egerton and Robert L. Paquette (Gainesville: University Press of Florida, 2017), 389–91.

13. *Richmond Enquirer*, June 12, 1812, quoted in Taylor, *Internal Enemy*, 132.

14. Philip J. Schwarz, ed., *Gabriel's Conspiracy: A Documentary History* (Charlottesville: University of Virginia Press, 2012), xxn21.

15. Michael L. Nicholls, *Whispers of Rebellion: Narrating Gabriel's Conspiracy* (Charlottesville: University of Virginia Press, 2012), 46.

16. Nicholls, *Whispers of Rebellion*, 52–59.

17. Nicholls, *Whispers of Rebellion*, 29, 37, 38, 40–44, 71–72; Sidbury, *Ploughshares into Swords*, 80–81.

18. Nicholls, *Whispers of Rebellion*, 46, 84, 115; Sidbury, *Ploughshares into Swords*, 6, 84.

19. Taylor, *Internal Enemy*, 100; Nicholls, *Whispers of Rebellion*, 125–26, 128, 131–32; Sidbury, *Ploughshares into Swords*, 136; Letter of James Monroe, February 8, 1828, MSS2 M7576a4, Virginia Historical Society, Richmond.

20. Taylor, *Internal Enemy*, 175–213, 245–73, 346 (citing *National Intelligencer*, April 8, 1815), 394 (citing Richmond Committee of Vigilance to James Barbour, February 3, 1814, Library of Virginia).

21. Egerton, *He Shall Go Out Free*, 136–37, 140, 155–58, 161; Egerton and Paquette, *Denmark Vesey Affair*, xxi.

22. Egerton, *He Shall Go Out Free*, 54, 145, 149.

23. Anna Hayes Johnson to Elizabeth Haywood, June 28, 1822, in Egerton and Paquette, *Denmark Vesey Affair*, 368; John Potter to Langdon Cheves, July 10, 1822, in Egerton and Paquette, 386.

24. Hartford, *Connecticut Mirror*, October 12, 1822, in Egerton and Paquette, *Denmark Vesey Affair*, 510.

25. Thomas Pinckney, *Reflections, Occasioned by the Late Disturbances in Charleston* (Charleston, SC, 1822), in Egerton and Paquette, *Denmark Vesey Affair*, 553.

26. Confession of Jack and Trial of Jesse, in Lionel Henry Kennedy and Thomas Parker Jr., *An Official Report of the Trials of Sundry Negroes* [Charleston, SC, 1822], in Egerton and Paquette, *Denmark Vesey Affair*, 178, 214; Johnson to Haywood, July 18, 1822, and Potter to Cheves, July 10, 1822, in Egerton and Paquette, 386; Egerton, *He Shall Go Out Free*, 137–38.

27. Johnson to Haywood, June 28, 1822, in Egerton and Paquette, *Denmark Vesey Affair*, 368; Potter to Cheves, July 10, 1822, in Egerton and Paquette, 386; Johnson to Haywood, July 18, 1822, in Egerton and Paquette, 397–98; Johnson to Haywood, July 27, 1822, in Egerton and Paquette, 421; Potter to Cheves, June 29, 1822, in Egerton and Paquette, 135.

28. Phocion, letter to the *Democratic Press* (Philadelphia), September 3, 1822, in Egerton and Paquette, *Denmark Vesey Affair*, 488–90.

29. *Newburyport Herald*, July 12, 1822, in Egerton and Paquette, *Denmark Vesey Affair*, 389–91.

30. A Columbian, letter to the *Southern Patriot, and Commercial Advertiser* (Charleston), November 15, 1822, in Egerton and Paquette, *Denmark Vesey Affair*, 522; Pinckney, *Reflections, Occasioned by the Late Disturbances*, 554.

31. White, *Encountering Revolution*, 145–48; Geggus, *Impact of the Haitian Revolution*, x, xiii; Hunt, *Haiti's Influence*, 3; David Brion Davis, "Impact of the French and Haitian Revolutions," in Geggus, *Impact of the Haitian Revolution*, 4, 8; Hilary McD. Beckles, *Bussa: The 1816 Revolution in Barbados* (Cave Hill and St. Ann's Garrison, Barbados: Department of History at the University of the West Indies and the Barbados Museum and Historical Society, 1998), 5–9.

32. Wim Klooster, "Slave Revolts, Royal Justice, and a Ubiquitous Rumor in the Age of Revolutions," *William and Mary Quarterly*, 3rd ser. (hereafter *WMQ*) 71, no. 3 (July 2014), 401, 421; Emilia Viotti da Costa, *Crowns of Glory, Tears of Blood: The Demerara Slave Rebellion of 1823* (New York: Oxford University Press, 1994), 176–84; Michael Craton, *Testing the Chains: Resistance to Slavery in the British West Indies* (Ithaca, NY: Cornell University Press, 1982), 295–96.

33. Davis, *Inhuman Bondage*, 212; Beckles, *Bussa*, 25–26, 42; Seymour Drescher, *Abolition: A History of Slavery and Antislavery* (Cambridge: Cambridge University Press, 2009), 259; Geggus, *Impact of the Haitian Revolution*, xii.

34. Davis, *Inhuman Bondage*, 219–20; Craton, *Testing the Chains*, 299, 300, 315.

35. Craton, *Testing the Chains*, 261; Beckles, *Bussa*, 25–26, 29, 42; Taylor, *Internal Enemy*, 346; Davis, *Inhuman Bondage*, 212.

36. Davis, *Inhuman Bondage*, 217–18; Craton, *Testing the Chains*, 269, 277; Da Costa, *Crowns of Glory, Tears of Blood*, xiii, 170–72, 182–97, 198–201, 238–42.

37. Gelien Matthews, *Caribbean Slave Revolts and the British Abolition Movement* (Baton Rouge: Louisiana State University Press, 2006), 135–69; Claudius Fergus, "'Dread of Insurrection': Abolitionism, Security, and Labor in Britain's West Indian Colonies, 1760–1823," *WMQ* 66, no. 4 (2009): 757–80; Edward Bartlett Rugemer, *The Problem of Emancipation: The Caribbean Roots of the American Civil War* (Baton Rouge: Louisiana State University Press, 2008).

38. Patrick H. Breen, *The Land Shall Be Deluged in Blood: A New History of the Nat Turner Revolt* (Oxford: Oxford University Press, 2015), 19–24; Davis, *Inhuman Bondage*, 208; Hunt, *Haiti's Influence*, 121; Clavin, *Toussaint Louverture*, 14–15; Peter P. Hinks, *David Walker's Appeal to the Colored Citizens of the World* (University Park, PA: Penn State University Press, 2000), 23.

INDEX

People and terms with identical names are distinguished by additional identifying information in parentheses.

ACKNOWLEDGMENTS

This book exists because many generous people and supportive institutions helped me at every stage. Most fundamentally, my teachers and mentors through the years challenged me and gave graciously of themselves: Fay Abernethy, James Axtell, Linda Colley, Ruth Hayes, Rhys Isaac, Alice Kay, Emmanuel Kreike, Joseph Miller, Philip Morgan, Paul Moyer, Ben Mutschler, Colin Palmer, Daniel Richter, and Peter Silver. More recently, Kathleen Brown and Bob Lockhart at the University of Pennsylvania Press guided this manuscript through a transformation that I would not have envisioned on my own. Gwen A. Burda copyedited this manuscript carefully and insightfully, and Margaret Puskar-Pasewicz indexed it expertly.

A great deal of time and money went into the development of this book. I am thankful that L. R. Poos, former dean of the School of Arts and Sciences at the Catholic University of America, supported this project and approved my research leave for 2012–13. I am also grateful to Ben Lowe, chair of the Department of History at Florida Atlantic University (FAU), and Katherine Jansen and Stephen West, chair and associate chair, respectively, of the Department of History at Catholic University, for arranging my academic responsibilities in configurations that allowed me to write efficiently. The financial support of many institutions gave me access to far-flung archives and time to write. I appreciate the funding I received from the Department of History at Princeton University, the Princeton Institute for International and Regional Studies, the Colonial Williamsburg Foundation, the Institute for Southern Studies at the University of South Carolina, the Barra Foundation, the McNeil Center for Early American Studies, the Robert H. Smith International Center for Jefferson Studies, the John Carter Brown Library at Brown University, the David Library of the American Revolution, the American Academy of Arts and Sciences, the Gilder Lehrman Institute of American History, the National Endowment for the Humanities via the Huntington Library, the School of Arts and Sciences at

Catholic University, and the Dorothy F. Schmidt College of Arts and Letters at FAU. Any views, findings, conclusions, or recommendations expressed in this book do not necessarily reflect those of the National Endowment for the Humanities, nor any other granting agency.

I am indebted to the knowledgeable librarians and patient staff members at the American Antiquarian Society, Ayrshire Archives, National Library Service of Barbados, Beinecke Rare Book and Manuscript Library at Yale University, British Library, William L. Clements Library at the University of Michigan, David Library of the American Revolution, Firestone Library at Princeton University, Geisel Library Special Collections at the University of California San Diego, Huntington Library, John Carter Brown Library at Brown University, John D. Rockefeller Jr. Library at the Colonial Williamsburg Foundation, Library of Congress, Library of Virginia, Mullen Library at Catholic University, National Archives of Scotland, National Archives (United Kingdom), National Library of Jamaica, National Library of Scotland, New-York Historical Society, Robert H. Smith International Center for Jefferson Studies, Albert and Shirley Small Special Collections Library at the University of Virginia, South Carolina Department of Archives and History, South Carolina Historical Society, South Caroliniana Library at the University of South Carolina, Sterling Memorial Library Manuscripts and Archives at Yale University, Van Pelt Library at the University of Pennsylvania, Virginia Historical Society, West Indies and Special Collections at the University of the West Indies at Mona, Widener Library at Harvard University, and the interlibrary loan office at Wimberly Library at FAU. In particular, Elizabeth Bennett, Charles Lesser, Kim Nusco, and Ken Ward went above and beyond.

Individual chapters benefited from the critiques of readers who participated in the following seminars: American Studies Seminar, American Antiquarian Society; American Origins Seminar, Early Modern Studies Institute, University of Southern California and Huntington Library; Atlantic History Seminar, Johns Hopkins University; Atlantic Studies Reading Group, University of Miami; Boston Area Early American History Seminar, Massachusetts Historical Society; Coffee Colloquium Lecture Series, FAU; Colloquium, Omohundro Institute of Early American History and Culture, College of William and Mary; Early Modern Global History Seminar, Georgetown University; Early Modern Seminar, Hall Center for the Humanities, University of Kansas; Faculty Colloquium, Department of History, Catholic University; Fellows' Forum, Robert H. Smith International

Center for Jefferson Studies; Luncheon Seminar, John Carter Brown Library, Brown University; Friday Seminar, McNeil Center for Early American Studies; Slavery, Memory, and African Diasporas Seminar, Howard University; and the Washington Early America Seminar, University of Maryland, College Park. I am fortunate that seminar participants took the time to engage with my work. I also appreciated the input from fellow panelists, respondents, and audience members during my presentations at the following conferences: Draper Conference at the University of Connecticut (September 28–30, 2006), Annual Meeting of the Omohundro Institute of Early American History and Culture (June 7–10, 2007; June 13–15, 2013), "Incarceration Nation" at the McNeil Center for Early American Studies and the Library Company of Philadelphia (April 3–4, 2009), Organization of American Historians Annual Meeting (April 7–10, 2010), American Studies Association Annual Meeting (November 15–18, 2012), "The World of Jenkins's Ear" at the Rutgers British Studies Center (May 28–29, 2015), Southern Historical Association Annual Meeting (November 7–10, 2017).

Parts of Chapter 1 appeared elsewhere as "Discovering Slave Conspiracies: New Fears of Rebellion and Old Paradigms of Plotting in Seventeenth-Century Barbados," *American Historical Review* 120, no. 3 (June 2015): 811–43; and parts of Chapter 3 appeared as "Hearing Whispers, Casting Shadows: Jailhouse Conversation and the Production of Knowledge," in *Buried Lives: Incarcerated in Early America*, ed. Michele Lise Tarter and Richard J. Bell (Athens: University of Georgia Press, 2012), 35–59. I thank Sir Francis Ogilvy for permission to use the Walter Tullideph Letter Book in the Ogilvy of Inverquharity Papers at the National Archives of Scotland.

Many scholars generously gave additional feedback and leads outside the formal venues. Others made my series of institutional homes enjoyable and productive. Thank you to Gergely Baics, Richard Bell, Evan Bennett, Chelsea Berry, Maria Alessandra Bollettino, Adam Bradford, Tim Breen, Holly Brewer, Christopher Brooks, Vincent Brown, Trevor Burnard, Brian Connolly, John Coombs, Stephanie Crumbaugh, James Corbett David, James Alexander Dun, Daniel Ellis, Stephen Engle, Paul Erickson, Ignacio Gallup-Diaz, Mark Hanna, Scott Heerman, Steve Hindle, Peter Charles Hoffer, Ronald Hoffman, Shona Johnston, Chin Jou, Marjoleine Kars, Julie Kim, Bruce Levine, Brendan McConville, Rupali Mishra, Lyra Monteiro, Hannah Weiss Muller, John Murrin, Michele Currie Navakas, Simon Newman, Sandra Norman, Dael Norwood, Lindsay O'Neill, Jennifer Paxton, Juan José Ponce-Vázquez, Justin Pope, Julio Proano, Cassandra Pybus,

Renée Raphael, Roy Ritchie, Justin Roberts, James Robertson, Brett Rush-forth, Elena Schneider, Mark M. Smith, Patricia Meyer Spacks, Owen Stan-wood, Antoinette Sutto, Alan Taylor, Anne Twitty, Megan Walsh, Laura Weinrib, Lev Weitz, Matt Wendeln, Julia Young, and Natalie Zacek. I am also grateful for the assistance of Kyle Dalton, Erica Fuller, and Maria Rodriguez through the research apprentice program at Catholic University.

Adrian Finucane gave endlessly of herself as I completed this book. I am thankful for her support, sacrifices, editorial insights, and intellectual partnership. I also appreciate the warmth and encouragement of William Finucane and Alice Santiago during the final revision of this project. Jenni-fer Reichenberg has always supported me with love and patience, and she has consistently given clear-eyed advice. The whole Reichenberg family—Jen, Rory, Aidan, Jonah, and Nathan—reenergized me whenever they were around. Finally, Tim and Dee Sharples ignited my passion for words and for the past. I am fortunate that they surrounded me with love and books, wrote stories with me at the kitchen table, and brought me to explore obscure historical sites. I wish my father could have seen this book, because he laid its foundation and left me with many of the tools that I used to construct it.

www.ingramcontent.com/pod-product-compliance
Lightning Source LLC
Chambersburg PA
CBHW030422100426
42812CB00028B/3064/J